ACROSS THE WATERS

ONTARIO IMMIGRANTS'
EXPERIENCES
1820-1850

Frances Hoffman
Ryan Taylor

Winter has already given us some palpable hints of his intended approach, in the shape of frost and snow, and we shall lose as little time as possible in wending our way, once more across the waters.

Henry Tyler

GL BAL
Global Heritage Press Inc.

First printing   1999
Second printing   2005

Canadian Cataloguing in Publication Data

Hoffman, Frances
    Across the waters: Ontario immigrants' experiences, 1820 - 1850

Includes bibliographic references and index.
ISBN 1-894378-00-8 (bound)

    1.   Immigrants—Ontario—History—19th Century.
    2.   Ontario Emigration and immigration—History—19th century
    3.   Immigrant—Ontario--Diaries
    4.   Immigrants—Ontario--Correspondence

I. Taylor, Ryan   II Title.

FC3071.H63 1999   304.8'713'09034   C99-900347-X   F1058.H63 1999

Additional copies available from:
Global Heritage Press Inc.
43 Main Street South,
Campbellville, Ontario, Canada L0P 1B0

Telephone: 1-800-361-5168 (toll-free order desk)
                     905-854-2176
Internet: www.GlobalHeritagePress.com

Made in Canada

FOR

RON AND MARILYN LAMBERT

whose work, encouragement and friendship
have meant so much to genealogists
in Waterloo and Wellington counties

ACKNOWLEDGEMENTS

First and special thanks go to Rick and Sandra Roberts, publishers of this book, who have supported the idea enthusiastically from the beginning.

Many people helped us in the their official capacities: Mary Bond, Don Carter and Mike MacDonald (National Library of Canada), Mary Munk, Michel Poitras, Patricia Kennedy and Jean Matheson (National Archives of Canada), John Kearon (Head of Shipping, Industrial & Land Transport Conservation, National Galleries in Merseyside), M. K. Stammers (Maritime Museum, Liverpool), Susan Bellingham (University of Waterloo), Karen Wagner (Wellington County Archives), Christine Bourolias and Carolyn Heald (Archives of Ontario), Suzanne Lout (Archives of the Roman Catholic Archdiocese of Toronto), Noel Alfonso (Canadian Museum of Nature), Paul Berry (Currency Museum, Bank of Canada), Bernard Katz (University of Guelph), Steve Leeson (Ontario Agricultural College), Susan Hoffman (Kitchener Public Library), Chris Masterman (Kitchener-Waterloo Record).

Among these official assistants, special mention should be made of Sandra Guillaume of the Archives of Ontario (she's a gem), and interlibrary loan helpers, Laurie Strome of the University of Waterloo Library, and Laura Eme of the Allen County Public Library, who went out of their way to help.

Many others gave us assistance by answering questions or offering encouragement or playing hostess to visiting researchers: Barbara Aitken, Linda Brown-Kubisch, Velma Cain, Martin Cordingley, Ian Easterbrook, Dr Jane Errington, Cheryl Hackworth & Don Rust, Robert Halfyard, Sarah Hoffman, Marjorie Kohli, Ron Lambert, Steve Myers, Doug Taylor, Velma Taylor, Mary Kearns Trace, Patricia Whitney, Curt Witcher.

We are grateful to Jim Rees of Arklow, Ireland, for generously sharing his vast knowledge of shipwrecks off the coast of Ireland.

The following official acknowledgements for use of copyright material are made:

to Thunder Bay Museum for use of W.C. Dobie's journal from the *Papers and Annual Reports* of the Thunder Bay Historical Society; to *Queen's Quarterly* for permission to quote from "Atlantic Crossing

1835" by D. D. Calvin, v. XLII, no. 1 (Spring 1935); to the heirs of William Stuart Cameron for permission to quote from *Some we have met*; to Penny Millar for permission to quote from the correspondence of John Millar; to Mary Kearns Trace for permission to quote from *Footsteps of a Highland Immigrant*, and the illustration from the same; to Barbara Bowles and Steve Brown for permission to quote from the diary of John Walker, and to Steve Brown for his photograph; to the University of Toronto Press for permission to quote from *I bless you in my heart*, the letters of Catharine Parr Traill, and Northrop Frye's "Conclusion to a 'Literary History of Canada'"; to Mary Bagg for permission to quote from the Andrew Hunter papers; to Elizabeth Gillan Muir for permission to quote from *Petticoats in the Pulpit*; to Garry Sherriff-Scott for permission to reprint Adam Sherriff-Scott's painting of an early postal delivery; to John Buttrick for permission to reproduce the diary of Leah Purkiss; to the Wellington County Historical Society for permission to quote from the reminiscences of Joseph Carder; to the County of Huron for permission to quote from *The settlement of Huron County*, by James Scott; to Irwin Publishing for permission to quote from *A Gentlewoman in Upper Canada: the journals of Anne Langton*; to the J. J. Talman Collection, University of Western Ontario, for permission to quote from *Western Ontario Historical Notes*; to Macmillan of Canada for permission to quote from *The Journals of Mary O'Brien*; to the Ontario Historical Society for permission to quote the following articles in their *Papers and Records*: "The United Empire Loyalist Settlement in Long Point," by L. H. Tasker (v. 2, 1900), The Reminiscences of Catherine White (v. 7, 1910), "Reminiscences of the Highland Pioneers in Eldon," by Hugh Ray (v. 24, 1927), "The Proudfoot Papers, 1833" (v. 26, 1930 & v. 27, 1931).

Every attempt has been made to trace owners of copyright material; anyone inadvertantly omitted will be gratefully acknowledged in future editions.

Contents

Introduction

Never in the history of the world had there been a migration such as occurred in the mid-nineteenth century, when vast numbers of citizens from the United Kingdom and Europe left their homelands to seek out new lives in North America. A good proportion of these migrants settled in Ontario. At first they came in a trickle, but as the decades wore on, their numbers would increase to tens of thousands per season. Among these numbers were people representing all occupations and professions as well as all personality types. Each, in his or her own way, contributed to the building of the new society. The results of their labours were bequeathed to future generations. Their stories and personal experiences may have differed, but in the greater scheme of things, each found their own place, and made their own mark.

The experiences of our emigrant ancestors are so far removed from those of modern-day lives that we tend often to overlook the extraordinary level of perseverance, sacrifice and selflessness that was essential to successfully establishing oneself during the formative years of Ontario. For, in the era explored in this publication, 1820 to 1850, it made little difference whether one arrived as a pauper or with pockets bulging. Certain fundamentals applied. The basic premise was that, providing a person was willing to work hard, rewards would be reaped. While this alone may have been sufficient to entice some, it was the promise of land, which in their homelands was such a scarce and much coveted commodity, which was the chief incentive, and which brought the dream to life for the majority of emigrants.

1

It was a dream that appealed to many, not just for those attempting to escape lives of drudgery and poverty. It also tantalized and enticed those with a whim to take up a challenge and those with a sense of adventure. Some simply came to see what all the fuss was about. Others came to write about their experiences with a view to publishing their efforts in the way of advice to prospective emigrants. And all along the way, letters, diaries, books and articles were created, which offer tremendous insight into the lives of these courageous people.

By allowing the personal writings of the early settlers to guide us through their own experiences, we come to better appreciate the process of settlement. By examining the various stages of emigration, such as preparing for the journey, ocean crossings, obtaining and clearing the land and building a house, we see the pattern of emigrant experience. Interspersed throughout, we catch glimpses of all manner of family and social life.

Several years ago, a lecture by Ryan Taylor called "Arriving in Canada West" described the process by which emigrants from Britain made the journey to Canada. Its focus was the period 1830 to 1850. The basis of the lecture was a series of contemporary documents—letters and memoirs—in which people who had actually made the journey described their own experiences. This book is an expansion of that idea.

Ontario changed its name during the time period covered in this volume. From 1791 to 1841, it was known as Upper Canada. It was Canada West from 1841 to 1867, and then Ontario. This portion of Canada would evolve in a grand fashion, mainly through the industry of these newcomers.

The life of an emigrant family was filled with hardship, but despite the hard work, their lives were not all tedium. Moments of joy, often aroused by their accomplishments, shine through in their writings, rounding out their sense of satisfaction, well-being and fulfillment.

All quotations are in their original spelling; occasionally, punctuation has been adjusted for clarity.

Preparations

Make up your minds and come to us
George Carpenter

It is usually true that many factors are involved in creating great tides of emigration. However, for the majority of British emigrants during the first half of the nineteenth century, the impetus to actually pack up and leave was primarily poverty and famine. For the ordinary people, this was a time of great discontent. It was also a time of shifting demographics and of extraordinary population growth. In a fifty-one year period, between 1780 and 1831, the population had risen from around thirteen million to over twenty-four million. In every corner of Britain, signs of desperation were evident.

A significant proportion of the nation's reserves had been channelled into sustaining the Napoleonic wars. When hostilities ceased, returning soldiers were frequently met with cold comfort in their search for work. It was a cruel twist of fate that, after serving their country through such terrible conflicts, there was no role for them except to swell the ranks of the poor. To add to the burden, the Corn Law of 1815, used to safeguard the interests of agriculturalists by inflating the price of British wheat, greatly added to the misery. Now the most basic of staples, a slice of bread, was often beyond the reach of society's poorest. Then, when the harvests of 1817-19 proved dismal, the labouring classes truly found themselves in tragic circumstances.

Changes had taken place on many fronts, each having an impact upon society's most vulnerable. Increased industrial-

3

ization and advances in technology brought cuts to the labour force. In particular the introduction of the spinning jenny and the power-loom ended a way of life for thousands of weaving families whose reliance upon small cottage industry had ensured their survival for generations.

One of the most poignant examples of this was the plight of hand-loom weavers in Glasgow, who, between 1803 and 1819, saw their wages shrink from twenty-five to five shillings a week.

> Working in their own houses far into the night, the weavers' families attempted to offset low wages by greater production; but the decreased demand soon resulted in a surplus. Emigration was the only means of escape, and many settled in Lanark County. [Edwin Guillet]

Such grim circumstances were experienced all across Britain. Rural dwellers found themselves totally reliant upon the mercy of landowners bent upon enforcing the land enclosure acts. Under these acts, landowners set about fencing and hedging their properties. Lands upon which many families had eked out their existence were quickly gobbled up and withdrawn from public use. In a general desire to improve financial returns per acre, farmers also began making use of advancements in mechanization and implementing modern farming methods. As well, over-eager landowners frequently included the privatization of forests, rivers and streams in their drive for wealth, causing great hardship by virtually eliminating the right of the common people to hunt and fish on those lands. Many were left with little choice but to quit subsistence farming, and request assistance from the parish or go to the workhouse.

While it is true that there remains some degree of controversy among contemporary historians as to the severity with which enclosure affected the average rural dweller, the misery of the labouring classes was widely acknowledged at the time. On 7 November 1821, William Cobbett, an influential radical writer, made the following comment on the deprivations suffered by the inhabitants of Cricklade, Wiltshire. His remarks conjure a picture far removed from the pastoral splendour one associates with rural Britain.

4

The labourers seem miserably poor. Their dwellings are little better than pig-beds, and their looks indicate that their food is not nearly equal to that of a pig. Their wretched hovels are stuck upon little bits of ground *on the road side*, where the space has been wider than the road demanded. In many places they have not two rods to a hovel.... Yesterday morning was a sharp frost; and this had set the poor creatures to digging up their little plats of potatoes. In my whole life I never saw human wretchedness equal to this: no, not even amongst the free negroes in America.... Fine fields and pastures all around; and yet the cultivators of those fields so miserable!

There was a gradual and significant shifting of rural dwellers to the towns where people sought work in the newly constructed factories that were springing up. Young children were very much a part of this work force until the first Factory Act of 1833 prohibited employing those under nine years of age. Until the Mines Act of 1842, little ones as young as six spend long days underground. Low wages, long hours and deplorable conditions were all part of life in the urban environment. There was little promise of improvement. Emigration, on the other hand, did offer hope.

Between 1847 and 1856, in an attempt to re-organize his 90,000 acre Coolattin Estate in south-west Wicklow, Lord Fitzwilliam cleared the property of almost six thousand tenants...Where did they go? The vast majority of these people were shipped to Quebec, but one ship load of 376 passengers went to St. Andrews, New Brunswick. Towards the end of the clearances some families went to Australia. Many of the Canada-bound emigrants, of course, crossed the border into the United States. Letters in the New Brunswick archives record that the authorities actually encouraged emigrants to seek work in the U.S. when work on the New Brunswick railroad became scarce... [Jim Rees]

The people of Ireland suffered on many counts. Absentee landlords and their drive for financial gain compounded an already desperate situation caused by famine, fever and crop failures between 1817 and 1821. Political reconstruction under the Act of Union of 1801, industrial competition, a tremendous population growth, sectarian animosity and dispossession all took their toll. Long practised in exporting her labourers as a means of coping with poverty and unemployment, Ireland was now poised for the commencement of what would become one of the largest migrations ever. A writer for the *Dublin Evening Post* summed up the Irish situation in 1818 when he said:

> It is a melancholy thing that emigration is necessarily restricted to the class immediately above the labouring order, who cannot raise the money to pay their passage.

All across the United Kingdom, an enormous outcry was heard from taxpayers, protesting that the cost of relief to the poor was beyond their means. Such dire straits provided fertile breeding grounds for the notion of using emigration as a means of ridding the nation of a large number of its poor. A motion to this effect was accepted by the Houses of Parliament in 1819. Britain was not prepared to run the risk of losing her prized artisans, however. The regulation preventing them from leaving was not relaxed until 1824.

Emigration was a topic about which there was no shortage of writers. Martin Doyle, who directed himself to the "middle and lower classes" advised the following:

> To those who are favoured with steady employment at home, who possess allotments of land, however small, which furnish them with comfortable subsistence, I say, 'be contented—make no experiments—remain where you are—and trust that a kind Providence will bring order and peace out of the present confusion and discord which distract these realms.' But to those differently circumstanced, Emigration is most desirable, and perhaps no country in the world is more critically suited than North America to the Irish and Scotch poor in particular...

It was the plight of the poor that gripped so many writers. John Murray feared that the system of the early 1830s was not designed with the welfare of the emigrant as its main objective.

> Those who are instrumental in inducing the poor to embark, by holding out to them the sure prospect of bettering their condition, merely for the sake of a parish riddance, would do

well to consider seriously what they are answerable for. If it is absolutely necessary, from over-population or other causes, that such emigration should take place, let it be their first endeavour to see them so provided, that they will have a small sum on landing, to enable them to reach the interior; where, indeed, they may be assured, that with honesty and industry they will not only be certain of being comfortable, but in a few years perfectly independent.

The earliest emigration scheme sponsored by the British government took place in 1815 when large numbers of Scottish settlers came to Lanark County. It was organized not only in an attempt to address issues of unemployment and destitution, but also in a desire to see Upper Canada inhabited by subjects faithful to the crown. Fears of renewed hostilities with the United States were ever present (the War of 1812 had just ended), particularly along the Saint Lawrence river between Kingston and Cornwall. Settlers who had migrated to this area from the USA were sometimes viewed with suspicion, their loyalty to the Crown brought into question. Improving security was of prime concern.

Increasing the population of this region by the importation of able-bodied and loyal workers held great appeal for the imperial politicians. A proclamation directed to all 'men of good character' was announced in Scotland. Under this scheme, providing a deposit of £16 could be found, a person was entitled to receive their passage in addition to those supplies deemed essential to successful settlement. They were also given a grant of land along with the promise that their male children would also receive land when they reached twenty-one years of age. As an inducement to industry, two years after settlement, the £16 would be refunded to those who remained upon, and were successful in settling, the land granted to them.

This was not a very successful enterprise. The emigrants, fraught with frustrations, were kept waiting in Glasgow for up to three months before setting sail. There were also delays when they arrived in Canada. Consequently it was the spring of 1816 before they were able to begin the process of establishing homes. They settled at Perth and by the time the first dwelling was ready for occupancy, many of them had been homeless for twelve months.

Following the first state-sponsored emigration scheme, societies began forming, particularly in those corners of the nation where unemployment and destitution were at their greatest. A number of people set about organizing with a view to seeking opportunities in Upper Canada. In January 1820, a group of Scottish societies commenced negotiations and petitioned the government for permission to emigrate to Upper Canada. They requested land grants and aid for each head of household or individual petitioner. The petition was approved, on condition that funds could be raised to cover the cost of passage and of provisions needed for the voyage. To this end, each society involved sought to assist eligible applicants from within their communities. Subscriptions were raised to help offset the cost for those who were unable to fund their own passage. About one thousand emigrants set sail in 1820.

A meeting took place at the Black Bull Inn, Glasgow, on 24 October 1820, during which local emigrant societies presented lists amounting to 6,281 individuals seeking emigration. The Colonial Office was only prepared to assist eighteen hundred. The desire to emigrate far exceeded transportation and settlement capabilities and the societies were advised to accept no more names until the backlog had been accommodated. Altogether, 2900 people emigrated to Upper Canada in 1820-1821 through the efforts of these Scottish societies. John M'Donald, a passenger on one of the vessels involved in carrying a large number of these emigrants, kept a diary of his experiences. It begins:

> Having, with many of my countrymen, determined to embark for Canada, little dreaming, from the flattering accounts which had been so industriously published respecting that country, of the hardships attending such an undertaking, I left Glasgow for Greenock, to embark on board the ship *David* of London, for Quebec, along with nearly 400 other passengers, where, having gone through the necessary steps at the custom-house, we left the quay on the 19th of May, 1821. A steam boat dragged the ship to the tail of the bank, and the wind being favourable we immediately sailed, and in 28 hours lost sight of land.

Not everyone supported the idea of assisted emigration. Where criticism existed, it was primarily aimed at the lack of assistance provided to emigrants after their arrival in Canada. Adam Fergusson had strong views on this subject, reinforced by seeing the situation of unfortunate emigrants in Montreal.

> I had a personal opportunity of witnessing the inadequacy of the arrangements, in regard to a large party from Somersetshire, that arrived in Quebec while I was there. I think there were one hundred and fifty, seemingly of the class of agricultural labourers, and they were under the charge of a respectable parish overseer, whose duty it was to have justice done to them on board ship and to land them at Montreal. There they were to be absolutely cast adrift, each man receiving £4; but no arrangements having been contemplated for locating them, or for providing them with work, they would be quickly relieved of their cash by the tavern-keepers, and left destitute, a heavy burden to themselves and a nuisance to the province.

It is worth noting that the money given to each man would have been insufficient to pay his own fare to Toronto, to say nothing of his family. By the time a person had spent a week on the road, unless they had additional money for food and shelter, they would be in a very sorry state.

Some schemes provided guidance right through to the point where people took up their land in the bush. In his account of the Petworth emigrants, James Marr Brydone portrays a well-planned and smoothly executed journey with no loss of life. Which is not to say he did not encounter some exciting incidents.

> June 6th...At noon, reached Lachine, a distance of eight miles....While waiting for her arrival, Mr. Gunn, and Mr. Hodges, took a row boat, and crossed the river, to view a large village, of native blacks....I declined with reluctance, ...it was as well I did, from what occurred with William West, who having got some beer, quarrelled with Henry Snelling, beat Snelling's wife, and becoming exceedingly cross, and stubborn, set off for Montreal, with the intention of returning to England, and, leaving behind him, seven children, under twelve years, and his wife very near the time of her confinement, with the eighth. I

immediately set out myself, in pursuit of him, accompanied by six men: after a diligent search, he was fortunately discovered, in some bushes, a mode of concealment, probably not new to him, being an old smuggler...

Prospective emigrants could seek financial backing from various sources. The Petworth scheme was sponsored by the earl of Egremont, but there were other schemes operating in much the same way. The marquess of Bath was responsible for aiding emigrants from Wiltshire, and Vere Foster helped with the emigration of women to the United States. Under a government initiative, Peter Robinson had supervised the resettling of over 2500 Irish immigrants to Upper Canada between 1823 and 1825. Fifty-four Irish families, with at least £20 capital each, had emigrated under the scheme organized by Richard Talbot in 1818. These people had settled in Perth and London township, and received free land grants. Some of these benefactors had noble motives, while others simply thought it worth spending money to rid their districts of the poor and destitute.

Their reason for this was that the poor law required landlords to support the poorhouse through their taxes. Like Scrooge (before his transformation), many wished the poor would simply die and be done with it. Although the sponsored schemes have the air of kind charity, there was also an element of cynicism in them, made clear by Robert Gouger in his aptly-named *Emigration for the relief of parishes practically considered.* He asks who should be selected to go.

We answer, the marriageble of both sexes, or the young married couple who have not yet the burden of a family upon them.

The purpose of this was to save money, because they would then have their children in the new land.

He justifies this with what is a credible argument:

That the time of marriage is a time of change, when two persons just united for life must, nearly always, seek a new home. [and also] that the natural time of marriage is one when the mind is most disposed to hope, to ambition...and to undertakings which require decision and energy and purpose.

10

He goes on to say that you must establish them in Canada, not merely abandon them on the docks, but also says they need not be independent but can continue to work for other people as they had in Britain. If this is how the governing classes in Britain saw things, the immigrants soon altered the idea once they arrived in Canada, where they perceived they could be independent through hard work along with their neighbours.

Land clearances also drove many to emigrate. The hard reality of this practice is that few received financial assistance. It seems extraordinary that by the act of purchasing stock and crops from the prospective emigrants, the landowner and emigration agent were viewed by the establishment as having acted nobly and benevolently. Some of these people may have received a fair price; most did not.

> Emigration has taken place lately to a considerable extent from South Unist [Uist], on the properties of Colonel Gordon of Cluny and Lord Macdonald. A fine large Clyde ship, the "Tusker" sailed on Tuesday from Loch Boisdale for Quebec, conveying 500 souls, and a second ship the "Mountstewart Elphinstone" was expected to sail later in the week with about 250 souls. The most, if not the whole of these people were from Colonel Gordon's property; and he assists them by taking their crops at a valuation, the emigration agent at Glasgow taking the stock also at valuation.

There were also a great number of single young men whose principal interest was excitement. Their heads were full of the 'wild romance and adventures of the Backwoodsman's life.'

> From a very early age the New World had been a favourite subject of my fancies and daydreams. Its primaeval forests, its boundless prairies, its exciting scenes of Indian prowess and adventure were all unspeakably delightful to my youthful imagination. Every work that told of travels undertaken and perils encountered in the wilderness, I used eagerly to devour as I could gain access to it. [Henry Christmas]

> So sanguine were we of returning in the course of six or seven years, with plenty of money to enrich, and perhaps bring back with us, our dear mother and unmarried sisters, that we

11

scarcely realized the pain of leave-taking, and went on board ship in the St. Catherine's Docks, surrounded by applauding friends, and in the highest spirits. [Samuel Thompson]

For a great many, whatever the initial impulse to consider emigration, the realization of the freedom they would find in the New World was the most significant idea.

> The hardships necessarily attendant on the voyage and first settlement of emigrants in a new country, have been represented as mere trifles when counterbalanced by their improved condition. [Robert Gouger]

> His honest toil meet recompense can claim,
> And freedom bless him with a freeman's name!
> [Susanna Moodie]

The idea that they could make a living and be free of the landlord was all that mattered, and they emphasized this in their letters home.
It is difficult to ascertain exact numbers of emigrants from Britain to Upper Canada because there were some who crossed on vessels small enough to slip by government inspection. There were also stowaways, slipping away once they reached Quebec, never to be detected. According to statistics offered by Edwin C. Guillet, between 1815 and 1825, 7,090 British people came on conducted emigrations, while 65,704 arranged their own passages. These people came from all walks of life. They were rich, poor, industrious or lazy. Sprinkled throughout were a number of adventurers eager to explore the backwoods of Canada. Of all categories of emigrants, young, healthy, marriageable ones were the most highly prized.

Emigrant Guides

Much was written in the way of advice to emigrants. Practical suggestions regarding what to take, and what to expect when one arrived, were of great benefit. Words of caution were also needed as a means of balancing some of the marvellously glowing, and in some cases unrealistic, reports about life in Canada. These guides were hugely influential.

> My picture of North America was principally drawn from that charmingly written book *The Backwoods of Canada.* [Mrs Edward Copleston]

> "Martin Doyle" was the text-book which first awakened amongst tens of thousands of British readers, a keen interest in the backwoods of what is now the Province of Ontario. ...My brothers Thomas and Isaac, both a few years older than myself, made up their minds to emigrate, and I joyously offered to join them, in the expectation of a good deal of fun of the kind described by Dr Dunlop. [Samuel Thompson]

John M'Donald's narrative, written upon returning to Scotland after a brief and decidedly dismal experience in Lanark County, quoted a countryman as saying, "That all the truth which had both been written and printed respecting Upper Canada, would not cover one-half of the lies which have been told." Patrick Shirreff, whose North American tour of 1832 was arranged primarily to investigate agricultural matters, concluded that

> Upper Canada has been much over-rated by some people who have visited the country. Many of the written accounts may be regarded as advertisements; and the statements have been the means of deceiving the unwary.

At the other end of the spectrum, Captain Charles Stuart exuded enthusiasm. His advice in suggesting

> If there be a means for the purpose, I would recommend the stranger to proceed immediately with his family to York. To wait upon the governor, producing his introductions, or introducing himself; and then leaving his family there, to undertake a tour of the province, in order to inquire or judge for himself

must have taken on shades of the fantastic for the average immigrant, who could barely scrape together the fare. Joseph

Sansom, the first American to write about travels in Canada, shared Stuart's enthusiasm. He concluded that beggary was unknown and thieving very rare. Emigrants whose bags and money had indeed been stolen would clearly have scoffed at this.

Despite the fact that opinions regarding life in Upper Canada ranged from euphoria to despair, most people were eager to believe that through emigration, their hopes and dreams would be fulfilled. Emigrant guides, good or bad, were devoured by the public. They served a useful purpose. However, the greatest inducement to pack up and leave came in the form of letters from family and acquaintances who had successfully accomplished resettlement.

> You will expect me to say something on emigration, we hear many accounts but chiefly favorable (in the Upper Country) to those who have a few hundred pounds if they be steady; but there are such numbers who come here with nothing and travelling being expensive they are often brought to distress before they fall in with anything, but gentlemen are forming societies for the instruction of those poor emigrants who want information. Any of our friends and acquaintances who have a little money and have counted the cost may do better than in England, but I will assure you the difficulties are many to those who have large families. Young women who are steady may do very well; two young women who came in the *Kingston* from Hull were hired immediately on their arrival for 25£ each for to keep houses for gentlemen [Robert Wade]

There was always the danger of immigrants embellishing their tales of success in an effort to induce friends to join them. But generally, words of caution were woven into stories of success. Robert Wade lived in the hope that more of his relatives would decide to emigrate.

> I think there is little doubt that you will live to see the wisdom of emigrating to America, as for England the good things of this world are so unequally divided that those who get the smaller share can scarcely get enough to keep body and soul together the short time they have to live in this transitory world.... [John Wade]

Nathaniel Carrothers sent a note to his friend Mrs Kirk of Maguiresbridge, at home in Ulster, notifying her that he had sent £11 via a merchant travelling to New York, where the money would be changed at the Bank of England and forwarded to her for passage and supplies. It was not uncommon for one or two members of a family to emigrate with the understanding that money would be sent home to finance the emigration of additional family members. Although it required great sacrifice, as poor as they were, funds were found. Such was the case with the Ritchie family.

> We take this favourable opertunity of writing to you to let you know that we are both well thank God for his mercies to us hoping that these few lines will find you in the same. you requested us to let you know if there was any chance of Getting a situation near us there is plenty of vacant land Close to us which you can purchase within 1/2 mile of us the price that it is sold is 8/- per acre there will not be much weaving here for some time as the country is new but you may fetch your loom as much of it as you can for you will have use for it after some time. It is not for the want of land here that I told you to fetch It as there is plenty of land to be got here there is no money to be paid down on it there is 8 years Given to pay for it in yearly installments. you can Buy any quantity of it you like. you want to know if the Crops is Good and If I would advise you to come here. the Crops is all very Good here this year and I would advise you strongly come out. You Want to Know If received your letter which you sent in the spring. I received your letter But it was too late for me to send any thing as you mistook the name in directing it. It was directed to Neelen in place of McNeelie as there is a man of that name some distance from here who received your letter and kept it for some time and then returned it to the post Office so that It was late before I received it as I was ankiously looking for it for a good many weeks before that I received it you can make preperation to come out in the spring and we will send you money in the course of three weeks or a month from this time as I have not Got all Gathered at present.
>
> Dear Brother you want to know the Directions to come Buy. From Quebeck to Montreal and then to Buytown and then to the Shaws and then to Portage du fort and then you are within six miles of my place. I am living in the township of

Ross and my mother is at present living in Ramsay. But is mooving up to my place in a few Days from now so that we will be Both there when you come out. When you come to Quebeck go to the Emigrant office and you will likely get up free. If you do they will give you a ticket to give to the Captain of the steem boat you wanted to know how that I got up, a single person will not get up free. I had to stop in Quebeck and work for money to fetch me to Montreal and then I worked there for money to fetch me to Buytown. do not spend any of your money on close [clothes] But come as saving as possible as you can get plenty of close here. Keep you minds to yourselves as much as possible till you be ready to come away....I have got £9 which will be sent in a few days through the Canada Company. it will make something more than £7 Sterling. [Mary Ritchie]

In weighing up the pros and cons of emigration, the first consideration was always financial. Whenever possible, an emigrant was advised to take sufficient money to tide the family over. In circumstances of dire hardship this was not usually possible. But for those emigrating under less frantic circumstances, a concerted effort was made to provide a nest egg upon which to draw during the first year of settlement. This was particularly important for those planning to take up occupations such as farming or similar labours offering little return during the first season. Besides travel costs, there was land to buy and buildings to erect. Stock and equipment had to be purchased, not forgetting that all along the family must eat.

That a man who had £100 currency, in addition to what he paid for his land, had a bare minimum. It would take £20 to buy a pair of oxen, a yoke, a logging-chain, and a harrow. £8 for a cow and a couple of pigs, £22 for a year's provisions, and £50 for erecting buildings and for hiring labour to assist in chopping and logging. Those who lacked money when they arrived in the new settlements had to acquire it by one means or another before they could expect to have a farm of their own.
[R. L. Jones]

The idea of their son emigrating to Australia did not sit right with the parents of John Boyd Taylor, but going to Canada was a different story.

I worked steadily all this summer and Fall with my father and how proud was I when I deposited a nice little sum in the bank of Scotland in Stirling, my first savings. There was glowing accounts coming across the waters from America, and south from Australia, and I had my mind fully made up to go south. Australia was the place for me. But when my father and mother heard of this, they said they could never consent, but would consent to my coming to Canada, as some of our neighbours had crossed the Atlantic in the spring previous, and another family was to go the coming Spring, so that decided me to try and seek my fortune across the water... [John Boyd Taylor]

When William Mullett, a tanner and currier of Ilminster, Somerset, his wife Mary Clothier and their eleven children decided to emigrate in 1821, great discussion took place among relatives and associates regarding the financing of their enterprise.

Brother Arthur I expect this evening, as by a letter Brother Sturge showed me on fifth day from him respecting brother Millett & family it is his intention to be at Frenchay Mo. Meetg to-morow to try if the ways & means can be accomplished to fit them out for Canada, but I am very doubtful the sum wanted is more than they will be willing to advance at once, I think Brother Arthur has come forward with a very generous offer of giving them 70£ towards it & was it in my power should most willing have done something for them also. [William Gillett]

The Mulletts were fortunate to have the backing of such generous people. They arrived in Canada in the summer of 1821 and soon settled on a farm near Adolphustown where the industriousness of this large family quickly provided them with a comfortable existence.

Once the commitment to leave had been made, it was time to begin preparing for the day of departure. Some might have property to dispose of and business matters to straighten away, as well as the procuring of whatever goods were needed. In the case of the poor, particularly during the early emigrations when Upper Canada had little to offer in the way of material goods, the government thought it necessary to outfit those

17

emigrants on assisted schemes with goods and tools necessary to their survival.

The Lanark emigrants of 1822 were provided with the following goods. Many of the larger tools were to be shared by several families.

> Implements among every 15 persons: 1 grindstone, 1 pit saw, 1 cross cut saw;
> 1 set of blacksmith's tools to each township;
> Implements for each 4 settlers: 4 felling axes in Canada, 10s. each, 1 broad axe, 4 hand saws, 4 locks and keys, 8 door hinges, 4 iron wedges, 4 pitch forks, 4 iron pots, 4 frying pans, 8 gimblets, 8 files of sorts, 4 chisels, 4 augurs, 4 scythes complete, 4 sickles, 4 spades and shovels, 4 pick axes, 4 broad hoes, 4 narrow hoes, 4 carpenter's hammers, 4 adzes, 4 drawing knives, 4 brush hooks, 36 harrow teeth, 4 planes;
> Building articles for each 4 settlers: 72 panes of glass, 7 1/2 by 8 1/2 inches, 6 pounds of putty, 4000 feet of pine boards to be provided in Canada for about 12*l.*, 48 pounds of nails, of sorts;
> Bedding for each 4 settlers: 4 paillasses and 4 blankets;
> Additional bedding for each member of a family: 1 blanket to each married woman, 1 blanket to each child, 1 paillasse to each family having more than 1 child.

Subsequent emigrants received far less. Government recommendations of 1825 were incorporated into Martin Doyle's ideas about items necessary to settlement in the woods.

> Tools: 1 American axe, 1 handsaw, 1 auger, 1 pick-axe, 1 spade, 2 gimlets, 1 hammer, 1 iron wedge, 3 hoes;
> Incidentals: 1 kettle, 1 frying pan, 1 iron pot, nails, small portable hand-mill for grinding corn, a gun, fishing nets

By the 1830s, as Canadian manufacturing had gained ground, it become less necessary to cart heavy tools, but people did have preferences. Some settlers remained loyal to, and relied heavily upon, their familiar British-made products. Others rated Canadian manufactures very highly, suggesting Canadian products held possible advantages since they were made specifically with Canada in mind. Emigrant guides and private correspondence provide much conflicting advice in this regard.

18

Martin Doyle recommended bringing a gun while W. J. Mickle of Wellington County sent the following advice to his father in England:

> You ask about bringing Tools &c. I wo^d not advise you to bring any or Guns as those suited to this Country can be had cheap enough at Hamilton th° a small box of Tools if obtained very cheap might be found serviceable.

Robert Wade, whose primary concern was improving his agricultural stock, kept his mind on more practical things when writing to encourage his relatives to emigrate.

> ...Dear brother if you or any of the neighbors come here provide well with clothes and shoes; do not bring anything to sell, it seldom pays well; bring apple pippins, plum stones, cherry stones, haws and a small quantity of seeds of all kinds, early potatoes, etc....

It was generally thought useful to bring some household items. In 1828, A. C. Buchanan suggested feather-beds—"the Irish peasantry generally possess a feather-bed," he reasoned. He also advised bringing spades, reaping-hooks and mechanical tools. In the needlework department, thread, pins and needles were essential. Last but not least, Buchanan, in company with many other writers, suggested bringing a strong pair of shoes for winter.

> A pair or two of stout shoes each; no iron but on the heels. Clothes of all kinds can be bought at Hamilton (U.C.) very cheap; blankets are not so...Wool is much cheaper than with you. [John Mathison]

In addition to cooking utensils, and those tools essential to hacking out a living in the backwoods, bedding, paillasses and blankets were deemed necessary. Emigrants arriving under sponsored schemes often received clothing. Fur caps, or Scottish woollen caps, cloaks for the women and girls, and woollen stockings for all were vital for surviving the bitter Canadian winters. It was reasoned that such articles could be manufactured locally, each community reaping some financial gain through the very act of preparing their neighbours for emigration.

> You should also have good warm frieze coats and jackets and worsted stockings and mittens for the winter; linen trowsers and jacket for the summer, as many linen shirts as you can afford to take out, (linen being dear in Canada) and a short flannel shirt to be worn next the skin, both in summer and winter. In the former season, it will be found most comfortable, as it absorbs perspiration: without it, the linen shirt becoming wet, and cooling the body, is apt to give cold and produce ague, the only complaint which the settler need dread; and this, I am convinced, is usually the effect of incaution, when heated, and of exposure to the air at night, when damp fogs are not unfrequent, but which disappear at sunrise, before which time no prudent person should be out. [Martin Doyle]

But first, appropriate clothing had to be organized for the voyage itself. Everyone wanted to know how they should dress.

> The kind of apparel I would recommend to male passengers would be, short jackets or waistcoats with sleeves, a dark handkerchief for the neck, and coarse trowsers; for women, a long bed gown, or wrappers with dark shawls or handkerchiefs, as cleanliness cannot be observed with any degree of precision. [James Wilson]

For a person who had never been to sea, there was much to consider in the clothing department. Salt water was very hard on coloureds, and everyone agreed that there was no point in wearing anything good.

> You should have a sufficient box to hold your bonnets, with nothing besides to crush them. Get three large flannel shirts. Have as few things open in your berth as possible; a bag to hold the clean, and another for the dirty. A cloth cap for yourself, and others for the children, as *bonnets* are not convenient at sea, and your dress should be of a warm description.
>
> Do not distress yourself preparing great store of things as if you could get nothing here. You can buy cotton prints, and cotton of all kinds, as cheap as at home. You may bring a few cuts of worsted for stockings, but we have far finer wool, and

cheaper, than you. We can have plenty of feathers as every one has dozens of geese, and they are plucked every month. You will have to supply your own bedding on board ship. Bring some blankets, as they are scarce here; 2 tea kettles, brander, and crook. Be sure to pack your dishes well. Keep your mind easy on the voyage and be always eating something. [John Mathison]

Every writer offering advice to emigrants included a section on clothing. The cold of the Canadian winter, and the heat of the summer, were far more extreme than the British climate.

Although some advised against it, there were some items worth bringing with a view to selling them in Upper Canada. William J. Mickle wrote to his brother suggesting he bring one or two good silver watches, providing he could buy them cheaply, since he might find a market for them. However, he strongly advised against bringing furniture because of the expense of carriage from Montreal to Lake Ontario. This was a constant theme played over and over in advice to the emigrant.

No heavy or cumbrous baggage ought to be taken; household furniture, iron utensils, implements of husbandry,—in short, all articles of considerable bulk or weight will cost, in freight and carriage, more than the expense of replacing them in Upper Canada; besides the trouble of their conveyance, the risk of damage, and the danger of articles carried from England or Ireland being found unsuited for use in America. The baggage of emigrants should consist only of their wearing apparel, with such bedding, and utensils for cooking, as may be required on the voyage; and any articles of clothing, not intended to be used at sea, ought to be packed in water-tight cases or trunks, not exceeding eighty or ninety pounds in weight. [John MacTaggart]

Most people had insufficient funds to consider carting heavy freight. Besides, it was well known that import duties, or taxes, would be levied on all manner of items.

John Mathison's publication of 1834 provided a great deal of advice with respect to equipping the family. Some of the items, while sounding rather poetic to modern ears, require the interpretation of a good dictionary.

Cooking utensils, crockery, clothes, and no furniture—two gridirons. Bring a bellows, shovel, and kitchen tongs, candlesticks, no lamps; pack some things into a tub or two. Tin water pails will be found useful, baskets, two tea-pots, coffee-pot, clock. No axes, for what we brought were of little use, so we bought others here, but a small one might be taken.... Bring a large tin plate oven, with feet. B— wants 1/2 doz. stout cotton pirns, a few balls of cotton thread, white and stout. Bring some flat and deep plates, two or three pudding dishes, with white-iron ones of the same size. A brass-pan. Soap and soda. Large oil flask—a tin candle-mould for three or four candles; twenty yards or so of narrow sacking; nine harrow teeth, 12 inches long, by 1 1/4 square, of good Swedish iron; one scythe, and mounting for three, the rings 2 inches diameter; a mason's small hammer; an auger 1 3/4 or 1 1/2; a light grape for the byre; two pitch-forks, one a size less than the other, with ferrils for them; cramp vice, glue pot, and glue; a wright's bench screw, and nut; two logging chains of Swedish iron, (for the oxen drawing away the trees after being cut) of the following dimensions—11 feet long, links 2 inch. made of 1 1/2 inch rod, or stouter, a strong hook at each end, 5 inches from the one end; the use of which is to put one of the hooks into.

A 'grape for the byre' roughly translates into a hook for the cowshed. This implement might have been used for jobs such as shifting hay. A ferril, or ferrule, was a metal band used to strengthen, and prevent splitting and wearing, on the wooden handles of tools such as spades and pitchforks.

A woman would be very proud of the few decorative pieces used to add interest to her home. It was often impossible to bring such finery since delicate pieces were likely to sustain damage. Deciding which of her few treasures must be left behind was heartbreaking for any woman. Since only the wealthy could afford to pay freight on heavy household furniture, family heirlooms were often left behind, auctioned off preparatory to departure. Many a tear was shed over such things.

But curtains, carpets, plate, glass and crockery, and especially bed and table linen, and blanketing, &c., may be brought, not only without detriment, but even with positive advantage; some of the latter commodities especially, being for the most part

22

dearer out here and not so good. Boots and shoes, cut out but not sewn, would be useful. [Henry Christmas]

Organizing and packing goods was another chore. Certain items would be kept handy for use on the voyage, others were tucked away until arrival. Security was a concern when it came to baggage. Goods could be stolen, lost, or accidentally taken by someone else.

It is necessary to provide strong chests or boxes for the voyage, well secured with good locks and hinges; or otherwise it is impossible to preserve property: I am sorry to have to say, in this vessel there has been much plunder committed, for want of being duly prepared against it. [James Wilson]

It was also necessary that articles needed on the journey could easily be identified once a person had reached the docks. Luggage stowed in the hold was virtually impossible to access during the voyage, but some produce might be placed in such a location that one could replenish the stocks.

You must have all your things packed up in boxes or barrels, so that you can replace them in safety. When you have to ship and unship them, have *locks* on all of them; have nothing in bags. I would warn you to look sharp, for sailors and passengers will sometimes make mistakes as to what is their own and what is not. Have all your tin dishes marked as they are apt to disappear without leave. Put your beef and your potatoes into the hold of the ship; your beer and cakes where you can have access; and those things most commonly applied to should be stowed away near your bed.... As soon as you can ascertain how many packages you have to go with you, call at the Custom-house, although it were some days before the ship is to sail, and give in the number of them, mentioning also their contents, whether clothing, books, utensils, tools, provisions, &c. then you get a permit, which you present to the searching officer at the ship, where one always attends. No duty, except shore-dues, on luggage. At Quebec, none at all, only on goods for sale, which are 2 1/2 per cent. The searching officers there are not very strict. Do not have your boxes too large, as we had; they will be easier managed. [John Mathison]

It was necessary for emigrants to take some cash. However, understanding the currencies used in Upper Canada required some effort. Charles Stuart's guide of 1820 explains that there were basically two systems at work, legal and practical.

Legal currency: 12 pence=1 shilling; 5 shilling=1 dollar; 20 shillings or 4 dollars=1 pound.

Practical currency (that of the state of New York, having the same name but different values): 12 pence or 12 1/2 cents=1 shilling; 8 shillings=1 dollar; 20 shillings or 2 1/2 dollars=1 pound.

It was advisable for emigrants to take gold sovereigns and Spanish or Portuguese gold coins which could be exchanged in Upper Canada. Once resident in Upper Canada, the emigrant would find the eagle or half-eagle of the United States, worth $10 and $5 respectively, to be the most commonly used gold coins. Since the currency of Lower Canada differed from that of Upper Canada, Stuart further advised that no shillings or sixpences of the lower province should be taken to Upper Canada and that no English silver coins should be carried beyond Montreal.

In view of the fact that many emigrants were uneducated, the prospect of coping with what appears to be a rather complex system must have appeared rather daunting. But they coped, and once the first payday arrived, it did not take long to sort things out.

New settlers were unanimous in their assertions that in Upper Canada, there were jobs for all able-bodied workers. This was a topic of endless epistles to family and friends back home. Naturally a higher value was placed upon certain occupations, but wherever a particular need arose in a community, note was taken, and everyone did their best to find someone with the required skills.

> I wrote a letter to brother William concerning John coming out and think he would do well as there is no clog maker in all the place and leather is only one and three pence per lb but if he comes to be sure and come by the way of new york.... [John Millar]

In 1820, Charles Stuart advised that "mechanics, particularly carpenters, blacksmiths, and shoemakers, may generally be sure of obtaining employment, with high wages."

Tiger Dunlop, with his own particular brand of humour, advised against bringing maids, especially young or good-looking ones, since in all probability they would get married within a month or two. The same applied to governesses.

> For the last five years, by an expedient similar to yours, the deficiency in the female side of my house has been made up by a girl which I brought up from Quebec. She left us a few weeks ago, having got married to a person in the neighbourhood, and we have in her place a stout Irish lass to whom we pay three dollars per month. [David MacLaren]

About Englishwomen in general, William Cobbett expressed little faith in their adaptability; many emigrant women would show how wrong he was.

> There is one other quality, without the possession of which, all the rest are of no use; namely, that quality which enables a man to overcome the scruples, the remonstrances, and the wailings of his wife. Women, and especially English women, transplant very badly, which is indeed a fact greatly in their praise.

Whether male or female, there were always folks who simply could not make up their minds about whether they wanted to come to Canada, or go to the United States. Happily there were always people such as Thomas Cather who helped to tip the balance in favour of Canada. In a letter to his father in Ireland, Cather wrote:

> From what I have seen of Canada I like it very much, and although inferior in several respects to some parts of the States, it is in others superior for the British emigrant.... The class of people who do best here are Labourers, Mechanics and working Farmers, the larger family of the latter, the better—these people are accustomed to hardship and suffer very little additional in the woods, which in the course of a few years they are sure of a comfortable competence, but the retired officers and reduced gentlemen, of whom there are a considerable number feel

25

severely the privations they must undergo, and sadly miss the society to which they have been accustomed. I met a gentleman who gave me an invitation to his house, he was a Lieut. in 10th Hussars and is now settled with his family in the Bush country, seventy miles from any market—he says he has to work as hard as a slave—there can scarcely be a greater contrast than life in the tenth Hussars and life in a log hut in the backwoods of Canada.

When all the bags were packed, and necessary business conducted, it was time to begin the round of bidding farewell to friends and associates. Sometimes, there was time for a last minute surprise, and perhaps a small parting gift.

I was invited to take a walk one evening by one of our members. When we went so far as Buchanan's Coffee House in the High St. Being invited in, I found all our members sitting around a table waiting for us and the table was well supplied with all that would satisfy them. We sat down and did ample justice to what was prepared. After spending a very pleasant evening, one of the members read a very nice address (which I am sorry I have not got a copy of), giving me at the same time, a Bible, also electing me an Honorary member of the Association.

This was more than I expected and although I prepared a sort of speech, it was of no use to me, for I could not say much. I babbled out a few words as they occurred to me, until I broke down when I began to think of the good young men who, thus clustered around and with genuine expression of kind regards, showed that I had in them good and true friends. This meeting I shall never forget, besides the many social and profitable meetings and excursions we had together, now to be separated perhaps for ever. [John McCorkindale]

When word got out that J. B. Taylor was emigrating to Canada, all his acquaintances wanted to wish him well. Some of the neighbours in his Perthshire community were ignorant of geography, and of other matters pertaining to life in the new country, but their hopes for his success were genuine.

...one old lady came to me and said: 'Our folk live in Canada, and if you see them tell them I was aye feared they would all a' eaten up with bears and bogles and are ye no feared of the awfu waves and muckle whales?' I said: 'Nay, Nay, my woman, God is on the mighty deep the same as on the land.' She answered, 'Aye, Aye, Weel tell them we're au' weel and brawly,' She evidently thought Canada was about the size of Perthshire.

Travelling to the docks was often a tedious affair, which, depending upon where the emigrant lived, might have involved a journey of several days. This often entailed significant expenditures, particularly so for large families. In addition to the fare, there might also be accommodations and meals to pay for, as well as tips for hostelry staff, the driver and baggage handlers.

The John Walker family sailed from Liverpool on board the *Queen Adelaide* on 27 September 1835, bound for Upper Canada. John, his wife Elizabeth Hextall, and their family children age one to twelve years, travelled from the village of Borrowash, three miles east of Derby. In his diary, John kept strict accounts of all expenditures incurred. [See box with expenses, on p. 28.]

There were various options when it came to overland travel to the seaport. The cheapest method would have meant plodding along at the rate of four or five miles per hour in the wagon of a friendly farmer. The advantage of this mode of transportation was that it provided a generous space for baggage as well as for large numbers of children.

There were two covered or tilted farmer's hay-waggons—one from a parish in Buckinghamshire, and the other from the neighbourhood of Northampton: they had joined company on the road. The women and children, with but few exceptions, occupied the conveyances, which were loaded with packages, bundles and boxes; a few of the more elderly females walked on the pathway by the side of their husbands and sons; the younger men trudging it with seeming glee, and carrying various articles we conjecture for immediate use.... The leafless tree and hedges—the miry road, with its long serpentine wheel tracks; the yellow waggons, with their inanimate and living freight, covered with light canvass; the women habited in blue or red cloaks; the men in their frocks blending in colour with the many hues of the bundles; and above all, the object of their journey was well calculated to excite human sympathy. Yet no

Expenses to America   Sept. 17. 1835

	£	s.	d.
Coach fare to Manchester	6.	0.	0.
Bread, cheese and ale	0.	1.	6.
Coachman	0.	5.	0.
Railway fare to Liverpool	0.	16.	0.
Pd. Kenworthy for goods from Derby to Liverpool	2.	1.	6.
Butcher for meat, &c.	1.	6.	6.
Baker for bread	2.	12.	0.
Groceries	1.	18.	0.
Porter, &c., spirits	3.	8.	6.
Byrnes for flour, meal, eggs &c.	2.	12.	0.
D. for Langhorn	0.	3.	0.
D for passage for 4 1/2 adults at 3£	13.	10.	0.
Hostable money each 4/6	1.	11.	6.
Mr. Barnes, lodgings, tea, bed, breakfast & dinner	1.	0.	0.
Lodgings	1.	12.	6.
At D. and coach fare	0.	15.	0.
Marnes for tea, bed & breakfast	0.	4.	6.
Travelling box	0.	4.	0.
Bread and meat	0.	10.	0.
Total	40.	12.	6.

[John Walker's addition is over by one shilling.]

John Walker's emigration expenses (see p. 27)

John Walker, ca. 1851 (Courtesy Steve Brown)

one appeared sad or sorrowful—on the contrary all seemed to be cheerful; and their clean and decent appearance bore witness of the propriety of their general habits; the whole looked remarkably healthy, especially the children.

Failing a friendly farmer, one might hire a local carter. The journey might be arranged to take place after working hours so as not to interfere with regular business.

Left Guisboro at 10 o'clock P.M. the 5th of April 1831. It be Easter that day. Hired Thomas Johnson Wagon & arrived at Port of Whitby at 8 o'clock in the morning. [Joseph Wilson]

One could also travel by Stage-Wagon. This cumbersome vehicle, pulled by up to ten horses, seldom exceeded three miles per hour. It was a practical way for large groups to travel, for depending upon the amount of baggage, it could accommodate as many as forty passengers. But for those with higher standards and, needless to say, more money, the prospect of whizzing along in a Mail-Coach, at the astonishing pace of twelve miles per hour, held far more appeal.

Patrick Shirreff's overland journey from Scotland to Liverpool began on 20 April 1833. He travelled the first leg, a distance of seventeen miles between Haddington and Edinburgh, by the Earl Grey stage-coach, drawn by a pair of thoroughbred bays in charge of Quinten Campbell. Shirreff expressed pleasure at having accomplished this distance in less than an hour and a half, and "without an application of the whip." In Edinburgh he joined forces with two companions with whom he would travel to North America. His party then connected with a coach for Manchester, travelling overnight to Carlisle. Here a quick change of coach took place before continuing on to Penrith where a hurried and highly unsatisfactory breakfast was served. Lancaster offered a twenty minute break during which the passengers dined. Then on to Manchester, arriving after nightfall. After such a tiresome journey, the prospect of being able to undertake the remainder of his journey by railway must have brought a modicum of relief.

One of Britain's earliest commercial railway lines was the thirty-mile stretch between Manchester and Liverpool. Opening in 1829 to service Manchester's ever-growing cotton industry, it also presented emigrants en route to Liverpool with a swifter and more comfortable overland journey. However, there were drawbacks:

> We travelled from Manchester to Liverpool by the railway, on the morning of the 22d, and accomplished a distance of thirty miles in an hour and a half. Several miles were performed in two minutes, according to my stop-watch. At the request of a friend, I occupied a place on the outside of a way coach, and was much annoyed by the current of air and coke from the engine. My eyes did not recover the effects of the coke for forty-eight hours afterwards. [Patrick Shirreff]

Another possibility was to travel part of the distance by water. Emigrants would make for the nearest major river or coastal port. A sailing vessel or steam ship would then convey them to the docks.

> We arrived at Gainsboro by Mr Foothill's Wagon about 1/2 past Six. got our baggage on board the Mercury Steam Packet. Breakfasted at my cousins John Hewitt's Bridge Street. took our Farewell of our Friends and embarked for Hull. Left word at Ferry by the boatman that we had commenced our long journey. Arrived at Hull and got on board the Ship with less trouble than I expected. Slept in the Ship all night. all of us rested pretty well in our new lodgings in the ship.
> [George Robinson]

The nineteenth century brought great advancements in shipping. Steamships made their appearance long before they were used to carry passengers to Canada. In 1812, a small steam-powered boat named the *Comet* began carrying goods and passengers along the river Clyde. The success of this very first steamship must have been an inspiration to other shipping companies, for it soon was possible to undertake journeys to the many points under the power of steam.

In 1816 a regular service was instituted between Brighton and Le Havre. A similar service was then offered between Holyhead and Dublin. It was immediately apparent that steam vessels held a great advantage over sailing ships. Crossing the

30

Irish Sea would take a sailing ship up to a week, whereas a steamer could make the trip in fourteen hours.

It was at this time that steamboats first appeared on the Great Lakes also; the first travelling between Kingston and Toronto were in 1817.

The first vessel to cross the Atlantic aided by steam was the *Savannah* in 1818. It would take several decades before the majority of trans-Atlantic passengers gained the benefit of this speedier mode of travel. Some consider the *Royal William* to be the first true steamer to cross the Atlantic. This Canadian vessel left Pictou, Nova Scotia, for London in 1833. In 1838, the *Sirius* and the *Great Western* commenced a regular steam-packet service between Bristol and New York.

> The passage on these boats took from fifteen to eighteen days. Setting out amidst cheers from Cork, the *Sirius* (703 tons) left Ireland on April 4th. On April 8th the *Great Western* left Bristol harbour in an attempt to overtake her. The *Sirius* arrived at Sandy Hook in American on April 22nd, fourteen days later. The next day the *Great Western* arrived, and, since she had taken less time, she shared the honour of being the first steamship to cross the Atlantic from England to America.

The advent of steamships meant that the emigrants of the 1820s and 1830s were at liberty to travel coastal waters, reaching large ports far quicker than they might by land. When John Frazer left his Scottish home to travel to Liverpool, he did so by steamer and was more than pleased with the speed of the trip.

> Sailed from Glasgow in the Vulcan Steamer at 5 o'clock P.M. for Liverpool, call'd at Greenock and remained for a few minutes then Mr John Gilmour late confectioner in Kilmarnock joined Mr Wm Robertson and myself we there by a previous arrangement had agreed to sail together. James Young late from Monger in Kilmarnock came on board and saw us off. 8 P.M. very much annoyed indeed with drunk people. Met with a Mr James Thomson and his son Robert from Garscube or Spring brow near Glasgow. They were bound for New York in order to recover property left by some distant relation in America. 1 o'clock Sunday morning passed Ailsa Craig felt a regret on having a last peep at my Father land. [John Frazer]

31

Travelling these coastal waters, especially in good weather, provided the passengers with wondrous sights, many of which had only been read of in books.

> 6 o'clock A.M. espied the Isle of Man at a distance. Steamer sailing 10 knots an hour 1/2 past 10 a.m. had breakfast on board paid 1/ 11A.M. passed the Isle of Man, seems a fine Island. came in sight of the Welsh coast about 12. entered the river Mersey at 2 P.M. and arrived in Liverpool at 1/2 past 3P.M. having made the voyage in 23 1/2 hours.... [John Frazer]

It was not always possible to sail directly from the port of one's choice. In March 1819, thirteen-year-old James Edwards emigrated with his parents and two brothers. Although James' father was a shipwright employed at the Portsmouth docks, and presumably knowledgeable about shipping procedures, the family was unable to obtain passage in a vessel in which they could sail directly to North America.

> When Sir George Grey who was Master shipwright of Portsmouth Dock Yard learned the intention of my father and others to leave England for America he sent for my father to ascertain his purposes in going to a country with which they had so recently been at war. My Father assured Sir George that he sailed to New York, but his destination was Upper Canada,— that he was obliged to go via New York there being no conveyance any other way at the time. This explanation seemed ample, and no more was said. It would appear as if the British authorities were very jealous lest skilled mechanics of their own should leave their shores, to build up wealth at their expense.... There being no Merchant vessel at Portsmouth the Emigrants were obliged to go on board a small sloop to ferry them across the Channel to Havre in France, where they found 3 vessels bound for New York waiting for fair wind. They got on board the "Comet," having as a convoy the two others. We soon lost sight of them however and each pursued its trackless path as best it could. [James Edwards]

William Hunter and his sister Janet experienced a mixture of excitement and anxiety as their vessel eased its way into the Solway Firth. The thrill of the moment was never to be forgotten, but, like most, the reality of bidding a final farewell to their homeland would momentarily dampen their sense of adventure. The Hunters were on their way to Liverpool, where they planned to book passage to New York. From there, they would travel to Upper Canada where they had relatives. William had worked hard and was rather proud of the fact that he had saved enough money to take Janet with him. First, they had to travel to Liverpool.

> Left Annan Waterfoot; had a pleasant passage to Liverpool; landed about 11 o'clock, lodged at a Mr. Lloyd's No. 29 Regent Street; did not think much of him. I think he is what we may call a respectable man catcher.

Large ports were often bewildering places. Surrounded by an extraordinary atmosphere of hustle, bustle, and confusion, even the most seasoned travellers were likely to become overwhelmed. Some emigrants managed to make the most of a few days in the big city. The Hunters 'spent the Sabbath walking about viewing the town of Liverpool.' William noted that he had seen 'many strange sights.' Despite their low opinion of the landlord, who was obviously one of the sort to take advantage of emigrants, William and Janet fared reasonably well. They managed to book their passage on the *Hottinguer* and to purchase items necessary for their voyage.

For the uninitiated, one of the greatest hazards of dockland areas were "Sharpers." Feigning friendship by offers of assistance, these fellows were highly skilled in the art of parting an emigrant from his money. There were numerous ways in which a person could be duped. Overcharging for lodgings and selling shoddy goods were common. Perhaps the most grievous mischief was wrought upon those unfortunate souls who were illiterate or ignorant about the geography of the country they were going to. In 1831, one Irish family did not fare well.

> June 25th, Michael Donnolly and wife paid £8 for their passage in the ship *Florence* to a person of the name of Yonge, who gave him a receipt without any date or ship's name filled into it, and he, not being able to read, did not find out the imposition until this morning, when Yonge told him that he was to go to St.

John. He complains of this alteration as he has some friends on board the *Florence*, and paid his money on the express condition that he was to go with them on that vessel. Michael McCormick was a witness to this transaction and certifies the truth of this statement.

I consulted the Mayor about this case, but he regretted that he had no power either to compel him to come before him or to pay back the money. Under these circumstances I thought it best for the interest of these poor people to try my influence and remonstrances with them, and Yonge agreed to pay £7 and Donnolly and family not having the means of proceeding returned to Ireland.

Emigrant guidebooks frequently warned of such happenings. People with some sophistication would have anticipated meeting such characters and dealt with them accordingly.

...was directed by the mate of the Steam Boat to a Mrs Johnsons Lodgins No. 10 Regent Street. the party now consisted of five with the Messrs Thomsons. had tea after which, went out to have a view of some of the American ships. the Docks where the Ships lie, are erected on a magnificent scale, we there met with one of the Sharpers, belonging to a class of beings who are continually prowling after, and ever ready to entrap the unwary and unsuspecting Emigrant. however we took care of them all, but it is no easy task to avoid them. we returned to our lodgings in the evening after having seen part of the Town went to bed a little fatigued. [John Frazer]

Liverpool became a magnet, especially to those fleeing starvation and fever during the years of the potato famine in Ireland.

The person employed by the parish authorities of Liverpool to provide coffins for the poor creatures who are dying daily from starvation and fever, states that he supplies 200 of these fragile tenements every week. He further stated that he received an order for 36 dozen on Thursday (last week). From the 1st of February to the 6th of April, there arrived in Liverpool, from Ireland, 88,812 persons. There are now on the parish books, 11,000 Irish getting relief. The number of emigrants since January is 29,000.

34

Not all these people emigrated to North America. Some remained in Liverpool, others moved on, seeking work in English centres, such as Manchester. For those who did leave on ships bound for Quebec, the possibility of contracting cholera, or ship's fever as it came to be known, was a frightening prospect.

Emigrants often sailed on packet ships, so called because they plied a regular route between two ports, carrying the mail, goods and passengers. Ships were classified in types; these classifications, such as brig, barque, schooner, were based upon the number and placement of masts on the vessel, as well as the formation of the sails. The length of a vessel, especially in the early part of the century, might be as little as fifty feet. Given the ferocity of north Atlantic storms, the prospect of sailing on such a tiny ship would have struck fear into the hearts of most. As the century wore on and shipbuilding increased, much larger vessels, some approaching two hundred and seventy feet, were carrying emigrants to North America.

While it was possible to arrange one's passage by correspondence with shipping companies prior to leaving home, most arrived at the docks having made no booking. Newspaper advertisements recommended that prospective passengers apply directly to the Captain on board for terms of freight or passage. This procedure often resulted in emigrants spending several days at the port, awaiting the sailing of the vessel.

> Make your bargain for your passage with the *owner* of the ship, or some well-known respectable broker or ship-master; avoid, by all means, those crimps that are generally found about the docks and quays near where ships are taking in passengers. Be sure the ship is going to the port you contract for, as much deception has been practised in this respect. It is important to select a well-known captain and a fast sailing ship, even at a higher rate. [A. C. Buchanan]

Some passengers had sufficient funds to ensure the best of everything. The Hopkirk family certainly appears to have fallen within that category.

> Having agreed for a cabin passage for New York for self, Mrs H servant and 2 children, for which I paid 50 sterling, in the

Tennessee an American vessel 415 tons Register, Capt. G.W. Robinson commander, we went on board this morning at about 10 minutes before 8 a.m., at the St. George's dock gates, and having been taken in tow by a steamer...to the mouth of the river...we made great progress so much so that by 8 o'clock p.m. we were off Skerries Head Light House. [James Hopkirk]

Unless a person kept his wits about him, he was in danger of being charged too high a price. A shrewd individual might approach several agents to enquire about availability, prices and sailing dates. It was not out of the question to bargain until the best rate had been achieved. Johnson noted in his diary, "took my passage in the *Thorntons* for Quebec. Seven guineas in the steerage. paid one guinea for my dog."

The cost of passage fluctuated, not only from ship to ship, but port to port, and from decade to decade. Johnson does not indicate whether his passage includes meals, but in view of the very much lower prices quoted in the 1820s and 1830s, one can only conclude that he did not entirely get his money's worth.

John Frazer may have obtained a particularly low rate by offering his services as ship's doctor. There was no requirement for a ship to carry a doctor, even under the Passenger Act of 1842, which improved conditions considerably. In case of emergency, the captain would make use of the stores in his medical box. Frazer's diary indicates his genuine concern for, and his involvement with, sick passengers. On 6 July, five hundred miles from New York, he was obliged to 'put one of the passengers in a straight waistcoat today (cause insanity).' Perhaps it was the same passenger who, on 23 May, threatened to commit suicide from 'Delirium Tremens or Blue Devils.'

John Frazer has provided such a detailed record of his Liverpool dockland experience in 1837 that the entire section of his diary devoted to this period is reproduced here:

Monday 15 May. After breakfast made enquiry regarding the first Ships that were to sail for N. York went on board of some of them. they are very splendidly fitted up. we found that none were to sail for some days which was a dissapointment to us all, went to several Agents found that the Ship Napoleon was the earliest the steerage was quite full of Irish. the second Cabin with a few Berths unfilled the demand for which was £5 but as five of us were going together we would have got for £4:10- Made some calls in Town today saw Mr Benjamin Smith from Kilmarnock. Drank Tea with Dr Craig and family in the evening then called on Mr & Mrs Snodgrass.

Tuesday 16 May. Went again this morning among the Ship Agents in order to make the best bargain we could. recommended by Dr Craig to Mr Sherlock who had freighted the ship Jacob Pennel and agreed to go by her for £3.10 a head and we have the choice of our Berth—he told us she would sail on Sunday following, after which we went into the Town accompanied by Dr Craig & saw the New Market &c which is fitted up on a very great scale. it contains all kinds of fruits vegetables &c &c. called again to Mr B. Smith who was kind enough to treat us to Two Tumblers of Scotch Whiskey Punch.

Wednesday 17 May. After Breakfast call'd on the Agent and fixed with him and deposited a sovereign a head and secured our births after which was met by Mr David Smith, crossed the river and had an excursion into Chesshire appears a fine county, saw then the interior of a Wind Mill for grinding flour for the first time to any of us.

Thursday 18 May. got all our heavy luggage on board hired a cart for which we paid 1/- called in the evening on Mr Snodgrass and Mr James Reid late Merch^{nt} in Sterling. Saw the Liverpool and Manchester Railway and the New Cemetery...

Friday 19 May. Went to the ship to see if all our luggage was secure. We met with Mr Cuthbertson, Farmer from Knockin Law his Brothers and Brother in law in persuit of a Brother who had eloped from shop in Glasgow. he had cleared out for New York the day previous to their arrival. he sailed in the ship

Saturday 20 May. Called again in the evening on Mr Sherlock the Agent he promised to send us off with the Napoleon which sailed this morning for 10/ a head more and sent us down the river in a Steam Boat on Sunday morning, we accepted. got some necessaries laid in for Sea and squared with our land lady—an accident occurred to myself this morning. Mr Thomson, his Son and myself went to see the Napoleon hauled out of the Dock and on standing in the Harbour the Steam Boat Tow line came around with a swerp where I was standing, and laid me flat on my face with the rapidity of lightning. My hat and wig was thrown into the river and myself very nearly. I had 3 of my Ribs fractured by it—so of course I lost my hat and wig and was thankful I escaped with my life. Young Mr Thomson was also knocked down but was not injured. An Irishman was knocked down at the same time but was not hurt either. I regretted very much the loss but could not help myself.

Doctor Frazer mentions no more of his accident. It is possible that the severity of his injury was less than he thought. On the other hand, he may have been one of those extremely stoic individuals who bear their discomforts silently. It would seem that of the two incidents, the loss of the wig gave him more concern.

By this time, wigs were no longer fashionable amongst ordinary people, but certain professionals, such as doctors and lawyers, continued to wear them.

On 21 May, in company with his chums, he boarded a steamer which took them to board the *Napoleon* four miles down river.

The authors have been unable to find reliable statistics to estimate the number of emigrants arriving in Upper Canada via New York. While it is safe to suggest that the greater proportion arrived via Quebec, it is evident from diaries and correspondence that a good portion did choose the New York route. Of the two, New York was more costly, but offered the promise of a shorter ocean voyage. In the 1820s, the average crossing took forty-five days to Quebec and forty days to New York. By the early 1830s with the advent of the railway, the overland part of the journey through New York state became considerably less arduous than travelling from Quebec. Consequently many established settlers advised prospective emigrants to take the New York route. It is also clear that by the 1830s, some poorer emigrants set upon living in the United States, chose the Quebec route because it was cheaper. Once in Canada, they hoped to make their way to the border, funding their travels by picking up odd jobs along the way. Among this group were many of those who found themselves admitted into the temporary accommodation at York sheltered in houses provided by benevolent societies, before resuming their journey to the States.

Some passengers expressed a preference with respect to sailing on an American or a British ship, possibly stemming from an experience on a previous trip.

FOR QUEBEC.

THE FINE
AND COPPER

FAST SAILING
FASTENED SHIP,

JEANIE JOHNSTON,

700 Tons Burthen,

Mr. JAMES ATTRIDGE, Commander,

WILL SAIL from the Port of TRALEE for QUE-BEC, on or about the 21st AUGUST next, (wind and weather permitting).

This fine Vessel is a well known and favourite passenger Ship, and has been most lucky and fortunate in all her voyages. She is, as usual, fitted up with every care and attention to the health and comfort of the passengers, is well ventilated, and has a capacious Life Boat in addition to her other boats.

For all particulars apply at the Office of the Owners, Messrs. JOHN DONOVAN & SONS, TRALEE: who have also for SALE a Cargo of prime Red and Yellow Pine Timber, Oak, Ash, Elm, Birch, Pine and Spruce Deals, Oak Pipe and Barrel Staves, Spars, Oars, &c,— which they have just landed from this ship.

An advertisement for an emigration ship

A. C. Buchanan, in company with most authorities on emigration during this period, recommended that people make the voyage in April or May. July and August were considered poor times, because of the likelihood of contrary winds.

A May arrival date provided a generous period to settle oneself before winter set in.

Martin Doyle expressed a preference for travelling the more expensive route, via New York. He reasoned that not only was the voyage shorter, but the dangers associated with the banks of Newfoundland were avoided, as was the navigation of the Saint Lawrence. More interestingly, he suggested that passengers could travel steerage and not let on they had.

> Those to whom money is an important object, (even though they be of a higher class of Emigrants, suppose half-pay officers with their families, or gentlemen of limited means with two or three hundred pounds in their pockets), they can bargain for part of the steerage accommodation, partitioned off for themselves, and when they land, it will be better for them to have the cabin fare (a large sum if families are concerned), in their pockets, for the purchase and improvement of estates— the money saved in this way by a single individual, would purchase in fee, fifty acres of estate. And who in Upper Canada cares, or will ever enquire, whether the new colonist slept in one part or the other of the ship which brought him, and, perhaps, his wife, and little ones, to the land of independence and peace; now would a real gentleman be lowered in the estimation of any one but a fool, for economizing funds, so essential to his future prosperity.

According to Doyle's information of 1832, the cost to steerage passengers between Bristol and New York was £5 while cabin passengers paid £25. Between Liverpool and New York, steerage was £5 and cabin £30. From Liverpool to Quebec, steerage was £4 and cabin £15.

Although emigration from Europe itself to Upper Canada was not heavy in this period, the one area which did contribute many emigrants was the German-speaking one. A great many Germans departed from Alsace, Hesse, Bavaria, Württemberg, Schleswig-Holstein and even Prussia itself with Upper Canada as their destination. In the 1820s they were motivated by economic hardship and the revolutions of 1848 encouraged another wave of refugees.

The early Pennsylvania-German settlers in Niagara and particularly Waterloo continued to speak their own language and organize life according to their traditional customs, which meant there was an essentially German society for emigrants to come to. In Waterloo they were attracted by the fact that they could live and work without having to learn English.

There were no direct sailings to Canada from Germany at this time, so these emigrants had to choose between crossing to Britain and sailing from there, or the New York route. There were regular boats from the Dutch ports and Le Havre, and this was their principal means of emigration. Once in America, they aimed for Buffalo and then Berlin (now Kitchener).

The Germans were regarded as such desirable settlers that Thomas Mercer Jones, in charge of the Canada Company office in Goderich in 1843 suggested offering them half-price lots as an inducement to emigrate. A German-language prospectus was produced in Berlin and sent to the British consul in Bremen for distribution.

Newlyweds Catharine Parr Traill and her husband Thomas sailed from Greenock in July 1832 paying £15 each for their passage to Montreal. Mrs Traill thought the fare rather high but was pleased with the comfort the vessel offered. The *Laurel* was "not a regular passenger-ship," she explained. They had taken her because "the only vessel in the river [Clyde] bound for Canada was a passenger-ship, literally swarming with emigrants, chiefly of the lower class of Highlanders."

Purchasing provisions for the voyage was often done at the port city. Besides the possibility of procuring items that would retain freshness longer than those carted from home, the emigrant was able to seek advice from ship's agents, merchants and chandlers about the best types of supplies to carry. The advice dispensed was not always the wisest. Passengers had to balance their needs against the limited storage provided on the vessel. In July 1819, Johnson "bought a cheese, gallon whiskey, tin-pot and wash hand basin" to supplement his supplies.

The Passenger Act of 1842 stated that passengers must be victualled by the ship. Supplementary stores were required since ship's fare, so far as that doled out to steerage passengers was concerned, was insufficient and generally of poor quality. Passengers had always had the option of paying for meals at the time of booking their passage. Steerage passengers could rarely afford to do so.

It was vital that passengers had adequate provisions in the event that their voyage was delayed. As a general rule, the voyage did not usually exceed six weeks, but, because of one thing or another, passengers did find themselves in the precarious circumstance of having run out of vital stores. The Resident Agent for Emigrants at Quebec, A. C. Buchanan, made many references to such occurrences. He ensured that semi-starving immigrants were fed before they left Quebec.

> Mr Buchanan, government emigrant agent at Quebec, gives many instances of the danger arising from being short-victualled, in his reports to the governor during the year 1841. 'In the brig, Lady Hood from Stornoway,' he says, 'were 14 families, 78 in number, all very poor; and landed here after a passage of 70 days, in great distress, from want of provisions. they had expended all their money in purchasing supplies from the master during the passage. 139 passengers in the *Cumberland Lass* from Belfast, were 66 days on the voyage. they purchased from Captain Smith as long as their money lasted, and he had to support from 40 to 50 of the poorest for the last three weeks. When he arrived here, all his ship's stores were exhausted, besides supplies which he obtained from different places in the gulf. [Samuel Butler]

It is interesting to note that the English, Irish and Scots were advised to take different supplies, the premise being that some were used to a richer diet. Many writers address this topic, affirming Doyle's assessment.

> Those who have been accustomed to use English diet, generally take with them biscuit, cheese, beef, pork, tea, potted herrings, split peas for soup, sugar, flour, onion, porter, ale, and gin, mustard, vinegar, pepper, and milk—which last, after having been boiled, should be carefully sealed up in jars, and if 1 lb. of loaf sugar be added to it, there is no danger of its not keeping fresh during the voyage. But the Irish and Highland Scotch, unaccustomed to so many good things, some of which they have perhaps, never tasted in their lives, are usually content with a supply for each individual, consisting of 4 st. of oatmeal, 4 st. of cutlings for gruel, 4 st. of biscuit, 1/2 st. of sugar, 1/2 lb of tea, 4 st. of butter, 20 st. of potatoes, and a few dozen of eggs, which should be well greased, to exclude the air, and consequently preserve them fresh. I must add a quart or two of whiskey, for emergencies, and no considerate agent would recommend or allow a much greater quantity.

42

In 1828, A. C. Buchanan proposed the following rations for a family of five persons:

48 stone of potatoes (if in season, say not after 1st June)
1 1/2 cwt of oatmeal or flour
1/2 cwt biscuits
20 lbs butter in a keg
a gallon of molasses
20 lbs bacon
50 lbs fish (herrings) in a small keg
1 gallon of spirits
a little vinegar
If the emigrant has means, let him purchase besides, 1 lb of tea and 14 lb sugar for his wife.

Buchanan also cautioned passengers:

When you contract with the captain for your passage, do not forget to insure a sufficient supply of good water. An adult will require five pints a day—children in proportion.
[A. C. Buchanan]

Since they were apt to rot if improperly stored, Samuel Butler warned against "trusting to potatoes as an essential article of food." Since generations of people had relied upon potatoes as the main staple of their diet, Butler probably realized the futility of his recommendation. He therefore added that if a person must take potatoes, they should be kept in a locked barrel, to prevent theft, and stored where it was neither too warm nor too wet, and monitored constantly by the passenger.

Some people managed these things better than others. Having lots of money certainly made things easier. Having sufficient foresight, as well as excellent advice about what to take, was equally important.

By authority from the Captain, I purchased a good little cow from a milkman in Liverpool; and the ship-butcher sent some four year old Cheviot wedders, *decidedly the best of all sheep for sea-stock*, and finer mutton for gravy and flavour never graced a board. The minor department of our live-stock was

43

well cared for, as our Captain took both a pleasure and a pride cramming his pigs and poultry to their hearts' content.
[Adam Fergusson]

Most people were not so fortunate. Going without milk for so many weeks could be especially hard on children. The youngest child of the Leeming family must have compensated by eating additional helpings of other calcium rich foods. She blossomed.

> The baby which if you saw you would hardly believe, she is so fat and plump and looks quite healthy, although she has not tasted milk since the first week were at sea, for, unfortunately, it was all spoiled, not having been properly corked up.
> [Sarah Leeming]

We do not know Sarah Leeming's method of corking milk, but Samuel Butler recommended the same method as Martin Doyle, given above. Another means was proposed by James Wilson:

> to preserve new milk for a voyage, take a large or small jar or jars, and clean them remarkably well, and when done, put the milk therein, and after securing it well by corking it close, put the jar or jars into a large pot of water, and boil them over a good fire, and when done, pack them in a hamper, or some other place, and it will keep sweet the whole of the voyage.

He reported that this recipe had been followed by a gentleman sailing to Philadelphia who has used the milk, even after his arrival, finding it still 'retaining its natural sweetness.'

By the 1830s the master of a vessel was required by law to carry prescribed quantities of foods for his passengers. The following, as documented by William Cattermole, were to be taken for each person:

> —bread, 2/3 lb; beer, 2/3 gallon; fresh meat, 2/3 lb; vegetables, 3/4 lb. Cocoa, 2/3 oz; sugar, 3/4 oz; tea, 1/4 oz. per diem. When fresh meat cannot be had, salt beef, 1/2 lb; flour, 1/2 lb; peas, 3/4 pint. On those days that flour is used, raisins and suet may also be substituted for a portion of the flour.

Cattermole also suggested:

a few pounds of portable soup, is an excellent thing on the voyage, and persons going in parties, may always arrange to take a pig or two, and if they will look after it, a sheep; many take fowls, but they are much trouble, and are often very sickly. Ducks will do well, some herrings, salt fish, eggs, suet, butter, rice, onions and carrots, with a few apples for puddings, &c. form the principal wants; portable soup, unless you take fowls, is good in case of sea sickness.

Anticipating the voyage had provided young master Dobie with a great deal of pleasure, and when the day of boarding ship finally arrived, he made certain that he missed no aspect of his family's preparations.

The next thing, after booking our passage, was to get supplies for the passengers who were going aboard. You may think £3 was very cheap fare, but they only provided us with water, fire and a bunk. Then there was nothing left for a single man to do but go up town and buy a chunk of hard tack, and if married with a family to provide for, he would get several bags of this hard tack. The longer these hardtack biscuits were kept the better they used to be, for in order to make them palatable we used to soak them overnight in fresh water, and then we would split them and fry them in pork gravy, then they were very palatable.... We had butter and a few potatoes, remember that it was August, and we had some cheese which did not keep very well. [W. C. Dobie]

Wherever possible, it was advisable to store foodstuffs in a container in which the bottom was wider than the top so that gravity might assist in keeping it upright. Some people never got as far as thinking about containers. Those living lives of hardship faced enormous difficulty procuring sufficient supplies for the voyage. The plight of a poor Irish family, preparing to set sail from London, is thus described:

...it was whispered that a few biscuits and a little oatmeal was all the provision they had made for the voyage. The captain, however, who had had some experience, considered that they were amply provided, and he had made the strictest inquiry. A

45

bag of coarse bread, which had been cut into slices and then browned in the oven, had that morning, he said, been send on board to assist them—it was the gift of a few poor Irish people who lived in the borough of Southwark.

The Trip

Adieu, adieu! my native shore
Fades o'er the waters blue
Lord Byron

Finally, after weeks of preparations and possibly days
spent in travelling to the docks, the time to board ship had
arrived. Baggage was separated into two piles, things needed on
the voyage, and those to be stored in the hold. Fortunate
passengers might find a good berth without too much difficulty.
Personal items would be organized and safely tucked away. Then
it was time to begin exploring the vessel.

> All now appear to be in a hurry and bustle and confusion on
> every side. The sun is shining bright and clear. The Quay is
> crowded with people, composed of Porters, Police, Beggars,
> children, emigrants & their friends & the different Articles of
> Luggage, hurried rapidly on board. Friends, parting with friends,
> some crying, some kissing, some shaking hands till all went on
> board, now numbering in passengers 320, and including the
> crew, 400. [John McCorkindale]

The Steele sisters, Millicent and Ellen, along with their
mother and brothers, sailed on board the *Thames* under the
command of Captain Griswold. Griswold inspired enormous
confidence in at least one passenger, and over the course of the
voyage earned great respect from the Steeles. There was
considerable confusion on boarding the ship.

April 27th 1833. Went on board the Thames about 2 p.m., Mr and Mrs E. Dollman and their daughters came with us to see us off—found Aunt Steele, Mary, Edward Cowcher, Mr and Mrs Dod and George there, Charles and the Kenningtons, never saw such a scene of confusion, the deck covered with packages of all descriptions, dogs barking, pigs squealing, we had hardly room to stand in safety; went down below and did not find it much better, saw some of our fellow passengers Mr and Mrs Fawcett a newly married couple, the brother of the lady Mr Rawlings, who intends going as far as Portsmouth with them.... We went over the vaults, on our return found Miss Taylor talking to a fat old lady in the cuddy, who it seems intends to be our fellow passenger whether we will or not, she says she is come all the way from Ireland to cross with Capt. Griswold with whom she has already made one voyage, and that she now finds there is no berth for her, but she says "I have calculated all along to go with Capt. G— and go I will—he is a splendid man and he must find me a place somewhere, I guess he'll do something for old acquaintance sake"— her name is Keating. We find that the ship cannot be ready to clear out tonight. The Captain left us at tea time, our friends did not leave us till the Docks were to be cleared for the night. [Millicent Steele]

After seeing that all was ready, and making sure that the pilot was installed upon the vessel, Captain Griswold proceeded to travel the distance from London to Portsmouth by coach, whereupon he resumed command. In Ellen Steele's view, this was a sly way of getting out of all the confusion.

After leaving port, a ship might make several calls before heading out to sea. On this particular voyage, the *Thames* anchored at Spithead, near Portsmouth, where more passengers embarked. While there, cabin passengers were given the opportunity to purchase a few luxuries when a cutter came alongside offering to carry them to the harbour. Only the men went, the women deciding that it was too rough to go to the trouble of climbing down into the little boat.

Once a ship left her moorings or drew up her anchor, it was time for a final wave of the hand and a last glimpse of a loved one. The distance between ship and shoreline slowly increased and faces in the distance became smaller. For some, this was an exhilarating experiences; for others, it was a moment of heartbreak.

> Now the little steamer "Robt. Bruce" is slowing towing up from the Quay and at half past five P.M. we are anchored in the Harbor, cheered by the crowd of spectators who cover where we left on the Quay, and we in return cheered, with Handerchiefs flying on all hands, but some looked on in Silence. The last I recognized from the shore was my poor Aunt, Flora, then the distance increased. I could see her wiping her eyes. At last I could distinguish her no more. [John McCorkindale]

For J. B. Taylor, the parting scene presented a moving spectacle. His father had travelled with him from their home in Blackford, Perthshire, to the Greenloaney Station where they bid each a fond farewell. Once on board ship, the young bachelor was at liberty to observe others saying their farewells. It was an emotional moment.

> We arrived at Glasgow at half past ten o'clock. We got down to the wharf and got ourselves and baggage into the vessel, and left the bustle at half past one o'clock in the night, and were taken in tow with a steamer. Here was an affecting scene. Friends were parting, families were dismembered a long adieu was bid with many a moistful hope of a prosperous voyage and a safe landing on the other side of the Atlantic. The salt tear trickled down the cheeks of not a few, others sobbed aloud with their faces buried in their handkerchiefs, and occasionally took a wistful look behind to the friends who lingered on shore. At length the wetted handkerchiefs were waved over head, and responded to by those on shore. In a few minutes we left Glasgow behind as we glided down the Clyde.... [John Boyd Taylor]

Living close to the coast made for an easier time. A person could arrive at the ship shortly after leaving home. P. Finan was able to board the *Lord Wellington* at Warrenpoint on the north shore of Carlingford Lough, close to his home town of Newry.

> The vessel removed from her anchorage, down the harbour, near Carlingford. Here I witnessed many an affecting party

49

scene. During the whole day boats continued to come along side, with passengers, or their friends, who came to take a last look of, and bid farewell to, their sons, daughters, brothers, sisters, relations, friends or acquaintances, whom, in most instances, they had little or no hope of ever seeing again....
[P. Finan]

The initial stages of any voyage brought great confusion. Steerage passengers were often unsure about which parts of the vessel they were permitted to frequent. Ropes and chains littered the deck while the crew lowered goods and baggage into the hold. This huge gaping hole was a source of immense interest, especially to the young. Many a curious child, out of the watchful eye of a parent, tumbled into its depths, some to dire consequence. Once there was some semblance of order, there would also be pressing details to attend to. Tickets would be checked once more, and a general search for stowaways was made. The Tide-Surveyor would have checked his list, ensuring there were only the legal number of passengers on board. Even so, it was not uncommon for an unaccounted for person to hide themselves away, and remain undetected until after the vessel left port.

> We hauled out from the docks [at Liverpool] at 11 o'clock (forenoon). Hundreds of people stood on the pier waving their hands as we came out into the River. As soon as we came out fairly we were all called on to the quarter deck and our names called over and our tickets shewn to see if they were stamped by the doctor. Five were turned out, as they had got no tickets. We were tugged out about 16 miles by a steamboat. then she left us and we hoisted all sail and went round by North Wales and a fair wind. I stood the fire amongst the Irish boys for the first time, and a fine company they are. The steerage is mostly of Pats. The second cabin, where we are, is a mixture of Irish and Welsh, but they are mostly a kind of genteel company. They are all in great spirits; some little sickness, but not much; we are about 130 miles from Liverpool, in sight of Holyhead; we went to bed about half past nine o'clock; slept very well. [William Hunter]

If it was proved that a stowaway had succeeded due to the Master not following proper regulations, a fine would be imposed when the ship reached its destination. Guards were sometimes hired in efforts to ensure that no stowaways boarded the vessel before she set sail.

> A woman, also, with the tact of her own sex, avoided detection until we had been a month at sea, and was only then discovered through the impeachment of one of her fellow-passengers. She had gone quite on the opposite tack to the 'poor orphan': so far from courting concealment, she had ever been observed to be cooking or loitering about the cabose, was the most noisy of all the females on board, and had once or twice even ventured upon the sacred limits of the quarter-deck. So proud a bearing blinded every person on board; nor could any one have imagined, even when challenged with the fraud, but that she had paid her passage, so menacing and formidable an appearance she assumed with her arms a-kimbo and a contemptuous toss of the head. Although the captain keeps a sharp look out (there being a fine imposed upon ships carrying a greater number of passengers than the law admits, according to the tonnage), yet few vessels sail from Liverpool without carrying more than their complement. Sometimes an affectionate wife introduces her lord and master on board in the guise of a trunk filled with old clothes, or in a crate, as her stock of crockery, in which he is half smothered, and tossed about most unceremoniously, during the confusion attendant upon weighing anchor. [Edward Coke]

The discovery of a stowaway was the cause of much excitement. Few were able to conceal themselves for very long, since hunger, cold or illness would drive them out of their cover. Then the captain would have to decide upon a plan of action.

> On the third day we were favoured with an unexpected addition by the discovery of a passenger amongst the hay provided for our live-stock. He managed to secrete himself while the ship was in dock, and, having lived very much like *bruin* by sucking his paws, was sufficiently wobegone when brought to light, and by no means cordially welcomed by the captain, who is bound, before getting rid of such volunteers, to grant security at New York that they shall not become burdensome as paupers. [Adam Fergusson]

51

Before the age of steam, a sailing vessel might sit at the dock for days, waiting for favourable winds. Later, in the time of steam power, ships could be towed downriver by smaller tugs or barges, sometimes for many miles. Once they were released, their sails would be hoisted in readiness, waiting to catch the first breeze that would set the vessel on its way.

After a detention of three days at Liverpool, owing to contrary winds with rough and boisterous weather, the packet ship, in which I had engaged a passage, hauled out of Prince's dock at daylight on the morning of the 23d of April, and stood down channel; but it was not until the fifth day from that time that we were clear of the southernmost cape of Ireland: a foul wind possessed, however, one redeeming quality, by successively displaying the fine bold coast of the Emerald Isle, and the picturesque mountains of Wales. [Edward Coke]

William Peters, his wife Elizabeth Blake, along with their children and a large number of Methodist associates, boarded the *Friends* at Plymouth, and found they had to wait seven days before sailing. Poor Elizabeth felt ill because of the ship's movement even while at anchor.

Came on board on Monday but returned to Aunt Denham's for the night. Felt peculiarly tired getting up by the side of the vessel and on Tuesday also, determined not to leave again on that account. Our close inhabitations make it trying for all, the children in particular, though I think they are as well or better than we could expect. So far they are able to eat and drink. 29th William was rather unwell, but today, the 30th is as well as before. In the day we are subject to much noise, but our nights are as comfortable as when on shore. As yet we have no cause to complain, but on the contrary, much to be thankful for. There are 23 on one side of the vessel and many more on the other side. The mate of the ship met with a sad accident on Wednesday which delayed us a few days. I feel anxious to be off. We have a doctor and his family on board in the cabin, of four children. With the motion of the vessel I feel at times indisposed, but have not been quite sick. [Elizabeth Peters]

It was far better for the faint-hearted when the ship set sail on schedule, so that anyone doubting the wisdom of their actions in leaving their homeland, might be diverted from melancholia by the excitement of the moment. For those who looked upon the whole affair with a great sense of adventure, a moment of quiet reflection might be in order.

We sailed immediately—towed out of the Mersey by a steam-tug some forty miles in to the Irish Channel—one's feelings and reflections on departing from England indescribable—trifling present to a poor emigrant family from Dumfrieshire called forth delight and gratitude. Well hath Dr Johnson remarked, "the spontaneous kindness of a fellow mortal is valuable"—involuntary tears—how inexplicable and mysterious our mental nature and emotions. [John Thornton]

The Dobie family lived at Birkenhead, a small town located across the Mersey from Liverpool. Their party amounted to fifteen, consisting of the diarist's parents and siblings, an aunt and uncle with five children, and a 'sailor uncle' who had worked on passenger ships in the India trade. It was very useful to have such an uncle, who could be relied upon to explain things.

On the date of sailing, we crossed from Birkenhead on a ferry boat. We got aboard our ship lying at the Princess dock, and we had a glorious time. It was a novelty. I well remember the bags of hard tack. I took one hard tack biscuit and ate one, and put two more under my pillow so that if I awakened in the night hungry I would have something to eat. Well, we hailed out of the dock in good time; weighed anchor in the middle of the river waiting for the tide to cross the bar, for vessels drawing 25 feet of water had to wait in those days for the tide. Things are different now: it is dredged out. The neap tide in Liverpool is 13 feet, the spring tides are from 25 to 26 feet. The morning of our sailing the anchor was taken up. Thirty men did the work, all by hand, no steam winches or windlasses then, and they worked to the tune of an old chanty, raising the anchor by main strength, not by machinery. One fellow, picked out by the rest as a singer, would stand up and would sing to the men who were doing the work. They would walk around singing in unison, and then the leader would improvise on the song. One of the songs was "Heave away, boys, we are bound for the Rio Grande," Then, after a while, away we went for the mouth of the river into the Irish Sea. When we got near to the mouth of the river sails were hoisted under the direction of the mate. The captain did not say a word to the sailors: he spoke to the mate and the mate gave the orders. [W. C. Dobie]

The Fergusson family appear to have been more than satisfied with their choice of vessel, for which they were paying a princely price. They were also very well pleased by its master.

After a lapse of several weeks, I finally pitched upon the *Eagle*, a vessel built in New York, of 520 tons burthen, known as a first-rate sailor, with a spacious roomy deck, and elegant cabin. Her commander, and part owner, Captain Lyon, we found to be a plain honest seaman, anxiously alive to his duty, attentive and accommodating to all on board, and desirous that his steerage passengers should equally partake in the cabin of the ordinary comforts and accommodations of the ship. My family consisted of ten individuals, including a man-servant. Three of my number were to be taken at a lower rate, on account of their youth; although I must candidly admit, that many an adult would have proved a safer speculation for the Captain's table than the very youngest amongst them. Including a state-room, for the exclusive use of Mrs F I paid in whole £212, 10s. Our accommodations were quite comfortable. A room fifteen feet square, entering from the cabin, fitted with four beds, allotted to three of my family and myself, while the others were distributed in the various state rooms off the cabin. [Adam Fergusson]

Although on separate voyages, Patrick Shirreff and John Frazer both sailed on the *Napoleon*. Shirreff proved to be less of a sailor than Frazer, finding little pleasure on the voyage. He reported that she carried eighty passengers in steerage and thirty in the cabin, eight of whom were ladies. England and Scotland furnished five gentlemen each.

At noon, on the 24th April, the *Napoleon* got under weight, and was towed down the Mersey by a steamer, in consequence of an adverse wind. In little more than an hour from the time of sailing, I became sea-sick, which afflicted me severely for nearly thirty days, and frustrated the little plans of recreation and amusement which I had formed on shore. Although appearing only once or twice at table, the attention of friends, and the situation of my berth, enabled me to know much that was passing on board. [Patrick Shirreff]

It was no time at all before passengers began to feel queasy, especially if the journey began on blustery days. Muster was usually called on the second day. Everyone with the exception of cabin passengers was required to scramble up on deck to be addressed by the captain. Those feeling ill, as many were, would have complained bitterly about having to get themselves up from their beds.

> Went on board of the Steamer at 9 a.m. and joined the *Napoleon* 4 miles down the river. the Ship was towed down the River for 15 miles. At 1 P.M. Wind blowing very fresh and right a head. at 4 P.M. Mr Gilmour got very sick but did not vomit. a great many of the other Passengers sick and vomiting. at 1/2 past 4 the Steamer left us. 1/2 past 5 Sailing with a side wind. 6 oclock Mr Gilmour vomiting. Wind N. In the Irish or St. Georges Channel. preparing for Tea 7 P.M. Ship tacking about. Wind N.W. steady breeze. 9 P.M. mostly all the Passengers sick. when the muster roll was called in the morning there were 219 Passengers on board besides Seamen 21 in number officers inclusive. [John Frazer]

Emigrants sailed from many parts of the United Kingdom. However, it should be stressed that Liverpool and Glasgow were the principal emigration ports. This was because they had tied up the transatlantic trade.

Cotton, timber and other raw products from North America were imported. Emigrants made a convenient and lucrative cargo for the return voyage. Other ports did play a role. London, Bristol, Plymouth and a handful of others saw substantial emigrant traffic, but far less than Liverpool and Glasgow.

Before steam, direct sailing from Irish ports was common, but with the development of faster steamships, Liverpool's importance increased. Eventually the fact that fares from Liverpool were lower than fares from Ireland tipped the balance.

It is impossible to list all ports of exit used by emigrants to North America, since some would have departed from relatively tiny places. The following list includes the most frequently used ports of exit, as well as those mentioned by diarists in this publication.

Scotland
Aberdeen
Boisdale
Dundee
Perth
Edinburgh
Glasgow
Greenock

Wales
Aberystwyth
Caernarvon
Cardiff
Chepstow
Milford
Newport

England
Bideford
Bridgewater
Bristol
Falmouth
Grimsby
Hull
Liverpool
London
Maryport
Padstow
Penzance
Plymouth
Poole
Portsmouth
Southampton
St. Ives
Sunderland
Torquay
Weymouth
Whitby
Whitehaven

Ireland
Ballyshannon
Belfast
Carlingford
Cork
Donegal
Dublin
Galway
Killala
Kilrush
Limerick
Londonderry
New Ross
Sligo
Waterford
Westport
Wexford
Youghal

There might be abortive sailings also. John Hicks Eynon had great difficulties but overcame them.

> After setting sail from Liverpool in October 1832, his ship was tossed about on the seas and blown to the coast of Ireland. There all his possessions were stolen. He returned to England where [Elizabeth] Dart and he were married the next March, and on the first of May they set sail from Padstow for Canada as a missionary couple. Storms forced them back to port, yet they persevered and set sail again five days later.

There were strict rules regulating the number of people a ship was permitted to carry. This was arrived at through a formula of so many passengers per burthen ton the vessel was licensed to carry. There were times when unscrupulous ships' owners, or brokers, paid little heed to rules and regulations, packing in as many passengers as they could with little regard to the safety of all on board.

> It is reported that the Hindoo [sailing from Kingsroad, Bristol] was "Libelled and duly seized," immediately after her arrival at New York, for carrying more emigrants then are allowed by the immigration laws of the United States. The passengers above the number are stated to be ninety; the penalty is 150 dollars per head for the first supernumeraries; but if these amount to be twenty the vessel is forfeited.

When travelling with young children, families learned quickly to be extra vigilant. The first few days of the voyage appeared to bring an endless round of enforcing rules of safety and preaching caution.

> ...the Captain came on board and had all things set in order for the vessel to sail, and we are now under way. The sea is as calm as it could possibly be. All appears hurry and bustle on deck, the chains rattling and the ropes drawing sails, hosting the pilot, etc. Captain and seamen all appear engaged. We have great difficulty in keeping the children below. The crew all appear to be anxious to know how far they are got on. We are now passing the breakwater. The sea is as smooth as glass. [Elizabeth Peters]

When Thomas Connon board the *Polly* bound for Quebec, he felt dismay at the thought of spending several long weeks on board this vessel. It was not so much his accommodation that distressed him, but rather his fellow passengers, and the incessant noise and confusion of it all. After the vessel set sail Connon attempted to find a quiet spot from which to observe the happenings around him.

> I was not long on the ship when I saw what sort of company I was to have. Their language would have told me although I had been blind. There were 260 Adults besides children and the ship's crew; altogether there were upwards of 300 souls aboard about 200 of them could speak Gaelic a good number of them could speak no English. A family or two were Irish. A great majority of them were drunk when they came aboard. and although it is against the government regulations they kept sucking away at the whisky the whole way...but such a swarming of men woman and children some of them had shipped before they were sure where their bed was and was wandering about naked seeking one; I went to mine clothes and all for fear that some strong fellow might turn me out. [On the next morning] ...we anchored about 2 miles of Greenock about 5 oClock, where we were visited by the Government Office and the Doctor. when called to pass the Doctor the highland passengers came up not only in families but in Clans. Camerons, McDonalds, McNeils, McNieske, and McBryde's; all passed the doctor but one man, he happened poor fellow to be too ill of the barrel fever, and was put ashore with his wife poor woman, and a child and a great mass of luggage.

Connon refers no more to the family that was put off the ship. Barrel-fever was a complaint brought on by immoderate use of alcohol. Consequently, few would have had much sympathy for the sufferer, but the wife and child must surely have deserved some compassion. Not only were they without a home, but in all likelihood, the money paid for their passage would not have been refunded.

Living space on board ship took some getting used to. Steerage passengers had little in the way of privacy, and in the early days, single men and women travelling alone were all mixed in together. By the 1840s, ships generally assigned singles to separate areas, one for men and the other for women, usually located as far removed from each other as possible. Wherever one's berth was located, the first job was to securely stow one's goods, and to prepare the bed.

> All the cooking utensils, which outfit had to be bought, were made of tin and sheet iron, because crockery would not last long on a ship which might roll from side to side, therefore everything had to be of iron and sheet tin so that it would fall about in a storm and not break. People had bedticks and they would buy a bundle of hay and also pillows, placing the hay in the ticks for bedding. [W. C. Dobie]

Some vessels accommodated steerage passengers relatively well. However it was often the case that a ship owner would charter his vessel to carry cargo. If for some reason the load was insufficient to fill the ship, the charter company might advertise for passengers in an effort to offset any losses. In such circumstances, accommodations often left much to be desired.

> We went down into the hold, which was fitted up with berths, if such a name may be given to the tiers of unplaned deal boards, which resemble large hen-coops piled one above the other; and stretched on mattresses upon these wooden gridirons we saw many emigrants, waiting wearily for the appointed hour that was fixed for sailing. It made the heart sick to picture that hold, when out at sea with hatches battened down, and the vessel driving through a storm. There were then little children running about, and playing hide-and-seek amongst the bales and casks—fair haired, red-cheeked, blue-eyed beauties, whose sun-burnt arms and necks told that they had had the run of the open village-green; and such we found had been the case when we enquired. Both father and mother were fine specimens of our English peasantry: the grandfather and grandmother were also there. They had fixed up the very clock in the hold, which had for years ticked in the old familiar cottage, and brought a few choice flowers in pots which they hoped to plant about their new home.

It was advisable to select one's berth very carefully. A person going to sea for the first time, without knowledge of life on board ship, might find themselves in a precarious predicament during high seas if they chose the wrong bunk. Those who knew better would take certain factors into consideration.

> Go in good time, and secure a berth in the ship to your liking. Do not take one, on either side, opposite the hatchway, because, when at sea, the water often rushes in, and be sure to close in your berth with boards, or get the captain to do it; the beds should not be narrower than three feet, on no account. [John Mathison]

Certain people suggested that pitching and rolling would be less noticeable in some areas of the ship. It was also a good idea, where possible, to find out a few details about those sleeping directly above.

> Choose then, if you can, a lower berth as far forward as possible, if you are a cabin passenger, or aft if a steerage one; because you will thus be nearest to the centre of the motion of the vessel, and so feel the least of the pitching. The only thing to be attended to in taking the lower berth is, if possible to avoid having a very sea-sick or awkward companion in the berth above you, or you may come in occasionally for a share of more benefits than you bargained for. [Henry Christmas]

The British social structure was indelibly printed upon the brains of all Britons. Class consciousness often resulted in snobbery, intolerance and insensitivity. It has often been said that, the moment a British person spoke, their countrymen immediately knew to which class that person belonged. In addition to class distinctions, there were old animosities. When crowded together on a ship, the habits, faults and eccentricities of fellow passengers, more often than not, were attributed to a person's origin.

> We have had a fine night for sailing; suppose we have gone about 8 knots per hour. We are not going quite so fast today, the wind being rather unfavourable, but upon the whole we are getting on pretty well considering all things and as comfortable as we could expect seeing there are about 28 of us stored up in a cabin about 8 yards by 12 our only room its dimensions is

about 2 yards by 2 and serves for every purpose except cooking. It serves for breakfast room, dining and drawing room, parlour, kitchen, pantry and sleeping room, storeroom wherein are 7 boxes, 3 crates and 3 barrels. There are about 22 passengers in the other end of the vessel chiefly the poor Irish. They seem happy and thoughtless as they are fiddling and dancing every night. [John Walker]

Having seemed relatively accepting of his fellow passengers on Tuesday, by Wednesday John Walker was much more morose.

A rough day followed with cross winds, indeed I cannot find any pleasure in a seafaring life. Believe Derby prison to be far preferable only for the name of it; what enjoyment can there be in such a place as this? Shut up with a parcel of beings many of whom have not so much as the form of godliness, much less the power. Thanks be to God that amongst all these commotions I do enjoy tolerable health of body and mind, but this is a very poor place for religion.

William Bell sailed to Quebec from Leith, which had long served as the main port for Edinburgh. During his preaching days at Leith and Edinburgh, Bell had become acquainted with the owner of the *Rothiemurchus*. It transpired that the son of this ship owner was the captain of the vessel. Bell elected to sail on her, reasoning that he would perhaps be more comfortable with the son of his acquaintance than with an entire stranger. The vessel was fitted out in rather a utilitarian fashion, offering some degree of comfort during the daytime.

On each side of the ship were ranged two tiers of stories of bed-births, the passengers providing their own bedding. Along the open space in the middle, were placed two rows of large chests, which were sometimes used as tables, and at other times as seats. When evening approached, a good deal of noise and confusion took place before all the passengers were arranged in their births, and the Captain was obliged to interpose his authority, and to determine which bed every one was to have. This was an arrangement which ought to have been made sooner, and the want of it occasioned much unnecessary trouble, both to the Captain and passengers. [William Bell]

By today's standards, passenger accommodation was far from comfortable. We might bear in mind that within most families, beds were shared. Three or even four little ones often snuggled up together. Robert Wade and his family sailed from Sunderland in 1819, and their places on the *William and Matthew* were no different from other vessels of this age.

> ...to give you an idea of our cabin, we are in the half deck, our bed places are 5 ft 10 in. in length 4 ft broad, two grown people lie together and three children 4 beds in length on one side and two in height, the ends two in length and two in height, and our room is only 5 feet high. we have 24 places for beds; after the bed places are taken off we have but 18 ft by 13 ft for 40 passengers, including children...

The minimal height between decks was five feet six inches, but as time went on, this was increased by law and practice. For tall people, this was not ideal. Although the narrowness of the berth did take some getting used to, it offered some compensation during the wild Atlantic weather. Without the narrow constraints, a body might be bumped and thumped, or rolled around like a barrel.

> Persons who have never been at sea, fancy that the wooden crib for the bed is too narrow in dimensions; but when the ship begins to roll and toss amongst the billows, they soon find error of the supposition. Were the beds not of circumscribed width, they would be tumbled about from one side to the other, and very likely hove out altogether. Many have their beds widened in harbour, but are glad to reverse matters again on the ocean. [John MacTaggart]

The Dobie family could look to their seafaring uncle for advice about life on board ship. He might also have secured for them the best possible situation in the ship. Even so, in 1849 when this family sailed, accommodations were still fairly primitive.

> A ship would come in to Liverpool from a foreign port, discharge cargo at one of the docks and then prepare for passenger service. Two tiers of bunks were put up. If any of you

have ever been out in a lumber camp in the woods, you will know what these wooden bunks are like. Just a bare board and nothing more, with a partition down each line of bunks marking them off and marking each bunk off from the next. [W. C. Dobie]

Before leaving the Thames, the *William Osborne* was already in trouble. Once at sea, a fearful storm put an end to her voyage and Joseph Carder was forced to dig in his heels and patiently wait for the voyage to begin again.

On Sunday, August 27, 1833, the good ship *William Osborne* was taken on tow by a steamer tug, who steamed us down the River Thames but had the misfortune to run on a sandbank, opposite Woolwich. Here we lay in perilous position. On the return of the tide we again floated and were steamed down to Gravesend. We had pleasant weather until Thursday p.m., when one of the most fearful storms arose, which continued until Monday morning. There had not been such a storm for 40 years. 136 ships were lost off the coast of France and in the British Channel. We lost all our sails, the windlass broke and away went our anchor. The bulwarks went. As the sailors were about to abandon the ship, a heavy sea swept off the jolly and all the other boats, sheep, hogs, poultry and everything, except the sailors. A second anchor broke away, a third, the last, held until Sunday afternoon. When the third went we were near the coast of Deal, who brought an anchor, took many passengers ashore. We went on. The storm moderated. We lay in Ramsgate Harbour for repairs for a fortnight.

Even when a ship sailed on schedule, the early stage of a voyage was often fraught with frustration, especially when winds were contrary and little headway was made. The prospect of sailing four thousand miles at a drearily slow pace cast a gloomy melancholy over the vessel. The Wade family left Sunderland on 12 May 1819 along with forty other passengers, including children. Four days later, they had tacked two hundred and seventy-seven miles up the northeast coast of England, to pass Peterhead on the Scottish coast. Taking the circumnavigation of shallow waters or rocky outcrops into account, in fair weather the vessel would have reached the same location sailing two hundred

63

miles. Between 12 and 16 May 1819, Robert Wade made the following entries in his diary:

> ...stormy, strong wind from the N.W., which carried away our jib-boom, all passengers sick except two, viz., Richard Oughtred and William Burlison, Shoemaker; sails to the north of Aberdeen when the wind changed to the N.E., which obliged us to lie to and we were driven to the south at 11 a.m. We saw Berwick upon Tweed where we continued till 5 p.m. when we again set sail.... Friday 14th, calm this morning till 9 o'clock when a light breeze rose from the S.W. and continued till 4 p.m.; passed some round hills near Leigth, one of which Richard Oughtred through was Roseberry.

> The passengers are nearly all well again; at 4 p.m. calm and continued so all night. Saturday 15th, fine breeze from the S.S.W. at 8 a.m., sailing four knots, or four miles, an hour to Aberdeen, on the South of which the land appears very barren, but at Aberdeen it looks very good. the passengers in good spirits.

> wind S.W.; at 9 a.m. passed Petershead, a fine town situated on a promontary; at 11 a.m. calm; passed a large shoal of mackerel supposed to be many millions; distance from Sunderland to Petershead 217 miles, but by contrary wind make 277 miles

A person might spend many days on board ship before the coast of Britain faded into the distance. When this finally happened, everyone was emotionally moved again. Perhaps Mary Gapper said it best:

> The coast is gliding rapidly past us and I must bid farewell to Charlinch without one more look.

The mood of the ship was often set according to the disposition of her Master. In the words of Samuel Butler, "A tyrannical or rude and boisterous master of an emigrant ship has it in his power to make the voyage very disagreeable to the passengers." This was certainly very true, but the actions of the crew might also enhance or detract from the pleasure of a voyage.

Much depends on the man at the helm for keeping a dry vessel. A bad steersman has her often shipping seas; he does not know how to meet her as the sailors say,—that is, to humour her with the helm. The sailors will sometimes *yaw* the ship for fun, when the passengers are walking the deck, and the surges will come lashing over them; but if grog has been given them now and then, the poor fellows will never play this trick. [John MacTaggart]

Samuel Thompson's ship sprung a leak during a storm long after the voyage had lost sight of land. Hard decisions were required and the captain remained calm.

Certainly courage is infectious. We were twelve hundred miles at sea, with a great leak in our ship's side, and very little hope of escape, but the master's coolness and bravery delighted us, and even the weakest man on board took his spell at the pumps, and worked away for dear life. My brother Thomas was a martyr to sea-sickness, and could hardly stand without help; but Isaac had been bred a farmer, accustomed to hard work and field sports, and speedily took command of the pumps, worked two spells for another man's one, and by his example encouraged the grumbling steerage passengers to persevere, if only for very shame. Some of their wives even took turns with great spirit and effect. I did my best, but it was not much that I could accomplish.

Despite the fact that they were approaching the Newfoundland Banks, the captain turned back to Ireland, where the ship was repaired in Galway. He took on more passengers there, and then safely sailed to Quebec.

It did not take long for passengers to realize that getting on the wrong side of the first mate was a foolish act. If he took it into his head to do so, he could make one's life most unpleasant.

Grouse [his dog] having offended the mate by some means or other was made fast on deck during the night. this mate is a sneaking low wretch, little in every sense of ye word. a very Iago! [— Johnson]

The mate on this voyage was a miserable character. His actions bring home the seriousness of abuses suffered by workers, not only at sea but in all manner of occupations during the nineteenth century.

> In serving out the allowance of water this morning the mate beat the steward most inhumanly. Is there no law to put a stop to such unheard of treatment? [— Johnson]

William J. Mickle's voyage on the *Pactolus* of Portland, Maine, which took him from Gravesend to New York, was not a particularly pleasant experience. There were personality clashes galore on board this ship.

> On the whole the voyage was very unpleasant for several reasons. 1st the boisterous & foggy weather. 2nd My bed or mattress was so excessively hard that I could not fix myself by sinking down into it but fetched away from one side to the other as the ship happened to roll & 3rd the Captn got cross & grumbling whenever there was a foul day which was tolerably often. all the troubles of the seas were nothing in comparison of the Yankee Captn (the Descendant of a Dutchman I believe) who was anything but a Gent^m & the 2nd mate a sneaking fellow brought up in the Cod fishery has set the Captn ag'st the first mate. the C. was constantly blowing him up & also swearing & blackguarding the Cabin Boy a Minister's son who was a careless and rather wild fellow; the term B—r being a favourite expression with divers additions always uppermost. he was also the greatest liar I ever had the misfortune to know & very much doubt wh^r he was naturally a brave man. he was very passionate & nearly killed the Black cook for a word or two, belting him with a stool tho' the poor fellow was 70 years old & had previously lost an eye by cruelty & his toes by frost whilst clinging to a wreck and with the C his chief offence appeared to be his color, as it is with all Americans. the C like the rest of his countrymen saying it was necessary every now & then to give them a good threshing if you had anything to do with them & then not to deceive them but to give it them well. The C used to give little things away & also make promises & offers which he would have been very unwilling to have performed.

A captain was certainly capable of surprises and could, if he put his mind to it, display great generosity.

> It was our Captain's birthday yesterday, and he provided dinner for us all, and such a scene, I wish I could describe it. It was one of our roughest days for it blew a hard gale at breakfast time which caused our Captain to take in every sail, and heave her too. This lasted until evening and we dined about two in the afternoon. Our first course was pea soup, second a boiled tongue, a beefsteak pie and a piece of boiled pork a plum pudding, and drank wine to dinner, and I am sure it was past seven before the vessel seemed to lurch more than usual even in a storm. In spite of all care every dish upset and turned out its thin contents, and often its solid ones are on the cloth. These of late are quite common scenes and on Sunday we had seven plates broken at one lurch of the ship. [Sarah Leeming]

It was unfortunate that the captain's birthday party turned into such a fiasco. The passengers may have recalled this kindness when for no apparent reason, they were faced with his mood swing.

> ...our Captain has turned out a very awkward unpleasant man. In the beginning he used to be sulky when we had foul winds, and now he has turned round on us and never speaks to us at all. He will not let us have anything but meat, and I suppose he dare not say he will not sell us that. After this you will fancy our supply of soup is stopped, and even to a bit of mustard he is so mean he told the steward to say there was none for us. [Sarah Leeming]

The social order on board the *Tennessee* was noted by James Hopkirk. He left Scotland on 21 July 1835, which he is said to have done because of reverses suffered by his family when the slaves on their Jamaica plantation were freed. Later, he would become Assistant Secretary of Canada West, a position he held from 1842 to 1846. Not being short of ready cash, Hopkirk ensured that life onboard ship was as comfortable as one could hope for. Hopkirk was quite delighted with the master of his vessel. He described Captain Robinson in the following manner:

a nice gentlemanay little man, and seems quite disposed to make us all as comfortable as he possibly can. He is very conversable and agreeable..... The Captain with whom we are every day more pleased.

The seven cabin passengers on the *Tennessee* consisted of Hopkirk, his wife Christian Glassford, two children, the family servant, and a Miss Bishop and a Miss Lynch. There were also eighty-three steerage passengers on board. Hopkirk remarked on them, but displayed little compassion.

> Except one or two decent-looking Welsh, the most filthy and abominable wretches I ever saw, all of the very worst and lowest class of Irish, covered with the Itch and Lice to a most inconceivable degree.

Once the immigrants were at sea, the days of the week had a way of melding into each other, one day seeming no different from the next. Those who put great store in setting Sunday aside as a special day for religious worship were frequently outraged by the antics of those whose lives did not run along parallel lines. Even the mildest of activities might cause comment.

> This was the Sabbath, and such a Sabbath as I never saw spent; whistling and singing throughout the whole day, and even playing on the flute. Our crew are also very wild; they are as ill as ever a navvy was on the Caledonian Railway; they seem to set their Maker at defiance. May God forgive them. We are all sick to-day but Charles Cowan, and it is an awful trouble for one cannot throw up much. What with the noise of the ship and the noise of about 400 people, no person has any idea of it who has not tried it. [William Hunter]

> Oh, it is pitiable to look at these poor sailors; how they are exposed to all weathers; and to see how they take their Saviour's name in vain, for they are awful swearers, and they swear always by Jesus Christ. I slept very little at night for it was very rough, and I had to hold on for fear of tumbling out of bed. [William Hunter]

The first sabath at sea. Prayer meeting in the morning & After noon & the scriptures read by the Captain.—An uncommon plesant day but quite calm—ship making no progress whatever—course northwest. Such a mighty din that I could neither read or think—A complete pig stye below. "Oh for a home for myself again secluded from this multitude." Never until now did I experience such an annoyance of a day I always set apart for meditation. "Lord send us a speedy voyage." [Joseph Wilson]

Religious services might be held on deck during good weather. Small groups often gathered together to read the bible and sing hymns. Cards bearing religious tracts were sometimes circulated amongst the passengers, particularly during stormy weather. At such times, even the most hardened of sinners would pray fervently.

There were occasional moments of upheaval when sensitivities and tempers got in the way of good relations. During William Hutchinson's voyage in 1850, a fight broke out on deck, whereupon the Captain ordered the culprits to be tied to the mast and a bucket of water thrown over them every half hour until five o'clock. Undoubtedly this was a tried and tested method of cooling hot tempers. Not all captains dealt with the problem in this manner.

A quarrel arose between two of the passengers, who appeared extremely anxious to terminate the affair by *force of arms*, or, at least, made all that boisterous and *valiant* display of the desire which is frequently assumed, when there is every reason to believe it will not be permitted to be indulged in, and as the Captain had been frequently tormented by similar disputes, he resolved to allow them to settle this in their own way. The quarter-deck was therefore cleared, and they stripped. While preparing for the combat, the wife of one of the parties, taking his coat &c. under her charge, animated him as much as possible to "mind what he was about—fight like a man, and not let that scavenger beat him." [P. Finan]

Women did not always display a levelling or calming influence on board ship. Certainly more than one writer was eloquent about their virtues, however. John MacTaggart's approving

69

words make it sufficiently clear that he was not witness to some of the fights among female steerage passengers documented by other writers.

> Strangers soon became acquainted with each other, for the natural disposition will show itself there sooner than any where else. How pleasant a voyage is, when a few good-hearted, sensible creatures meet together; and how disagreeable, when they are otherwise, as they most commonly are. He who has had what some will term comforts ashore, finds them not aboard—then the poor wretch frets himself to death; while the wanderer, who has *roughed out life* in many a dismal climate laughs at such trifles. Females are always our best companions both on sea and land; although they may be more troubled with sickness in ships than we, still the soft-soothing remark, the resigned state, and sometimes cheerful smile, counterbalance that. the ladies often make cowards of us there; they brave storms with fortitude, at which we tremble.

The weather also had a great impact upon tempers. Rain dampened spirits because it meant that everyone had to stay below deck. When confined in this way, it did not take long for nerves to begin jangling and the most trivial of incidents could cause upheaval. When bodily harm was the result, folks were thankful if there was a physician on board ship.

> a row occured between the sailors and second mate. the latter threatened to shoot them. they immediately seized a hold of him and disarmed him and threw the Pistol over board. he then drew a knife and got cut in the finger in the struggle. I had to dress them. [John Frazer]

Most passengers became restless and impatient as the weeks wore on. This was particularly evident during calm stretches when the ship appeared to be making little progress. A feeling that the voyage would never come to an end would envelop the ship, and frustrations would cause even the most innocent and mundane remark to cause a stir. A discussion on political or religious topics was liable to ignite into a volatile situation, greatly offending some sensibilities.

...our progress to the West very slow. This being the King's birthday part of the passengers have got their minds set against King and Government; they seem thankful that they have made their escape from the Land of Egypt, and out of the house of bondage. Our Captain is what all Englishmen should be "to love their country with all its faults." [Robert Wade]

Perhaps the most devilish influence on board ship was drunkenness. It was disturbing to most people, especially if the person were in a nearby berth.

In a calm, the Welsh and Irish kept the whole vessel in an uproar with their broils and fighting, which ever arose from national reflections; and each man having brought a store of liquor on board with him, as part of this sea-stock, the combatants were generally more than half intoxicated; while in rough weather, the self-same parties would be leagued together singing psalms, in which they were assisted by the English and Scotch, who kept aloof during the storm of words and war of fists. [Edward Coke]

Little was understood of dietary matters until the last decades of the nineteenth century. Some people ate well, but it was not because they had specific knowledge about balanced nutrition in order to maintain healthy bodies.

Scientists of the day debated all manner of questions. Some promoted ideas sounding quite bizarre to modern ears. In 1842 a French scientist presented a theory suggesting that human milk from brunettes was far more nutritious than that from blondes. As absurd as this sounds, many people accepted his conclusion.

The average diet of the urban working person was ill-balanced and monotonous. Country folks were accustomed to seasonal treats courtesy of Mother Nature. Her bounty could be reaped from the hedgerows: blackberries, raspberries, elderberries, apples and nuts, as well as other vitamin-rich foods. Once at sea, unless they had paid to be victualled by the ship, which few could afford, emigrants had only the produce they had packed to see them through the voyage.

With the emigrants' welfare at heart, the Passenger Act of 1842 stipulated that passengers must be victualled by the ship. Even so, ships' stores were generally of such poor quality, and in such meagre quantities, that passengers continued to take their own supplies. There were countless incidents of ships running out of food and of passengers arriving at Quebec near starving.

> I was very unfortunate in choosing the Glasgow emigrant ship as a means of conveyance; both as regards the company, accommodation, and length of time required for the voyage. I did not expect to be much more than 3 weeks on the way from Greenock to Quebec, but instead of that, I was a dreary six, three of which was spent on the way from land to land and the other three I may say we required to go up the Gulph; the provisions we got on the vessel was not first rate, the tea was very coarse, and I think damaged, and neither the oatmeal nor the biscuits were a great luxury the rice was altogether useless as we could not get it cooked, the beef cheese and herrings that I took with me were not enough for half the time so that although I had good health I did not fare very sumptuously toward the end of the voyage. [Thomas Connon]

Cooking at sea was not a particularly pleasurable activity. To begin with, there was little joy in waiting one's turn in a crowded and cramped galley. The whole process called for great patience. As provisions dwindled, turning out appetizing meals required great depths of culinary wizardry. Consequently most people made do with the most basic fare.

> The cooking department is the only means of excitement onboard that is likely to be permanent during our voyage. Men, women and children must have the cravings of nature satisfied. The struggling, squeezing, grabbing and pushing that always occur from day to day is enough to satisfy us that this mode of accomodating Emigrants is sadly deficient. So early as 3 or 4 o'clock in the morning, crowds are seen gathered at the Galley door, some with pans to make Porridge, some with frying pans & kettles, Tea Pots & Coffee Pots, some with Bannocks or cakes for toasting and all sorts according to the individual tastes, but this is comparatively nothing till the hours of 12 or 1 o'clock arrive. It is then that the real climax may be witnessed.

Poor old John, the Sailor, is always trying to suprintend and during these struggles makes a show of maintaining order in this Galley, but too often he is disregarded and his power does not extend further than threats and curses. His hand was badly scalded lately. Two men fought today because one of them shifted the other's kettle from its place. Two women fought for the same reason. They pulled each other's hair and screamed. A little girl, glad to have her porridge ready for use, ran out of the crowd, fell, spilled the contents over her face. Afterwards I saw her with her nose skinned red. [John McCorkindale]

Later in the voyage McCorkindale, who appears to have made a point of observing this sort of thing, reported another fiasco—the outcome of which might lead one to wonder whether the whole scene was contrived.

Two women quarrelled, fought and scratched each other for the same reason. They threw hot water at each other and in the heat of the conflict the Galley was cleared when the hot water began to fall, and after all, the combatants had a better room to cook their meal.

Trying to find a place to warm up, if one were cold, was virtually impossible.

...on Tuesday morning we had a heavy swell and I was very cold but there was no comfortable fireside to warm myself at for although there were 2 fireplaces on deck it was altogether out of the Question to get near them they were lighted from 6 oclock in the morning till 6 oclock in the evening and all that time they were crowded with pots, kettles, frying pans, and girdles [griddles], above and before and surrounded with cooks male and female striving sometimes fighting about the best place on the fire. [Thomas Connon]

Even though meals at sea were often less tasty, the very act of preparing them, at least on good weather days, offered a diversion which helped to break up the monotony. Food formed a major topic of conversation, for no sooner was one meal done, than preparation of the next must be considered.

The ship allowance for the week was given out. It consisted of beans, oatmeal, flour, rice, and biscuit. We took the half of our flour and the other half of rice but they are very bad. We can make little use of them. [William Hunter]

The ship allowance was given out to-day. It consisted again of oatmeal, rice, beans, biscuit. We took beans and rice. They are better this time, and the beans make a good dish when well boiled with a little butter in them. [William Hunter]

On the following day, three pounds of salt-pork were given to each person. Hunter was not pleased with the ship's rations, remarking that he was thankful they still had plenty of their own.

Passengers were frequently ill-prepared, sometimes resulting in depravations virtually amounting to starvation. For families such as the Peters', whose financial circumstances enabled them to procure good quality provisions, the journey was not too arduous. Even the most carefully prepared meals had a way of becoming monotonous.

Generally we have been comfortable, and as we have been able, have everything we wish except water, which seems to be bad, but the sailors say it is very good, and I suppose it may be, as it tastes very well in broth and gruel. We have a variety of things. Sometimes we have ham and water for tea and potato cakes etc. Puddings we make, as we like it much better than the ship biscuit. We make stews and pasties, pies, and bake puddings. It is generally done well. We have eaten more ham rasher than we ever did before. We like nothing better than fried potatoes. We can have raw potatoes, at times fried, and pancakes we have had for several meals. Since we have been on board ship, have all our things at hand. We have not the trouble to run for milk or butter to the dairy or to the parlor for our best things, but we have it all common...

I am not so well accustomed to the ship that if we could get fresh water, I should not at any time dislike a sea voyage. It is not so bad to be in it as it was in anticipation. I will give you this day's fare. In the morning we had fried rasher and pudding. For dinner we had roast potatoes and meat and baked pudding, and for tea had gruel and potato cakes. We had our bellies filled with fish. It is so delicious, better than whiten pullet. The

74

children could hardly be satisfied, and they ate so heartily. We have met with some losses since we have been here. The cider, as we were told, was robbed, and wine, a bottle or two, was missed. There is no trust to the sailors, and the forecastle passengers are not all honest. There are some that make but a mean appearance. There is one man sent by the parish, a young man he was not very much preferred. Should any young man come, he would be better off in the cabin in every respect he would have plenty of attendance, get a plenty of provisions and very good. They live very well. Mrs Aily who has been very communicative tells me they are supplied with everything except their bedding, and of course are furnished with a great deal of information.

It is astonishing to what expense the Captain is to on account of his men. They will not eat or drink any but what is extravagantly good. They have strong tea and coffee with rum in it. Nice potatoes swim in fat, and their puddings are generally filled with suet and butter and sugar. They are allowed besides 2 pds of beef a day per man. [Elizabeth Peters]

Sarah Leeming echoed Elizabeth Peters' sentiments concerning the Captain's table. For those who were short-stocked, especially if they had young children to feed, the spectacle of officers tucking into regal fare must have been hard to bear.

You can form no idea of the way the Captain and ship officers live they have such a set out. For breakfast & tea, quite extravagant, we should think for diner that we have looked quite shabby. They have soup of some sort every day of which we generally partake, our poor fowls were nearly drowned in the storm of last week. They killed them that they might be eatable & we had a couple yesterday and today.

It was quite customary for passengers to take livestock on board ship, which might be killed and served up at table. This was perhaps more usual amongst cabin passengers, who in general had more money than those in steerage, and who had more freedom to roam the deck areas to keep an eye on their stock. Steerage passengers might club together and purchase a pig or some other animal to be divided amongst them. Sarah

Leeming had taken live chickens, but she still lamented her shortcomings in arranging supplies.

> We have had a poor idea of laying in provisions, for we have had sadly too many trifles and very little substantial food, and you would hardly believe the things we like are so different to what we like on shore. I cannot bear the taste of tea or coffee yet, and if it were not for the cocoa I do not know what I should have done, and cream, I cannot taste. We found a day or two after we came out, that our beef that you had been so kind as to get us was quite bad, and we could not eat it, the same was so bad that we could not account for it except it was the ketsup we had in it. So there were several days meat lost at once, and we lost one of our fine legs of mutton last week it having been washed overboard in the storm. The piece of ham you gave us was delightful.

Several weeks later, Sarah reported that she had become quite tired of salt-meat. The passengers had tried fishing, in the hope of producing an appetizing meal, but without success. Fortunately, the Leemings had money left to purchase something special from the Captain. Sarah reflected upon culinary matters.

> We have bought a nice ham from the Captain weighting 27 lbs., and we have a good many eggs left, together with puddings make a nice dinner. I seldom taste anything but a cup of cocoa until dinner. I have not tasted butter since the first week we came out and I begin to long for bread beyond anything I ever felt to want in my life. You have no idea of our wishes and longings when we are anticipating getting on shore again.

Fresh meat was perhaps out of the reach of many emigrants. The Robert Wade family had planned very carefully for their voyage. They kept a round of beef fresh for nearly three weeks by periodically dipping it into the ocean.

> ...I will give you an account of how we live; in the cookhouse are two coppers and one oven and a large fire place for the use of the passengers; we have every privilege that we can wish for; by rewarding the cook with a little spirits we make ready a good deal of our victuals; we brought two bushels of bread meal

which we find very useful, potatoes and oatmeal also for the children being easily cooked; we make yeast so that we have brown and white bread. we bought a round of beef, and by dipping in the sea a few times it kept fresh for nearly three weeks; tea and coffee are not good; oatmeal barley and rice are best; raisins, prunes and preserved berries are very serviceable; we have need to treat ourselves on account of sickness, and we have reason to be thankful that hitherto we have lacked nothing. [Robert Wade]

A supply of fresh fish became available to passengers on the *Hottinguer*. Since it arrived early in the voyage, most people would not have recognized their good fortune.

Towards evening a boat came alongside and sold a good deal of fish to the crew and passengers. They were real Paddies from Cork, a set of poor naked wretches. We are sixty miles past the Irish coast, standing out into the Atlantic. [William Hunter]

Ships' biscuits were taken by everyone. Most people complained about them, often saying they were too old. Those with sufficient patience and ingenuity could work out a system of making them quite palatable.

Jenny's bisquits are quite a treat to us as they are so thick & well baked. Those we got in Whitby we can not eat—they are complained of by all the passengers. We have found out an excellent plan for cooking them which is to just steep them about a minute in water & then toast & butter them & they are fine & light as a cake & afford a fine treat to us who like cake. [Joseph Wilson]

Joseph Wilson's assessment of biscuit ('fine and light as a cake') was higher than others, who acknowledged that this was still the basis for most meals at sea.

Biscuit is much used by seamen, and the only way for passengers to take it is to pour boiling water on it, and when steeped a few minutes toast it before the fire, then butter it, and it will eat as pleasant as loaf bread, but not otherwise. [James Wilson]

During the voyage of the *Tennessee*, the mate, Mr Williams, harpooned a large porpoise which was cut up and distributed among the steerage passengers. This would have been a splendid treat, relished by all. On the next day, the talented steward prepared a succulent breakfast feast for all the cabin passengers consisting of a stew made of potatoes and porpoise sweetbreads along with 'cakes made of the brains which also tasted well.' They were unusual treats, but did not go unappreciated.

> One would never have discovered they were fish, of which they had no taste. The sweetbread was something like kidneys, but a good deal more delicate, the brains tasted like those of lambs—We had to dinner today steaks made of the flesh of the porpoise. In appearance it was exactly the colour and look of beef steak it more nearly resembled wild duck than anything else, had my eyes been blindfolded I should have taken it for this. It was a little tough and dry perhaps...had no doubt a pasty made of it and eaten with red currant jelly could be scarcely distinguished from a venison pasty....[next day] a sort of stew or hash made of pieces of porpoise and potatoes, which with red currant jelly—was most excellent. I should scarcely have known it from hare. [James Hopkirk]

Captain Griswold ensured that his steward and kitchen staff went to great lengths in looking after the cabin passengers on board the *Thames*. The meals were quite delicious. In addition, those with queasy stomachs received special attentions, unlike their counterparts in steerage.

> A very fine day, but quite calm. Mamma came on deck. All the steerage passengers also. They are very quiet and orderly. When we go down to dinner at 4 o'clock they are allowed the whole of the deck, and as we are in general a decent time at this meal, they enjoy it very much. Our table is served in the most liberal manner. We have claret, sherry, port every day, with the addition of champagne on Sundays and Thursdays, and those that are ill may have sago, gruel, arrowroot, lemonade, as often in the day as they like to order them. [Ellen Steele]

William Bell and his family fared extremely poorly. Some of his children became so weak they were unable to get out of bed, even in fine weather. There was much alarm when one of the boys began to lose his sight.

> As soon as we were fairly at sea, our situation every day grew worse and worse. Our porridge was sometimes so abominably dirty that it was impossible to taste it, and sometimes shamefully burnt; ...Brose of oatmeal was some days served up, for breakfast, and nothing to it but water. For diner, we had beef, so old and ill-preserved, that it was black, stinking rotten and bitter to the taste. My family could not touch it or the biscuit which was also rotten and full of vermin... The Captain admitted the biscuit was more than a year old, and the beef older still... It was said that both had been purchased the year before at a government sale of condemned stores. [William Bell]

The one hundred and thirty-five emigrants on board the *British Tar* were well looked after, mainly due to the organizational skills of James Marr Brydone. Brydone drafted a list of rules and regulations to be observed by all the passengers. To avoid any confusion regarding the doling out of rations, the following information was posted:

> 1st, The Bread and Water will be issued daily, between six and seven in the morning.
> 2nd, The beef or pork, on Sundays, Mondays, Thursdays, and Saturdays, and at ten in the forenoon; and on those days, brandy, or rum and water, at two in the afternoon.
> 3rd. The flour, raisins, cheese, and butter, on Mondays, Wednesdays, and Fridays, at ten in the forenoon.
> 4th. The tea, or coffee, and sugar, on Saturdays, at four in the forenoon.

Water is something the body cannot do without. It was a great problem if the ship's water was bad, having an offensive odour or a nasty taste. Sailors became accustomed to it, claiming there was nothing wrong with it. This was small comfort for passengers who found that the only way to get it down was to mix it with something that was strongly flavoured. Conse-

79

quently, most people agreed that, when at sea, coffee was better than tea, its stronger taste going some way towards disguising the nastiness.

> Coffee is much preferable to tea, the water being so bad, as to render the tea rather insipid and tasteless; bottled ale is good for a drink, but in my opinion, cyder when mixed through water, is a much better and cooler drink for the stomach than any other; a constant thirst being common to all on sea. [James Wilson]

Even before the ship sailed, Elizabeth Peters' queasy stomach made it impossible for her to drink the ship's water. She was not alone in this. Emigrants who knew about the water situation made sure they brought a variety of additional beverages on board. Those who were taken unawares had to make do.

> My sister Mary here had fried beef for diner. I fear we shall be deprived of good water. The coffee tastes well, but the tea I cannot relish. All of us like the cider and find it quite an indulgence. [Elizabeth Peters]

Later in the voyage, Elizabeth benefited from the generosity of a fellow passenger when she was presented with a collection of dried herbs.

> The tea I cannot let down, nor coffee. I've had a little dried herbs of Sarah Dumble, who followed Doctor Stevens' advice in bringing it. It was a mixture of herbs: agrimony and sage, thyme, balm, peppermint, rosemary, and pennyroyal, all chipped up and dried together. It was so good that I could drink it in preference to any other, and now it is all done, I am obliged to have recourse to gruel. We can have oatmeal of the Captain. Pease we like much. We did not bring any ourselves, but have been able to exchange 2 lbs. of flour for pease from those that were tired of them. Our appetites are such that most of us are longing for what others have got, and what we have of our own, we cannot touch. Many things that I had I've been able to sell on account of the length of our voyage, such as butter, and bread, figs, sugar, etc....

A supply such as Elizabeth mentions would have been easy to produce, easy to pack and light to carry. It is therefore quite surprising that none of the emigrant guide manuals, with all their instructions about the water situation, suggested producing and bringing a collection of dried herbs. One or two writers did mention mint-tea, but none of the other herbs on Elizabeth's list were referred to.

Much has been written about ships' water, mainly because it was such an important issue and because the water was universally despised. There was an endless litany of complaints, such as storage barrels reeking of former contents which might have been almost anything, impure water drawn from the river in which a vessel stood at anchor, improper testing prior to sailing, as well as a whole array of other unfortunate circumstances.

Vinegar was frequently mentioned as being highly valued at sea. Some writers claimed that it was beneficial when mixed in small amounts with water, in coping with the dreadful thirst so frequently experienced at sea, particularly in association with sea sickness. It did not do the trick for everyone.

> I cannot omit to mention here, as it was at this time I suffered most from it, the disgusting water, to which we were obliged to resort, in our extreme thirst, there is no disguising its abominable taste by any mixture whatsoever, it baffles all the efforts of wine, spirits, raspberry, vinegar, tea, or coffee to render it at all palatable. We should have brought with us a filtering machine, and this may be a useful hint to others.
>
> ...I would encourage all emigrants who can possibly afford it, to be profuse in their store of bottled ale and porter, as the only wholesome and agreeable beverage to rely on— temperate advice you will say from a delicate lady!!—but the more delicate the ladies, who may have occasion to avail themselves of it, the more applicable the recommendation. [Mrs Radcliff]

One of the most frightening occurrences at sea was receiving the announcement that water rations were to be reduced. For no matter how bad it tasted, intake of fluid was vital. Laws regulated the amount of water to be supplied to each

81

passenger and although the amount per person fluctuated slightly, in general it was about three quarts per day, infants excluded.

> Yesterday we were cut short of our allowance of water, from three quarts per day to each passenger, to five pints (government allowance), and from the badness of it, together with the small quantities given, serves to increase the distress of mind which arises daily... [James Wilson]

One must consider that this amount must satisfy drinking, cooking and washing needs. In view of this, it is small wonder that steerage passengers were often unable to maintain a decent level of cleanliness.

> We are put upon short allowance for water, only 3 pints per day owing to us losing about 6 portions of water during the rough sea, having leaked away. [John Walker]

James Marr Brydone drew on past experience when dealing with the difficulty of unpalatable water by producing a soothing drink which also had the property of providing much needed warmth to the passengers.

> Finding that all the people, more especially those affected by sea sickness, were suffering much from thirst and cold, during this tempestuous weather; and that the latter, was increasing as we approached Newfoundland, and knowing, from experience, that the water on board of a ship, is, at no time, a very palatable beverage, I procured some peas from Captain Crawford, and caused to be made for every person a pint of excellent soup, which was so generally liked, that I induced to continue it, every Tuesday and Saturday, until we reached the river St. Lawrence.

There was no doubt that drunkenness was an acute problem, not only among some passengers, but also among the crew. It was not unusual for a captain to sell liquor, often at greatly inflated prices, thereby pocketing a nice profit for himself. It was then in the best interests of a captain to encourage the passengers to indulge to their hearts' content. Grog, the famous reward of the sailor, was often dispensed to the crew at the expense of discipline. Recognizing the problems associated with unruly behaviour led to the banning of all alcohol on the *Eagle*.

> The crew consisted of twenty steady men. Not a drop of grog or spirits was served out, as the *Eagle* was a "Temperance ship," an arrangement now becoming very general in the American ports. The men have coffee in lieu of grog, and the difference of price is reckoned to them in their wages. [Adam Fergusson]

Many of the regulations under the Ships Passenger Act of 1842 came about because of abuses on the part of passengers and crew alike. One of the regulations, although perhaps a difficult one to enforce, was that there be no sale of liquor, on pain of a fine of £100. There does, however, seem to have been a distinction made between cabin and steerage passengers. Since a person was still free to take their own supply of liquor on board, which many tended to do, the mischief element was not entirely eliminated.

> We bought a quart of brandy from the Captain. It cost us four shillings, that is sixpence each, as there are eight of us in the two rooms without Janet. We got two other Scotchmen in Liverpool named Burnet and Robson, and seven of us name the nine. And a jovial company we are altogether. We often have an hour or two singing before we bed, sometimes church music, sometimes a good old Scottish song to cheer our hearts. [William Hunter]

Cooking on the high seas required the skill of a culinary artist and the dexterity of a contortionist, for even the simple act of preparing and serving a hot drink could bring nasty consequences.

> Rather more calm but one of the passengers met with an accident his wife was very anxious for a little tea & sent him up afloat for the Kettle & in going down the steps fell and scalded his face, neck and [illegible] [Julia Bird]

Everyone recognized that galley work could be a dangerous occupation. The motion of a ship frequently upset cooking utensils as well as people. If a person were in the midst of stirring a pot of hot liquid, dreadful scalds might result. Those sailing on vessels without a doctor on board were aware that, should they suffer burns or scalds, their only chance of relief would depend upon the contents of the Captain's medicine chest.

> The ship rolling much, the cooking coppers were upset before dinner, without other injury, than that of dirtying the beef, and frightening John Barton, the cook, whose post was immediately filled by Job. Hodge. [James Marr Brydone]

When the sea was very high and it was far too dangerous to cook, there was nothing for it but to try and bribe someone else to take over the responsibility of preparing your food.

> Sunday 7 May 1831. Winds still contrary. Weather still cold & rainy with a heavy sea which makes it hazardous & disagreeable to cook meat at the fire & there is a great deal of mischief about getting any thing done in the cook's galley. He is an old snarling curmudgeon unless you bribe him with spirits. This we will not do. [Joseph Wilson]

Caution was important in the cooking department, for the danger of fire was of enormous concern. Since a ship was mostly constructed of wood, once a fire caught hold, it would be virtually impossible to extinguish.

> 6 A.M. Still squally. 2 P.M. was suddenly alarmed by the cry of fire in the steerage. the Cambooze or Cooking place was upset by a sudden heave of the ship and Tumbled it fire & all into the steerage. the fear and alarm was dreadful and produced a sad sensation among all. it was soon put to rights by the activity of the Mate and hands. a little afterwards a fight took place among some of the passengers in 2d Cabin but order was soon restored by the interference of others. some of the steerage Passengers provisions entirely done. some of my medicine bottle broke in a chest at the same time that the Cambooze was thrown over. our fears increased regarding the provisions on board being a month to morrow since we sailed and neither hope of land or fair wind as it still blows right a head. [John Frazer]

A fire at sea might be caused by all manner of things. Naturally the cooking department might be the cause, but candles, too, which were often used to brighten dark areas, might lead to dreadful consequences should they be handled carelessly. On 2 September 1848, the *Ocean Monarch* burned on her voyage from Liverpool to New York. She carried three hundred and ninety-six passengers, of which one hundred and seventy-seven were lost. In examining the cause of the fire, survivors put forth several suggestions, including that of a burning candle. For weeks, bodies washed up on shore at places such as Blackpool.

Keeping on the good side of the captain, cook and first mate was a wise move, since a person never knew when they might need a special favour. One month into his voyage, when shortages on the *Napoleon* became obvious, John Frazer noted in his diary that "my cakes are now nearly done at which I grumble." He was afraid that the vessel would run out of food and that the passengers would starve. Frazer was not a seasoned sailor so may have been overreacting. Taking matters into his own hands, he arranged to have a private word with the mate. He thought that a little gentle coaxing would not go amiss. His efforts were to no avail.

> ...called the Mate down and gave him a glass of rum and told him the necessity of running into the Western Isles for provisions but could not prevail. he says, however that they will hang out a flag to the first ship that appears in sight for a supply. as yet no abatement of the gales.... Rum now done. every thing getting more scarce on board.

Once it was clear that a ship would not reach its destination on time, a wise captain began to think about conserving whatever he could in the way of food and water. This sort of scenario was not unusual, for ships could be delayed by all manner of things. Sometimes a situation became quite desperate, as it did on the *Napoleon*. During the last three weeks on the voyage, John Frazer continued to document the hunger situation. His concerns were primarily for the steerage passengers, thirty of whom had developed a fever. The threat of starvation, compounded by illness, became intolerable. Passengers with an excess of potatoes began selling them at exorbitant prices. Out of desperation, Frazer, along with another cabin passenger, persuaded the captain to conduct with them an inventory of the ship's stores. After the completion of this, the situation was deemed slightly less critical than had been thought. An appeal was directed to the passengers requesting them to share whatever provisions they had amongst themselves. All through this episode, a lookout had been mounted for other ships. At last, one came into view.

> Scarcely a breath of wind scarcity of provisions staring us in the face. a melancholy prospect before us. so many people being on board. espied a ship at a distance at 2 P.M. hung out a distress flag. was returned in good faith by her. she neared about 6 P.M. the Captn lowered his boat and sent the mate on board in quest of Provisions. He returned with 2 Barrels of Beef 2 Barrels of biscuit and a small keg of molasses. This vessel was the Cherokee of New Bedford bound on a whale fishing expedition to the South Seas.

Everyone was greatly relieved to learn that some provisions had been procured. However, at this time the Captain was unwilling to share anything with the passengers. Tempers began to flare and the captain fell under much criticism.

> A passenger applied to the Captain this morning for a few pounds of beef but was refused. This shewed that if he got himself secured he cared not for others, whether they starved nor not, but it is determined if a famine occurs he shall suffer as well as the rest.

The voyage continued thus for three more weeks. For his own needs, Frazer arranged to get some biscuits baked by the servant of a fellow cabin passenger. Throughout the ship as a whole, fights took place, passengers begged for food, gale force winds were experienced, but finally and happily on 16 July the ship arrived safely at New York.

Once the passengers had been at sea for some days, they usually began to gain their sea-legs. When this happened, they were ready to commence activities. For those suffering heart pangs from missing their loved ones, time could be spent in writing letters or journals detailing life on board ship. The Leemings sailed on board the *Alicia* in May 1840. Sarah Leeming filled many hours in this way.

> I cannot express to you, the feelings of pleasure and emotion on this, my first time of sitting down to address you when I think that every breeze is wafting me further from those I so dearly love. It is only since the 3rd., of this month that I have been in any degree able to be out of my berth.... You will be glad to know that John has not been sick at all which has been well for me as I have been scarcely able to raise my head, or do anything for myself.

Life on board ship was not always doom and gloom. The ocean was intriguing, providing endless fascination, especially for those who came from inland communities. Male passengers were always keen to receive informal tutorials from the captain, thereby learning something of nautical matters. Searching for marine life was great sport, and the antics of whales and porpoises delighted almost everyone.

> I was informed last night that three whales were seen a few nights ago by the side of our vessel, one of them as large as our ship; what a mercy that we are preserved to the present moment. [John Walker]

> Last Friday night we discovered the new comet to the northwest. The other day we saw another great shole of porpoise, some hundreds if not thousands came about our vessel. [John Walker]

There was pleasure in observing the animals on board.

> Mr Woodward's ewe brought forth a fine young lamb which was viewed with pleasure by all the passengers. [Joseph Wilson]

Since lack of exercise was a problem, calisthenics might help alleviate the tension.

> Constant exercise will keep a man in good health better than all
> the physic on board. It is generally from want of it, and from
> over-feeding, that sickness occurs at sea. Make a point of
> walking the deck as much as possible; but you require to use
> your arms also. For this purpose, get a spar fastened athwart the
> deck, as far above it as a man can reach. Grasp it with both
> hands, and lift yourself up till your chin can touch it. Go on
> practicing till you can lift your whole body above it with your
> arms straight. Then learn to throw yourself completely round it.
> [William Kingston]

He also suggests skipping, swinging, fencing and boxing.

In an economic climate where nothing was wasted, even
the most mundane items could be put to use. William Kingston
suggested utilizing leftover bones from roasts of meat to produce
functional objects.

> A variety of very beautiful articles may be manufactured from
> the meat-bones saved from your meals. Bones from fresh meat
> are the best. The French prisoners during the last war used to
> make most elegant models of ships and other objects, many of
> which exist perfect to the present day. The only tools they had
> were their knives, some of which they turned into saws, to cut
> up the bones more easily. Save all the bones at dinner, and first
> scrape them thoroughly, and get all the marrow out of them.
> They should, where it is practicable, be boiled in turpentine to
> get all the greasy particles extracted. When this cannot be done,
> hang them up to dry in the sun, but not long enough to let
> them crack.

Although none of our diarists mention bone work, Kingston was
convinced of its usefulness. Among other artifacts, he suggests
making knife-handles, paper knives, heads of walking sticks or
whip-handles, rings, rulers, letters for teaching children to read,
spoons and salt-cellars.

For the sedentary, there would be card games, reading,
quiet handwork, or simply relaxing with a group of companions.

> The weather much finer—walking on deck almost all day, all
> but Miss Taylor, Mrs Keating and myself very ill, but they got
> better towards evening as they generally do, and we had a great

deal of music—Mamma, Mrs Keating and Mrs Hargraves, after
the gentlemen were gone, sat up telling long stories, which were
overheard and repeated to them next morning by the
gentlemen, to their great discomfiture. [Millicent Steele]

Women could find something to do since there was
usually a basket of mending and other handwork to do. The
Steele sisters, showing their youth, did not entirely approve of
this sort of pastime.

Mrs Keating does nothing but knit all day long, counting
stitches as she goes on, to employ her mind as she says, all the
rest find something better to employ theirs. Mr Fawcett has
been singing very much to-day, his airs amuse us almost as
much as his voice, which is very good. [Millicent Steele]

Knitting was at the time an occupation enjoyed by both sexes.
However, there is no evidence of male passengers on the voyages
recounted here taking part in this simple pleasure. This is
unfortunate, since in the view of one writer, the women busy at
their handwork appeared content.

Many of the women were on deck, some knitting, others
mending, and all who were not disabled by sickness, exhibiting
a striking contrast to the listlessness of the men. [James Logan]

The most functional of articles was that made by Jane
Wade, who, recovering from a broken arm, set about making her
mother a black silk cap. This colour was necessary because the
ship was carrying coal.
James Hopkirk whiled away tedious moments by making
himself a broad-brimmed hat out of old sails and succeeded "in
making a most capital one." Besides hat-making, there were
other occupations with which men could busy themselves. When
passengers became aware that some activities were taking place,
they might line up to avail themselves of a talented person's
services.

...as we get in to a more southern latitude the weather is
warmer, the sea very smooth, and our two shoemakers are at

work mending boots and shoes, those women who have no families are sewing, and knitting, the carpenters are at work making kreels to take the bottles out of the ship, others reading, etc. [Robert Wade]

The atmosphere on board a small vessel was certainly more restful than that on a large emigrant ship. However, the lack of companionship did begin to weigh heavily on Catharine Parr Traill. Besides the crew there were only two other passengers, the captain's fifteen-year-old nephew and a clerk, neither of whom provided much in the way of diversion.

Though we have been little more than a week on board, I am getting weary of the voyage. I can only compare the monotony of it to being weather-bound in some country inn. I have endured the horrors of *mal de mer* and except when the weather is fine I sit on a bench on the deck, wrapped in my cloak, and sew, or pace the deck with my husband and talk over plans for the future... Every space is utilized in a ship. The bench on which the bed of cloaks is spread for me covers the hen coop. Poor prisoners to be killed and cooked as needed!

Mrs Traill found much pleasure in the captain's pet, a pretty goldfinch, who had been on twelve voyages with his master. She made a great fuss over the bird.

I have already formed a friendship with the little captive. He never fails to greet my approach with one of his sweetest songs, and will take from my fingers a bit of biscuit, which he holds in his claws till he has thanked me with a few of his clearest notes. This mark of acknowledgement is termed by the steward, "saying grace." But his master views my attentions to his beloved "Harry" with a jealous eye. He has neither wife nor child to love him; he says, "I cannot afford to lose the least bit of Harry's love. I want it all."

It did not take long for someone with musical talent to surface on board. Once a willing volunteer offered to make music, dancing, singing and generally kicking up the heels was the order of the day. Sometimes the men, no matter how much they were coaxed, could not be induced to perform. The women were far more agreeable, even a clergyman's sister.

> ...while we were on the lookout, a fiddle was heard somewhere below, which suggested the propriety of a dance. Joseph and the young man from Mull, who, having been a teacher, may be named the Dominie, were the first to volunteer; but the other young fellows could not be persuaded, excepting one or two. The captain went down to the hold and brought up for his partner the preacher's sister, an old woman of 60. Stewart, Ewing, junior, and I, kept up the dance with the girls and wives until nine o'clock, when I sent the steward with a bottle of rum to give all the women a dram, but with strict injunctions not to let the men have any, saying, that since they would not 'shake a fist, I would not wat their whistles.' [James Logan]

When a calm overtook the vessel, remnants of giddiness and nausea were quickly chased away. Storms were forgotten and all seemed right with the world.

> This is the very Temple of Idleness, and the waves to-day seem to have caught the infection. The sea looks like a blue lake with scarcely a ripple on its surface. We had music all day—two violins, three flutes, the Captain, Mr Fawcett and Mr Woolsey's and one of the ladies every now and then at the piano. This calm has done wonders for our poor invalids, but, unfortunately, will not bring us an hour nearer New York. After tea we danced to the violin, and sang glees on deck. The gentlemen persuaded Miss Taylor, Millie and me to stay on deck. The moon was shining so beautifully and the air was so fresh and pure to what it is in our confined cabins that I think we should have stayed all night if Mama had not sent for us. Mr Marshall declared he should not go to bed at all. [Ellen Steele]

A calm offered landlubbers the opportunity to mingle with the rest of the passengers. Then, a party-like atmosphere reigned, unless the calm lasted too long.

> Still lovely and calm. We sat up till 2 o'clock, Mamma not excepted. The whole of the steerage passengers, one hundred and forty, on deck. All the gentlemen sang by turns. I never saw

anything to equal the beauty of the scene. Even Mrs Keating was pleased and ventured to walk about without support. the gentlemen ran after each other up and down the ladders and ropes. But I must say I think this a very dangerous amusement and far from amusing me. They frightened me to death. I expected to see one of them overboard every minute. The sails were festooned up so gracefully and they looked so beautiful in the moonlight. I begin to think a sailor is quite right to be proud of his ship. We went to bed in high spirits. Indeed the gentlemen told us we talked and laughed so much in our rooms that we prevented their sleeping. [Ellen Steele]

Climbing the rigging was a sure-fire method of attracting attention. Perhaps it was the daredevil quality of this activity that made it so irresistible. Whatever the attraction, few young men seemed willing to forego the pleasure.

Stewart and I took a race up the shrouds, to the great amusement of the passengers. The second mate followed us, and getting hold of one of my legs, tied it to the riggins, demanding, as a customary fine in such cases, a bottle of rum for the ship's crew, on granting which we were allowed to descend without further molestation. [James Logan]

If another ship passed close by, some communication might even be possible. In some cases, the two ships might trade or purchase goods.

It is now five days since we have seen any vessel; the last we saw was one from New York; came so close to us that the Captains spoke to each other. They informed us they had had a very bad passage... [John Walker]

During James Logan's voyage, a sailor from a passing ship came across in a dory to request drink and news. He said he was a Dane, but the excited passengers quickly decided he was a more exotic Russian and they craned to get a better look. In the end, they concluded he was a pirate, but he departed without ravishing anyone.

The tobacco habit was much in evidence on the *Napoleon*. Cigars and chewing tobacco were in common use and it is almost certain that many people would also have used snuff, since this product, made of powdered tobacco, was still popular during the nineteenth century. Tobacco frequently met with disapproval.

> In some cases, the use of tobacco was immoderate, one gentleman smoking a hundred and fifty segars in fourteen days; the saliva in many parts of the vessel was copious and disgusting. Some of the passengers seemed to spend much of their time in sensual gratification, there being a little reading or card-playing indulged in. [Patrick Shirreff]

Nautical folklore abounded on all sorts of subjects, tobacco included. Had tobacco-loving passengers on the *Napoleon* been superstitious, they might have modified their habits, at least for the duration of the voyage.

> It is said that the shark cannot suffer the smell of tobacco-smoke: he is not singular in this respect, for there are human beings who do not relish it either,—at least they pretend so. The Indians are aware of this fact, and dare not smoke while they are crossing the bays of the Gulf of St. Lawrence, or the river itself, lest they rouse the ire of the shark. [John MacTaggart]

Having copious amounts of tobacco juice swilling the decks would have been unsightly, but this was only one aspect of the unpleasantness on board ship that may have contributed toward poor hygiene. Without making an enormous effort, maintaining a decent level of cleanliness was difficult, especially for steerage passengers. Cramped in appalling conditions, they had little hope of successfully coping with undesirables such as lice and bedbugs, let alone the potential dangers posed by infections. After twenty-one days at sea, Mr Johnson noted, "I have not shaven since last Sunday. A frightful specter!" He was not alone. Almost everyone suffered from the discomforts of uncleanness.

> we had 348 second Cabin & Steerage passengers beside first Cabin passengers & sailors. 300 of them were Irish. we were

packed so closely together then 2 weeks before we got to New York we were almost eaten up by Lice & I was so pestered with them that I cast off my flannel shirt & drawers Like other people did and I fear by so doing that I have catched a Cough & a Cold that I shall carry with me to the Grave. [John Hallas]

One might think that keeping clean would be a relatively simple matter when surrounded by the ocean. Here, several forces came into play. In the normal course of things, people did not bathe as frequently as modern day folks. Also, salt water did not make the ideal bath. Some suggested that adding a little oatmeal to sea water would improve the quality and make it suitable for washing. It is doubtful that this idea was promoted in any serious way, especially among steerage passengers who would have viewed the idea of using precious supplies of oatmeal for such a frivolous purpose to be totally absurd. Advice dispensed by A. C. Buchanan might more readily have been followed.

> Keep yourselves clean on board ship, eat such food as you have been generally accustomed to (but in moderation), keep no dirty clothes about your berths, or filth of any kind. Keep on deck, and air your bedding daily when the weather will permit; get up at five o'clock, and retire at eight; take a mug of salt water occasionally in the morning.

Every captain knew that the fate of his passengers lay in maintaining careful housekeeping. It was not uncommon for steerage passengers to be expected to assist in cleaning those areas set aside for their use. These would include berths and eating space, the cooking area, part of the deck, and most importantly, the water closets. Men and women had separate water closets. With a high level of traffic, and large numbers of upset travel tummies, they required constant attention. There sometimes were additional toilets located on deck. When things got out of hand, drastic measures were called for.

> Old Beersley [the Captain] made an awful morning among the crew and passengers. He cleaned out the two weather water-closets and padlocked them with his own hand, all for health. He is a perfect devil to his crew, but I think he tries to promote

94

the health of his passengers as much as possible. [William Hunter]

Later in this voyage, Captain Beersley and the first mate got into such an altercation that the captain nearly had the mate put in irons. In Hunter's words, the captain "is a very passionate man."

When the captain of the *Rothiemurchus* ordered passengers to commence cleaning on a Sunday, there was a great deal of grumbling. This was not due to lethargy or a dislike or sprucing things up, but had everything to do with the fact that the 'Sabbath' was being desecrated. Earlier, objections had been registered when the same captain ordered the sailors to spend Sunday battening the hatches in preparation for a storm. In the minds of many passengers, Sunday was sacrosanct.

A conscientious captain would enforce housekeeping rules such as airing of bedding. This was a chore which could only be done on good weather days, since it entailed dragging the straw-filled ticks onto the deck, and giving them a good shake. Some extended this routine to include other items.

> Every day the Captain ordered all his passengers to bring up their clothes, and air them. The sick passengers were also all ordered above, those who were unable, being assisted. The Captain was much afraid lest an infectious fever should get in amongst us, and he himself, after landing at Quebec, was confined for some time by severe indisposition. [John M'Donald]

Cabin passengers, who often had the luxury of a steward or even a servant to tidy up after them, were not general very sympathetic when it came to the dismal conditions steerage passengers had to contend with.

> The captain caused the steerage passengers to bring up their blankets and other articles of clothing, and shake them over the sides of the vessel. It was only, however, after repeatedly urging them, and sending the mate among them, that they were induced to make a clearance, although it seemed probable, that from the filth which had accumulated, and the noxious effluvia that vitiated the air in the hold, disease might otherwise have arisen in a few days. [James Logan]

95

There was always someone on board with extraordinarily fastidious habits. In an environment such as on board ship, where maintaining a high level of personal hygiene required great efforts, the primping and preening of an individual might become the cause of much hilarity among fellow travellers.

> This has been another calm day; scarcely a breeze. Nothing of any consequence has occurred to-day; the passengers are all very merry. We have a very proud Irishman in the second cabin; he has been at the looking-glass three times, brushing and dressing for the space of half an hour; he is a real pup, poor blockhead. [William Hunter]

Then there were eccentric creatures who braved the elements with a fortitude that put even the most seasoned sailors to shame.

> ...I used to make it a practice as often as I could, to go before breakfast on the forecastle, and have sundry buckets of salt water dashed over me, using a good rough towel after the ablution. I continued the practice with decided advantage, until after our arrival in the St. Lawrence, when some of the mornings were very chill, and even the hardy seamen declared I should take my death of cold, though I derived benefit instead, thank God, from the operation. [Henry Christmas]

To deal with the vermin, various remedies were tried.

> Report comes from below that a thief is at work there, and that an army of lice from below will soon be here.... We begin to fortify ourselves against them by thoroughly cleansing our abode and holding no communications with those below. We also put a circle of water round our Cabin to prevent the 'crawling ferlies' from passing to our abode. [John McCorkindale]

Most emigrant vessels included young families and so it was not uncommon for children to be born during their voyage to the new world. In the general run of things, the arrival of a new baby was the cause of celebration. On occasion, things did go wrong and a child would not survive. When this happened sadness prevailed and the child was dropped into a watery grave.

Accommodation in the steerage was cramped, even for the average family. For a pregnant woman there was little comfort and very little privacy, even when labour commenced. A curious sequence of events happened aboard the *Rothiemurchus* during her voyage from Leith to Quebec in 1817. It began with a storm.

> Those who had young children, found it difficult to avoid crushing them to death in their beds. About midnight a woman lately married was taken with premature labour, and added much to the horror of the scene by her dismal cries. But before morning she was safely delivered of a male child, and in a few days was as well as before. The surgeon's situation, during her labour, was scarcely less embarrassing than her own. He was several times thrown down by the violent motion of the ship, and at one time the birth [berth] in which she lay, went to pieces with a crash which made some people think that the good *Rothiemurchus* herself had uttered her last groan. [William Bell]

But this was not the end of the tale. Several days later:

> An inquiry was set on foot to ascertain why the wind was generally against us. Some imputed it to the man who had forgotten to pay his debts, others to a party of smugglers who had escaped from the clutches of the excise, but the cook determined the question, by affirming in the strongest manner, that it was the unchristened child that occasioned our detention. [William Bell]

It is to be hoped that the captain of this vessel quickly put a stop to such foolish notions, and that he did his best to ensure that the new child received a warm welcome from all on board.

When a new baby girl arrived on board the *Napoleon*, the parents settled on a name to the ship's honour.

> ...a cabin passenger, gave birth to a female child. In compliment to the ship, this little nymph of the sea was to be christened Josephine! A name memorable for conjugal affection, and the

poor return such a virtue will sometimes receive. [Patrick Shirreff]

Most women gave birth without the aid of a physician, whether at home or at sea. If a ship's doctor were in attendance, a woman might think herself quite fortunate. Mrs Ditton obviously coped well with the birth of her child:

> A remarkably fine day; the people enjoying themselves dancing on deck, to the violin. Mrs Ditton, who was confined on the 28th. ultimo, (seventeen days since) and her husband, the most actively engaged in this exercise. [James Marr Brydone]

Robert Wade was of the opinion that breast-feeding a child would sap too much energy when a woman was at sea. He recommended planning the family around a voyage across the ocean.

> ...Our passengers are all well of their sickness but Mrs Oughtred who is a very delicate woman and has a child sucking above a year old. I mention this for the sake of those who may follow us for to wean their children when 6 or nine months old for children can endure the fatigue better than their mothers who have both themselves and children to provide for.

In the event of illness at sea, folk remedies were often counted on. While it was true that most people attempted to plan for any eventuality, there was a limit to the amount of supplies they could bring. As one might fear, items most needed were frequently missing from the medicine chest. When many passengers on the vessel took sick with coughs and colds, Joseph Wilson regretted not having brought along "Spanish Juice," an old sore throat remedy, produced from licorice. Later, when stricken with strong symptoms of gravel, a condition resulting in the passing of tiny stones from the bladder or kidney which he blamed on ingesting bad water, he regretted not having brought a little spirit of nitre. As a precautionary measure for that most common of complaints, seasickness, the general advice was to keep a full stomach. In the event that one did succumb, the most

98

frequently mentioned remedy was ginger. It could be used in various forms: cookies, cake, tea, wine or brandy.

Seasickness was a nasty business that very few people escaped. For some, it struck as early as one hour after leaving port and continued intermittently for the duration of the voyage. When the weather was very bad, the consequences could be dreadful.

> It has been an awful day in the ship, nothing but throwing and vomiting in all directions. When we tried to walk our heads were so light with the rocking of the ship that we felt like flying up; we were all like drunken people. [William Hunter]

The wisest thing, providing it was not too dangerous, was to take some fresh air, up on the deck. For those who were truly suffering, bed was the only place.

> Ship rolling fearfully. Pig iron rattling on deck and under our berths, empty bottles, cans, Jimmeys & chambers are rolling and dancing through the house. a shoe here and a boot honder, some half full of water. Caps, hats, and all sorts of moveable articles are scattered on every side and saturated not with water alone, or Brine, but with the contents of all the "Jennies" that form a part of this ugly horrible confusion, mingled with vomit and its accompaniments. All are in their beds below and mostly all sick. [John McCorkindale]

There was no escaping it. Even the grandest of ladies succumbed, despite all the comforts her station provided.

> ...After the two first days of beauteous weather, succeeding our embarkation, and which made us in love with Sailing, and *the Herald*, and in *good humour* with our accommodations, and with every body, and everything!—and during which, we were all very busy arranging our books, writing, and *deciding* on a variety of occupations, and rules to be observed during our passage, in order to the passing our time profitably and agreeably when the whole scene changed and for the rest of our six weeks passage till we were fairly in the lovely St. Lawrence we enjoyed only the pleasing variation of Gales *head sea*—fogs off Newfoundland, becalmed or squalls—extreme indisposition

became the lot of most of us—for myself I was reduced to a pitiable state of weakness not exactly sea sick, but truly exhausted from being unable to keep my feet for days together none of our party were able to walk on deck. My maid fortunately proved a every good sailor and we had another female on board accustomed to the sea, and very useful in our Cabins—I never dined at table for a month, and seldom could go on deck you may readily conceive our joyous feelings, when we sailed with as fair wind up the magnificent St. Lawrence.... [Lady Aylmer]

A large family might have all its members laid low. A. C. Buchanan reminded passengers not to forget to carry medicines suitable for young children. In the case of sea sickness, the young generally recovered first. No matter how dreadful a parent was feeling, unless they had kindly neighbours to take over their charge, they must look after the children. Fortunately, Elizabeth Peters fared quite well.

I have neglected writing for some time, owing to the sickness on board. William has been very sick almost all the time, at least when it is at all rough. Maria and Thomas Hoskins really ill. They could not help themselves. Maria soon got the better of it, but Thomas is much worse than William. We have had a gale of wind since we have been here. It lasted the both times rather more than a day and night during which time we could scarcely stand to dress or undress, and it was really dangerous for a female to walk the deck, and the children require all the attention it was possible to give them. We have many times said to each other how little did we know about our voyage. Our friends thought we should have nothing to do but to make observations and write them, but I assure you so far the contrary that we have as much as we can well do, all of us, even those who have no children. For my own part, I am as well as when on shore. I have felt a little uneasiness at times, and my appetite is sometimes delicate owing to the inconveniences we are subject to, having to dine and sleep so many of us in so small a place. However, we have the deck for a drawing room, and thither we repair to dine or tea in fine weather. [Elizabeth Peters]

William Bell "took a draught of salt water, which operated as an emetic" upon the advice of a sailor, as a result of which he soon got better. But, for most people, there was little to do but patiently wait it out. While doing so, one might analyze the way in which seasickness affected the body.

> most of our neighbors sick & we, although not sick, yet are quere.—The sensation of sea sickness is the most curious I have even experienced. It is as though the blood in the extremities of the feet was urged up by a certain jerk into the bowels & the bowels altogether pushed into the head & then returning back again into the feet. [Joseph Wilson]

When calm was restored, it was time to replenish the body. Fluids were vital, though ships' water held little appeal. After a long bout of seasickness, Joseph Wilson declared, "Wine or ale would now be very desirable." Mary Gapper, relieved that she had recovered, said "A most happy change has taken place in my digestive organs and I can laugh again."

Serious illness was apt to develop at any time, often bringing dire consequences. Such was the case with the Robinson family. They did not immediately recognize the seriousness of their father's complaint.

> Most of our family sick though not quite so as yesterday. Calm again about noon. towards night after my Father had partaken a very hearty tea he was taken ill and complained to me of his inside being painfull, but most of us being ill with the sea sickness and he too had been sick but not so bad as some of us yet through this we the less noticed him and he made no particular complaints. Mr Bicker being very ill. [George Robinson]

When it became apparent that Mr Robinson was critically ill, George did everything he could to make his father as comfortable as possible. As the illness progressed, and it became certain that death would occur, the family gathered around the bedside offering what comfort they could to the dying man. George documented his father's illness in his diary. This record offers modern readers a first-hand account of the progression of cholera. It also provides testament to this family's strength of faith, and

101

expresses in a very Victorian way, the glory and hope of Christianity.

...I was called upon to attend him and to my great surprise and grief I found him very bad of the Cramp in his leg which soon reach'd his thighs and from thence upwards and to his arms and fingers which was most grievous to see. His flesh and joints were drawn in such a manner as I never before beheld which caused him to call for us to rub him in the parts most painful. We made every exertions in our power to relieve him but nothing had any effect to stay his pain. He said to me he must die. but I still hoped he would get better has I have seen him very bad before but I saw to my great concern his strength gradually though quickly to fail, the pain of his body caused him to often cry out for us to help him by rubbing the parts most afflicted. The Sailors and Captain were very kind rendering every assistance in their power thus he continued untill morning when I left him a short time being much fatigued by sickness and trouble of mind and body but he soon enquired for me as he never seemed to wish for me to be out of his company...amid all this severe afflictions I never heard a murmuring word escape from his lips. it was seen that night that the complaint was the Cholera which much alarmed us and I was afraid to tell my Dear Father of what was suspected but I need not have been afraid for he seemed to be resigned to the will of God to live or die.... I told him we should be left fatherless and ask'd him what we must do, he told me many were left younger than we, and said the Lord would provide for us.... he seem'd much parch'd with thirst and constantly beg'd us to give him cold water but we durst not fearing it would hurt him we gave him a little brandy and water which seemed a little to quench his thirst but it soon return'd.... towards noon our Captain...proposed to run down to Scarboro as we had not got far past, ...there to procure a Doctor if any relief might be had... I told my father we were going to Scarborough and should there get a Doctor on board but he said a Doctor would do him no good. I can see a better Doctor than him he said which truly rejoiced my soul to see him resting on Christ whom I know alone would sustain him in his time of trial. as soon as we came near the place the boat was sent out on shore for the Doctor. even before the ship was near as the wind was slack and our anxiety very great for a Doctor. but before the Doctor got on board the other man left this mortal scene and entered his eternal state. My dear Father also was just quivering on the brink of eternity.... I therefore asked him if he should be as content for his body to be swallowed up of the sea has to be buried on the land. His answer to me was in three words just the same, just the same. O what a mercy that he was thus comforted and borne up in his departing moments on seeing my sister Margaret approach his bedside he asked who she was if it was his Margaret on being told it was he began thoughts with a fathering tongue to give his last helping and advice commencing with her... He then proceeded to the rest according to their age until he came to the youngest after which he addressed my dear mother in an affecting manner and lastly commended his own precious soul into the hands of his Redeemer thus he was enabled to give his last blessing unto each one of us separately and commend us to God in a manner which greatly astonished me considering the state he was in though affliction of body. [George Robinson]

Describing the death scene was a common practice in Victorian times, since it was important for people to know that the dying person had made a good death. George may have copied excerpts from his diary for inclusion in letters informing relatives and acquaintances of his father's death.

There was very little in the way of treatment for cholera. A good diet would have help to increase resistance to the disease, but poverty was not conducive to a good diet. Those who took sufficient supplies on board ship, might have produced an "Anti Cholera Diet Beverage" by boiling a gallon of water, to which one pound of rice (without washing), a tablespoon of barley, and one of tapioca were added. This was boiled for half an hour, drained through a sieve, pressing the liquid from the rice with a spoon. A little powdered cinnamon and two ounces of sugar candy were then added. The patient might drink this whenever thirsty.

The manner in which a sea captain dealt with a death could enhance or destroy his relationship with the passengers. In ensuring that a dying person's physical needs were met, and by offering support and comfort to the relatives of a sick person, he would earn great respect.

...I think it my duty to make some observations on our captain, and am of opinion, that no man could possibly take more pains to secure the comfort, health, and protection of the passengers at large than he did; night and day he left nothing undone to hasten us on our way; and when almost all the people were sea-sick, he failed not to visit them daily in their respective berths, to enquire after their health, and to administer such medicine or food (whether meat or drink), as he judged might recover them speedily; his attention to the deceased young woman who left this stage of time, deserves to be noticed. He attended her faithfully, and freely gave her of his wine, fowl, or any thing else he had, and evinced much trouble respecting her; and confident I am, that his knowledge and skill in conducting and bringing passengers to America cannot be exceeded, or perhaps equalled. And I am further of opinion, if Captain Cunningham is disposed to bring passengers next season to Quebec, it would be wise and safe in all my countrymen who can to embark with him in preference to any other...[James Wilson]

A doctor might show his compassion in various ways. John Frazer did what he could for a woman suffering from fever, to no avail. When medical help was of no further use, he attempted to add a small speck of brightness to her last hours by bestowing a small gift.

Several people sick in steerage. One woman not likely to survive sent a little remaining jam I had to her she seemed quite delighted with it. Her family was very grateful. wished I had a little more of it. this evening at 6 she died. her body was carried up and deposited in the long Boat to await the ceremony of heaving into the deep in the morning. a good many leery of being ill of Fever... [John Frazer]

...the body of the woman who died last night was consigned to the deep and the English service read over the remains by Mr. Henry Close and Englishman. an impressive scene. [John Frazer]

In June 1836, Robert Cromar, along with his sister Ann, and his father Alexander, sailed on the *Hercules* from Aberdeen to Quebec. There were 154 passengers on board. Within twelve days, the first death had occurred.

104

Doctor John Frazer, photographed by S. Hays. (Courtesy National Archives of Canada, PA 202763)

The death of a fellow passenger might induce a variety of responses. Some felt fear, especially if the death was the result of a contagious illness. Others felt sadness or anger. But perhaps the death of a child was the most moving. Compassion at such times was not always evident in a captain. Cromar's description of Captain Duncan Walker's officiating at the first of the funerals presents a grim picture.

> Child belonging to one of the Passengers died in the afternoon and rolled up in the fashion of the dead at Sea...
>
> ...the child put overboard at half past five in the morning none on deck but the Child's father two of the Passengers and the Seamen. I was too late of getting up to see the funeral Ceremony but one of the Sailors told me that the Corpse was merely laid on one of the Hatches and turned over-board into the Sea without any other ceremony whatever than a hearty Curse from the Captain to one of the sailors for not turning the Hatch in the proper way. I thought he might have let the cursing alone untill the corpse was out of site at any rate. The child's mother appears to be very sorry about it but no word nor appearance of any kind among the Passengers of any such circumstance taking place... [Robert Cromar]

More illness and death occurred on this unfortunate voyage. There were reports of scarlet fever in the foremost hatch. However, Cromar thought this a misdiagnosis, saying the afflictions were more likely to be some "scurilous flush reaction to foul air." Measles developed later on in the voyage, affecting a large number of children.

> ..A child belonging to one of the Passengers died this morning at Two A.M. and was committed to the Deep at 1/2 Past 4 A.M. A good many of the Passengers on Deck at the time and all seemed to be little concerned about it. [Robert Cromar]

> [On the 17th, another child died. Cromar gave no details] ...A child died in the afternoon 5 P.M. and was committed to the deep at Ten P.M. I stopped out of bed to see the ceremony it being the first of the four that I had ever seen put to the water. There were about 12 or 14 Passengers on Deck at the time. [Robert Cromar]

People frequently died without the cause of death being established. For even at the best of times, physicians might have been unclear about an illness. While sea sickness was sometimes suggested as a cause, dehydration may have been a great contributor. But whether at sea or at home, any number of things could go wrong.

> This morning one of the passengers a little girl about 7 years old died of sea sickness, the first instance I ever saw. the breath was scarcely out of her body before she was bound up in a blanket and thrown over board. What indecency. [— Johnson]

Fourteen days into her voyage, the *Caroline* had already lost fourteen of her passengers to illness. Cholera was suspected, causing everyone on board to feel extremely anxious.

> ...many of our company in the ship began to sicken with a disease, if not cholera something very much like it. On Monday a death of a woman and on Tuesday another child died. the same thing again with another child on Wednesday [of] the disease and caused great alarm to all the crew and passengers— which I should have mentioned consisting of between 80 & 90

German steerage passengers with myself & family & of 3 other intermediate pass. 13 of them men women child paid a great debt of nature as also one of the sailors of the name of Hopper whose Brother is Master of the Marinia the most healthiest in the ship. This up to 9 Aug making 14 deaths. On seeing the disease gain strength I took upon me to recommend the Capt to put back in order to have a medical person on board before we got out of reach of such aid but without success...[Joseph Brown]

If a clergyman or preacher happened to be on board, they may have been called upon to sit with the dying person. While there was little to be done for the physical well-being, the soul had to be tended to.

I visited Phoebe Dagg, (the young woman already spoken of) about twelve o'clock this morning, but found her speechless, prayed with her for the last time, and commended her soul to the Lord; she died about two hours after. She was allowed to remain in her bed till night, when about nine o'clock she was put into a sheet of canvas and brought upon deck. I was sent for by the captain to have prayer on the occasion. It was a serious time! After prayer she was let down into the sea, there to remain till morning of the resurrection, when the sea shall give up her dead, and body and soul be united again to receive its final sentence, and I hope to inherit a crown of glory. The distress and anguish of her sister on the occasion were truly lamentable. This young woman was from Ahowle in the Co Wicklow, about 23 years of age, and whilst in health, was agreeable, friendly, and truly pleasing in her manner. [James Wilson]

In recounting matters of life and death, James Hopkirk documented five births and two deaths during his voyage. The first death was "natural" and the second a "drowning." Hopkirk also made note of happenings within the animal kingdom. When his "cocker, Minna, had five puppies, four pretty and one little ugly wretch..." he threw the runt overboard, keeping the rest. There were a surprising number of dogs on board ships, but no mentions of cats.

..a small black terrier dog of the captain's which had been very sick last night and had drunk a quantity of salt water was found dead in his kennel and committed to the deep.   [James Hopkirk]

A fine morning & fair wind but the sea runing tremendously high. We yet feel the effects of the storm & can eat nothing I never felt so weak & languid in my life. We are comforted today with a fair & brisk breeze.—ship runing 8 knots an hour Lost a small favorite dog of the chief mate over board.—No chance of saving it... [Joseph Wilson]

Birds were also made into pets. Not just singing canaries, for whatever landed on deck became vulnerable when spotted by people desperate for signs of life beyond the ocean. But when the little creatures died, as they surely did, great ceremony might attend dealing with the remains.

Several, however, of the smaller birds were caught to make pets for some of our younger fellow-passengers; but they invariably died before they had been kept in cages twenty-four hours, however tenderly treated, as indeed the captain said they would. I was much amused at the tender care of one amiable young lady, who made the neatest imaginable little shroud for one of her feathered favourites when it died, and sorrowfully handed it over to one of the young officers to consign to a watery grave. [Henry Christmas]

Providing the weather cooperated, once a vessel reached the Banks of Newfoundland, everyone's thoughts turned to fish. When the weather was still, the captain might order small boats to be lowered for the purpose of fishing expeditions. When the catch was good, delicious feasts were prepared and everyone had their fill. Cod was particularly relished.

Cod-fish are caught on the banks of Newfoundland by hook and line; one man can attend to four lines, although fishing in forty fathoms water; the bait is generally a piece of white pork. Thus, as the poet says, "They wind them up by barrelfulls, To feed a hungry world." [John MacTaggart]

The offerings of the sea were many. Some required more skill in catching; others decidedly took more talent to land.

> ....there has been a herd or shole of porpoise or sea hogs come all around the vessel. Our second mate succeeded in spearing one with his harpoon. We had some difficulty in getting it on board. Suppose it weighs about 16 stone. the lean part of its flesh is very good to eat; the fat part makes excellent oil to burn in lamps. &c. [John Walker]

Everyone resigned themselves to the possibility of fog, once they reached the banks. This part of the ocean was famous for it. When a fog did descend, there was little to do but try and keep dry and warm, and wait it out.

> Fogs off Newfoundland Banks generally arise with a little westerly breeze. They are extremely dense; so much so, that the bowsprit of the ship cannot be seen from the quarter-deck. While the fog continues, the weather is very cold, and the thickest woollen clothes and mitts that we have, are in request. Often it will not clear away for a month or six weeks after it comes on: such duration, however, is rare about Midsummer; in the spring and fall it is more common. Fog-horns are blown in the ships at intervals, night and day, so that they may not run foul of each other. Lights of any kind cannot be seen very far off; the sun is quite obscured, and about the summer solstice the day is nearly as dark as the night; in order to read, we must burn candles. The sailors argue that the fogs raise the seas,—that is, create a commotion in the waters.
> [John MacTaggart]

Eventually, the weather would clear, and after weeks of nothing but ocean, the first sighting of land was made. Far in the distance the shores of Newfoundland slowly came into focus. The mood on board ship, which formerly had been one of impatience and frustration, quickly switched to that of optimism and gaiety. Gradually, quiet resignation would resume, with the realization that the voyage was far from over.

On a fine, mild afternoon—the first we had been favoured with since the shores of England had sunk into the waves—there was a cry of 'land a'head!' from the fore-top gallant yard. Every one in an instant was upon deck, some for the first time during the voyage, and the rigging was covered with those who previously had not courage to mount the ladder of the hatchway. Every eye was in vain strained to gain a glimpse of the long-wished-for coast of America, and three cheers greeted the captain as he descended upon deck; the women crowding round him, dancing and singing, as though he had rescued them from some imminent danger. [Edward Coke]

The first sailings of the season always ran the risk of running into difficulties due to ice. Late spring thaws were especially menacing for vessels approaching Newfoundland. Never underestimating the danger, a round-the-clock watch was mounted at the first glimpse of an iceberg. While passengers were generally in awe of these massive creations during the daytime, once darkness fell, a strange eeriness enveloped the ship.

We were roused earlier than usual this morning by the cry "an iceberg" Before us it lay two or three miles ahead of us and after breakfast we passed it within 1/2 a mile. It appeared about the size of our ship above water, and they are considered to be two thirds under water. It looked almost like a mountain of snow stuck in the sea, being quite white, it was a beautiful sight. There is a man set to watch today for fear we come unexpectedly upon these masses which are sufficient to break our vessel. [Sarah Leeming]

At 9 A.M. a mass of ice appeared just a-head, about two hundred yards distant. We instantly altered our course a little. The novelty of its appearance brought every person on deck, who was able to get out of bed. It was of an oval shape, and appeared to be half a mile in length. We had scarce time to look at it when another and a larger mass was announced. It was as high as our top mast, and probably reached near the bottom of the sea. ...At a distance we observed a large mass of ice, which we had passed in the night unobserved. It had much the appearance of a great castle in ruins. [William Bell]

In the spring of 1847, the *Albion, Great Britain, Eromanga* and *St. Andrew* ran into winter storms and ice about thirty

110

miles off Newfoundland. For three of these vessels, this was the beginning of a long, cold and tedious period. Eventually they stuck fast in the ice, where they remained for several weeks.

As the ship approached the latter stages of the voyage, any number of situations could arise. There was always a possibility of gale force winds, cold rains, turbulent seas, fog or freezing temperatures, adding misery to the trip.

> This cold state of the weather continued till we approached the mouth of the St. Laurence when it became so warm, that I was nearly suffocated from the smell and heat below deck. I was consequently compelled to sleep on deck, together with many others, who were in a similar situation. [John M'Donald]

When the weather cleared, and a festive mood resurfaced, it was time for a gesture of kindness on the part of the captain.

> A very fine morning but the wind quit ahead of us. Land in sight to the right of us but at a great distance. The Captain made a present of 4 gallons of rum to the passengers this afternoon which was equally divided & us & two or three of our neighbors had an excellent bowl of punch made to drink to his health & each others prosperity... [Joseph Wilson]

As the voyage of the *Friends* neared its end, everyone was relieved. The Peters family, along with their Methodist colleagues, gave thanks in prayer for their safe delivery across the wide Atlantic.

> ...Newfoundland on the north and Capt Breton on the south, 31 days after losing sight of Old England. All hearts were cheered and our spirits enlivened, but we did not get up to land in the evening as we expected in to morning on account of a calm. Blessed by God, we are all well, and they that love God are happy—10 o'clock and now going to bed Glory be to God. [William Peters]

> By this morning we had passed the land we saw last evening and have in sight of other islands. All day under a calm, and the Captain hove to and about 11 o'clock we began fishing, when one of the passengers soon hooked a very large fish which the

111

mariners called Hollowbut. weighted upwards of 60 lbs, a flat fish of very good flavor. Many other of the passengers caught cod fish, and I was one of the successful fishers. Caught one about 10 lbs; so that we have one more fresh meat to feed upon, and yet I feel a heart tuned to praise God and can say "Surrounded by thy power I stand; On every side I feel they hand. I own thy goodness, I feel thy power, Thy hand sustains me every hour." [William Peters]

There was a great contrast between sailing to New York, where one was on the wide ocean until the very last, and to Quebec, where the watery depths disappeared more gradually. The sense of this was poetically described by Northrop Frye.

But Canada has, for all practical purposes, no Atlantic seaboard. The traveller from Europe edges into it like a tiny Jonah entering an inconceivably large whale, slipping past the Straits of Belle Isle into the Gulf of St. Lawrence, where five Canadian provinces surround him, for the most part invisible. Then he goes up the St. Lawrence and the inhabited country comes into view, mainly a French-speaking country, with its own cultural traditions. To enter the United States is a matter of crossing an ocean; to enter Canadian is a matter of being silently swallowed by an alien continent.

Once they had passed into the Gulf of Saint Lawrence, one of the emigrants' first experiences of the Canadian landscape was Anticosti Island. Long, dark and deserted, it passed them in silent majesty—or silent gloom.

It might be an interesting object were it settled, but it present for the most part the aspect of a gloomy and fearful wilderness—an unbroken continuity of swamp and forest, replete with wild and fearful traditions of old wrecks and hunger-perished mariners. [Henry Christmas]

It does not appear very inviting. I can't get any information regarding it. It looks black and deserted and that in connection with this chilly contrary wind, I must say I don't like it. [John McCorkindale]

In case of shipwrecks, a single family lived on the island, which had always belonged to a single owner. It remains largely unsettled even today.

Shortly, more appealling habitations appeared on the riverbanks and a sense of welcome could be felt on board.

When a vessel entered the Saint Lawrence river, it was time to take a pilot on board. In the early days, these men often farmed in addition to their nautical work. The captain would have hoisted a flag or fired a gun to indicate his need of a pilot. If things went according to plan, there would be little delay before the pilot-boat set sail from shore. Once on board, the pilot assumed responsibility for taking the vessel to Quebec.

> Ships coming up the St. Lawrence, generally meet with pilots off Cape Chat, which is about three hundred miles below Quebec; but these persons take no charge of them until they are past the Isle of Bie. They are French farmers, and but poorly informed. Their knowledge of the seaman's art is, indeed, very small, and few of them can speak English so as to be understood by those who know no other language. They are obliged to undergo a kind of apprenticeship to the pilotage business; and during that time must make at least one voyage across the Atlantic. They are generally very snug-looking, and warmly clad, smoke their pipes, and swallow their grog, extremely comfortably. They make, at an average, about 250£. per annum, conducting about twelve ships up and down. They live to a good old age, and are considered rich by their countrymen. The daughter of a pilot is fancied to have more charms than any girl else on the coast—the reason is obvious. [John MacTaggart]

Many people were moved by the grandeur of the scenery, and filled with the joyful anticipation of finally reaching Quebec. The last few days meant scraping the barrels, since provisions were just about run out.

> ...we are now sailing up one of the noblest rivers in the world, 90 miles wide at its mouth and no soundings for two or three miles up; several whales playing round us and four schooners in sight; sold flour and potatoes to some of the passengers, few of

them having anything but biscuits and tea; but the greatest outcry is bad water and want of tobacco. [Robert Wade]

Wade need not have worried about dwindling tobacco supplies, for two days later the pilot came aboard and "supplied us with what we most wanted, viz. tobacco." Later the ship weighed anchor near Hare Island.

...with seven ships in company, two with emigrants, the one from Ireland, the other the Kingston from Hull; she was the first ship we spoke in the Western Ocean... Mr. Evans, John and two of the sailors went on board of one of the ships called, the Governor Milne London, for water; but they could not spare us any, after which they went on board the Kingston, and the first thing their passengers asked for was tobacco, having had none for a fortnight; she had 99 passengers, and one family consisted of 20 persons, viz., grand-father and grandmother, fathers and mothers all going to the expected land of peace of plenty. [Robert Wade]

Storms and Shipwrecks

A memory for the perish'd ship!
A love-thought for the drowned!
A prayer to God for all who sank
Into the sea-profound!
F.W.N. Bayley

Most of the letters and journals written by emigrants document storms of varying degrees. Generally people began to feel seasick within twenty-four hours of leaving port, whereupon accounts of "seas being mountains high" fill the pages. One of the authors of this book, having had the good fortune of crossing the Atlantic Ocean between Britain and Quebec on five occasions, can attest to the fact that once a vessel reaches offshore waters, the greater swell of the ocean can indeed cause seas to appear mountains high. But the severity of the swell was sometimes magnified in the minds of those sailing for the first time. Having said that, in fairness to those emigrants who did indeed face dreadful storms, it should be noted that emigrant vessels of the nineteenth century were often surprisingly small, and their stabilizers were far less sophisticated than those of our modern luxury liners. It is small wonder the emigrants felt they were at the mercy of the elements as their ships pitched and tossed their way across the ocean.

A great many sick below. I can't walk on deck. One tremendous gush of wind and a sail is torn to rags. Sea washing over board. None allowed to stay on deck but sailors. It is truly awful and

grand. I cannot call them waves, they are great upheavals of the ocean, more like mountains, moveable and moving ragged with foaming caps, threatening to engulph our ship as we descend into the watery Glens and Valleys of this mighty Deep, and the top masts of our Ship don't appear so high above us as those mountains that frown upon us on all sides.
[John McCorkindale]

Sketch of Captain Tilly from the diary of John McCorkindale (by kind permission of Mary Kearns Trace)

The young are usually blessed with a natural sense of immortality enabling them to float above the tribulations of storms. This is certainly evident in the storm scene portrayed by Ellen Steele during her voyage on board the *Thames*, a scene reaching comic proportions.

Oh! the sea is the most inconstant of all inconstant things. When the hustle had a little subsided I went down to see what they had thought of it below. Millie had lain down for an hour, and had just fallen asleep when she was roused by the noise on deck and by no small bustle in the ladies' room. She looked out and saw Mrs. Hargraves, who had been very unwell, tottering towards the sofa with a glass of water to sprinkle Mrs. Keating, who had fainted. She jumped up to assist her and poor Mrs. Hargraves nearly fainted herself with her exertions. It was some time before Millie could get at the right of the story. It seems that in the height of the squall the Captain called out three times in a thundering voice to the man at the helm, "Luff, luff, luff!" and then again, "D__ it, will you luff!"

When Mrs. Keating heard the Captain swear, she exclaimed, "Oh God! we are lost!" and fell back in a swoon. She was just recovering when she saw me. She exclaimed, "Oh! what has been the matter, my dear child! Do tell me. Were we not in great danger. It must have been dreadful to make the Captain swear. He never did it before. Never once on board the Florida, though we had some bad storms too," "Did he swear, Ma'am?" said I. "Indeed I did not hear him." "Not hear him, my child? What could you have been thinking of? His voice was like thunder. I thought the vessel was going to pieces. I was so terrified that I fainted. Did I not, Mrs Hargrave? Did I not Miss Millie? quite dead away, and I am all of a tremble still."

Captain Griswold was quite in despair when he heard all the mischief he had done. But as he is a great favourite with Mrs. K he was soon forgiven, particularly when he told her that if the man at the helm had not obeyed him when he did it might have cost us all our lives. [Ellen Steele]

The fear of sinking was very real. When the brig *Minstrel* en route from Limerick to Quebec went down, taking all but a very few of her one hundred and forty-one passengers, one-third of which were children, there was an outcry. This wreck, along with dozens of others sustaining large loss of life, helped to bring about the provision under the 1842 Act stipulating that lifeboats be provided for all steerage passengers.

To the emigrants, an increasing gale was a source of great tribulation and alarm; the deck resounding with their groans and prayers until it moderated. The captain and myself were walking upon deck one squally day, when seeing several of the steerage passengers sitting on the fore hatchway, exposed to every sea which came aboard, yet at the same time apparently regardless of it, we had the curiosity to ask them, what they were doing there, and why not below in their berths? "Why sure now, Captain," said the spokesman, an Irishman, "and isn't it that we are waiting here, so that we will be ready to get into the boats, if the ship goes down; for we know you wouldn't wait to call us..." [Edward Coke]

John Walker noted several days and nights of rough weather during his crossing on board the merchant vessel, *Queen Adelaide*. His description of this sorry state of affairs would do little in the way of enticing his relatives to follow in his wake.

After a stormy day, we found we had a worse night approaching. I never experienced such a night in all my life and hope I never shall another like it. Captain and his men were all at hard work all night but such a night for thunder and lightning with wind and rain as themselves had seldom witnessed. We were all confusion below, our tinware like so many bells, ring a dumb peel, potatoes and eggs running up and down our cabin in all directions exhibited at once one confused mass such heaving, reaching [retching], moaning and vomiting as can scarcely be imagined, driven back 50 miles on the Isle of Man coasts, but praised be the name of the Lord on Tuesday morning He stilled the tempest. [John Walker]

...Towards noon the sea began to be very heavy and swelled very much. It appeared to run mountains high. I really thought at times we must be all dashed to the bottom. We were thrown from one side of the vessel to the other, as in a moment some of our experienced men on board say it was the most dangerous part of our voyage passing between the Welsh and Irish coasts... [John Walker]

John MacTaggart displayed a keen interest in all about him, absorbing much in the way of nautical folklore. In view of the fact that he anticipated publishing an account of his experiences, it is probable that he went to additional pains in recording the happenings on board ship.

When fully out to sea, we fall in with the stormy petrels, better known by the name of Mother Carew's chickens: on the eve of a storm, they gather in to the wake of the ship in great numbers. Mother Carew was an old witch, it is said, good at raising the wind. These birds are about the size of the swallow, only their tails are not so long; with brown plumage, short bills, feet not webbed, they keep on the wing—sometimes they let their little legs droop, and trip along the water with their wings extended, but at rest they seem to be fond of any little crumbs of food that fall from the ships. The sailors will not shoot them on any account; they pay them great respect, that their mother's wrath may not be roused. [John MacTaggart]

We have some Stormy Petrel Birds follow us almost all our way which is always considered a bad omen. [John Walker]

Stormy petrels, variously described as Mother Carey's Chickens, Old Mother Kerry's children and Mother Carew's chickens, were noted harbingers of storms. Mystical powers were also attributed to other creatures. Sharks, however much they might amuse some passengers, were said by some to be a sign of a death to come. To others, they were a sign of poor weather ahead. But signs or no signs, storms arrived and they had to be endured.

Awoke between 12 & 1 o'clock this morning to the wind which was blowing a terrible gale—could not compose myself to sleep again.—3 o'clock felt rather alarmed at hearing the sailors called on deck & ordered into the rigging.—the ship was heaving from one side to the other at an awful rate. We were apprehensive of being thrown out of bed & it was all we could do to keep in.—9 o'clock A.M. the storm now at its greatest fury; the water breaking over the bulwarks & pouring down our hatchway in torrents. the people in the lower cabins were almost floated out of their beds, articles of all discriptions flying about like shuttle cocks. Many of the passengers who were foolish enough to get up & go upon the deck were thrown down the hatches & upon the deck & some got sore bruises & lamed. We were confined to our beds but in great jepardy of being thrown out until 3 o'clock P.M. at which time the storm abated & we got up. [Joseph Wilson]

Severe storms brought many consequences. Not only was there discomfort in being tossed about, and the general feeling of debility produced by motion sickness, but cooking, or the simple action of making a cup of tea, were completely out of the question due to the possibility of accidents. For those who sailed well, and whose appetites were enhanced by the bracing sea air, hunger pains during a storm were most unwelcome. Cooking was not allowed, even if one could brace oneself and remain in an upright position. William Bell offered a most poetic description of a meal taken during a storm:

> No cooking could be accomplished, and no provision were served out, except rotten Dutch cheese, as bitter as soot, and bread partly alive.

> The wind rose, a heavy gale commenced, and the waves rolled mountains high, and made a mighty noise. To see a ship making her way in the midst of a storm, over these Lofty billows, is both grand and awful. We now became like drunken men, reeling and staggering to and fro. To walk on deck was impossible, and the places where the pots were erected for cooking, tumbled down, so that we could not get any victuals made ready, and some of our associates were compelled to mix a little meal and molasses, and use this composition as a substitute for better fare. The comparative want of food, and the storm together, rendered us very weak. This storm continued nine days. The captain affirmed, that he had never witnessed a tempest of such long continuance at that season of the year. [John M'Donald]

Cabin passengers may have enjoyed greater luxury than steerage passengers, but they frequently had to contend with floods. On board the *Clio*, high seas broke through a cabin window, soaking everything.

> A great lurch the Cabin window bursts in & filled the place with water. Papas & boys clothes were all floating and my shoes swimming about like little canoes. Boys obliged to lay in bed while their clothes were drying in the rigging. [Julia Bird]

When this sort of thing happened, there was nothing for it but to rig up a temporary covering. This was far from satisfactory since the covering would eliminate daylight from the cabin.

After this we had to be in darkness, our window being covered with thick canvas. I feel to have little news to tell you for the weather being so rough we cannot either speak vessels or anything else. We are drawing nearer to the ice in some directions, for, some days it is so cold we can hardly bear. Our Captain think we are about 200 miles from the banks of Newfoundland, and we are in the sixth week since we last left Liverpool. [Sarah Leeming]

Death was sometimes the consequence of a storm for sailors must do their work, in spite of the elements.

Very stormy indeed. A sad accident one of the poor Sailor Boys fell over board he was doing something the anchor chain & a wave washed him over it was too stormy to render him any assistance the waves were mountainous high. [Julia Bird]

Once a person had found their sea-legs, a storm might bring a sense of adventure. For the younger crowd, less concerned about formalities and etiquette, much mirth could be derived, though often at the expense of others.

As we felt much better to-day, and indeed very hungry, Mrs Hargrave and I we determined to join the party at dinner, the Captain was very gallantly handing us up to the table, when a sudden lurch sent a piece of roast pork and a couple of fowls well covered with melted butter rolling at our feet, these were followed by plates, glasses, sauce-boats, more things than I can enumerate, the noise, the laughing, the screaming (for I think Mrs. Keating thought it was all over with us) was enough to frighten poor Mamma to death. As for me, though the unfortunate fowls slipped by me two or three times, I really laughed too much to secure them, but Mrs Hargrave, who by-the-bye had been talking all the morning about preferring fowls to anything else on board, caught up a fork and held one of them fast till Mr Fawcett came to her assistance. As this was her first appearance at table she has been well laughed at for her extraordinary alertness. [Ellen Steele]

There are many noted trouble spots around the coasts of Britain and certainly the Irish sea had its share of them. William

121

Hunter, who sailed on the *Hottinguer* in May 1849, kept a small news clipping telling of the wrecking of this vessel less than a year after his voyage. The *Hottinguer* went down on 12 January 1850.

> The *Hottinguer* sailed from Liverpool, for New York, on the 10th January. She had on board 230 cabin and steerage passengers, together with a Captain and crew of twenty men and boys, and had a very full freight of various descriptions of goods. On the morning of the 13th, the ship floated off Blackwater Bank, and bore away before the wind, and struck Arklow Bank, where she afterwards went to pieces, and Captain Beersley, and twelve of those who determined to be last in the ship, were drowned. At the time the passengers left the ship the hold filled with water, and the sea made clear breakers over her. The passengers were unable to save anything from the ship, unless the clothes they had on at the time.

The Blackwater, Arklow, Glasgorman and Seven Fathom banks, located off the coast of Counties Wicklow and Wexford, posed formidable threats to shipping taking the Saint George's Channel route from Liverpool. The banks off this part of the Irish coast have claimed countless ships, including the *Pomona*, which in 1859 hit the Blackwater Bank, taking 388 passengers. Under gale-force winds, it was virtually impossible to steer clear of these shallow sandbanks.

When Isaac Booth, master of the *Exmouth* sailed from Derry on 25 April 1847, he could not have foretold the tragedy waiting to unfold. In heavy weather, Booth lost his direction, the ship drifted and caught on the rocks off the Isle of Islay. Only three sailors survived the wreck. The *Exmouth*, of Sunderland, had been carrying a total of two-hundred and forty emigrants. Most were small farmers and tradesmen, with their families. In addition, there was a large number of females and children on board, going out to join their fathers and other relatives already settled in Canada. There is no doubt this ship was overloaded since it was only registered to carry sixty-five and a half passengers. Children only counted as half a person, infants did not count at all.

The loss of an emigrant ship was not an uncommon occurrence. A glance at nineteenth century newspaper columns devoted to shipping soon confirms the precariousness of ocean travel during this period. Between 1847 and 1851, at least forty-four passenger vessels out of Britain suffered shipwreck.

The causes of these disasters were numerous. Besides losses due to storms or fires, collisions were sometimes to blame. The Victorian age brought extraordinary growth to the nautical field, part of the price of this expansion being congestion of coastal channels. Once in the ocean, heavy fog might set the scene for a collision. This was the case when the *Charles Bartlett*, carrying 162 steerage passengers from London to New York, was hit by the mail steamship, *Europa*, on 27 June 1849. Captain W. Bartlett, master of the ill-fated *Charles Bartlett*, estimated there had been one hundred passengers on deck at the time of the collision, fifty of whom were instantly killed.

Investigations into this disaster, which took the lives of 135, concluded that no blame could be attached to either party. Six months earlier, the *Europa* had made her passage from New York to Liverpool in twelve days. This included a stop at Halifax to land and take in the Canadian mails and passengers. Newspapers of the day report this crossing as being the shortest ever made between New York and Liverpool. High speed received no mention during the inquiry.

Whatever the cause of a disaster at sea, the loss of life was often high. Assistance to survivors of shipwrecks was minuscule. It was possible to purchase insurance prior to setting sail, but most did not. Survivors of the *Charles Bartlett*, in addition to losing luggage and tools, lost cash averaging from £20 to £40 each.

After the packet ship *Great Britain*, built at Quebec in 1839, sank on her outward passage to New York on 30 March 1843, her Master, Captain Shaxton, reported: "The cries of the women and children, of whom you know there were many, sometimes fell on our ears...the horrors we endured were dreadful." For three days, the crew fought to keep this vessel afloat, losing one sailor in the effort.

To his great credit, Captain Shaxton was able to transfer all passengers to another vessel, which happened to be in the

123

vicinity. All baggage and cargo were entirely lost. As traumatic as this situation was for all on board, the emigrants, suffering the loss of precious goods, found themselves close to destitution.

> Captain Shaxton and thirteen hands of the ship Great Britain, bought from the wreck into Philadelphia, by the Bremen barque, Philadelphia, have been clothed and supplied with necessaries by the British consulate at this port. A Welsh family, named Harris, nine in number, from the same wreck, are in this city in much distress, having lost all they possess.

Some vessels weathered such horrendous storms that their survival was nothing short of miraculous.

> ...early on the morning of the 12th a tremendous storm came on so sudden as not to allow the sailors to take down their sails. The vessel shipping very heavy seas and being in dead of night we were literally washed out of our berths and our bedding completely soaked with water indeed for some hours I considered ourselves in the greatest danger which afterwards was acknowledged to be the fact not a single sail had scarcely a piece left as large as a pocket handf. [handkerchief] and the decks covered with them. The bulwarks beaten in the Jolly Boat & oars lost in this sad situation most of our things were driven from their places badly broken to pieces... [Joseph Brown]

Experiencing a storm was anything but pleasant. But after it was over, most people felt a sense of exhilaration. In years to come, recounting the experience would fill endless hours of fireside stories, fine-tuned to impress and delight eager grandchildren. In Donald McKay's opinion, most emigrants "found the voyage more uncomfortable and tedious than horrendous."

Here is the full account of a shipwreck off Newfoundland:

Narrative of the loss of the Ship "Hebe" Captain Straughan, bound to Quebec, from London, on the Brazil rocks, near Cape Ray, Newfoundland July 10, 1833, by one of the passengers.

The morning was cold, damp and foggy, as it had been for several days previous, and the ship was going about four miles an hour, when, just after breakfast, I heard a great shouting and noise on the deck above; I immediately ran up to ascertain the cause, when, to my great surprise and horror, I saw we were close to the land and rocks, the waves dashing over the latter in a most terrific manner and not more than twenty yards from us. The bustle and confusion which now took place both above and below, were far beyond description, and dismay was visible in every face. The captain ordered the anchor to be immediately lowered, but it could not be done in time. For a while we hoped we should have got out of danger, as the wind was so moderate, when all at once I heard several exclaim, "it's all over with us, as we are getting on a reef of rocks." I immediately ran below with feelings not to be described, and told my family, and begged of them to lose no time in coming upon deck. I then secured my watch and what little cash I had on board, when the vessel struck on the rocks—the shock was like that of an earthquake and threw many of the passengers down—there was now a general screaming and shrieking from the females and children, and a rush upon deck. I got Mrs. T. and the children up with difficulty, led them to the mainmast and told them to hold on by the ropes, while the ship continued to strike and roll about in a most dreadful manner; many persons were thrown down and much bruised, and others dashed about from one side of the deck to the other. A rope was now thrown ashore, and two or three sailors got to land, who were soon followed by several of the passengers, and we all then began to hope that our lives would be saved. After some time I got all my family near the place where the landing was effected; my poor children I threw towards the shore, and most providentially they were all caught by one or another without any accident. Mrs. T. following, they all got safe to land, and my feelings were most highly excited when I saw them all ascend the rocks free from farther [sic] danger. I staid on board some time longer till most of the passengers got on shore; I then

125

left the others. A tent was now put up as soon as possible, formed of the spars and sail cloth saved from the ship, but it was a poor protection from the weather, and it most unfortunately proved a very rough night. In the morning we all got to a sheltered place among the rocks, and got a breakfast as well as we could.

About two o'clock in the afternoon, the Captain ordered all the females and children should be immediately got ready to be sent off to a place called Payte Bay, about twenty miles distant, for better accommodation, but that they must walk a mile to the boats acordingly in great haste we all got ready.

I hired a man to carry a bed and bedding, carried our babe myself, and partly led one child by the hand, all the others took something with them—a more rugged path I think impossible, on our right lay the ocean foaming dreadfully, on the left, high black barren hills, our path lay almost all the way in a bog, and in places up to the ancles in water.

Having arrived at the creek, we had to wait nearly an hour for the boats: and when they arrived I saw my family safely embarked, and then returned to the tent. We continued upon this desolate inhospitable rock eight days—our provisions had become very short, when to our great joy, our Captain came again to us and informed us he had with great difficulty procured a vessel to convey us Sydney in Cape Breton, at which place we all arrived on July 15th,—The passengers and crew altogether about one hundred and fifty individuals.

> Francis Thomas
> Sydney, July 25, 1833.

Quebec and Montreal

I was called on deck to *smell the land*—
and truly the change was very sensible...
It was the breath of youth and hope and love.
Diary of Mary Gapper

Life was far simpler in the days before quarantine, when ships were welcome to drop anchor and visit the islands along the Saint Lawrence. The inhabitants of these tiny communities were glad of this, for it meant that they were able to earn money by selling food to the emigrants.

> We are now at anchor 36 miles below Quebec & the Captain and a few passengers went ashore to an island in the river & brought us a bottle of excellent milk. We had warm cake & tea with the milk which was a great treat. [Joseph Wilson]

The brightly painted houses, so different from British homes, attracted a great deal of attention, as did the white churches with their steeples rising into the sky. It was all novel and very striking, especially to those who hailed from British communities constructed of grey stone and slate. Few had been prepared for the vastness of the river, but all were impressed by its majesty. John McCorkindale wrote, "This is a noble river. Clyde is a stream in comparison to it."

The names of the islands soon circulated among the passengers. Everyone would remember Green Island, with its "smooth lawns and meadows of emerald verdure, with orchard and corn-fields sloping down to the water's edge." Further along,

127

Grosse Ile, another of the river's treasures, also would draw pleasing comments. But in 1832, with the coming of quarantine, its beauty belied its sad function.

A deadly epidemic of Asiatic cholera surfaced in India in 1826. Over the course of the next few years, it gradually spread to parts of Europe. By 1831, Britain was also plagued with outbreaks. Port cities, where trading vessels frequently off-loaded sick crew along with their cargoes, provided fertile breeding grounds for illness. With increasing migration, vast numbers of people, many of whom were undernourished and therefore vulnerable to illness, congregated at the docks, awaiting berths on a ship. It was only a matter of time before the disease reached North America. It arrived in 1832.

On 25 February, in anticipation of the arrival of spring shipping, the Assembly of Lower Canada, under pressure from various groups, enacted a provision that funds be set aside for caring for sick immigrants, and that a quarantine station be established for this purpose. Grosse Ile was selected as the perfect spot. The island, located thirty miles below Quebec, providing a convenient stopping place in which emigrants could be screened by medical officers and, where necessary, held in quarantine. It was a system designed to prevent the sick from continuing their journey, thereby halting the spread of disease. Inspection of all emigrants commenced during the season of 1832.

In this first season, approximately fifty thousand people arrived at Quebec. Most had gone through the vetting process on the island.

> We reached Grosse Isle yesterday evening. It is a beautiful rocky island, covered with groves of beech, birch, ash and fir trees. There are several vessels lying at anchor close to the shore; one bears the melancholy symbol of disease, the yellow flag; she is a passenger ship, and has the smallpox and measles among her crew. [Catharine Parr Traill]

Louis Henry Ferrier, a widower living near Linlithgow, west of Edinburgh, had received an offer of the office of Collector of Customs at Quebec in 1829. He accepted. In April 1830, along with his family, which consisted of three daughters and a son, their governess, two women servants and manservant with his wife and children, he boarded the *Rebecca* at Greenock. Their crossing was long and stormy, but in the capable hands of Captain Rob Laurie, the vessel reached Quebec in safety.

Ferrier's son, Alexander David, obtained work as a clerk, staying in Quebec for several years before moving to Fergus, Upper Canada. He wrote of the cholera epidemic at Quebec City in 1832.

> ...sad were the scenes that took place. Many of the merchants' offices had only one person in them. For weeks I was the only clerk in our establishment; one of the partners was ill with the disease, and seventy or eighty people were buried daily. My friends, the raftsmen, brought their rafts into the various coves and hurried back as fast as possible to the woods of Upper Canada. Large sugar kettles burned day and night with tar at the corners of the street, and a coffin maker started a shop close to our office. Many a time I walked home to our pleasant place, but following a coffin, as a new cemetery was just made on the roadside leading home...

Many attested to the fact that the quarantine system was greatly flawed. While it is true that everyone recognized the necessity of attempting to control the spread of illness, the way in which emigrants were processed at Grosse Ile drew enormous criticism. Besides the nuisance element of being detained when eager to continue the journey, confining healthy people in this place of sickness was surely a recipe for disaster.

> We have already seen the landing of the passengers of three emigrant ships. You may imagine yourself looking on a fair or crowded market, clothes waving in the wind or spread out on the earth, chests, bundles, baskets, men, women, and children, asleep or basking in the sun, some in motion busied with their goods, the women employed in washing or cooking in the open air beside the wood fires on the beach; while parties of children are pursuing each other in wanton glee, rejoicing in their newly-acquired liberty. [Catharine Parr Traill]

It did not take very long for Mrs Traill to appreciate the falseness of her initial assessment of life on the island. Later in the day, a resident officer came on board. He provided her with a far truer picture.

> Believe me, in this instance, as in many others, 'tis distance lends enchantment to the view. Could you take a nearer survey of some of those very picturesque groups which you admire, I think you would there behold every variety of disease, vice, poverty, filth, and famine—human misery in its most disgusting and saddening forms; such pictures as Hogarth's pencil only could have portrayed, or Crabbe's pen described.

Figures for the year 1834 show that by the end of June, 17,737 emigrants had arrived at Quebec. Almost all of them would have passed through Grosse Ile. This year brought another epidemic of cholera. The authorities were dismayed, and those placed under quarantine at Grosse Ile were disheartened. Such was the case when the *British Tar* weighed anchor at Grosse Ile at the end of May 1834. On board were one hundred and thirty-five emigrants from Sussex and the Isle of Wight, making up part of the Petworth migration. Under the direction of James Marr Brydone, the voyage had gone according to plan. Supplies had lasted, discipline amongst the passengers was reasonably upheld, the weather had not been too dreadfully wild, and illness had been at a minimum. Still, measles was serious enough to require enforcing the quarantine regulations and to require fumigation of the ship. It was not a happy experience.

> Here we counted twenty eight vessels, at the anchorage. At 9. A.M. Captain Nicholas, the harbour master, came along side, and furnished us with a copy of a Proclamation, of the executive council of Lower Canada, dated at Quebec, 27th March, 1834; directing that all ships with cases of Asiatic cholera, fever, small pox, or severe cases of scarlatina, or measles, shall be put under quarantine; and all patients under the above disease sent to the hospital. At 10, A.M. the inspecting Physician, Dr. Fortie, came on board; mustered the passengers, directed us to hoist the yellow flag, and to send the convalescent, and the four recent cases of measles, to the hospital. We were thus placed in durance vile, at a time, when the same disease (the measles) prevailed, both at Quebec, and Montreal,

and probably in half the Townships of the Lower province. [James Marr Brydone]

Within two weeks of the *British Tar*'s quarantine, the first cases of cholera for the year 1834 were reported at Quebec. The disease came on 11 June, arriving with the *Constantia*, from Limerick, which had lost three passengers during her voyage. On the following day, the *Elizabeth and Sarah* dropped anchor. This vessel had come from Dublin, bringing two hundred passengers with cholera. Before the year was out, Quebec City would witness the loss of 2900 lives.

This sequence of events continued. Ships arrived and passengers were placed under quarantine. After the required length of time, providing they were deemed healthy, they were permitted back on ship. The greatest flaw in the system was that while some passengers seemed well at Grosse Ile, many were stricken en route afterwards.

> After encountering some rough seas & contrary winds we arrived at the Quarantine Ground 30 miles below Quebec on Tuesday 16 Sept [1835]. where we was obliged to continue till the 24 when in the Even. we took all our things back—namely every thing we took out and was compeled to wash every article of Linen in and air all our other articles. A task neither small nor easey and on 25 we raised anchor at 9 and at 12 we arrived at Quebec amid a most heavy Rain. [Joseph Brown]

On 24 August 1836, the *Hercules* from Aberdeen arrived at Grosse Ile. At least four children had died during the voyage. Robert Cromar documented the activities of the passengers during their three days of quarantine.

> Got up to the Quarantine station at 1/2 past 3 P.M. and was visited by Dr. McKenzie from the quarantine station who ordered all our luggage to be taken shore and washed owing to the measles being in the ship altho none of the Passengers are ill at present. [Robert Cromar]

> Got up at 5 A.M., & began to land the luggage, we got off one boat load when the Doctor came & stopped the landing of more until the sea calmed a little, it being very rough at present

131

owing to the run of the tide. there is a great deal of convenience on Gross Isle for quarantine Passengers being a large Shed and beds with a house for cooking in and a stove in it and plenty of fire wood. there is a party of Soldiers on the island and a store with all sorts of provisions for the Passengers. Got the rest of the passengers landed at night & began to wash some of the clothes. [Robert Cromar]

Got up early and washed the whole of the dirty clothes dryed them on the rocks was inspected by the Doctor, cleared, got aboard the Hercules and set sail at 3 P.M. [Robert Cromar]

Cromar's depiction of the scene at Grosse Ile in 1836 differs little from that documented by Catharine Parr Traill in 1832. Things were much the same by the time James Logan arrived sometime between 1843 and 1848. Logan was particularly critical of the practice of holding whole vessels when only a few passengers were ill. He reasoned that while waiting, more people would become sick. Besides, people had to eat during this time. Additional costs were incurred which meant that many people reached Quebec and Montreal more or less destitute.

Nothing but scrubbing, to prepare for the inspecting officer of quarantine, who came on board, when, a breeze having sprung up, we proceeded five miles further, and anchored off Grosse Isle. The inspector was a tall dark Englishman, of the name of Poole. Having ordered all the steerage passengers on deck, and arranged them on one side, he caused every individual to pass between him and the captain, while he took the number. After this he went down to the hold, then to the cabin, and questioned the captain, ordering him to whitewash the hold with lime. The cabin passengers were permitted to go on shore at the fort, and walk along the east part of the island, but were warned not to have communication with the passengers of the other vessels at anchor, two of which had disease on board, there being fourteen passengers ill of fever in one, and in the other a few cases of measles. The passengers were landed on the Island, where they washed their clothes. [James Logan]

Those who had slept on bed-ticks filled with chaff or straw were ordered to turf them overboard in consequence of the

132

regulations. It was feared they might prove contagious. The sight of his charges going about this task was distressing to James Marr Brydone. Nevertheless, he remained quite philosophical about things.

> Having conducted the people thus far, in safety, I cannot avoid remarking, how much they were cast down, and annoyed, by having been detained under quarantine, for nine days, landed, with all their luggage for inspection, at Grosse Isle, and obliged to remain on shore there, all the night; without any other shelter, than that of an open shed, with barely room sufficient for the women and children. I do not blame the authorities of Grosse Isle, for any of these occurrences: I am satisfied, that the accommodation, and assistance, at that place, is not adequate, to the duties of the station; and I believe they have little, or no discretionary power. The principal place, where persons in quarantine, at Grosse Isle, are sent to wash, and clean their clothes, and themselves, is a continued succession, of small, rugged, projecting points, of rock, where the filth accumulates, in the hollows, and eddies until the winds scatter it abroad, over the clean, and the unclean; instead of the ground being levelled, and the filth, swept into the river St. Lawrence. [James Marr Brydone]

There was little in the way of medicines to ease the symptoms of the fever. The best defence was a nourishing diet. But once the illness took hold, survival depended upon a person's constitution. Those whose bodies were depleted of reserves stood little chance. For a person of means, quinine was generally relied upon. Others might mix a teaspoonful of sulphur in a wine-glass of brandy. But for most of the sick at Grosse Ile, there was nothing.

The authorities mounted fierce efforts in an attempt to contain disease. Some years saw heavier casualties than others. In financial terms, the cost was enormous. Money to help offset the cost of providing care to the sick slowly began to reach Quebec. It came from various sources, although the amounts were perhaps insufficient. In 1842, £5000 was approved by the House of Commons for the relief of sick and destitute emigrants arriving in Canada from the United Kingdom between 1 April

133

1842 and 31 March 1843. This meagre sum was but a drop in the bucket

Things were to get very much worse. Nobody was prepared for the summer of 1847, when horrors of unimaginable dimensions occurred. In May of that year, the *Syria* arrived from Liverpool, carrying mainly Irish passengers. Several passengers had died during the voyage, and fifty-two were ill with typhus by the time she arrival at Grosse Ile. This marked the beginning of the nightmare season. Before it was over, 17,477 lives would be lost. Most of the unfortunate victims were Irish, forced out of their homeland by famine, poverty and disease. They came to Canada searching for a better life. Instead they found suffering, anguish, heartache and death.

In 1848, a royal proclamation ordered that every vessel carrying more than thirteen passengers must stop at Grosse Ile and undergo inspection. From the tone of the British media and their use of phrases such as "dirty immigrants," one might conclude that the thinking of the day, amongst certain people, was that the unfortunate emigrants had brought it all on themselves.

> Every vessel having more than thirteen passengers on board is to anchor at the quarantine ground; if there has been any disease on board during the voyage, or if the vessel has sailed from any port where infectious disease prevailed, the vessel is to undergo a thorough purification, and the dirty emigrants are to be landed on the island and they and their clothing and baggage to undergo a compulsory scrubbing. The island is placed under the authority of a military commandant. It is stated that the new legal enactments respecting emigration will increase the passage money from Ireland to America to £5, at the least, per head.

Once a ship was given a clean bill of health, it was time to resume the journey. The vessel would be towed out, sails were hoisted, and with a good breeze, it was not long before the Ile d'Orléans, the tidal mark of the Saint Lawrence river where salt and fresh water mingle, came into view. Upon the approach, John Leeming described it as "the greatest variety of enchanting scenery we ever saw." Others agreed.

...On leaving the quarantine station, you are soon in view of the fertile Island of Orleans, between which and the south shore of the river, you pass up to Point Leni....the city of Quebec is in full view. You now immediately find yourself amid the bustle of steam-boats, shipping, and all the apparent confusion of a crowded business port. [John Murray]

A dazzling spectacle awaited those who arrived at Quebec after dark. Lights from the town offered a backdrop to a busy waterfront, where steamboats spewed sparks like fireworks out of their funnels.

At ten last night, August the 16th, the light of the city of Quebec were seen gleaming through the distance like a coronet of stars above the waters. At half-past ten we dropped anchor opposite the fort, and I fell asleep dreaming of the various scenes through which I had passed. Again I was destined to be disappointed in my expectations of going on shore. Pity my disappointment! The captain promised us a treat of new milk, white bread and fruit. Alas! it was not to be. The words came to my mind, and only too true they proved: The best laid schemes of mice and men Gang aft agley. [Catharine Parr Traill]

When the sun rose over Quebec, the church spires and rooftops shone. It was a sight to impress most.

At a bend of the river, a short distance below Quebec, that city gradually presented itself to our view. From its elevated situation, it produces at first sight, a striking effect, especially to a stranger who has not seen it before. It stands on an extensive and rocky hill, the highest part of which is crowned by the fort or citadel. The side next the St. Lawrence presents a high and precipitous rock. But the north side slopes down gradually to the St. Charles, which at the lower side of the town falls into the St. Lawrence. The spires of the churches, and many of the roofs of the houses are covered with tin, which causes them, when the sun shines, to glitter like silver. Just as the evening gun was fired at the fort, we dropped anchor before the town. [William Bell]

Quebec consists of two towns, the Upper and Lower, and is adorned with a cathedral, whose metallic roof glitters in the sun

135

like a vast diamond. Indeed the tin-roofs of the churches and public buildings give this city a splendid look on a bright sunshiny day, testifying, moreover to the dryness of the air. [Samuel Strickland]

Some found the architecture strange. John McCorkindale had said of Grosse Ile, "I never was in a wooden village or town before. What a blaze it would make if it were to catch fire."

Of Quebec, he said, "I don't like the appearance of the city. It is low and dirty, the houses are so scattered."

Montreal, with its stone buildings reminiscent of home, pleased him very much.

Those arriving in Canada prior to quarantine enforcement sailed straight to the harbour at Quebec

The ship anchored in the harbour, to the great satisfaction of all on board; particularly some of the old men and women who, having run short of tobacco, had not spoken a good-natured word for some time previously. The safe arrival of the vessel, however, was a subject of general congratulation among us. [P. Finan]

After 1832, when strict regulations had to be followed, passengers had to stay on board ship until the medical officer of health checked that quarantine certificates were in order, and the tide-surveyor had checked the number of passengers on board. Baggage then had to be taken to the "Searching Office," a place of inspection where taxes, or duty, might be levied on particular items. Mr Johnson had reported paying three shillings as a duty on his guns and a camp-bed before leaving England in 1819. Most would have dealt with duties after their arrival.

Anchor got up at 4 A.M. and was dropped again at 6 A.M. about a mile from the Port of Quebec when the inspecting doctors came on Board and got our quarantine papers when our Ship was cleared and we was permitted to go ashore. After that time 6 or 7 of the passengers went on Shore and engaged the Canadian Eagle Steamer to take us to Montreal. She came along side of our ship at 4 P.M. and took us and all our luggage on board, along with ourselves up to the town, when the Steamer took 140 Passengers from the Portsea Ship from

136

London, we slept on board of the Steamer stern about as we had to watch our luggage by turns, and as long as the Steamer lay at Quebec it was just one continued moabs on her and rioting the Passengers from the Portsea quareling among themselves, and 50 or 60 Blackguards from the Town looking after what they could catch or take. There can no person have any idea such a hurry & confusion as prevailed here as long as we was at Quebec. [Robert Cromar]

The diarists all told stories of drunkenness and fighting amongst passengers. Occasionally the sailors joined in. It was a well recognized problem, and one most captains attempted to control. At times, things really did get out of hand.

...the Captain and several of the passengers went ashore, having ordered the Mate not to suffer any ardent spirits to be brought on board. Nevertheless, some of the passengers who had gone ashore, returned with some rum, which was taken from them and thrown over board. This circumstance caused no small disturbance, and produced blows between the sailors and the passengers, and even also amongst the sailors themselves; and till the scuffle terminated, it was indeed a very disorderly night. [John M'Donald]

On monday forenoon we came to Anchor in the river at Quebec, immediately there came alongside boats selling brandy at a shilling per bottle, it was bought and drunken to an enormous extent by the passengers; in the afternoon they were nearly all drunk, and I never saw such brutal fighting among human things before, I thought they would kill each other. [Thomas Connon]

For most of the women, other things took priority. Their attentions were turned towards making their families look presentable. Since the ocean voyage had taken its toll on clothing, the job at hand was by no means trivial.

Elizabeth and I have been trimming up a little bit this week, but you will easily think what sort of plight we are in to go ashore after nine weeks voyage, and particularly our bonnets, which we have had to see about hanging on nails the whole of the time. But many thanks to you my dear sisters for all your counsel and advice in rigging me out for my journey, for I have found all my things which I prepared as comfortable and useful. My green dress looks well yet though the colour is a little changed, but this you will expect when I tell you that twice I have been quite drenched with going on deck when it has been blowing a gale, to look at the grandeur of the scene which is more than I can describe. I have worn nothing but the old black cap, which is now hardly to be called black. [Sarah Leeming]

In February 1831, Adam Fergusson sailed to New York. His intention was to tour part of the United States and Canada to eye things up with regard to bringing his family to settle here. This he did in 1833. During his first trip, he made his way from New York in a leisurely manner, visiting acquaintances along the way. He reached Quebec later in the spring.

> Upon reaching the quay we found still many formidable relics of winter. The ice upon which we stepped ashore was fully ten feet thick, and huge masses of it lay scattered along the beach. Whatever inducements Quebec may hold out to the stranger, comfortable hotels are assuredly not of the number...our accommodations fell considerably short of what might have been reasonably expected.

Poor accommodation was only one of Fergusson's concerns. He soon made it his business to look into emigrant affairs.

> The influx of emigrants at Quebec is very great, and a large proportion landing in a state of destitution, the inhabitants are subject to a most vexatious burden in providing some temporary supplies. Fifty thousand have been landed at Quebec this season and probably ten thousand more have passed on to Montreal without being regularly reported.

It was also expensive.

> Things, however, seemed very dear in Quebec—dearer by far than at any other part of Canada that I have visited; with the exception of dray-hire, which is reasonable enough... [Henry Christmas]

138

In the early days, emigrants in need of assistance might have approached the Quebec Immigrant Society, where benevolence in the form of food, shelter, and even funds towards the cost of transporting an emigrant family to Montreal, or further afield, was frequently extended.

> It costs a good deal for a family to come out, but the Emigrant Society in Canada will forward any who apply to them and find their own provisions, free of expense to York; and from thence the Government will send them on in schooners, supplying them with rations; and when they arrive near the lots to be distributed, they will have their goods conveyed in waggons, free of expense, also.
>
> This is peculiarly advantageous to the poorer emigrants; and even the rich can have their luggage carried free, from York, by an order from the Government. [Thomas Radcliff]

Quebec had other advantages for the poor emigrant.

> Quebec contains several nunneries, for the French inhabitants are mostly Roman catholics. The nuns are very useful to emigrants, who have often been bountifully relieved by these charitable vestals, who employ themselves in nursing the sick and feeding the hungry. [Samuel Strickland]

When the British Parliamentary Emigration Committee of 1826-27, appointed Alexander Carlisle Buchanan as the first Resident Agent for Emigrants at Quebec, another source of assistance became available. Prior to this appointment, Buchanan had served as a passenger agent in the north of Ireland. He was considered to be most knowledgeable and experienced in matters of emigration. He was also a seasoned sailor, having made sixteen voyages to America. Over the next few years, Buchanan worked tirelessly towards bettering conditions for emigrants. He also wrote much in the way of advice.

> Dress yourself in light clean clothing. Females frequently bring on sickness, by being too warmly clothed. Cut your hair short, and wash daily and thoroughly. Avoid drinking ardent spirits of any kind, and when heated do not drink cold water. Eat

moderately of light food. Avoid night dews.... Previous to disembarkation, should sickness overtake you, proceed immediately, or be removed to the Emigrant Hospital in St. John's Suburbs, where you will be taken care of, and provided with every thing needful until restored to health. Medicine and medical advice can also be had at the dispensary attached to the Quebec Charitable Emigrant Society. This society will grant relief to all destitute emigrants.

Buchanan's office was open daily from ten until two o'clock. Here, a person might make inquiries regarding the availability and price of land and arrange to receive a ticket, to be later presented to the Location Agent in the appropriate township. This ticket entitled the settler to choose a lot, providing suitable financial arrangement were made. In 1830, Buchanan's office was greatly promoting settlement in the township of Cavan. Advice was also dispensed regarding travel arrangements, and general currency matters. Those with limited or no means could look to Buchanan for guidance in employment opportunities in and around Quebec.

James Wilson met up with a fellow from the Bay of Quinte, a merchant who advised him to go to Upper Canada, where he would be among British, rather than to stay in Quebec.

Accordingly having an opportunity of the steam boat going in a day or two to Montreal, I determined to embrace it, taking care first to draw up a petition to the governor for the privileges granted last year to my countrymen, namely, a supply of rations (or food) to bring us up to the ground; but the governor being from home, my presenting it was rendered useless. My mind became deeply exercised respecting my trying situation, now in a strange land, with a wife and five children, only one guinea and a half in my pocket. However, I got my grant for land from the governor's secretary, with a ticket directed to a commission at Perth on the river Rhedo, who is appointed to shew the different lots to the settlers.

Wilson had brought letters of introduction which he presented to several clergymen in the hope of obtaining guidance and financial assistance. He obtained enough at Quebec to set off on the next leg of his journey, to Montreal.

140

After business had been dealt with, it was time to begin exploring the city. Strolling about the streets was not only an interesting pastime, it also was a good means of clearing the head and of regaining land-legs. A body accustomed to the rolling and pitching of a ship would still feel as though the ground were heaving and swelling beneath the feet, a sensation which could take days to fade.

> We arrived safe, ...at Quebec....strongest desire to go on shore and having applied to the captain, a few of us were allowed that liberty, but requested to return in a few hours, the ship not yet being examined as to the state of passengers' health, &c. We got into the boat, and in a few minutes arrived on shore, when the joy that each of us felt was inexpressible. We could scarcely walk, the earth appearing to bend under us....[James Wilson]

Words of warning were still called for. Quebec was, after all, a port and as such, there was hustle, bustle and confusion. In such places, there were always people out to get what they could. Some people suggested it unwise to leave the vessel at all, except to board a steamer to Montreal.

> On leaving the ship, remember that you come into immediate contact with many people who will take every advantage over you which they can, so look sharp in your bargains, and after your luggage. Keep a strict watch over these picaroons wherever the boats stop in your voyage up the river, or on the lakes; for, on these occasions, crowds of people assemble, and come on board ostensibly to assist you, but often to carry off any handy article. Even on leaving the ship at Quebec be on your guard, and call a muster of your various articles, in case the sailors should take a fancy to any of them. [John Mathison]

On 13 June 1840, after a tedious voyage of 63 days, the *Alicia* finally anchored at Quebec. Apart from Sarah Leeming's old back complaint, the family were in good health, some of them sporting tans from the hot sun. Safe in Quebec, Sarah was at last able to indulge herself with much-dreamt-about food.

> John and Joseph have been into the town this morning, and brought us some provisions. the first thing I tasted was bread

141

and butter, which I thought were very good I assure you. Butter is 9d per pound.

There was also the French language to deal with. Surprisingly few emigrants mentioned having any difficulty in this regard.

> The French language very generally spoken among the lower orders, and the general appearance of the city is very strange. Its outward appearance poor, the river is magnificent in the extreme, and the neighborhood around it is exceedingly beautiful.... the price of provisions in Quebec is cheaper than in England generally. Butter 10d currency per lb of the very best quality eggs 6d per doz, beef 5 ditto, fish a fine fresh water perch weighing 1 lb. 3d. [John Leeming]

The sense of relief at having survived the journey and of having finally landed at Quebec must have been extraordinary. But, upon reflection, many emigrants came to view the remainder of the journey as the hardest part of the trip.

> We arrived at Quebec on the 25th of June [1821], when we were all inspected by the surgeon, and then passed through the custom-house. We all slept that night on board, and by 6 o'clock in the morning the steam boat was laid along side of us, when we all set to work to get our luggage on board of it. We continued all that day at Quebec, and then went off in the steam boat at 11 o'clock at night. As we were setting out, a tremendous storm of thunder and lightning came on, the most dreadful that ever I either saw or heard; the rain was also uncommonly heavy. There were nearly 400 people on board of the steam boat, the greater part of whom were obliged to sit on deck all that night.... I can assure you, I myself and the greater part of all who were on deck were as thoroughly drenched as water could make us, and we all had to remain, drenched as we were, in our wet clothes, till they dried on our backs. We had no alternative, access to our chests being impossible, as they were all locked up in the hold; and in this state we continued till we reached Montreal! [John M'Donald]

Part of the Quebec experience involved replenishing supplies. Even if a person did not leave the vessel, they might purchase foods from other passengers. A really organized person might set about cooking up a storm to ensure the family had enough to eat during the next stage of the journey.

> The emigrant before going on board the steamer, should boil as much pork or beef as will serve him for a day or two, which he can do before leaving the emigrant vessel. In a few minutes he can procure fresh bread, and if he has a large tin tea-pot with a few tins, he can with ease obtain hot water in the steamer to make a little tea to refresh the members of his family on their journey up. [Thomas Rolph]

Quebec to Montreal was a journey of 180 miles which took between twenty and thirty hours by steamship. In 1847, the steamships left daily at five o'clock, docking at Three Rivers, Port St. Francis and Sorrel. The trip was much disliked by everyone. Cramped and crowded, the level of discomfort was virtually intolerable.

> Steamer started for Montreal at 4 O Clock this morning and in the forenoon we passed Three Rivers, took in some firewood at it. It is a nice looking village with about 200 houses some of them very fine & a roman Catholik church...[on board the steamer] there was upwards of 300 passengers and a good deal of them raftsmen who was drunk the most of the day. & two women selling apples & gingerbread to good account. [Robert Cromar]

The number of passengers reported to be on some of the steamers is very large.

> The steam boat sailed at eleven o'clock at night, having near five hundred souls on board, consisting of the 37th regiment of foot, and part of another also, which, with their wives, children and luggage, produced such a scene of confusion and distress as to exceed any thing I ever before witnessed. I thought the misery I passed through on the sea could not be exceeded, but when I compared it with my voyage from Quebec to Montreal, I

143

felt my comforts of body and mind were then much greater, as I was now surrounded with the most unruly cursing, swearing mortals I ever beheld. [James Wilson]

The total cost to James Wilson for this leg of the journey was 9s. each, and 4s. 6d. for each child under fourteen years of age. He reckoned that the reason the fare was so moderate was because the government had contracted with the steam boat owners allowing the emigrants to travel for half the regular price.

Joseph and Hannah Wilson and their two sons, Robert and Charles, who were no relation to James Wilson, also found the journey tedious, but, attempting to maintain an optimistic mood, they soon began to appreciate certain things.

> Set sail for Montreal at 10 o'clock A.M. On this boat we are indeed uncomfortable. We had a crew of dirty looking Irish a many of the Canadians who come down to Quebec on the timber rafts. They are a thievish set & we were obliged to watch our goods upon deck all night. [Joseph Wilson]

> The prospect up the country is really grand. Cultivated land on both sides & neat houses. We made very slow progress having to tow 2 brigs & a large boat up with the wind right ahead. A child died this morning & the father with the utmost sang froid made a coffin himself & got drunk with whiskey. [Joseph Wilson]

In 1842, Charles Dickens made his first tour of the United States and Canada. He sailed to Boston, leaving England on 3 January. By springtime he had arrived at Quebec. He commented upon the newly arriving emigrants, "grouped in their hundreds on the wharfs, about their chests and boxes," and later wrote:

> The vessel in which we returned from Quebec to Montreal was crowded with them [emigrants], and at night they spread their beds between decks (those who had beds, at least), and slept so close and thick about our cabin door, that the passage to and fro was quite blocked up. They were nearly all English; from Gloucestershire the greater part; and had had a long winter-passage out; but it was wonderful to see how clean the children

144

had been kept, and how untiring in their love and self-denial all the poor parents were.

Although the steamboats made several stops, people were advised not to leave the vessel until arrival at Montreal. This was usually for fear that tardy folks might be left behind. But there was also a question of luggage, which must be guarded at all times.

> After leaving Quebec, the first place the boat stops at is a small town called Three Rivers...ninety miles distant, or half way between Quebec and Montreal. The boat merely stops here, to land and receive passengers, and to take a fresh supply of fuel; so that you had better not go on shore, as they start at a moment's notice, and will not wait for any one. There is nothing to engage your attention here, but I have heard of many persons being separated from their friends and their baggage by gaping about, and suddenly finding the boat gone without them. [John Murray]

It would have been far simpler if ocean-going vessels had sailed right to Montreal. We might wonder why they did not. John Howison provided the following reason:

> At present, comparatively few vessels come up the St. Lawrence as far as the latter town, for they cannot move from Quebec unless by the help of the tide, or a strong breeze directly astern. But the tide flows only to Three Rivers, about sixty miles below Montreal, and when they have gained this place, they must lie at anchor until a favourable wind enables them to stem the current, which is very rapid. However, six steam-boats now ply between the two cities, and transport all sorts of lading much more safely and expeditiously than square-rigged vessels can do.

> When we had got as high as Lavaltrie, the wind became light and baffling; and the tide water having ceased as far below as the three rivers [Trois Rivieres], we brought up with one or two other vessels to wait for a steamer to tow us up the remaining distance. [Henry Christmas]

Thomas Connon took very little pleasure in his journey. From Grosse Ile to Quebec he found that his fellow travellers left much to be desired. Things were very little better at Montreal.

...since sabbath till last night I did not get a sleep but in my day clothes sitting on the top of my luggage which has given me the cold very much the reason of this was that on sabbath when we came to the Quarantine station (Grouse Island) our beds were all thrown overboard, we were a night after that before we got to Quebec the highlandmen which were on the ship got drunk on the brandy when lying at anchor there and were in such an outrageous condition that I was easily advised by the captain not to go that night to Montreal with the steamer so I stayed on board the ship another night, next night when I did go with the steamer it was the same thing there were about 1200 persons aboard of many nations English, Irish, Scotch (highland and lowland) French Dutch Canadians and Yankee; there was really not room for every one to lye down on deck irrespective of beds I would have got my supper and a bed in the cabin for 3 dollars or 12 shillings but I was in no want of meat having taken 2 hearty meals in Quebec and I thought this rather dear for a bed; so instead of going back to the steerage I went through the cabin passing for a Gentleman until I got to a saloon where the Gentry's luggage lay and on top of some luggage I took up my nights quarters and took a sleep, at 7 o'clock in the morning we arrived in Montreal when I made myself scarce, and went to see about a conveyance to Hamilton.... I fully intended to write when at Quebec or Montreal but found it equally impossible in both places, at Quebec I required all my time to get myself made clean (every shirt and stocking that I wore on the passage were covered with lice the coat trousers and vest that I wore were in the same condition, so I packed them altogether into my provision box and now wonder how I will get them cleaned.) [Thomas Connon]

The moment of arrival was a tumult.

Landing was neither so delightful, nor so easy a business as I anticipated. Such scrambling, such confusion; all the kindly feelings which fellow-passengers entertain for each other vanished at this moment; our mutual sympathies, now all danger and sickness had passed, came to a sudden end; each seemed now to be on the look out for No. 1, yet when each had secured his own, curiosity, not unmingled with interest in a stranger's lot, again reigned predominant. [Mrs Edward Copleston]

For some, reaching Montreal was like gaining a new lease on life.

We arrived this morning at the wharf in Montreal. I like the appearance of the city better than Quebec. The houses are built of stone like the old country houses.... I must try to get something to eat. I don't think I shall care to eat any biscuits for years to come. Some of us went to a baker's shop, got some splendid fresh bread and lemonade till we were satisfied. I never ate as much before or since. [John McCorkindale]

Most people complained of being fatigued by the time they reached Montreal. This is not surprising since, in many cases, people had sat up all night on the deck.

We arrived at Montreal the second day about eleven o'clock, being much fatigued for want of rest, having slept but little for two night. On leaving the vessel, our boxes, chests, and beds were all measured, and a charge laid on, only a small allowance made to each passenger. The expense of this journey amounted to £3. 5s. which sum I could not have paid, but for the kindness of my friends in Quebec. Here my first object was to look out for a temporary lodging, but on enquiry I found that the king's barracks were open for the settlers to remain awhile; this was very timely, as it saved some expense, lodging being very high in this place. I hired a waggon and brought my family and luggage into the barracks, as did also the rest of the families who came over with me. We remained here about a week, during which time my wife employed herself in cleaning the wearing apparel, bed-clothes, &c. after the severe distress and filth contracted on sea. [James Wilson]

The splendour of the city was appreciated by most travellers. On bright clear days, if one had sufficient energy and time to linger, the pathways and byways, with their markets and

147

stores, made an enchanting diversion from the hardships of travel.

> Montreal has a most brilliant appearance on a sunny day as you see it from the river approaching-the site of the city is on a gentle ascent to the mountain, and the city, with its most conspicuous buildings, as the towers of Notre Dame Cathedral, the dome of the Market Place, and the various towers and spires of the churches, and the public and private edifices, with the roofs of tin gleaming in the sun's rays, offer a view rarely to be met with, and the whole backed up with the wood and verdure of the Montreal mountain. [John Thornton]

Getting from the wharf to the hotel might be a tricky business.

> We arrived in Montreal at a very early hour in the morning. From my fatigue, and William's having been very ill in the night, we were obliged to make use of the only carriage in waiting to bring us to the hotel. This was termed a calash.... It would have been luxury to us, but for the miserable road we had to traverse...So dreadful is that [road] from the wharf to the hotel in Montreal, that I really thought I should go distracted before we arrived; but I thank God we did arrive, without having broken down or been upset; I was however, sadly shaken, and poor William very ill—whether from the water of the St. Lawrence, the fogs of Newfoundland, or the general change of climate, I cannot say. [Mrs. Radcliff]

The Mullett family found themselves comfortable arrangements. Mary Mullett's description makes it sound as though they were quite spoiled.

> Having a few hours to spare, which I have not had for some time past, and knowing the pleasure thou wilt derive my dear Grandmother at receiving a few lines from me I avail myself the opportunity. We are now in lodgings at Montreal very comfortable they are equal to most of our English Hotels.—We pay six dollars and half per day for lodging and board which is half a crown each, one with the other, not as we think an extravagant charge. William Falconer & family are at the same place, the children, both theirs & ours, take their meals together with the landlady. I looked in on them this morning at breakfast, and

they were sat round the table very well pleased with Raspberry's and milk, and tea and bread & butter, which thou mayest suppose was quite a luxury to the children having been so long deprived of their liberty. Our table are elegantly laid out. The custom of the country is to have three meals a day. We breakfast at eight, dine at two, drink tea at seven.—We are sadly anoyed with Bugs here—they have served Father and William very bad....

Since everyone had been advised that prices in Montreal were considerably less than those in Quebec, a great deal of comparison shopping went on. Consequently, letters back home were filled with prices. John Mathison suggested bringing farthings (valued at a quarter of a penny), since they were accepted at the same rate as pennies. They were especially useful when it came to purchasing small supplies such as "milk, or other refreshments, in coming up the river." He also suggesting laying in the following stores at Montreal:

> ...—some soap; 2 lb. of tea (young hyson); 1 lb. black tea; (we shall soon have plenty of sugar from our own trees.) Some fresh provisions, which are cheaper there than at Quebec.

When Joseph and Hannah Wilson arrived at Montreal, their first task was to unload their baggage from the steamer onto the wharf. Later it had to be loaded onto a batteau from the Durham Boat Company.

> The change to this heat was very sudden, consequently with us moving luggage 3 times, which we had to do, we were all fatigued as much as possible. Our company made 3 loads & 2 of them set off this evening but we thought best amongst ourselv to sleep at the store tonight, which we did—We opened our beds on the floor & enjoyed a comfortable sleep, made so by our previous hard labour. [Joseph Wilson]

Unaccustomed to the strength of the sun, the emigrants felt their energy sapped, but there was no rest for the weary travellers.

Went into Montreal to look about & had work again offered. Purchased a large brim hat for me & the children. The sun was so scorching & our own would not keep the sun from our eyes. Many passengers suffered very much having the skin burnt off their faces, noses, & their eyes swell like the sting of a bee, particularly Mary Walker & her children. [Joseph Wilson]

It was possible to proceed directly downriver, if the travellers had the strength and presence of mind. Most would have required at least a day to compose themselves, but John Murray's suggestion was that they go straight on.

If on your arrival at Montreal, ...your object is, to save money by proceeding directly on to Upper Canada, five minutes' walk will take you from the steam-boat landing to the starting place at the Lachine Canal; which, indeed, (looking up the river) is in view from where you land. If your luggage is heavy, a carter may be engaged by two or three of your party together, so that the whole may be taken for about one shilling. Here you are to determine whether you will proceed by the River St. Lawrence, or by the Ottawa and Rideau Canal, both which routes take you to Kingston; where, as first observed, they meet....

The stores of the forwarders, or in other words, established companies, for the purpose of forwarding goods and passengers to the upper Province, are situated at the sides of the canal. Here, you can deposit your luggage, and arrange for your immediate departure by canal-boat. These boats are of the burthen of from fifteen to twenty-five tons, mostly open, or half decked; the passage-money by them to Prescott, one hundred and thirty miles distance, is one dollar, or 4s. 4d. sterling. From Prescott, you can take a steam-boat to any part of Lake Ontario, or Bay of Quinté.

There was much competition among boat owners. Some gave better deals, including food and lodgings.

When we arrived at Montreal, several men came to us wishing to engage to take us to Prescot. If you come, make the best bargain you can with them. We employed M'Pherson & Co. who keep a store three quarters of a mile above the place where the steamer stops on the side of the canal. Our luggage cost 2s. 6d. per cwt. All sorts of provisions free. Each adult 10s. 2d.

They were at the expense of carting us all up from the steamer to their store, where we lodged, till the boat sailed, which was next morning. We paid nothing for lodging, there being great opposition among the boat owners. We sailed in what is called a Durham boat, which was partly covered.... [John Mathison]

For John M'Donald, who seemed to be on the receiving end of all that was nasty, the journey seemed to progress from bad to worse. But eventually he did reach Lachine.

Here we arrived in 24 hours, a distance of 190 miles. Having stated our difficulties on the passage from Quebec to Montreal, I may add, that this was the first of our trials in going up the country; and I can safely aver, to my certain knowledge, that it was the source and cause of their trouble who are now no more in this world. Nay, to show you further our distress, the beds of those passengers who were stationed on the lee side of the boat, between the engine-house and the paddles, were made literally to swim with the rain water. Every thing was spoiled, our very meal and bread being reduced to a state of dough. We now began to carry our luggage from the steam boat, Government having provided waggons in abundance. We mutually assisted each other in loading them with the women and children; and all who were unable to walk got on the top of them as far as the village of La Chine, ten miles up the St. Laurence from Montreal....

For most, Montreal was a mere stopping point on the journey and they were keen to progress on to Lachine and down the Saint Lawrence.

It is highly injudicious to waste any time in Quebec or Montreal, as living is very expensive in both cities, and as nothing but general information can be obtained in them, the people knowing as little about the exact nature of the different lots of land that are open to settlers as we do in this country. [John Howison]

For those whose money was running short, Montreal was a place to regroup. It was possible to obtain short-term work there, which many did to obtain the cash for the rest of their journey. For others, whose needs were more pressing or who had friends in the city, charity might be a possibility. Writing in 1820, John Howison saw many poor people stranded in Lower Canada and proposed a solution.

> When I was in Quebec and Montreal, I had opportunities of knowing, that many of the hovels of these cities contained crowds of British emigrants, who were struggling with those complicated horrors of poverty and disease, whom the hope of being exempted from such evils had induced to abandon the clime of their birth. The greater number of these people, when they first landed, had funds enough to carry them to the Upper Province, and even settle them comfortably on their locations; but they knew not where the "promised land" lay, and were detained in Lower Canada, by anxious and unavailing efforts to obtain correct information upon the subject. All the misery occasioned by this circumstance, and various others of a similar nature, might be easily prevented, and thousands of active settlers annually added to the province, if the supreme government would bestow a moment's attention upon the matter, and place in Quebec, Montreal, and the other towns, an agent, to whom the emigrants could apply for advice and information. I am aware that Emigrant Societies have already been established in the principal towns of Lower Canada, but such owe their existence entirely to the benevolent exertions of private individuals, and are, comparatively speaking, superficial and limited in their operation. Nothing but the interference of the supreme government can effectually rid poor emigrants of the difficulties they have at present to encounter when the arrive in Lower Canada.

These agents were established, but his further suggestion that the government run a cheap mode of transportation for immigrants from Quebec to Toronto was ignored.

It should be clear that a great many of the emigrants were naive and might easily be duped by sharpers who plied the docks. These people would offer to buy tickets for the rest of the journey, offer food or lodging, and then disappear with the funds. If an example is needed of precisely how ill-informed some of the travellers might be, there is the example of a group who arrived at

Charlottetown presuming they were at Charleston, South Carolina.

As we saw in Mary Ritchie's letter cited above, she found that families who needed funding could apply at the emigration agent's office in Quebec, but she, as a single person, had to stop and work for a time there before proceeding.

> you will see I intend remaining here for the Winter, and getting something in the Spring when business commences...Montreal is preferable to Quebec on account of its being a richer & larger place & the settlements settled by other than Canadians within less than a days journey [William Mickle]

Those with influential connections in Britain or Ireland might have a letter of introduction which would lead to assistance. For others, church friends would provide help.

> Having a letter from the preachers of Quebec to the preachers of Montreal, I proceeded to their house,.... On reading the letter, they made enquiry respecting my means and design. Having laid the state of my affairs before them; I was requested to call next day, which being done, Mr. Booth presented me with the sum of £3. which he raised by going through the society and friends, and procured such means of relief as enabled me to proceed on my journey...[he also obtained a letter from Sir John Johnson, to a magistrate, a Mr. Finclay, at LaChine]
>
> ...On delivering the letter above mentioned to squire Finclay, he prepared to seek for a free passage for my family to Prescott by water, and having consulted with two or three gentlemen, they agreed to pay my fare, and send me free of expense. A large boat being about to sail, I got my family and luggage into it, and so proceeded on for Prescott, a distance of nearly one hundred and eighty miles. [James Wilson]

For everyone whose goal was Upper Canada, eyes turned longingly westward. They had completed the longest and worst part of the journey, but it was far from over.

Up the Saint Lawrence

the passage of emigrants and their families up the St. Lawrence
frequently exhausts their means, depresses their spirits and...
produces sickness among them...
James Fitzgibbon

As we have seen, from Montreal the emigrants travelled overland nine miles to Lachine, where they began another journey on water. They might hire some vehicle to make the short trip with their luggage. Most people seemed to enjoy it, perhaps because it made such a pleasant change from the miseries of shipboard life.

In travelling from Montreal to La Chine, a village nine miles further up the St. Lawrence, I could not but remark the warm and glowing appearance which every part of the country exhibited. The air was so pure and transparent, that every beam of the sun seemed to reach the earth in unimpaired brilliancy, quickening the luxuriant verdure that covered the fields, trees, and shrubbery. Beautiful and improved farms lay on each side of the road; and instead of being immured among forests, as I had anticipated, I saw extensive tracts of land waving in all the gayety and loveliness of harvest.

After an amusing ride, which lasted more than an hour, I stopped at La Chine. There is a portage between the two places, for the Rapids of the St. Lawrence interrupt the navigation, and consequently all stores and goods, intended for the upper country, are conveyed from Montreal to La Chine by land. At the latter place, they are put into flat-bottomed boats, called *batteaux*, which are rowed up the river, with incredible labour, by Canadians, whom the forwarders engage at a certain sum during the season. La Chine is thus rendered a place of some importance, which otherwise it would not be; but still it merely consists of a few dwelling houses, and several large stores for the reception of the goods. [John Howison]

On Saturday 31st of July hired carts to take us to Lachine, distant 9 miles, for which I paid 4 dollars. The land is chiefly gravel soil, and cucumbers, melons, pumpkins, French beans, etc. grown in the fields; the orchards from one and a half to four acres. This is the finest country I have seen in all my travels except this country [meaning his own farm in Hamilton township], and if I had to settle again I would settle about Montreal; the chief objection is they are nearly all French. [Robert Wade]

We are going to set out from here tomorrow in some covered conveyance to La'Chine, nine miles from here, and then we shall proceed afterwards by Boats again. [Mary Mullett]

It is worth noting the varied forms of transport hired for the purpose. Although Mr Howison does not tell us how he travelled here, it was obviously comfortable enough for the ride to be 'amusing'. He reveals later it was a *calèche* (or calash in Georgian English), which was mentioned by other travellers between Montreal and Lachine. That is quite different from the cart used by the Wades or the 'covered conveyance' which Mary Mullett anticipated. Her sizable family no doubt travelled with plenty of luggage.

The Radcliffs seemed to have enjoyed their coach ride.

They are of the most extraordinary construction—not unlike the lord mayor's state carriage, except that in lieu of its profusion of glass, are substituted curtains which are occasionally looped up to admit the air.

The new coaches are very showy, and by no means ugly in their appearance. There are three rows of seats in each; the centre seat moves on a pivot so as to clear the doorway, and allow of free ingress and egress, for those who occupy the other two; for this a broad strap of leather, well stuffed, is contrived to hook on, so that the mid-passengers may have something to lean against. Each seat holds four moderate persons, but three Radcliffs. [Mrs Radcliff]

Joseph and Hannah Wilson had already loaded their luggage on a Durham boat in Montreal, and set off in it at ten in the evening, towed up the canal through the five locks by one horse, arriving at La Chine in the evening.

As at each other stage of the journey, there were those who tried to take advantage of the travellers.

14 Seper. I was going to sail with Mr White and family but found I could not [illegible] take Grouse [his dog] with me in the bateau. La chine is a place of hellish extortion.a [illegible] is sure to be cheated out of his money. there is not an appellation in the English language that I can use that can fully describe the infamous conduct of the inhabitants to poor Strangers!
[— Johnson]

Some few would continue their trip down the Saint Lawrence in a private carriage (as John Howison does in his calash), but for most the trip would be divided between riding on the flat-bottomed Durham boats or batteaux on the water or walking along the shore beside it.

I took my passage in a Durham boat, bound for Kingston, which started the next day. We had hard work poling up the rapids. I found I had fallen in with a rough set of customers, and determined in my own mind to leave them as soon as possible, which I happily effected the next evening when we landed at Les Cedres. Here the great Ottawa pours its might stream into the St. Lawrence, tinging its green waters with a darker hue, which can be traced for miles, till it is ultimately lost in the rapids below.

I now determined to walk to Prescot, where I knew I should be able to take the steam-boat for Kingston, on Lake Ontario. At the Coteau du Lac I fell in with a roman Catholic Irishman named Mooney. We travelled in company for three days, and as I had nothing else to do I thought I might as well make an effort to convert him. However, I signally failed; and only endangered my own head by my zeal. [Samuel Strickland]

157

We were charmed to get on dry land, to follow our batteau along well-beaten paths, gathering nuts, stealing a few apples now and then from some orchard skirting the road; dining at some weather-boarded way-side tavern, with painted floors and French cuisine, all delightfully strange and comical to us; then on board the batteau again at night. Once, in a cedar swamp, we were enraptured at finding a dazzling specimen of the scarlet *lobelia fulgens*, the most brilliant of wild flowers, which Indians use for making red ink. [Samuel Thompson]

From Lachine to Prescott the navigation of the river is very difficult, and nothing but small vessels can get up; they are of two kinds, one called Durham boats and the other Batteaux; they have to push them with poles and the labor is very tiresome. We took passage in a Durham boat for 2 dollars a passenger and 1 dollar a cwt for baggage. We had 26 hundred weight; they are the most wicked men I ever saw. We were eight days in going from Lachine to Prescott, distance of 130 miles; the land is chiefly stony on the river side and barren; their crops are chiefly wheat and white peas; the quantity from 10 to 15 bushels per acre; they are certainly very bad farmers; one third of their crop being thistles and weeds... [Robert Wade]

Both William Bell and John Howison also mention the uncivilized nature of the men who worked the Durham boats. Howison describes them as 'disgusting,' but Bell cannot prevent a measure of admiration entering his description.

I may here inform you how the boatmen are lodged on these occasions. After selecting the place at which they intend to spend the night, they make the boat fast to the bank. They then collect wood to make a fire and cook their supper. When that is over, they drink their grog, and go to sleep upon the ground, with one tarpaulin under them for their bed, and another over them, fixed in a slanting direction to send off the water if it should rain. They carry their provisions along with them, consisting generally of pork and pease. They are a savage-looking race, and are capable of enduring a great deal of fatigue.

Bell and his family were travelling free of charge, thanks to the generosity of Presbyterians in Montreal. They spent their nights in passing farmhouses but the quality of both food and accommodation did not meet his standards. Others did not mind.

> 15 Sep I stopped at an Irishman's house in a village upon the river lisle, got mashed potatoes and milk for supper & had a good bed and slept well. [— Johnson]

Poorer immigrants could not have afforded to stay in houses on the riverbank, and would instead have done what the boatmen did, curling up on board or on the riverbank in whatever circumstances they could manage.

> here allow me to say our worst part of the voyage began—of course economy was my object and after much enquiry I found the durham Boats to be the cheapest. I accordingly went to the Wh [warehouse] of Macpherson Henderson & Co. and engaged at a very heavy charge to convey myself & goods up to Toronto (late York) and the conduct of this house is notoriously shameful this I had to learn instead of the accomodation agreed for they filled up the Boat to the top and we had no place of rest or refuge further than we could get by creeping under the Turpauling which covered the food in the boat. In this sad state we continued till 8 October when after a journey of 402 [miles] we quitted this vile boat and proceeded to finish our Journey by steam [Joseph Brown]

At Saint Ann's on Ile Perrot, they passed the mouth of the Ottawa (mentioned by Strickland above). John Howison was also impressed:

> The house was situated in the midst of an orchard, and the boughs, loaded with blossoms, clustered round the window, through which I had a view of the Grand River Ottawa, rolling majestically, and glittering in the sun. In the midst of the river was the island of Perrot, so luxuriantly wooded, that the foliage of the trees descended to the surface of the water, and completely concealed the bank on which they grew. Numerous birds fluttered in the sunshine, sometimes plunging into the bosom of the forest, sometimes issuing from its recesses to revel upon the surface of the water...All was glorious, animated, and beautiful.

159

Howison then mentions that this was where his calash plunged into the untouched forest for the first time. For the emigrants, used to the tidy copses of Britain, the sight of huge trees, numbering thousands to the horizon, must have been a thrilling experience.

The next spot of note was *Les Cèdres* (or The Cedars), where the Saint Lawrence has another set of rapids.

> ...the Rapids of Les Cedres, which present one perturbed expanse of foam, rushing over a rocky bed with terrific grandeur and vehemence. The river is half a mile broad here, and such is the rapidity of the current, that the water, when it strikes against the projecting rocks, is thrown up in large jets many feet high. [John Howison]

In all, if the immigrants were not ill, they seemed to have found the river trip a pleasure to some extent, since it was beautiful and exciting, and they did not have to endure the difficulties of life on board ship.

> Nothing of interest occured during this part of our journey, save the great beauty of the noble river, its innumerable islands and diversified scenery; occasionally meeting scooners with Barrels of Flour piled high on the deck on its way to Montreal & Quebec suggesting the immense importance of an outlet to the great Western country before us, that this river must eventually be. [John Leeming]

> We afterwards passed the Longue Saut, through a channel so full of rocks and shoals that no vessel but a flat-bottomed boat could possibly have lived in it. Sometimes we seemed on the point of being dashed against the land, till, snatched away by some unseen eddy into another direction, we were twisted down a watery precipice, and carried across a bubbling field of waves and breakers, till once more in open space the lessening roar of waters died upon the ear... [George Head]

It was possible to switch back and forth between land and water vehicles, depending on the safety of the river at various points.

At La Chine we deserted our land conveyance, and with the appetite of morning travellers enoyed a good breakfast on board the steam boat under way for the cascades—a distance of twenty-three miles—there we took coach again for a village called Coteau de lac, (sixteen miles) and *there* embarked in another steamer, which brought us (36 miles) to the town of Cornwall. [Mrs Radcliff]

Along the way, it was necessary to stop at rough wayside inns for meals or to rest. Even in the towns these were not up to standard.

The hotel at Cornwall is a wretched place; bad attendance, worse rooms, ill furnished—vile beds, and no rest'—not a very good preparation for a long day's journey by land to Prescott, (50 miles,) commenced, however, before five o'clock, with a great delight at quitting our uncomfortable station... [Mrs Radcliff]

An encounter at one of these establishments is one of Susanna Moodie's most famous stories.

It was unanimously voted by all hands that we should stop and breakfast at a small inn by the roadside, and warm ourselves before proceeding to Prescott.

The people in the tavern were not stirring, and it was some time before an old white-headed man unclosed the door ,and showed us into a room, redolent with fumes of tobacco, and darkened by paper blinds. I asked him if he would allow me to take my infant into a room with a fire.

"It guess it was a pretty considerable cold night for the like of her," said he. "Come, I'll show you to the kitchen; there's always a fire there." I cheerfully followed, accompanied by our servant.

Our entrance was unexpected, and by no means agreeable to the persons we found there. A half-clothed, red-haired Irish servant was upon her knees, kindling up the fire; and a long thin woman, with a sharp face, and an eye like a black snake, was just emerging from a bed in the corner. We soon discovered this apparition to be the mistress of the house.

"The people can't come in here!" she screamed in a shrill voice, darting daggers at the poor old man.

161

"Sure there's a baby, and the two women critters are perished with cold," pleaded the good old man.

"What's that to me? They have no business in my kitchen."

"Now Almira, do hold on. It's the coach has stopped to breakfast with us; and you know we don't often get the chance."

All this time the fair Almira was dressing as fast as she could and eyeing her unwelcome female guests as we stood shivering over the fire.

"Breakfast!" she muttered, "what can we give them to eat? They pass our door a thousand times without any one alighting; and now, when we are out of everything, they must stop and order breakfast at such an unreasonable hour. How many are there of you?" turning fiercely to me.

"Nine," I answered laconically, continuing to chafe the cold hands and feet of the child.

"Nine! That bit of beef will be nothing, cut into steaks for nine. What's to be done, Joe?" (to the old man).

"Eggs and ham, summat of that dried venison, and pumpkin pie," responded the *aide-de-camp* thoughtfully. "I don't know of any other fixings."

"Bestir yourself then, and lay out the table, for the coach can't stay long," cried the virago, seizing a frying-pan from the wall, and preparing it for the reception of the eggs and ham. "I must have the fire to myself. People can't come crowding here, when I have to fix breakfast for nine; particularly when there is a good room elsewhere provided for their accommodation." I took the hint, and retreated to the parlour, where I found the rest of the passengers walking to and fro, and impatiently awaiting the advent of the breakfast.

To do Almira justice, she prepared from her scanty materials a very substantial breakfast in an incredibly short time, for which she charged us a quarter of a dollar per head.

The Radcliff letters paint a better picture of tavern food:

At all the poorest taverns alone the line of road, they set out a plentiful dinner, not of the best quality of meat, excepting veal, which is very good; the cooking but middling. Pies and puddings abound, and uniformly a dessert succeeds, of raisins, almonds, biscuits and wild fruits. The red currants are large, but sour; the strawberries and cherries scarcely eatable. The raspberries are better, and served up in milk, with sugar.

James Wilson was probably not alone in finding that his luggage was switched from one mode of conveyance to another. This placed it in danger of going astray, either by chance or because of being stolen.

> After sailing a few days, we arrived at a part of the river called the Cascades, called by some the Rapids, and by others the Split Rock. In this place the water swells and rises to such a degree that every boat or vessel coming up against these Rapids are obliged to be unloaded, and the property sent by land carriage to a place called the Cedars, and here my increasing sorrow, I may say, commenced: for being obliged to lighten the boat I and my family were in, amongst the [not printed] of the property delivered up by the proprietor of the boat to carriers waiting on shore for that purpose, my valuable library of books, packed up in a large box, with another larger one of clothes, &c. were given in charge to the waggoner, to be brought forward to the Cedars; it being rather late in the day, this carrier left my two boxes, with two puncheons of rum, in the yard of a tavern, about half a mile from the place where he took them in charge, and as I supposed them safe, remained with my family; in the mean time, my box of books was stolen in the night: and thus, after bringing them safe across the sea, and flattering myself that I should have much comfort in reading them from time to time, in one night I lost my valuable library, which I had for years been collecting... [James Wilson]

Wilson's experiences in Brockville also illustrate the catch-as-catch-can nature of finding a place to stay.

> Bring uneasy to get forward in my tedious journey, I agreed with a waggoner to bring my family and luggage to Brockville, a distance of twelve miles, for which I gave him 12s. 6d. and coming in the evening, I expected to take up my abode for a few days with Mr Hazlewood, a wheelright, who came over in the same vessel with me, and arriving some days before me in Brockville, had taken a house and commenced his trade; this friend had his house so filled with several families who came over with us, that I would not allow my family to take shelter with these people, whom Mr. Hazlewood had kindly received, arising from a knowledge of their sinful and very improper conduct on sea....

Not being able to find a lodging for my family, I sought out a convenient place near the riverside, and unloaded my little property, and paid the carrier for carriage to Brockville. Resolving thus to sleep with my family in the open air, I procured, through Mr Hazlewood's means, leave to put my beds and other effects into a workshop, belonging to a Mr Skinner, who carried on the carpenter and joiner business very extensively...

James Marr Brydone quotes a long account of the river trip, written by William Phillips who went to Adelaide in 1833:

In the morning, we with our luggage, went on board two large Durham boats, and was carried through the locks in the Lachine canal, there we were forced to unload the boats, to have every thing weighed; it was six in the evening, before we left this place, and got to Lachine at eleven at night; could go no farther, for the lock: we expected some place to go to, but no place was provided for us; so we sat in the boat all night: in the morning the men went, and stole wood, and made a great fire. The next day, being Sunday, we stay all day and night, we made tents, and slept on the ground. Monday morning, at break of day, sailed the remainder of the canal, and crossed a small lake, into another canal, called the cascades; with a great many locks, every one taking us several feet higher up a hill. This canal, is but through a rock, to miss the rapids in this place: we were not drawn by oxen, up the rapids, they walked at the edge of the water, taking us as near the outside of the water, as the boats could go: out travelling this way is very tiresome, and took us eight days, to get to Prescot; the first night we reached a village, and after begging hard, we prevailed with them to let us lay on their floor: we carried our beds, and slept there, at the charge of 6d. each: at break of day, we went on board, and stopped at night, where there was no houses: we borrowed the sail, and as many as could get under did: the others, made a large fire, and sat, or slept by it; the next day, it rained all day, and at night we stopped at a village, and prevailed with some poor people, to lodge us, a house full, on their floor; they let us make tea, and dryed our clothes: in the night, I was taken ill, with the spasms, and a fever followed; I did not eat one mouthful, of food, for eight days; only drinked a little port wine often. I could not hardly get in, or out of the boat, nor did I think I should ever see Adelaide. We at last came to Prescot; sleeping on the ground every night, but two: The boatmen were all French-men, and no way obliging; we could not make the kettle boil, by the fire. When we came to Prescot, we were all very wet with rain, and went to a tavern, hoping to dry ourselves; but we were so many, standing in their way, they did not want us there, so we was forced to remain, as we was. At five o'clock, we went on board the steamer, to Cornwall, in a close room; should have been comfortable, if we had been dry. We got to Cornwall, about five in the morning; the boat-men said, we must walk nine miles, the rapids run so strong: a great many walked; but myself, so ill, I could not; so myself, and Ellen, and three more women, with small children, hired a waggon, and two horses, to carry us twelve miles for two dollars: these waggons are not like yours, they have one straight board, on each side, one at the head, and one behind, just like a great chest, without a lid; they are like this all the country through; but we had spring seats, and a man to drive; the boats did not get here until the afternoon: the roads are very dirty, and rough; but this is one of the best, being where the coaches run. The men walked on, but the women and children got in the boats, for we were as much in the rapids, as before; the middle of the stream, is worse, by far, then the edge of the water; where we were drawn by oxen, when we got at last to Prescot, we took the steamer for York, across Lake Ontario—I have told you wrong; we came to Cornwall, before we came to Prescot; the other place's name, I have forgot: Prescot is where we took the steamer, for York.

With the river being so wild in places, and the boatmen also, there was a chance of accidents.

Notwithstanding the dangerous nature of these Rapids, the Canadians pass down with boats and rafts almost every day, and very few accidents happen; but when a boat does fill, or upset, the crew inevitably perish. [John Howison]

The steamer 'Passport' collapsed her boilers on the morning of June 29th, at Cornwall near Montreal, by which accident nine emigrants were instantly killed and fifteen persons scalded.

Finally they reached Prescott, where they might pause before the next stage of the journey.

165

Prescot is a fine little town, and daily increasing—it is a military station. Two churches are building here, the one an episcopal chapel, the other a presbyterian meeting-house. ...The majority of the inhabitants are Irish and French, and increasing fast. Here the mail-coach stops, this being the only road to Kingston, which is 62 miles straight up the river. [John M'Donald, 1820]

...I remained two or three days at Prescot, waiting the arrival of my baggage, which I had left on board the Durham boat. I amused myself during the interval by taking walks in the neighbourhood. The land appeared very sandy, the timber being chiefly hemlock: the situation of the town is good. Steam-navigation commenced at this place, and now that the Welland Canal is completed, it affords an uninterrupted navigation to the head of Lakes Huron and Michigan. [Samuel Strickland]

The time taken on this trip varied greatly according to the kind of transportation used, the state of the river, the time of year and any number of other factors. John Howison stated categorically that it took seven days from Lachine to Kingston, but he was travelling in a private carriage. Robert Wade, above, says eight days from Lachine to Prescott. The diarist Johnson took nine days from Lachine to Kingston, but he was walking without luggage. The batteaux carrying his bags took longer to sail down the river than he did to walk the riverbank with his dog.

If I were ever to travel down the course of the St. Lawrence again, I should take the land conveyance from Prescott to Cornwall, though I never enjoyed myself more than during the five hours I was on board the bateau this day, and we outstripped the coach two hours and a half in the journey of fifty miles. [Edward Coke]

One diversion at Prescott was the chance to go across the river and thus enter the United States. In the 1820s memories of the War of 1812 were still fresh and the Americans occupied an unusual position in the minds of many English. They were no longer seen as having things in common with the mother country; they were 'different.'

John Leeming made the crossing and reported:

We arrived at Prescott a town on the British side of the river, and having to wait here several hours before we could proceed to Kingston, we took the opportunity of crossing the river to Ogdensburg exactly opposite on the United States side of the river, and here it was that I first set my foot on Yankee territory. The river here is about 1 mile wide and very deep....Ogdensburg is a neat good town, and thro it many goods are smuggled from each shore.

Leeming's principal remarks about the town have to do with relics of the war, among them marks of cannon balls on a windmill, which are

> very conspicuous objects as we pass up the river and are allowed to remain untouched as a warning to the disaffected, numbers of who are still on the opposite shore.

The English visitors who wrote about Canada often had either critical or satirical things to say about Americans. The immigrants may not have continued in the same vein for long, because the common social ideals of all North America had their effects. Canadian society would develop similarities with the United States as well as Britain. The new Canadians would quickly stop seeing the Americans as so very different from themselves.

James Logan spent the journey from Montreal to Cobourg alternately in a coach on shore and a steamer on the river or lake. The highlight for him is the 'highly romantic' vision of the Thousand Islands.

> ...the most perfect fairy-scene in the world,—the Thousand Islands [James Dixon]

They came to Kingston, a substantial place with a fort and bustling docks.

> At Kingston we changed steamers, and here I was "let in" unnecessarily for a quarter of a dollar (an English shilling), by the carter who conveyed my packages from the one vessel to the other. I afterwards found that the transfer is made at the expense of the company. it was partly owing to my own fault,

however, in going myself to bargain with the carter, who dishonestly took advantage of my ignorance. It cannot be too strongly impressed on every traveller, the desirableness of picking up from some one whom he may find most qualified to inform him, the probably charges which may meet him at every succeeding stage of his journey. Had I thought of inquiring of the clerk of the boat, or of the obliging gentleman who so kindly volunteered to stand sentinel over my luggage, this imposition could not have been practised upon me. [Henry Christmas]

The effects of this trip, first on shipboard and then via the various possible vehicles down the river, were very wearing on the immigrants. Many of those who met new arrivals at the end of their journey in Toronto or the backwoods describe them as pale, tired and ill. It might be disastrous if one of the family took ill while they were travelling on the river.

on our arrival at the village of Prescott, 120 miles above Montreal, I was sezed with a bloody flux, which desease continued about ten days with me. I had just got the turn, when our society was ordered for Brockville, a small village 12 miles further up the St. Lawrence. The fatigue of the removal &c, brought on a relapse of my Complaint, which detained me and my family in that place for about a month. the first and second week of my stay there, I was tottering on the brink of grace, but thanks to God, I recovered contrary to the expectations of my physicians, having been given up for lost, one consolation was still left one during my illness, which was, all the rest of my family were in good health,—On the 31st day of August last, I was located for my land, when at that time, I was unable to walk without the assistance of a staff.
[William Dowie]

The worst might happen.

here our little William died after a very tedious illness and was buried amongst the soldiers that fell in the battle of Ogdens-burg. It was a great trial for us to leave him behind; it would be well for us to be resigned to the will of God. We stopped here 5 days and then took to Kingston. [Robert Wade]

The number of digestive upsets on the trip, which might be attributed to the journey or variances in food, were caused by the water itself.

> Those who go to Canada ought to beware of drinking too much of the fresh water of the river St. Lawrence, when they come first up to it, as from its effects on those who are not accustomed to it, it is liable to cause a flux. [A. Bell]

> The water of the river [Saint Lawrence] is exquisitely pure and transparent, and when it sparkles round the oars, one is almost induced to drink it, whether he feels thirsty or not. The effects which it produces on those unaccustomed to its use, are rather difficult to account for. It occasions nausea, pain in the stomach, and diarrhoea; but the boatmen, who use it every day, never experience any of those effects. Several gentlemen who live in the western parts of Upper Canada, and are in the habit of going to Montreal once a-year, told me, that they regularly had an attack of the kind I have described during their passage down, but never suffered at all on their way back again. These effects probably proceed from the extreme softness of the water, which, being mingled together in such prodigious quantities, and exposed so long to the influence of the sun, loses its carbonic acid, and likewise the greater part of the atmospheric air that is loosely combined with it. [John Howison]

Howison later comments on the wan countenances of new arrivals in Toronto, as do Samuel Strickland and Tiger Dunlop. It is hardly surprising after such a journey, but the effects of the water of the Saint Lawrence when they were already in a weakened state perhaps emphasized their sickly appearance.

For some, there was the pleasure of meeting old friends as they travelled, either because they knew where they lived in the new country, or by chance.

> The evening of the 28th, I went to Niagara & met my two sons, Archy & Jasper, very well & I was delighted to reunite with them: they are promising lads.
> The 29th & 30th I went to Queenston, the Falls & Chippawa, & saw my old friends Clark, Duff & Street, of other & bygone years, who lived in those places. [William Gilkison]

you have acquantance in nearley all the towns you pass trough
in Canada who will give you free quarters for anight and when
you come to Toronto there you will have Mr Rutlege
[Nathaniel Carrothers]

It was at Kingston that the two routes from Montreal, via the
upper Saint Lawrence and via the Rideau Canal, met.

Rideau Route

Early settlers arriving at Quebec and wishing to continue
to Upper Canada had little choice but to take the Saint Lawrence
river to Lake Ontario. In 1832, with the opening of the Rideau
Canal, it became possible to consider an alternative route.

> For emigrants of small means I should consider this route to
> Upper Canada much preferable to the other (by way of the St.
> Lawrence). The boats on this line are larger, and being decked
> completely over, you are not exposed to the weather, as you are
> by the other, where the boats are open, and you are exposed day
> and night... [John Murray]

The promise of a higher degree of comfort on board these
vessels, as compared with those plying the Saint Lawrence,
might have appealed to families with small children, since one of
the more unpleasant parts of this sort of journey was the
possibility of becoming soaked to the skin and having no access
to dry clothing.
Travelling between Montreal and Kingston along the
Rideau would take four or five days, depending upon the weather
and the number of hold-ups at locks. As with the Saint Lawrence
route, it was sensible to stock up on provisions at Montreal and
avoid having to pay exorbitant prices on the way.

> On leaving Lachine, the steamer passes along the shores of the
> Island of Montreal, through the St. Ann's Rapids, and up the
> Grand or Ottawa river to Carillon, a distance of about forty
> miles; you then pass through the Grenville Canal, and arrive at
> Grenville, situated at its extremity, and distance from
> Montreal, sixty miles, the same evening. The next morning you

170

embark in another steam boat which takes you to Bytown, and Hull, situated opposite each other; the former, being on the upper, and the latter, on the Lower Canada side of the river; here, you arrive towards evening of the second day, after stopping at Longuiele, Petite Nation, Alfred, Plantagenet, Lochabar, Clarence, Templeton, Buckingham, and Gloucester, having an opportunity of enjoying by full day light the delightful scenery of the Ottawa.   [John Murray]

From this point on, the Rideau Canal, which consists of a large number of interconnected lakes, continues for 123 1/2 miles before reaching Kingston harbour. In terms of the overall journey from the United Kingdom, this was a brief stretch, but things were still liable to go wrong.

The first adventure occurred when the steamer sprang a leak and it became necessary to borrow a pump from a barge in tow to keep the water under control. Two days later the engine broke down and the captain took two of the Durham boats, which the steamer was also towing, and started for Kingston to secure assistance. Meanwhile those on board ran short of provisions and had to make good the deficiency by fishing. They even tried to capture a deer which appeared on the bank, but failed in the attempt. The situation was not made brighter when the cook mutinied. Finally the captain returned with help and provisions, and the *Enterprise* was able to reach Kingston by the thirteenth of May, seven days after leaving Bytown. [W. L. Smith]

John Murray's portrayal of a journey through the Rideau system may have enticed a number of travellers for no other reason than to experience the exotic journey described in his guide of 1835. Within these pages, each leg of the trip received a detailed study.

Proceeding up the Rideau river, and having passed through the locks at the rapids; you enter upon a beautiful sheet of water, called the Rideau Lake, through which, at its extreme, length, about twenty miles, lies the course of the canal; the breadth of the lake varying from half a mile, to six miles; and abounding with the most delightful and varied scenery. [John Murray]

The journey continued through descriptively named waters. From the 'dark and turbid' Mud Lake, to the 'beautifully transparent' Clear Lake, then on to Indian, Opinicon, Sand, Whitefish and Cranberry Lakes.

The canal winds through territory that was well known to John MacTaggart. He worked as Clerk of Works on the canal project under Colonel By. During MacTaggart's tenure he developed strong opinions about the health hazards associated with swamps and lakes. Summer heat brought the fever.

> In the summer of 1828, the sickness in Upper Canada raged like a *plague;* all along the banks of the lakes, nothing but languid fevers; and at the Rideau Canal few could work with *fever* and *ague;* at *Jones's Falls,* and *Kingston Mills,* no one was able to carry a draught of water to a friend; doctors and all were laid down together. And people take a long time to recover amid these hot swamps; it is not two or three week's ills, and then up and well again, but so many months. The Ottawa is conceived to be a very healthy river; the people on its banks are seldom or never sick; and the Lower Province is much freer from distemper than the Upper. Stumps in a certain state of decay are said to be dreadfully obnoxious to health.
> [John MacTaggart]

Of Cranberry Lake, or 'Cranberry Marsh' as he called it, John MacTaggart wrote:

> This infernal place lies between Rideau Lake and Lake Ontario; the route of the Rideau canal goes directly through it. The dimensions are about eighteen miles long, and in some places about two miles broad. It is almost covered with extensive *flats* of cranberry bushes; these have long tangled roots above eight feet long; so the bushes, although rooted in the marsh, swim on the surface of the fetid waters.

Whether emigrants were dissuaded from travelling these waters on the basis of MacTaggart's view is debatable. It is clear that this was the most sensible route for those set upon settling in places such as Perth and Smiths Falls.

The main canal had forty-five locks with a difference of 437 feet between beginning and end. Passing through these took a long time, with much waiting. For emigrants, many of whom had been travelling for six weeks, or more, and who were anxious to arrive at their destination, the whole process must have seemed very wearing.

On to Toronto

From Kingston the steamboats went along the north shore of Lake Ontario. Robert Wade describes his arrival in Port Hope (then known as Smith's Creek) in 1819:

> On Thursday morning arrived at Smith's Creek; it is a small harbor on the lake and has its name from the first settler who is still living. There are four stores, two taverns, two breweries, two distilleries, grist mill, saw-mill and a carding-mill; it is the chief market town between Kingston and York, situation 116 miles from the former and 64 from the latter. We intended to go to York, but being recommended here and well fatigued with our journey, and appeared the finest country we had seen, and after looking at several farms, I bought one joining the lake three miles from Smith's Creek, two miles from Cobourgh, where court is kept and three miles from Hamilton, half a mile from a school and good roads...

The earliest steamers sailed from Prescott and their destination was Niagara, the stops being Kingston, Ernest Town, York, Niagara and then on to Burlington. By the mid-1820s, they had changed to Brockville, Kingston, Cobourg, Port Hope, York. This indicated the change in status of the towns, Niagara and Ernest Town being in decline, Cobourg and Port Hope rising as the land around Rice Lake was settled.

After 1830 this was a settled route, with transfers in Toronto for Hamilton/Burlington and Niagara. There, people could go on to Chippawa for a Lake Erie steamer to points west. Once the Welland Canal was built, travel between the lower great lakes was easier and quicker.

As well as rough quarters for ordinary travellers, there were luxury facilities for the rich and respectable.

There were no trains in this period. Railways were first discussed in Ontario in the mid-1830s, but the plans did not come to fruition for some years, with the first railway leaving Toronto in 1853.

The migrants' first view of Toronto was of the lighthouse on Gibraltar Point, built in 1809 and fifty-four feet high. In 1833 the height was increased to sixty-six feet. It guided ships into the harbour, which was protected by a sandy peninsula. This piece of land was constantly in a state of change wrought by the weather, which added some here and washed away parts elsewhere.

In 1854, Captain Thomas Smith said,

> I have lived in Toronto for over forty years, and been connected with sailing the greater part of the time...When the lighthouse was built by my grandfather and uncle the materials for building it were landed within 25 feet of where it now stands; but the land extends now over a quarter of a mile to the south and three-quarters of a mile to the west of the lighthouse.

Before 1820 the docks were inadequate for the first steamships, so they anchored in the harbour and Durham boats would come out to them. Passengers and goods would then be transferred to shore.

The growth of traffic and Toronto's importance caused the construction of wharves and the creation of other facilities for the reception of immigrants as well as anyone else who was travelling. By 1834 there were three wharves, but a map of 1841 shows thirteen and by 1847 there were eighteen. In his history of the city, E. C. Guillet indicates that some of them were showing signs of age by then.

In fact, in 1844, the Toronto board of trade issued a report which was critical of the way the port was run, summing up with,

> The general aspect too of Toronto from the water must be, to all strangers, very unpromising.

This surprising assessment echoes John Galt's first impression from 1825, when he arrived in a snowstorm from Queenston and stayed at the Steamboat Hotel on Fleet Street facing the harbour. It had a steamboat painted across the front of the building on the second floor, which must have made it an

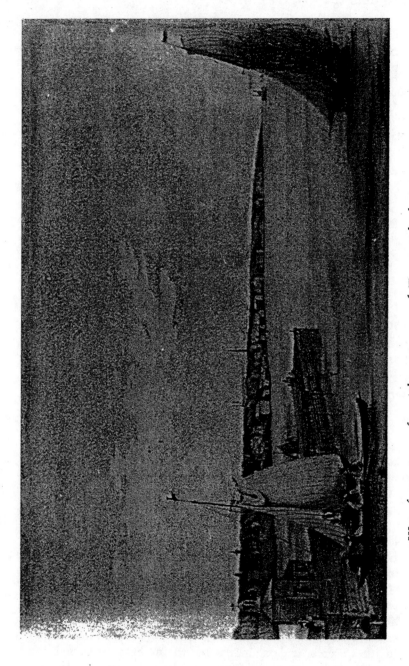

Waterfront scene from the entrance of Toronto harbour, ca. 1840 (Courtesy Archives of Ontario, Acc. 1696 S 1156)

175

attraction from the water. He wrote,

> The general appearance of the town was such as I had expected, but the place less considerable by at least half than I was prepared to see.

The docks initially had no one managing them; only in 1833 was an act passed to improve it, and the first Harbour Commissioners were appointed in 1850. The immigrants who set foot on the eighteen wharves in the 1830s and 1840s stepped into noise and chaos. In 1841 on Maitland Wharf, already showing its age, Sir Richard Bonnycastle was

> jostled almost into the water by rude carters plying for hire on its narrow bounds, and pestered by crowds of equally rude pliers for hotel preferences.

At the corner of Yonge and Front streets, the runner for a steamer between Toronto and Rochester shouted its best qualities, and rivals would be doing the same around him. There were people selling food, carriages for hire, hotel touts, and undoubtedly those with less savoury intentions.

However, the town did dispose people favourably, despite those who had been unimpressed with the view from the docks.

> Toronto is a very fine city. The streets laid out at right angles, and since I left here I have not seen any place I should like to reside in as well as Montreal yet in first seeing Toronto, the difference in society, now being all English, and English customs instead of French as we have it down here, was exceedingly grateful to me. King Street Toronto is a very splendid street, and the shops are more uniform than generally found in America. It would be a credit to any town in England, not even excepting Leeds. Rents here are tremendously high, and property greatly increased and increasing in value. It is strongly surmised that the United Parliament will sit here, and the good people of Toronto are so full of it that they are going ahead furiously on the strength of it. There are a great number of coloured residents of Toronto, who have escaped from slavery in the States and a many of them have obtained very considerable property and have good business establishments. I

sold one, Mr Harris, a quantity of goods for cash. He could have paid into cash for 500£ worth of goods if he liked. He was formerly a slave in the States. They have 3 chapels in Toronto for their own race. For the shame and discredit of many of our fellow countrymen, they despise these simply because of their colour. To a person who had time or who took much interest in the matter, Toronto is place where much information might be obtained from slaves personally of the nature of American Slavery. [John Leeming]

The society in York is equal to any provincial town in Britain, and on Sundays the different congregations present as gay an appearance as in this country, both as regards fashion, handsome carriages, and attendance of servants; who, by the bye, bad as they are, even there, are full fifty per cent better than in New York, or any part of the states I ever visited. The place is well supplied with ministers of most denominations, Episcopalian, Roman Catholics, both of whom have bishops frequently residing in town; Presbyterians, Methodists, and Independents. [William Cattermole]

Toronto at this time was quite a small place, but there were a number of pretty cottages and villas. It still well deserved the name of muddy little York, and indeed, there was one particular hole just at the corner of King and Yonge street, which was well known, and at that time was full of dirty water with a green scum on top, and there was a little, sluggish creek creeping through the town pretty much of the same complexion.
[A. D. Ferrier]

Those who needed information, guidance or even money had a place to go.

...It is a matter of much encouragement to the poor class of emigrants to know that the legislature, aided by the assistance of some gentlemen in and about York, have this year erected a commodious building in York, for the temporary use of such emigrants as may need it, and to prevent the inconvenience which has happened from their not being able to find accommodation at inns on their first arrival, it is the duty of the superintendent of that establishment to seek employment, and direct those who wish it, to persons in the country who require servants....

All emigrants on arriving at York should go first to the emigrants' asylum, and they will learn particulars of the country, &c. and if they have children they wish to provide with situations [employment], the editor of the Courier paper will always put in an advertisement gratis, and I believe, the columns of the Advocate and the Canadian Freeman, are also open to them. [William Cattermole, 1831]

Any person, however humble his station, bringing a character from his parish minister, and presenting himself to any of the clergy in Toronto or elsewhere, would instantly meet with the kindest advice, support, and attention; and, if in want, his necessities would be relieved till work could be obtained, to which he would have a ready recommendation given him. Of course, where emigrants of the poorer classes come out in large numbers, nothing could be done for them usually at the outset, beyond the ordinary provision for their comfort and protection in landing, but as they gradually get settled, and spread themselves over the country, such recommendations as those referred to could scarcely fail of being of use to them.
[Henry Christmas]

For most, the aim would be to find a piece of land in the backwoods which they could claim, clear and work, and then call their own. The land grant system was complex, but there were both civil servants and agents in Toronto to explain it and then people could set out to find their own patch.

When the emigrant reaches York, he should go to the Land Office there, where he will be informed concerning the steps that must be taken, before he can be entitled to a grant. It is unnecessary to detail these farther than by stating, that the chief object of them is, to make the applicant prove himself a British subject.

Government gives fifty acres of land to any British subject, free of cost; but, if he wishes to have a larger quantity, he must pay fees to a certain amount. In Canada, fifty acres are considered as a very small farm, and, therefore the emigrant should procure at least twice as much, if he can afford to do so; however, he will not easily obtain more than one hundred acres, unless he proves himself possessed of the means of soon bringing a larger quantity under cultivation. All lands are bestowed under certain regulations and restrictions. The settler must clear five acres upon each hundred granted to him, open a road in front of his lot, and build a log-house of certain dimensions. These settling-duties, if performed within eighteen months after the location-ticket has been issued, entitle him to a deed from the government, which makes the lot his for ever; and are so far from being severe or unreasonable, that he will find it necessary to perform them in less than the time specified, if he proposed to obtain a subsistence from the cultivation of his farm. [John Howison]

Charles Stuart also describes the same settling duties, 'in default thereof, the whole to be forfeited.'

The casually impending forfeiture above-mentioned is never exacted, except in cases of extreme remisness, or of total abandonment.

This meant that the settler who had a bad year, or fell ill, might hope to recover and continue without an immediate threat of losing his property.

Via New York

The very first welcome accorded to passengers on board the *Thames* came from a butterfly. As it flew high overhead, the passengers gave a shout of joy, delighted that such a pretty creature should be the messenger telling of land ahead.

Everyone is dressed for landing. The gentlemen have doffed their fur caps for fashionable hats. All the steerage passengers are on deck quite smart. Even the sailors look clean, and I can hardly recognize our old friend Charley. Every one seems in that happy humour that is ready to laugh at anything. The land looks beautiful; but we must not leave the ship till the doctor comes from the island to see us. We hear cannon firing. All the ships in the bay are covered with colours. The pilot tells us the President makes his *entree* into New York to-day. He passed us in the American steamboat. Bands of music playing. Streamers flying. It is everyone's gala day as well as ours. At half-past 4 P.M. the doctor came, and after seeing every one, complemented the Captain on the healthy state of our ship. He told us he was the more surprised as the *York* who had come in three days before us had twenty sick, and one had died the day after their arrival. They had also a mutiny and the cabin passengers quarrelled all the way out. [Ellen Steele]

James Buchanan, who served for many years as the British Consul at New York is reputed to have met the newly arrived ships with a view to encouraging emigration to Upper Canada. It is said that it troubled him to see his 'fellow Irish Protestants lost to the empire,' purely because they were ignorant about prospects in Upper Canada. Besides Buchanan, a Canada Company agent might also make himself available to those intent upon going to Upper Canada, providing information regarding land and job prospects.

when we landed we found that work was as scarce in new york as it is [in] England so made a determination to proceed at once into Upper Canada a distance of nearly 600 miles which we can travel by steam packet and fly boat to rochester for 13 shillings we then cross Lake Ontario 90 miles across for 8 shillings it is a fresh water lake and contains fish of all sorts and then we reached Toronto a City in British American as all upper canada belongs to Queen Victoria. [John Hallas]

The Dobie family sampled local fare on their first day in New York.

I saw and tasted water-melons for the first time in New York. My father and uncle went up town in New York and carried back a big water-melon. I ate a little too near the rind and was not very well after it. In the evening we went aboard a little vessel, then we went up the Hudson and up to Albany. I remember seeing the Palisades there quite well. I saw my first mosquito there, that night on the boat. [W. C. Dobie]

Emigrants arriving prior to the days of railroad travel had a far more difficult time of things. The Edwards family, who arrived in 1819, had a tedious journey ahead of them.

By this time the month of September had arrived and the Emigrants began to shape their courses Westward. This they did by getting on board a sloop for Albany, which when reached there were no other means of transportation by land but by wagons, and sufficient of these were engaged to carry us to Sackett's Harbour—a port on Lake Ontario opposite Kingston, Upper Canada. The journey by land was tedious, but by the appearance of the country at that period loaded with fruit by the roadside impressed the Emigrants favourably as to the fertility of the soil. At the harbour a sloop was engaged to take us to Kingston. When nearing Kingston we discovered the Union Jack flying at Fort Henry. My Father felt delighted that once more he was under that flag which had "Braved a thousand years. The battle and the breeze." [James Edwards]

The German immigrants bound for Canada were often short of funds by the time they reached America and paused here to work for a time, as some did later in Albany, Syracuse, Rochester and especially Buffalo. Some had, or lost, children while in New York state, and many did not complete the journey but stayed there.

While the navigation on the Albany river was very smooth, I got sick. The water-melon referred to was the cause. I could not look another water-melon in the face for many years. Railways were not exceedingly plentiful in those days; they were like steamers; a great deal of traveling was done then up the Erie canal by canal boat. On the canal boat by which we traveled there were 70 passengers. The vessel was not very large and the accommodation was not very good. It took us eight days from Albany to Buffalo by mule power. Three people had to be taken off the canal boat at Rochester with cholera. [W. C. Dobie]

Once a person arrived at Albany, the tedious part of the journey commenced.

The Steele family took the train between Albany and Schenectady. Travelling in the new land was full of discoveries, some of which turned out to be more memorable than others.

> At 7 o'clock, A.M., we got into one of a train of steam-carriages on the railroad, which took us in an hour to Schenectady. We seemed to fly. Mamma and the gentlemen went to enquire for a canal boat for the Erie Canal. Millie and I remained in a sort of lumber room, when who should come in but our old friend Julia Bird, the daughter of a surgeon at Chickhowell; Only fancy our mutual surprise, that we, who had left England at different times, should meet in this little room so far away from our own country. She told us that all the family were with her, and that they were going on to Lake Huron. To our great sorrow we were obliged to part from our newly found friend in a few minutes. [Ellen Steele]

The Erie Canal to Buffalo, which was very busy and along which boats whizzed at five or more miles an hour, was the principal thoroughfare for people heading to western Upper Canada.

> The Erie canal, which runs up to the borders of Canada, at Buffalo ends, is mostly open till near Christmas, when the water is let off; about the first week in April it is filled, when the greatest bustle commences towards the western country and Canada. The vessels generally go out in ballast, in order to return with cargoes of timber and other bulky articles, the produce of Canada, and are often of large dimensions, and being in ballast, have extensive accommodations for steerage passengers. [William Cattermole]

> ### Three routes from Albany to Canada
>
> 1) Railroad from Albany to
> Syracuse, 147 miles,
> Syracuse to Oswego 35 miles;
> Oswego to Kingston by
> steamboat, 643 miles;
> or to Toronto, 140 miles.
> Total distance from Albany to
> Toronto, 322 miles
>
> 2) Railroad to Lewiston,
> 356 miles.
> Lewiston to Toronto by
> steamboat, 43 miles,
> total of 399 miles;
> from New York 546 miles.
>
> 3) Railroad direct from Albany to
> Rochester, 251 miles.
> Rochester to Toronto by steam,
> boat. 97 miles.
> Whole distance from Albany to
> Toronto 348 miles.
> From New York, 493 miles.

Some people devised their own itinerary and route.

On Monday 28th May I arrived at Queenston after having passed through Syracuse, Geneva, Canandaigua, Rochester, Lockport & Lewistown. I spent a day at Canandaigua with John Grieg & was delighted with his kindness. The towns through which I passed have become extensive, compared with what they were a score of years ago, & the people seem contented with their comforts—comforts such as theirs are only to be had under a republican Govt where man stands on a footing of equality—rational equality in government. [William Gilkison, 1832]

William Hunter found the canal very slow. He attempted to break the monotony by hopping off at intervals and walking alongside. The weather was dreadfully hot but the scenery was pleasant. He remarked that the villages were "all clean, and everything about them has the appearance of happiness."

> Landed in Rochester about eight o'clock in the morning; took off our luggage; went away to the steamboat landing; too long for the Canadian boat to Port Hope. Waited all day; took our passage in the evening to Lewiston. Set sail at seven o'clock; landed in Lewiston about three o'clock in the morning.
> [William Hunter]

The Hunters then took the ferry to Toronto.

On the alternative route, William Fraser took the Erie Canal to Buffalo in 1834.

> We arrived here by the Great Erie Canal a few minutes before sunset.... And after a very pleasant though sometimes rather tedious voyage of 8 days we are safely arrived at this beautiful town at the lower end of Lake Erie.

He continued on to London by boat, which met a storm on Lake Erie. They sheltered in the mouth of the Welland Canal overnight, then went on.

Joseph Carder provided very little detail of his experience in travelling from New York to Upper Canada.

> We arrived in New York. Our next start was for Canada. We secured a passage on a schooner, belonging to Mr. VanNorman who owned a blasting furnace at Long Point. Our host at the hotel, harnessed up a double cutter and we had our first sleighride. We were in Long Point by daylight and after three months travel we were on Canadian soil. We had 2 canaries and a goldfinch and they sang the whole way.

At Rochester, the Steele party boarded the steamship together and soon the shores of Upper Canada, and then Toronto became visible. The distance travelled from New York to Toronto was 493 miles.

At last the boat reached the wharf. It was crowded with people, and who should we see among them but our dear father. We could not get across to him, but he soon jumped over, and we took him into the ladies' cabin to have him all to ourselves. [Ellen Steele]

Arriving and Clearing

On Wednesday, *Deo volente*, I mean to sleep at Need's,
and on Thursday under a cedar on my own land.
John Langton

Once the emigrants had arrived, their first task was to
obtain some land on which to settle. They may have come with
an idea of where they were going, either because they had friends
in the new land or because they came with an emigration society
who would guide them.

> Suppose, for instance, that a dozen friends and acquaintances agree
> to form a settlement. They choose a colony where improved farms
> can be bought, and also where cheap Government land can be
> acquired. The man with 1000*l*. [pounds sterling] or 2000*l*. can
> settle down comfortably at once on a made farm, while his poorer
> friend would content himself with uncleared land. It is not to be
> supposed that a dozen men will all grow rich together; but if even
> half that number remain together, a pleasant society will grow up
> with the settlement. A society like this may take England with
> them, and individuals will be spared the wrench of parting from all
> old friends. [John Rowan]

Certainly the history of Ontario is dotted with the stories
of those who came to join old friends or simply those they knew
were from the same locale. The clumps of settlers from Devon in
Darlington and Whitby townships and in Huron county give
evidence of this, as do the Scots in Lanark and Glengarry, the
Mennonites in Niagara and York, the Poles in Renfrew and,
overwhelmingly, the Germans in Waterloo.

The attractions of being with your own kind should be obvious, especially if you spoke a language different from that of the dominant group (as the Germans and Highland Scots did). Perhaps no one put this better than Mr McNab, with whom William Bell travelled from Perth to the St. Lawrence.

> To all the Highlanders we met Mr McNab talked Gaelic. He said a mouthful of Gaelic now and then was quite a luxury,...it warmed his mouth on a cold morning. [William Bell]

As we have seen, there was a possibility that emigrants without a definite objective could begin to sort out their problem in Quebec or Montreal. However, they would have to proceed to Toronto to begin the process, or some other place where they knew people and could organize the first step in getting a grant. As John Howison has told us, the initial grant would be for fifty acres.

The fifty-acre size of the immigrant's farm had been arrived at after consideration by the authorities and those who knew what was possible. It was regarded as a 'good unit for beginners', especially those with little money. It was enough to provide sustenance to a family and later, once more clearing had been done and some secondary activities added to the basic ones, an income also.

Later, the 100 acre farm was seen as the basic unit, with 'arable land, garden, orchard and a patch of woods.'

Although the dollar values of land at that time mean little to the modern reader, the reasons for variation in prices is interesting. This is in 1821:

> In Upper Canada, waste land varies in value according to its situation. Near villages, and populous parts of the country, its price is from £4 to £8 an acre; however, when it lies remote from any settlement, and has no particular local advantages, it may sometimes be purchased in tracts at the rate of two or three shillings an acre. Cultivated land sells much higher, particularly when bought in small quantities, its price being then sometimes £20 or £30 per acre. [John Howison]

Which more or less says that the circumstances are very similar to today.

Although some emigrants came with sufficient funds to set themselves up and see them through the first lean times, most had limited cash in hand. Rowan, writing much later, offered the same advice as many others. Emigrants with funds should not be precipitate in investing them in real estate; they should have a look around and consider carefully their own abilities as well as the land and businesses available before plunging in. Many people would lose what little they had by spending it too soon, and there were always those ready to lighten even the poorest purses.

> Contrary to an impression rather prevalent among later generations, a considerable amount of money or credit was necessary for getting a start in the backwoods. It was estimated that the man who had £100 currency, in addition to what he paid for his land, had a bare minimum. It would take £20 to buy a pair of oxen, a yoke, a logging-chain, and a harrow, £8 for a cow and a couple of pigs, £22 for a year's provisions, and £50 for erecting buildings and for hiring labour to assist in chopping and logging. Those who lacked money when they arrived in the new settlements had to acquire it by one means or another before they could expect to have a farm of their own. [R. L. Jones]

Some men left their families behind while they went to choose and buy their plot of land.

> When you arrive in Canada you had better leave the Family in the old Settlements while you come on to me & look abᵗ & make arrangements. the propriety of wch [which] you will at the first House you ask to be accomodated at after going into the Woods. I am 23 miles in a direct line from Sumners Tavern on Dundas street. Whatever you do don't buy land without first seeing it... [W. J. Mickle]

John Stuart's experience as recorded in his journal in 1820, is worth quoting in full:

> I left Montreal on Sat. 27th, arrived at Prescott Sept. 1st. I left Prescott on the 3rd, on board a steamer to Kingston. On the 4th

from Kingston on board of ditto, and arrived at the head of the Bay of Quinte on the 5th. Went to Smith's Creek [Port Hope]— and on the 6th went to Cavan—bought John Nichol's lot of land.

On the 7th came back to Smith's Creek—on the 8th to the Bay of Quinte, arriving on the 11th. On the 13th to Kingston—on the 14th to Prescott: travelled about 20 miles— got into a boat and arrived at Montreal on the evening of the 15th. Left Montreal on the 22nd Sept.—got my children, myself and luggage on board a drum boat at Lachine and arrived at Kingston on Sat. Oct. 7th. Sailed from Kingston on the 10th on a schooner.

On the morning of the 11th a most terrible storm arose, so they were obliged to lash the helm, and lie to for 25 hours in the middle of Lake Ontario—expecting every moment that we would go to the bottom. May this day never be forgotten by me. There were about forty passengers on board.

It pleased the Lord to have mercy on us and changed the wind so that we came back to Kingston, after being drive to within 20 miles of York,—and lost our boat, with one of the hatches and a valuable chest belonging to a passenger all swept from deck. Arrived evening of the 12th at Kingston.

On the morning of the 15th, sailed from Kingston on the Steamboat, arrived on the 16th at the head of the Bay of Quinte. Hired a wagon for the luggage and children, and came to Smith's Creek on the 17th.

On the morning of the 18th went to Cavan,—slept at Mr. Page's.

On the night of the 19th, lost my way in the woods and slept all night in the trunk of a tree.

On the 20th in the morning got to John Nichols, where Alex Speers, John Bowe, and Robt. Deckie had been for some time expecting me. On the 21st I gave up my bargain of John Nichol's lot, and came that night to Mr. Page's. Left on the 23rd and came to Smith's where I had left my two children. On the 25th went to Hamilton Courthouse and drew the East half of Lot 14 of the Township of Otonabee. On the 27th went to [illegible] and returned again on the 31st of October. On Friday the 3rd came with my luggage and children to Rice Lake, but was detained at the ferry by bad weather until Tuesday 7th, when we crossed over and remained at Mr. Foley's shanty until our own shanty was ready. On the 15th we got into our own in health,—thank God.

190

A later county historian reconstructed the pioneer's journey to the interior in this way:

> Let us try to follow one of these stalwart men as he leaves some outpost of civilized life and starts out into the bush, in search of a location on which he may settle, clear a few acres of land, erect a shanty, and thereby establish a squatter's claim to the lot of his choice. Before he starts he carefully prepares the pack he has to carry. This contains a supply of provisions, a few necessary cooking and eating utensils, a blanket, an axe, and possibly an auger and a chisel; some, in addition to these necessaries, took also a gun. After a weary tramp through the woods along a surveyor's "blaze", a spot that seems somewhat near the ideal he is looking for is reached. The land, he notes, is covered with heavy hardwood timber, a safe indication that the ground on which it grows is good; the soil, exposed where some ancient monarch of the forest had stood, but now fallen and uprooted, seems all that could be desired, and a spring flowing clear and cool fairly captivates him. Here his search ceases. After securing his provisions in the hollow some tree, so they may be safe from rain or the depredations of wild animals, he proceeds to do some underbrushing, and erect a shack or shanty, which has to be made of timber of such a size that he unaided can lift it into place. Cutting the logs into suitable lengths and notching each one for the corners, he erects after much hard work his shanty. A narrow opening is made for a doorway; planks split from cedar logs are made into a door. The chinks between the logs are filled with splints and stuffed with moss or clay. The roof is covered with elm bark. His bed of hemlock boughs is placed in one of the corners. The table is made by driving four crotched sticks into the earthen floor, on which rest, supported by crosspieces, a couple of split or hewed planks. With a block of wood for a seat, his furniture is complete. [Norman Robertson]

Guides were available to show you to the available lots. You might even employ 'a young man of considerable respectability' :

> At Owen's Sound, for instance, the individual whom you would be sure to hear of as a guide is a gentleman's son, whose father has filled the office of sheriff of one of the other districts. [Henry Christmas]

191

In John M'Donald's estimate, it was worth employing a guide to ensure you saw the best acreage available:

The ground is measured out into lots of 100 acres each, and in every township the ground is divided into concessions or grants, and each concession is again subdivided into a proportionate number of lots. A post is fixed in the ground to mark the limit or boundary of each concession, both in front and rear. For this reason the most of those who go to view their lots, take a guide with them, and two or three go commonly together, which diminishes the expence to each individually, because they have to pay their guide five or six shillings every day that they are employed for the above purpose; which commonly occupies three days when they go out on a journey of this nature. The sooner they set out, the better, on account of the great distance which they have to travel through the woods. Each emigrant generally gets two lots to view, and if three set out together, there are 600 across to be inspected. I thought that this toil would have almost finished me, and even stout young men were so completely worn out with the toil, that they could scarcely return home, and were afterwards confined to bed, and fevered, from the great fatigue and exhaustion of bodily strength occasioned by excessive perspiration during the intense heats of the day, and from sleeping all night in the woods, exposed to the cold and heavy dews.... One of our companions, a young man, leaving a wife and family, died after such an excursion, in the course of a few days.

Everyone who had had to choose land had their own story about the experience:

I arrived here a week ago last Monday & on this day Wed^y week went to look ab^t for some Land. I got to the Head of Burlington Bay in ab^t 6 hours by which time it was morning (Thursday) & walked on to Galt where I arrived by sun down & next day looked at some Land for which the owner asked 4 Dollars part down the rest in 4 or 5 years. they were cutting the road thr^o it or what is here called a road but like nothing you ever saw. This land was covered with pine trees and plenty of Huckleberries so you may guess the rest. I got as far as Guelph the next day and on Monday to Eramosa where the land appears to me to be excellent. I walked by the next day to East Flamborough to see the owner of some in that part but alth° I made the utmost speed a man had got & he promised of it two or three hours before but there is plenty of Land fur' up to be had upon the same terms names 2 Dollars per acre with Int at 10 years credit. The C[anada] Company say their lands in the London District are from 2 to 3 Dollars per a[cre] & at Goderich on the Huron Tract one & a Half in fact you are very much mistaken in thinking Land may be had at a Dollar but I believe the Government gives out some at that rate to poor Emigrants, but it is on Lake Simcoe away north. [William Mickle]

Mickle's comment, "This land was covered with pine trees and plenty of Huckleberries so you may guess the rest," might be a mystery to the modern reader, but his father understood. When choosing land, observation of the kind of trees which grew there was essential, because it indicated the type of soil and its abilities to grow certain crops. The first Mennonites who came here from Pennsylvania looked for the black walnut. Samuel Strickland's advice was:

> The best land is timbered with oak, ash, elm, beech, bass-wood, and sugar maple. A fair mixture of this species of trees is best, with here and there a large pine, and a few Canadian balsams scattered among the hard-wood. Too great a proportion of beech indicates sand or light loam: a preponderance of rock-elm is a sign of gravel or limestone-rock near the surface.

> When you are upon it, see that it is chiefly covered with hardwood, such as beech and maple, and beware of pine, unless you want it for a saw-mill; otherwise pine land is always very severe land to clear, the stumps an interminable time in rotting out, desperately hard to grub up, and the land sometimes miserably poor when you have done all. [Henry Christmas]

The land of 'superior quality' was that with predominately maple and basswood.

Lack of ability to make this judgement about timber could be financially disastrous. When William Lunn bought his first piece of land in Clarke township, it adjoined the farms of his wife's family, some of the best soil in the area. After her death and his remarriage, he chose to relocate, giving up the prime land

on Concession VI for sandy soil covered in pine on Concession X.
His family did not prosper there.

> My visit to this spot, however, when only about ten days arrived
> in the country, convinced me more and more how very
> incompetent a settler, unless perhaps he be an experienced
> agriculturist, which I did not profess to be, is to judge of a place
> when newly come out. I felt completely bewildered with the
> aspect of bush and water, and had no eye for 'privileges,' viz.,
> creeks with water power for machinery, &c., (all rivulets in this
> country are called creeks, probably from the early settlers
> having kept near the shores, and having been unable to
> distinguish between a stream and an inlet of the sea or inland
> lakes). Neither was I at all versed in the mystery of
> 'hardwood'—blocks of land, cedar swamps, swales or pine tracts,
> except from books, which of course, was very different from
> practical knowledge. [Henry Christmas]

Even cedar swamps might be worthy, according to John
Langton, who said you could clear them down to the rich soil,
clear the river so they drained, and the result was good land for
agriculture. A side benefit was all the cedar logs for fence rails
and shingles.

For those who wanted to settle where there were no land
grants available (because it was near friends or in an area deemed
more desirable), there was always the possibility of buying land
which had been cleared and was ready for some sort of planting.

> There are always plenty wanting to sell, for, even in that land of
> abundance and plenty, the careless, the idle & the dissatisfied,
> and they are always ready to part with their farm for money.
> Others sell for profit, and after having cleared a farm from its
> original wilderness of forest, sell the improvements, and again
> take forest land which they get for a mere trifle. [John Leeming]

> Settlers, with capital, who prefer establishing themselves on
> land, on which partial clearings have been made, and log-
> houses erected, will generally find lots with such improve-
> ments, for sale. This arises from persons going originally in a
> very destitute circumstance, who, having succeeded on their
> lots, are willing to sell their land, with a reasonable profit, to

194

new comers, at from 4 to 6 dollars, with the improvements on the same, houses, barns &c. These individuals generally remove further westward, having acquired sufficient knowledge of the country... [William Cattermole]

Some fifteen years prior to the time I speak of, the tract of country now constituting my parish was a wild wilderness of woods, untrodden by the foot of man, where the bear, the wolf, and the panther, the fox, the deer, the beaver, and raccoon, held undisturbed possession, save when a solitary trapper or a wandering Indian invaded their wild domain. At length a bold adventurer, with a little capital, so little that it would not have availed him much in an old settlement, where land was of greater value, bought as large tract of land and came to live upon it. He built a house and made a "clearing." The first settler is soon obliged to hire labourers, when one or two, with perhaps large families and very poor, will come and built a hut, and make a little clearing, and "locate" themselves beside him, so as to be near their work. These persons are called squatters, and generally, when the land is sold, they either purchase a small portion comprising their improvements, or sell these improvements to any one else who may have bought the land. The purchaser, at any rate, must pay for their labour upon the land before he can turn them off and get possession. [J. Abbott]

While there were many reasons why those who had already cleared their land wishing to move along to start again, one point of view divides the first settlers into two groups: pioneers and farmers. The pioneers liked the challenge of clearing while farmers truly wanted to settle. For some, moving from place to place was part of the pleasure.

It has been remarked of the settlements of Upper Canada, that the first settlers were not destined to be the permanent occupiers of the land, and that in the course of a few years, the original settlers are almost uniformly superseded by an entirely different class of persons.

The task of clearing land—of converting a tract of unbroken forest into a cultivable farm—is a very different operation from that of tilling and cultivating the land, after it is brought into that state in which it may properly be called a farm.

Those different occupations, to a certain extent, require different tastes and capacities, and have a tendency to require, and to form a distinct class of persons for each vocation.

Hence it often happens, that when the "original pioneers" as they are poetically called, have cleared their farms and brought them into that situation in which the mere *farmer* would consider them just fit to begin to live on, they become dissatisfied with their lot, they do not relish the different kind of labour which the altered state of their farms require, and they long for a new settlement—for the excitement of chopping, logging and burning brush.

...Many of the earlier settlers in Huron and Kincardine, have within the last three or four years sold out their improvements, and repurchased in the newer townships of Elderslie, Bruce, Saugeen and Arran; no other lands in these townships were brought into the market—and some of these very same persons, as well as others, are now contemplating another move into the new lands of the peninsula, as soon as they are offered for sale. [John Lynch]

John Rowan looked at the question from a more agricultural point of view:

The original settlers in Ontario were not as a rule good farmers. Even if they were, the process they pursued spoiled them. They found land which when cleared of forest produced splendid crops of wheat. So they grew wheat year after year till the land would grow wheat no longer. Then, when they discovered that in order to make their farms reproductive it would be necessary to farm in a more scientific way, many of them, instead of taking the trouble to establish a system of rotation of crops, flitted to other localities where they cleared new farms on which they were able to repeat the process of scratching the soil for wheat. Even at the present day, although there are many good farmers in Canada, this system is still pursued, and the consequence is that there are always in the market numbers of farms, well situated, with good buildings, fences, orchards &c., the soil of which, although temporarily unfitted for one particular crop, is admirably suited for many others, and is capable, with a very moderate outlay of labour and capital, of being brought into a high state of fertility.

196

Those arriving in Montreal and setting off down the Saint Lawrence would find friendly persons aboard with farms to sell.

I must not omit telling thee of an offer father had of a farm from a person who has three to let or sell. One he tells father of is one hundred and eighty acres with a good commodious house and outhouses, &c. on it which we may go into immediately, and remain there if we please for a twelve month at the expiration of which, should we not like it we may leave it without paying any rent or anything else. He will also give us an acre or more if we wish for a Garden. [Mary Mullett]

If a ready-made farm with a 'good commodious house' was chosen sight unseen, the first glimpse of it could have been similar to Susanna Moodie's experience:

"I guess," quoth our Yankee driver, "that at the bottom of this 'ere swell you'll find yourself *to hum;*" and plunging into a short path cut through the wood, he pointed to a miserable hut, at the bottom of a steep descent, and cracking his whip, exclaimed, " 'Tis a smart location that. I wish you Britishers may enjoy it."

I gazed upon the place in perfect dismay, for I had never seen such a shed called a house before. "You must be mistaken; that is not a house, but a cattle-shed, or a pig-sty."

...The driver, however, was well used to such roads, and steering as dexterously between the black stumps, at length drove up, not to the door, for there was none to the house, but to the open space from which that absent, but very necessary, appendage had been removed. Three young steers and two heifers, which the driver proceeded to drive out, were quietly reposing upon the floor.

At length we arrived at our destined home. Hitherto I had not been to inspect, and I felt, I must confess, very much aghast when I saw it. It had to me the appearance of a mud-hut; but it was a fair specimen of a log-house or shanty, rough cast, and all the interstices between each log well filled with mortar. These kind of houses are always warmer than the more comely-looking frame buildings. [Mrs Edward Copleston]

197

Others found themselves pleased with what they found, even by chance:

half a mile from a school and good roads; it contains 200 acres, 30 acres cleared in grass; I bought the hay and eatage along with it and two log houses for 1200 dollars, £270 sterling and got immediate possession; the hay and eatage work 25£, the late owner having another large farm he has paid little attention to this and we have been very busy burning old logs and stumps. The land is of the first quality and a small creek runs through it; the wood that it grows is beech, elm, basswood, oak, birch, ash, maple, cedar and asp [ash]. [Robert Wade]

Those who arrived to join family who had gone before to prepare the place often found the prospect pleasant also.

Though the road is bad our little driver and his Canadian horses make nothing of it. When we arrived at a place where it branched off to the left, papa exclaimed, "this is my road." The waggon turned in and rolled gently along on a road much better than the one we had left. Indeed were it not for a few stumps it would not frighten even an English horse. I assure you, dear uncle and aunts, it was great pleasure to turn round and say, as we looked at the fine land covered with noble trees, "this is all ours." No one can deprive us of it. And when we caught a glimpse of our pretty house through the trees, we did indeed feel thankful to the Almighty who had brought us in safety to this happy home in the wilderness. Our dear John ran to meet us. We were together again after our long separation...
[Ellen Steele]

After more than a quarter-century in the country, Samuel Strickland had a considered opinion on the subject. He thought that buying a ready-made farm was better for most than starting in the bush, because inexperience would lead to error. Also he did not think that people coming from well-established places in Britain would know how to survive in the bush. However, he was very much in favour of the emigration of the working classes, who were often viewed with disfavour by other middle-class emigrants.

Thomas Radcliff summed up the pros and cons of choosing cleared land or bush. He thought the bush was cheaper, and in starting from scratch settlers could be sure of a clear title in their own choice of district, and the chance to choose one's neighbours to some extent. On the other hand, the bush was far from everything, including neighbours, mills and markets, without church or doctor. One was alone and the road was bad.

Life in the clearings offered immediate accommodations, no heavy labour in chopping trees and brush, with both mill and market nearby, and perhaps church and doctor also. Its disadvantages were the danger of a clouded title and liability for a predecessor's debts, unfortunate neighbours and no room to bring in one's friends from home.

As John M'Donald had warned, the initial experience of finding the land and claiming it had many unpleasant aspects. The weather always seemed to be too wet or too humid, and various beasts intruded.

> This will not, however, prevent reptiles, such as snakes and lizards, from getting in. I saw a snake myself sucking a frog nigh my tent, but we killed it, and when it got a stroke on the head, it shot out its poisonous fangs. After this we grew more afraid of the venomous reptiles. We saw numbers of squirrels running about our beds; and we were frequently deprived of sleep from the unwelcome intrusions of oxen and cows, which, straying from their owners, came close to our tents, and we were much terrified, lest they should have pulled down our tabernacles about our ears. The swine would come to our very heads, and take away any thing they could find or see; and they seemed to be very fond of their own flesh, seizing what flesh meat we had, and running away with it in their mouths, so that we were obliged to pursue them, in order to recover it. [John M'Donald]

> Either a mink or an otter found out our thawing process, and more than once walked off with our joint bodily, and I well remember a 'company day,' when I went to the box, the joint was gone—a fine haunch it was too, and we had to wait till another one was thawed. [Alexander Ferrier]

199

In addition to these annoyances, we had to encounter another, and that a very serious evil, especially to those who have never previously known or experienced it, namely, the musquitoes. This is a very aggravating and distressing circumstance, as they tormented us both by day and night continually. The only remedy left to avoid this serious inconvenience, was the kindling of fires, which tended greatly to keep them away. Whenever they stung, it pierced through the skin. I have had my legs all over pierced with the fangs of these tormenting and mischievous insects.... The only cure was to bathe them in cold water, and rub them with salt. [John M'Donald]

For three days I had been disgusted with the dirtiness, noise and grossness of the Canadian boatmen, and during as many nights, had been prevented from sleeping by the fumes of rum and tobacco, the bites of musquetoes, and the hardness of the planks which formed my bed. [John Howison]

John Rowan added blackflies to the mosquitoes:

There is only one drawback to the perfect happiness of the angler on these rivers, and that is the flies. I suppose they are sent to prevent him from being too happy. There are days in the fishing season when the sun is obscured by a sort of haze—dull, close, sweltering days—when the thin-skinned man (especially if his hair be of a reddish or ginger hue) is unable to endure them. Ointments, veils, gloves, tobacco-smoke! nothing can protect him. He is reduced to a state of temporary idiocy, and unless he wishes that state of misery to be permanent he had better fly to his tent, where, sitting of a smoke of burning cedar-bark, so pungent and stifling that the tears flow from his eyes and blood-stains trickle down his punctured cheeks, he may experience some alleviation of his suffering.

Rowan goes on to suggest keeping to the open, using a complicated system of veils, and finding the dirtiest possible unguents. He particularly recommends a mixture of half tar and half pork fat against both mosquitoes and blackflies. The mosquitoes trouble him most at night, and he names leech-like blackflies and tiny sandflies, but neither house flies nor horse flies, perhaps because they do not bite as much.

Either at the point where the settler was searching out his lot, or soon after when he had to go to the mill or the town, or simply to a neighbour's, he would find that one of the worst aspects of working and living in the bush was getting lost.

We soon left the cleared land, and now for the first time I found myself in the virgin forest, or as it is universally called in U. Canada 'the bush'. The novelty of the situation very pleasant and exciting we rode on following the rode, sometimes only consisting of an Indian trail but at length we had the mortification to find our guide did not know where we were, and here we wandered about till dark, and had every prospect of spending the night in the forest, had we not fortunately met with a settler returning from Coburg. We were quite out of our course and going exactly the wrong way. We followed him for 8 miles, and he then treated us and our horses with his homly fare in the log cabin, and sent his son along with us on our way to Aldersville [in Alnwick township] thro the bush. [John Leeming]

A story from another part of the County is of a settler's wife who blew a horn in the evening to guide her husband home from another clearing where he was working. One night when she had been blowing the horn longer than usual, a stranger who had recently arrived in that part of the 'Queen's Bush' came out of the forest, hurrying towards her. He had been lost since the day before and hearing her horn had followed the sound, hoping and praying that she would not stop blowing it until he had been guided to her clearing. [Edward Marsh]

When the settler arrived at his land after the necessary formalities, his first task was to arrange a shelter for that night. On the following day he could begin to clear, consider where to put the house and so on.

A settler upon getting posession of his land, general erects on the most convenient spot, a shanty, which is a temporary hut, made of any materials at hand, with a rude roof, it is commonly open on one side, nigh to which during the night the inmates who sleep within, raise a great fire to keep themselves warm.

This shanty is put up in a few hours, and affords a protection to the settler, while he examines for a spot to build his log-house, and preparing the materials necessary. [William Cattermole]

About an hour before nightfall preparation is made for sleeping, and what is termed a camp is formed for this purpose, in a summary way, by placing a ridge pole of ten feet upon two forked sticks six feet in length, and stuck firmly in the ground. Against this ridge pole are laid, at one side, a set of poles, obliquely; leaving the other side which forms the front, entirely open, not only to admit the heat of a large fire, which is lighted up before it, but the smoke, also, to banish the musquetos. A thick coat of hemlock boughs, or of bark stripped quickly from the standing trees, and covering the poles, keeps off the rain or dew. [Thomas Radcliff]

A bundle of spruce boughs laid across the extreme end, with a sack of potatoes for my pillow, formed my bed; and if I had no door opposite, all the cold that got in necessarily passed through the fire and smoke. [George Head]

Wretched habitations indeed! and utterly insufficient to prevent the torrents of rain, ...from penetrating these temporary tabernacles. Such substitutes, when the branches wither, are almost complete open at the sides. Some, who are able, cover them with blankets, or whatever else they can obtain, on the roof; others have them covered round about. [John M'Donald]

Samuel Strickland suggested that fresh boughs made a fine bed if combined with 'a preventive.'

...I prepared our bed, by breaking a quantity of fine hemlock-brush to thatch the bottom of the camp, to keep us from the damp ground, which it did quite effectually. I have camped out, I dare say, hundreds of times, both in winter and summer; and I never caught cold yet. I recommend, from experience, a hemlock-bed, and hemlock-tea, with a dash of whiskey in it, merely to assist the flavour, as the best preventive.

Building the house deserves a chapter to itself, which follows ("Our House").

However, even before the house, some land would have to be cleared of trees and the dense bush which surrounded them. This task required a certain know-how.

The light brush, which included trees up to six inches in diameter, would be cut as close to the ground as possible and piled, either in heaps or windrows. They were allowed to dry for a time and then burnt. The best time for doing this was in the autumn, once the worst heat of the summer had abated but before the onset of the snow, which hampered movement in the bush.

After the small growth was removed, the heavy chopping began, and this continued through the winter. Some people thought that it was easier to kill the trees first and then chop the deadwood.

> Some persons take a quicker mode of clearing land, though not so seemly in appearance, by girdling, that is cutting down all the light timber, brush, &c. and simply chopping a notch round the heavy trees, deep enough to destroy future vegetation, leaving it standing 2 or 3 years, when it may be easily cut down, better prepared than green forests, subject however to this inconvenience, that cattle are often destroyed by the falling trees; about half of the labour in burning, &c. is saved.
> [William Cattermole]

The object in chopping was to place the tree as close to the piles of underbrush as possible, because it would cause less work hauling them later.

> I began & chopped down some trees this morning but the greatest art is in laying the trees the right way, labour chopping it up for logging making it into heaps for burning. [William Mickle]

Both heaps and windrows needed to be well packed to ensure the best burning. Windrows were difficult to control once they were aflame, and often resulted in uncontrollable forest fires, which were one of the greatest fears of the pioneers, who might lose all they had in a few minutes as a result of one.

For a Methodist minister in eastern Ontario, who perhaps dealt too closely in visions of the fiery depths of hell, the sight of a burning 'slack,' or heap of dried underbrush, was almost more than he could bear:

> When ye burn a slack, the roaring of the fire is fearful to hear, and the sight awful to behold... [Joseph Abbott]

The great trees, once down, had to be cut into logs. There were too many to be of any use, so they were set on fire if possible (one reason for laying them in the windrows) to clear away the smaller branches. The charred remains could then be hauled and piled for another fire.

It was demanding work. One book of advice stated, "But, say you are determined to go on wild land, I am far from advising this, especially if you have never been accustomed to hard manual labour." The surprising suggestion for those overcome by the exertion is to recover by "sucking the underdone leg of a partridge."

Some of the best logs would be kept, especially if the live trees were well placed near the site of the house or barn. No doubt the wise woodcutter would also be keeping an eye out for trunks which would make suitable fencing material.

Fence rails needed to be long and straight; those with too big a curve would offer animals inside the enclosure the opportunity to stick their heads through and upset the whole structure. Although rail fences were not the first concern of the pioneer, he probably heard of them early and began to keep watch for suitable trees.

If the pioneer had a knowledge of wood, he might also select certain kinds of trees for special treatment in case he wanted to use them for the building of furniture, in shingle making or to sell to craftsmen.

This activity was hard labour and parts of it, such as hauling logs, could not be done by a single man alone. He had the choice of hiring someone to assist him or relying on the communal work of the neighbourhood, where people helped one another, usually in the form of bees.

Finding labour to hire was not always easy, there being both a shortage of workers and a high price to pay for them.

Labor will always be dear as long as land is given away.

Robert Wade's observation is true, for why should men work for others when they could be doing the same thing on their own land which was available to them at no cost?

Even with land grants, there were other expenses in setting up house, as we have seen, and so there were usually young men about who could be hired. They would come to help clear the underbrush, but as well as being paid they had to be lodged and fed also. Abbott observed that if they had families, they would simply settle nearby, living in the rudest of log houses for the time they worked there. James Scott suggests that if the pioneers hired too many men to help, they could fall into serious debt.

The government expected that those who received land grants would begin clearing immediately; they also had to clear a certain amount to make the grant final. In addition, most people needed to clear several acres to ensure they had space for planting in the following seasons. The exact amount which was possible and the rate of clearing were a matter of disagreement. Thomas Radcliff claimed to have cleared thirty acres after only a few months on the land, a sum which his editor places in doubt by quoting a rate of two acres a year, derived from local assessment rolls.

According to Robert Wade,

We have cleared 75 acres of land, and a man will chop an acre in 8 days and five men will log it in a day if the weather be dry.

After taking possession of his property in mid-July 1831, William Mickle was able to report in September,

I have ab^t 3/4 of an acre chopped up ready for logging but in consequence of the very wet fall I am not able to burn the Brush which must be done before it can be loged and so am unable to set in any fall wheat but must depend upon spring wheat, Barley, Oats, &c.

One of the dangers of the clearing process was that working with an axe might result in serious injuries.

> John Plews called at our house about a week since, he was then very well; we have heard since that he cut himself with an axe. [Robert Wade]

If a man had an axe injury, he might well bleed to death before help came, or if he survived there was little useful medical treatment to help it heal; infections were common and their causes not understood. Added to this was the loss of working time while he was laid up. Samuel Strickland told of assisting a wounded man to a neighbour's, where he remained for ten months!

> I have been working on a farm, chopping, and other work; but I have been very unfortunate, I've cut myself four or five times; I cut my hand in the summer whilst mowing with Meredith Orman, on Mr. Silcog's field; I cut my foot very bad four weeks ago, its not well yet. I cut two of my toes off; Mr Silcog sewed them on again; they seem to be getting on very well considering the time. You must not think that I dislike the country on account of my misfortunes, for if I was to cut my leg right off, I should not think of returning to Corsley again, for I could do much better here with one leg than in Corsley with two [William Singer]

Logging was hard work but if the labourers were a group of high-spirited young boys, even a little play might come into it.

> The MacPhersons were strong, rugged men, but James became crippled with rheumatism, and Andrew went blind. One day, his boys nearly grown up, were bringing home large logs of wood which they wanted to pile up to take less room, one of which they could scarcely put up, he being blind but out talking to them, came to their aid, and when he got ready for a lift they not only quit lifting but one of them got on top of the log and he put it up alone with the remark that 'it *is* pretty heavy.' [Hugh Ray]

Aside from the humour in this story, it also demonstrates the great strength which these men built up working in the bush.

Once the logs were gone, the fields were left, dotted with stumps. These could not be removed right away, and so the farmer worked around them for a time using an A-shaped harrow, an adze or an axe. The stumps remained for several years.

> I believe most land requires three years to get it into profitable cultivation, and seven years before the stumps are all cleared off, excepting pine stumps, which remain many years an eyesore to the neat farmer, long before which time the emigrant is equal to his new life, having a due regard to preserving all his manure, till he finds the land requires it... [William Cattermole]

Naturally there were entrepreneurs who tried to come up with a technology to deal with the stumps.

> Scott's 'monkey', a machine which he invented to pull out stumps, was long celebrated. It was like the big wheel of an old-fashioned spinning wheel, and just about as well adapted for pulling out stumps as a spinning wheel would be.
> [Alexander Ferrier]

Eventually, the stumps would have rotted enough to remove them. All the auxiliary roots would be severed, then the oxen would be brought in, with chains attached either to their shoulders or their horns and heads. They would pull and break the tap root and the stump would be free.

The loose stump was valuable and not wasted. Set on its side, it created a good barrier, and numbers of them lined up created a fence, sometimes more than six feet high. With their dead roots intertwined, they were solid and worked well as a form of early fence for pioneer fields. They kept stock in (or out, as needed) and also created a nook where brambles could grow, providing wild berries in future years. Songbirds, game birds and small mammals also took advantage of the shelter.

Our House

when we caught a glimpse of our pretty house
through the trees, we did indeed feel thankful
Ellen Steele

The first area for clearing was the site of the house and its surroundings.

The wise settler would choose the site of the house with various qualities in mind. To begin, it would need to be dry underneath for reasons of health. Those who had lived in Britain knew that living in a damp area was unhealthy, because the open hearths which were the basis for heating were inadequate for keeping a damp building fully dry. What they may not have realized was that the summers in Upper Canada were both hotter and more humid than Britain, and swampy surroundings would intensify the discomfort.

On the other hand, there needed to be water nearby. The housewife would not wish to carry her water for cooking and washing from a long distance. Most settlers would choose to build near enough to a stream or pond. It was unlikely that the difficulties inherent in digging a well would be among the new settlers' first priorities.

I am five miles from a mill, have good water within 50 yards of the door [Robert Forrest]

The other consideration was proximity to the road. For many, ease of transportation would have been a good reason for having the house near the thoroughfare. This might mean that

209

the source of water was more distant, or that the workmen would have to walk far each morning to reach some fields. There was an argument for putting the house in the centre of the plot of land also, for ease of access to all worksites. The difficulty with this choice was that at certain times of the year—spring and winter—the long lane which led to the house would be almost impassable because of mud or snow, making getting in and out difficult. Descriptions left by itinerant preachers and travellers indicate that many of the first-generation log cabins were still near the road.

As we know from the sites of modern farmhouses, first built in the later nineteenth century, the next generation of builders chose to work well back from the road but still in sight of it. Since they had wells they did not have to consider the placing of streams quite so much.

The remains of the original house at Lot 9 Concession X in Manvers township, for example, lies a great distance from either of the nearest roads, but near a stream. Even now, the stream runs through a wooded area, but at the time the house was occupied, there would have been no near neighbour. The house which replaced it, a spacious Italianate yellow brick of the late 1800s, sits on higher ground about a hundred yards from the road, and until the 1960s was reached from the road by a lane closely lined with trees to make using it easier in winter. The builders of each house had differing priorities.

The Scottish settlers in Lanark were given suggestions for the design of their houses in Lamond's *A Narrative of the Rise & Progress of Emigration* but the charming cottages pictured there were based on old-country ideas, where lumber or even bricks might be easy to come by and there would be roads for transporting them where necessary. For people who had to find the materials readily at hand and then erect the buildings themselves, these plans were more fantasy than practical reality. They may have been useful for those who built the next generation of farmhouses.

Settlers may well have had dreams of the kind of habitation they would like, but the pressure of getting something up which would provide the necessary shelter was all that mattered. They needed the house in place quickly so they could continue with clearing the land and preparing to plant during the next season.

John M'Donald has this to say about the first houses:

> Their method of building their huts, or log-houses, is the following: they take the small logs, and cut them to certain lengths and breadths, and lay them one above another, notching them into each other at the four corners of angles. In this way they proceed till this substitute for a house is finished. The front wall is commonly made highest.—The method of roofing the houses is this: They take the hollow trees, as there are many of these rotten internally, and split them through the midst, and lay them close together, one is laid on every joint, with its mouth down, which is the hollow side, and the rain is thus received into the hollow of each side. They proceed thus till the roof is finished. Many of them are very roughly constructed, but a tradesman could make a very good job of the same materials, by jointing them together.—Others again cover their roofs with the bark of trees, but in my judgement the other method is preferable.
>
> The gaps in the walls must be closed or filled up with pieces of wood and clay. This however does not stand long, and they are not at all nice as to the method. The only light which many of them have, is by the door and a wide chimney. But whenever a farmer has it in his power, he builds one more durable and substantial, the logs being squared and laid one upon another.

In some cases, the walls would be more finely finished.

> I have a well-finished log-house, lathed and plaistered in the inside, with a brick chimney, the house containing a kitchen and two rooms, besides the upstairs. My garden is at the side of it, surrounded by a picket fence. My barn is built of good logs, which, with a new addition to it, is ninety-six feet long by twenty-six wide, covered with shingles, and contains my stable... [John Kelly]

Martin Doyle gives a more explicit description of the way the logs are laid to ensure the rain runs off:

Bush Farm near Chatham, 1838, by Philip John Bainbridge (Courtesy of National Archives of Canada, C-11811)

The roof was formed of logs split into four lengths, then hollowed out, and laid with the concave and the convex sides alternately upwards and downwards, so as to overlap one another, like long tiles sloping from the ridge to the eaves, so that each alternate log formed a gutter or channel to carry off the rain. The openings between the logs forming the walls were closed by mud and moss mixed together; and sometimes these shanties had a window, sometimes not.

Doyle was of the opinion that it took two men two days to build a log house.

In his book of advice to potential emigrants, William Cattermole says:

The usual dimensions of a log-house are 18 feet by 16 feet; the roof is covered with shingles or bark, and the floor with rough hewn plank; the interstices between the logs, which compose the walls, being filled up with pieces of wood and clay, and a hollow cone of coarse basket-work does the office of a chimney. The whole expense of a house of this kind will not exceed from 10/. to 12/. [shillings] supposing the emigrant puts the work all out, but much of this work is done gratis. I have seen great numbers erecting, it is done by what is termed making a bee, which is, collecting as many of the most expert and able-bodied settlers to assist at the raising, by which the walls are put up in a single day, without peril of life or limb among the workmen, and in that case, the whole expense often does not exceed 4/. or 5/. But I should state that a superior log-house, to a farm of 150 acres of land, will cost from 20/. to 25/.

Robert Forrest wrote from Lanark County in 1824 about his house:

I must now say something of our selves. we have no reason to complain having always had good health—We have put up a good house lately which has hindered our Clearing considerably. It is 26 feet long, 18 1/2 wide and is 24 feet high from the floor to the rigin. It is well furnished and has a good Stove Chimney in it altho this [has] been rather a large undertaking for a new begginer. the frequent accidents of fire made me resolve upon doing it—we have two good Cows and a calf. 12 acres of cleared land and under crop.

213

The size of the house would depend on the ambition of the builder, his experience and the number of hands involved in the construction.

Once the walls were up, the roof had to be covered in. Shingles were often used, created by peeling elm bark and allowing it to dry. This was done first, so the drying could take place during the cutting of the logs and erection of the walls.

M'Donald described a more elaborate form of roofing shingles:

> ...then in place of slates, take cuttings of clear fir, eighteen inches long, and split them up to the thickness of 3/8ths of an inch in the one end, and very thin and tapering in the other; these they call shingles. Some dress them well with the plane, and others with a drawing knife; but they are nailed on in the same manner as slates, and when properly done and painted blue, they look like slates.

Samuel Strickland added another dimension:

> A log shanty, twenty-four feet long by sixteen, is large enough to begin with, and should be roofed either with shingles or troughs. A small cellar should be dug near the fire-place, commodious enough to hold twenty or thirty bushels of potatoes, a barrel or two of pork. etc.

Robert Wade was an early arrival in Hamilton township, and was fortunate enough to find a ready-made dwelling:

> I could have bought a farm cheaper with better housing, but situation makes a great difference in this country. We never had reason to repent settling here unless we had settled near Kingston or Montreal; about York is very unhealthy on account of a great deal of marsh land and stagnant water. When we came to this place there were no buildings but two old log houses, the one we repaired up for ourselves and the other for our cattle. The size of our house is 22 x 18 ft.; we have partitioned three small bedrooms off below and we have built an addition which answers for dairy and kitchen. Sawn boards are 25s [shillings] per thousand feet, but joiners' work is very dear; we have done all our work ourselves; we have lined the inside with boards and we have a boarded floor. It is true that

many of the houses are mean and the inhabitants poor, but it need not be the case, the farmers are their own landlords and stewards and their farms and houses are done in so slovenly a manner that you can have no idea of it; but we ought to make a great allowance for them, when they came here they had nothing to begin on, and as I have said before, no landlords to assist them to build their houses. The country around here is improving very fast; there have been seven frame houses built within a mile of us since we came here. We intend to build a house in two or three years' time...

Wade's ambition was not misplaced, for in five years, a short enough time in the pioneer period, he was able to report:

We have had a very busy summer; we have built a brick house 44 ft long and 20 ft wide, with a stone cellar under it. Cellars are very necessary here to keep out the cold in winter and heat in summer; the house is two stories high; we shall have two rooms and a passage through the middle in the lower story and three rooms in the other.

Samuel Strickland did not care for log dwellings, but contradicts himself in his suggestion about making an early move:

As soon as the settler is ready to build, let him put up a good frame, roughcast, or stone house, if he can possibly raise the means, as stone, timber, and lime cost nothing but the labour of collecting and carrying the materials. When I say that they 'cost nothing' I mean that no cash is required for these articles, as they can be prepared by the exertion of the family.

Some did indeed have both the ambition and know-how to create an immediate house one step up from the log shack, as Joseph Carrothers observed:

Dear Willy I have been very busy this summer building a house and I am living in it now. I have a neat Cottage House 30 feet by 20. The out walls 10 feet high of mud and inside walls of brick. It is well thought of in this country (stones is very rare in this place). I have a dislike to the timber Houses. The are very cold in winter and very hot in summer and the are allways sinking and twisting. I got help from Brothers and Cosins but I

215

was Brick layer and Carpenter my self. The wondered I done the fireplaces so well.

Inside the house it was always smoky. Initially there may not have been a regular chimney, as William Cattermole's and Robert Forrest's comments above make clear. Chimney-making required some expertise and the time to put it into effect, and even then may not have worked well. As William Mickle wrote to his brother in 1832 from Eramosa:

> my chimney is built of split cedar & daubed inside with mud but smokes so badly that I have been obliged to keep the door open there all winter not having any one to advise me when I built my Shanty. It is not by any means so commodious as it might have been...

However, keeping the door open might not have been a good idea, as Alexander Ferrier observed:

> Everything froze in our house, and we daren't leave the door open in case the wolves should come in, although our fireplace smoked dreadfully.

Even in the shanty, there would have been some attempt at making a bed. John Weldrick's first day in Osprey township was spent in creating a place for his wife to sleep:

> Father then cut down some browse for the cattle, tied them to the sleigh at the door, and started to make a bedstead by boring holes in the logs, using a crotch stick for the third post, sharpening the other end and driving it down in the mud floor. Cedar branches formed the mattress; on these were put their blankets, and they were soon fast asleep. [Edward Marsh]

The first bed was a very primitive affair, with the new arrivals sleeping on cedar or hemlock boughs, which smelled fresh and good at a time when both the house and people probably did not. They were also easy to refresh simply by cutting more not far from the door.

Once the pioneers were more settled, they could 'fill the bed-ticks with moss,' which had the advantage of greater softness. Within a year or so, they could transfer to straw ticks and feather quilts and pillows, which would remain the norm for a century or more. The straw came from their own cutting and the feathers from the many ducks killed for food, or from the poultry they raised themselves. There would also have been a great many feathers from pigeons also, but pigeon-feathers in pillows were considered bad luck.

Some of those who came to the log house were not arriving from across the sea, but only from their parents' dwelling in a more settled part of the country. These lucky people would have been able to put up the log house ahead of time, and then arrive with an assortment of furnishings which would seem rich beside their emigrant neighbours:

> A house was built—a log one, of the Canadian rustic style then much in vogue, containing one room, and that not very large either; and to this my father brought his young bride. Their outfit consisted, on his part, of a colt, a yoke of steers, a couple of sheep, some pigs, a gun, and an axe. My mother's *dot* [dowry] comprised a heifer, bed and bedding, a table and chairs, a chest of linen, some dishes and a few other necessary items with which to begin housekeeping. This will not seem a very lavish set-out for a young couple on the part of parents who were at that time more than usually well-off. But there was a large family on both sides, and the old people then thought it the better way to let the young folk try their hand at making a living before they gave them of their abundance. If they succeeded they wouldn't need much, and if they did not, it would come better after a while. [Canniff Haight]

When Sarah Hallen married John Drinkwater in October 1840, she went to the house he had already built, but the furnishings compare with those described by Canniff Haight above, including things lent by the older generation:

> We began with nothing but the farm which consists of between 40 and 50 acres cleared, some cows, steers and heifers and oxen, a barn and cattle shed. Our house is square: a kitchen, parlor, a bedroom; no rooms upstairs are finished as yet. Our furniture consists of a table, two chairs borrowed from Mr. Drinkwater [her father-in-law]. We now sport six chairs of our

own painted a most brilliant color, glazed curtains, 2 guncases, basket work bottle hung on the log work; the chimney is nearly built, its small and in the parlour, but quite big enough to heat the room which is square. There are curtains at the windows in the bedroom, a bed, a barrel with a board on it for the wash hand stand, hanging looking glass, a rough shelf with a book on it, trunk with my clothes in, also some on strings. When my things came had two or three more boxes and two pots de chambre. A small entrance at the front and back room a kitchen with a nice chimney, two windows made like the parlor, rough shelves, a carpenter's bench for a table and five spare barrels, a clock (a treasure), two iron pots, one kettle, a saucepan to hold about a pint [i.e., small], a large iron spoon, one dozen knives and forks, four German silver tablespoons, six teaspoons, two German silver candlesticks, snuffers and tray, a black tin teapot, one dozen cups and saucers, seaweed pattern blue and white, half dozen small plates, four dishes, two pie dishes, soup tureen, two vegetable dishes, half dozen tumblers, two salt sellers, two water jugs, cream jug. Our larder consists of a piece of fresh pork, some salt and a dried fish, a keg of butter and flour and potatoes. My mother sent me also some onions which were most acceptable as I stewed our meat, which made it last until they killed four pigs, which we did ten days after we were married... Oh dear, I have forgotten to mention we have 3 lbs. white sugar, a little pepper and mustard, a dozen white candles, all of which Mr. Drinkwater was kind enough to give me until we got more, and 2 lbs. of tea. Anna milks and gives us milk and butter—very kind as we have no girl.

Eventually they would separate the house from the outbuildings and surrounding forest by a small yard and fence. Many families, unlike the Wades, remained in their log house for years. Around it grew outbuildings and the elements of a happy farm, as Canniff Haight described:

The houses were almost invariably inclosed with a picket or board fence, with a small yard in front. Shade and ornamental trees were not in much repute. All around them the 'boundless contiguity of shade;' but it awakened no poetic sentiment. To them it had been a standing menace, which had cost the expenditure of their best energies, year after year, to push further and further back. The time had not come for ornamenting their grounds and fields with shrubs and trees, unless they could minister to their comfort in a more substantial way. The gardens were generally well supplied with currant and gooseberry bushes. Pear, plum and cherry trees, as well as the orchard itself, were close at hand. Raspberries and strawberries were abundant in every new clearing. The sap-bush furnished the sugar and maple molasses [maple syrup]. So that most of the requisites for good living were within easy hail.

The first concern of a thrifty farmer was to possess a large barn, with out-houses or sheds attached for his hay and straw, and for the protection of his stock during the cold and stormy weather of fall and winter. Lumber cost him nothing, save the labour of getting it out. There was, therefore, but little to prevent him from having plenty of room in which to house his crops, and as the process of threshing was slow it necessitated more space than is required now. The granary, pig-pen and corn-crib were usually separate. The number and extent of buildings on a flourishing homestead, inclosed with strong board fences, covered a wide area...

Haight goes on to remark that the log house was coloured, outside, only by nature. Inside, the more ambitious might find a way to plaster and then tint the walls, but by and large it, too, was as nature left it.

The second house was another matter, but according to Haight, who wrote in the late 1870s, it too had vanished by that time and been replaced by 'more modern' structures. His point of view was that of the Bay of Quinte, one of the earliest areas settled and so perhaps somewhat ahead of parts of the country farther inland.

So the first house was of log and quite simple, but here is the second house (of the 1830s in Quinte) described by Haight:

I hardly know in what style of architecture they were built; indeed, I think it was one peculiar to the people and the age. They were strong, substantial structures, erected with an eye to comfort rather than show. They were known afterwards as Dutch houses, usually one story high, and built pretty much after the same model; a parallelogram, with a wing at one end, and often to both. The roofs were very steep; with a row of dormer windows, and sometimes two rows looking out of their board sides, to give light to the chambers and sleeping rooms up-stairs. The living rooms were generally large, with low ceilings, and well supplied with cupboards, which were always filled with blankets and clothing, dishes, and a multitude of good things for the table. The bed rooms were always small and cramped, but they were sure to contain a good bed—a bed which required some ingenuity, perhaps, to get into, owing to its heights; but when once in, the great feather tick fitted kindly to the weary body, and the blankets over you soon wooed your attention away from the narrowness of the apartment. Very often the roof projected over, giving an elliptic shape to one side, and the projection of about six feet formed a cover of what was then called a long stoop, but which now-a-days would be known as a veranda. This was no addition to the lighting of the rooms, for the windows were always small in size and few in number. The kitchen usually had a double outside door—that is a door cut cross-wise through the middle, so that the lower part could be kept shut, and the upper left open if necessary. I do not know what particular object there was in this, unless to let the smoke out, for chimneys were more apt to smoke then than now; or, perhaps, to keep the youngsters in and let in fresh air. Whatever the object was, this was the usual way the outside kitchen door was made, with a wooden latch and leather string hanging outside to lift it, which was easily pulled in, and then the door was quite secure against intruders. The barns and out-houses were curiosities in after years: large buildings with no end of timber and all roof, like a great box with an enormous candle extinguisher set on it. But houses and barns are gone, and modern structures occupy their places, as they succeeded the rough log ones, and one can only see them as they are photographed upon the memory.

It is interesting that these Dutch houses, which would have appeared as palatial to the occupants of the log cabins, are cramped to Haight, whose grandparents lived in an even larger place. The old folks occupied the original settled property, while his parents had penetrated into the forest when they were newly married:

The old home, as it was called, was always a place of attraction, and especially so to the young people, who were sure of finding good cheer at grandfather's. What fun, after the small place called home, to have the run of a dozen rooms, to haunt the big cellar, with its great heaps of potatoes and vegetables, huge casks of cider, and well-filled bins of apples, or to sit at the table loaded with the good things which grandmother only could supply. How delicious the large piece of pumpkin pie tasted, and how toothsome the rich crullers that melted in the mouth! Dear old body! I can see her now going to the great cupboard to get me something, saying as she goes, "I'm sure the child is hungry." And it was true, he was always hungry; and how he managed to stow away so much is a mystery I cannot now explain. There was no place in the world more to be desired than this, and no spot in all the past the recollection of which is more bright and joyous.

When the second house was built, it was often very near the original log shack. The old house would then be used for something else, perhaps as storage for grain or a home for chickens. Old log houses survived for a long time under their new uses, and in the Ottawa Valley it is still possible to see them, decrepit but still useful now.

One visitor's conclusion was that the larger second houses were more than the occupants needed.

...amongst the farmers, who own perhaps thriving places, and have risen, with the improving value of land, from the primary condition perhaps of ordinary labourers and choppers, there prevails a curious taste for building a considerable sized two-storied brick or stone house for a show, putting curtains or blinds, the latter figuratively as well as literally, to the windows, and then living in the kitchens, furnishing none of the upper portions of the house, into which if you take a pilgrimage, you will probably find one room half full of dried apple shreds, another of Indian corn, another of pumpkins, and so on.

For the more genteel settler, some attempt would be made to recreate the qualities of the old-world house in the new. While they might look down on their neighbours for their 'slovenly' ways, as Robert Wade did, it was probable that these poor people had never lived with very much and would not have considered that even the rudimentary comforts of Catharine Parr Traill's house would be within their grasp:

In the parlour we are kept warm and cheered by a Franklin stove a very handsome adornment to our room. The floor is covered with an Indian mat plaited by my friends the squaws from the inner bark of the cedar. We have a handsome sofa with brass railing which also serves as a bed for one or even two persons. I have made blinds for windows of green cambric with white muslin draperies which have a light and pretty effect. These with the white painted chairs, a stained table, book case and some large maps and prints of General LaFayette, Kosciusco, Fox and Brougham form the tout ensemble of our log sitting room.

In fact, people from varying backgrounds in the old country might well see the same place in quite different ways, as the agricultural historian Robert Leslie Jones observed:

Women of refinement, like Mrs. Moodie, found life in the bush intolerable. On the other hand, it cannot be doubted that to emigrants from the Hebrides or from the famine areas of Ireland even the remotest backwoods of Upper Canada must have partaken of the character of an earthly paradise.

Life in the Clearings

Every country is a home to the brave.
Robert Gouger

Once the first days had passed, when shelter had to be built and the initial arrangements made for food and fuel, the pioneers could begin their new day-to-day life. They established their home, met their neighbours, discovered what sort of community they lived in, perhaps reached out to the family they had left behind. They established their own roles in the area: as labour, as members of church or school, as consumers.

The trip from Montreal to wherever they eventually stopped, whether it was Glengarry or on the shores of Lake Huron, must have seemed puzzling, endless and exhausting. Once they had stopped, they would discover what day-to-day travel in their new land was really like.

Transportation

From the descriptions of emigrants' voyages from Montreal to their new homes in Upper Canada, we have some idea of the situation of transportation at the time. There were basically three modes: on the water, on horseback or via horsedrawn vehicle on the roads, or on foot.

Ideas about the acceptable nature of the long distances between farms or settlements might vary even within the same family. James Mullett wrote to his grandmother about the family's impending move:

We are all looking forward to remove up the County on our new farm it is 20 miles back from any village or store and a Lake to cross of three miles. I suppose thee wilt think it a great way but we do not. Unless it was 60 or 70 miles and that is not far in this Country.

William Mullett (Courtesy National Archives of Canada, MG 24 I 132)

Five days later, his sister Deborah also wrote:

We had two of the fatest geese I ever seen and a fine large piece of roast beef, as we have always killed a fat cow the week before as yet, but I don't know how it will be when we get into the woods, where we are going the latter end of next month. I hope it will answer father's expectation. there are none of our friends scarcely like our going there I do not like it at all myself as there are no friends and the nearest friends that will be to us is forty miles and its eighteen miles back through nothing but woods.

Throughout the accounts of both settlers and visitors there are tales of lengthy walks. In fact, our own ideas of what constitutes a lengthy walk might conflict with theirs.

> We lived about a mile and a half from the lake shore, and I took advantage of my vicinity to the water to bathe daily. I found great refreshment in this, for the weather was very hot and dry. [Samuel Strickland]

> On foot, and alone, I set out for the village, five miles off. I never considered it a hardship to walk five miles on a good road, but on this occasion, tired and exhausted as I was, it proved a formidable undertaking. [Joseph Abbott]

For those whose daily round involved travelling, there was a great deal of walking to do. This was very true of some early clergy, who were too poor to afford a horse when they first began preaching. Here is William Fraser's experience at a time of family excitement:

> I immediately set out and walked down from Grant's to Clarke Helicks, 7 miles. This far Mr. Grant very kindly accompanied me. I lay just an hour on the floor, and at daybreak set out again. It rained incessantly for half the day and the roads were extremely bad. I found it impossible to obtain a horse on the way and was obliged to walk completely through 38 miles—I reached home completely fatigued about 6 o'clock—where I found Mrs. F. [his wife] and her son doing extremely well. [His son had been born unexpectedly while he was away.]

Despite these difficulties, the easiest way to journey along the roads was on foot. Even the best road in the colony, Yonge Street, was treacherous. Any others were a constant source of comment. In summer they were rutted and dirty, with holes which might well have gone across the width of the track. In spring they were impassable with mud, and often the same in autumn. That left winter, which, surprisingly, was the best time to travel. Sleighs or other conveyances on runners could make headway in the snow and people found journeys became quite

pleasant. Once you were bundled up, the cold could be kept at
bay.

> It may be observed that the winter season is the most favorable
> to land carriage, as the roads then admit of sledging in all
> directions, which is a very expeditious mode of conveyance, and
> attended with but little draft; so that one horse or ox can, in
> this manner, easily draw double what he can upon wheels.
> [Martin Doyle]

Those fresh from England found the depths of the
Canadian winter dazzling. George Head described the scene as he
drove down the Saint Lawrence in February:

> Although the air was piercingly cold, the sun shone forth with
> great brilliancy, shewing signs of his increasing power by the
> icicles which, in many warm and sheltered situations, already
> fringed the eaves of the houses....The foaming rapids, the heavy
> roaring of the waters, the huge slabs of ice ripped from the
> summits of the rocks, whose black desolate looking points
> formed a striking contrast with the overpowering whiteness of
> the snow,—all these were objects which irresistibly rivetted the
> attention.

> The weather was fine and clear, but so cold that the bay horses
> might have been mistaken for iron-grey, so powdered over were
> they with frost. [George Head]

Some new arrivals did not find winter as picturesque.
They found the cold more than they could bear, as Mrs Jameson
observed despite being 'well wrapped up in furs and buffalo
robes':

> I returned trembling and shuddering, chilled outwardly and
> inwardly, for none of my fur defences prevailed against the
> frost and the current of icy air, through which we glided, or
> rather flew, along the smooth road.

Despite feeling this way, Mrs Jameson was able to provide
a romantic vision of a well-stocked conveyance for freight:

The wood-sleighs are my delight; a large platform of boards is raised upon runners, with a few upright poles held together at the top by a rope, the logs of oak, pine and maple, are then heaped up to the height of six or seven feet. On the summit lie a couple of deer frozen stiff, their huge antlers projecting in a most picturesque fashion, and on these again, a man is seated with a blanket round him, his furred cap drawn down upon his ears, and his scarlet woollen comforter forming a fine bit of colour. He guides with a pole his two patient oxen, the clouds of vapour curling from their nostrils into the keen frosty air...

Mrs Moodie also had a romantic vision of winter sleighing:

It is the favourite afternoon drive of young and old, and when the wind, sweeping over such a broad surface of ice, is not *too cold*, and you are well wrapped up in furs and buffalo robes, a sleigh ride on the ice is very delightful. Not that I can ever wholly divest myself of a vague, indistinct sense of danger, whilst rapidly gliding over this frozen mirror.... Still it is a pleasant sight of a bright, glowing, winter day, when the landscape glitters like a world composed of crystals, to watch the handsome sleighs, filled with well-dressed men and women, and drawn by spirited horses, dashing in all directions over this brilliant field of dazzling white.

The Bay is now strongly frozen over and presents today an enlivening scene. Last night there fell about an inch of light snow but the sportsmen have swept off a considerable space nearly opposite this house and then the active and fashionable game of Curling is being played by some scores of light hearted Spirits—Parties of pleasure in gallant sleighing equipage are constantly passing and repassing to and from the Peninsula Hotel. There is a shooting match just opposite our door on the Lake & the skaters borne on speedy foot are abroad in abundance. All appears to be hilarity & joy. [William Fraser]

However, not everyone agreed about the gliding and flying, especially if they were used to the well-established thoroughfares of Britain.

On the morning of this day we set out in the midst of a fall of snow and after a not very agreeable drive of 6 or 7 hours we arrived safely at this place [London]. The roads of this part of Canada are by no means good. In fact in many parts the ruts were so deep that I could not believe but that we were in imminent peril though we were constantly assured by the driver that there was no danger. However we have fought our way through & are now in safety, for the present at the end of our journey. [William Fraser]

The condition of snow-covered roads depended a great deal on how much they were used. If there were many sleighs going back and forth, the snow would be packed down and the 'gliding' would be comfortable. In December 1840, Aitcheson Brown, a farmer in the Huron District, noted in his diary that he had "driven all the cattle up & down the road to improve it," thus flattening the snow in preparation for passing sleighs.

This presumed that you had a proper road or track to drive on; paths in the bush might be too narrow and cluttered with stumps to provide space for a sleigh.

The sleighing, about which we hear so much, is I am convinced unpracticable for us who have no beaten track; at least unless the ice most materially improves. I have had experience of it once and do not wish to repeat the experiment. About seven in the evening I set [out] to bring home some forty or fifty pounds on a handsleigh from McAndrew's, a distance of four-and-a-half miles, and I cannot have been less than four-and-a-half hours on the road—the last mile, I am convinced, took more than two hours. An unlucky cramp seized one of my legs, which would not hold out more than ten yards without a rest, and when I was ready to start again the sleigh was always frozen to the snow; the worst of it was that I could not keep myself in exercise long enough to keep warm.
[John Langton]

Here is a description which captures the full experience of driving in newly-fallen snow on these roads, a clergyman's account of struggling to reach a waiting congregation:

Sometimes, indeed, they were bad enough even in winter: on one occasion I had a fearful journey of it. There had been a heavy fall of snow the day before, accompanied by a high wind, which drifted up the roads very much. In one place, about four miles from my destination, my horses fairly stuck fast: I sent my servant to a house, at a little distance, for a shovel, to cut out a path for my leading horse; for I was obliged to drive two, one harnessed in front of the other, as one horse would not have been able to drag my sleigh over the heavy roads; but the trifling favour was denied me, with many ill-natured remarks, on the "sinful' practice o'breeking the Sabbath that gate; forbye travelling on that holy day." They "did na ken why sax days i'the week should na satisfee ony reasonable body." We had therefore to trample down the snow with our feet for more than a hundred yards, when the noble animals, as if instinctively aware of my anxiety to get on, plunged gallantly through of their own accord, after me. We soon afterwards got into the woods, where, of course, there had been no drifting, and at length arrived at our journey's end within a few minutes of the appointed time. The people, at least the greater part of them, had been waiting for me for hours. They had no clocks, they were all too poor in that settlement to buy them, and they were afraid of being too late. Our substitute for a church, a rude log-hut covered with bark, was crowded to suffocation. I read prayers and preached, and then administered the Sacrament to nearly twenty communicants. After which I christened three or four children, and churched as many women.... On one of my subsequent visits to this settlement I had to cross this very lake on the ice. It was the latter end of the winter, and the ice was not throughout strong enough to bear a horse. When I got to the shore I met eight young men, who were watching my coming, to warn me of my danger and to assist me. They took my horses out and tied them to a tree, and then dragged me over in my sleigh themselves; and after service in a house on the opposite shore, they brought me back again in the same manner. [William Bell]

Even walking in newly fallen snow could be especially tiring, but as on any journey by foot, there was the chance to meet a stranger and chat on the way.

As there appeared to be no chance of any sleigh going towards the Talbot Settlement, I resolved to set out for it next morning on foot. This was rather an arduous undertaking. The road lay through

229

seventeen miles of uninhabited forest; it was bad and but little
frequented, which was the more unfortunate as I had to carry a
portmanteau on my back. However, after taking a good breakfast,
and receiving directions about my route, I began my journey. Just
as I struck into the woods a man accosted me, and requested
permission to bear me company, as he was going the same way.
We found the snow very deep in the middle of the road, and not at
all beat down, only two sleighs having passed since it had fallen.
The roughness of the ground underneath rendered our walk
inexpressibly tedious and fatiguing; however, my companion
contrived to beguile the time, by telling stories of the murders that
had been committed by the Indians, during the last American war,
on the very road where we then travelled. About sunset, we heard
the axes ringing in Talbot Settlement, and never was any sound
more delightful to my ears. However, I had still two miles more to
walk before I reached the house where I intended to sleep, and I
accomplished these with the utmost difficulty. [John Howison]

A day or two later, the same traveller again met a stranger on the
way, but this time he had hired a horse to make the way easier. The
stranger wanted to buy the horse, pressing the traveller so urgently
that he began to fear for his safety.

The secret to comfortable walking in the snow was wearing
the right footwear (then as now).

Bushwalking in winter is rather hard work, particularly for
those who like me could not get their boots and were obliged to
put up with worn out moccasins, which, except for the
appearance of the things, is much the same as walking in one's
stocking feet; but a dinner of porcupine repaid us for all our
fatigues. [John Langton]

In summer the more primitive roads offered a cut above the
virtually impassable forest, but not much more. If you were walking,
you could watch where you trod and make some slow progress.
However, with a wagon and oxen or horses, every bump became an
agony. James Logan describes going from his brother's farm to the
town, twelve miles distant. It took six hours, because the road was
swampy and the corduroy parts were so rutted. Roads in bad
condition offered special difficulties because, if the wagon broke
down, there was often no one for miles to help fix it. Both axles and

230

wheels suffered from the rough paths. Goods which were left behind on the broken wagon might be stolen, either by people or animals.

If the passenger were energetic enough, he would walk along beside the wagon which contained his goods.

> Next day, I started in the stage (a common lumber wagon) for Guelph, and an awful shaking we got. One of the passengers put a bottle of whiskey in the pocket of his swallow-tail coat, but alas, it was smashed before we had gone a mile. There was an English gentleman, who afterwards settled near Guelph, in the stage, and when we got a mile or two out of Dundas, he and I resolved to walk. The woods looked so high and dismal that we each hunted up a good, big staff in case of meeting a bear. The travelling through the pine woods then was, bump against a stump or the big roots, and then thump into a hole, with a pleasing variety of little steep gravel and sandy knolls now and then, especially after getting into Puslinch.
>
> I never travelled that road in a waggon again, except once, and then it was because I had cut my foot, and so I could not help it. [Alexander Ferrier]

There were two early methods to improve the basic cleared road: corduroy and plank.

Plank roads had large sawn boards placed as runners along the road. The idea was that coaches and wagons could run along the planks, above the bumps and mud. The first of these roads was laid in 1835-1836 running east from Toronto, but it was done with more enthusiasm than science, using twelve foot planks. In the next ten years the government of Upper Canada installed 192 miles of plank roads and another 250 or so were built privately. The idea was that the smooth planks enabled the horses to pull their burdens easily. The theory was interesting, but the practice did not necessarily fit.

> The place in Hamilton where you bought your ticket and took your seat was an old hotel on King street west of Charles. If you were a lady you might hope to keep your seat, but hardly if you were a gentleman—you'd be out pushing long before the stage reached Ryckman's Corners. First there were the hazards of a narrow, unguarded road up the mountain; then the mudholes and broken patches of corduroy beyond that. Although four stout horses had been put on the coach they were tired out before they reached the

231

Corners. They had to be replaced at Terryberry's big inn. In 1842 the plank road was opened to Caledonia when the stage-coaches rolled along on the hardwood with a thunderous roar. But these planks also got bad-tempered and stood up on end. They proved disappointing and were not long in use. [Mabel Burkholder]

The fact was that if the planks were not on a proper base, they would shift or rot. On a steep grade, they had a tendency to slide from under.

Corduroy roads were even more interesting. This involved felling large trees and placing them side by side across the road. This was meant to provide a firm base, which would not move about and would last a long time. The difficulties were found in the round shape of trees and logs, which meant the roads were very bumpy, hence their name. Sometimes the drainage of the soil around the logs caused one to sink, making a very large gap in the road. Anna Jameson observed such a gap, which had been filled with newly cut tree branches, with the leaves still on. The effect was that the hole had been filled, but in fact it was mostly air and the wagon-wheels fell right in.

In swampy marshy places the roads were bridged over with corduroy; this was done by laying logs of cedar, or some other wood, six or eight inches in diameter, close together across the road. Sometimes these corduroy roads be extended for as much as a couple of miles when the nature of the causeway required. They fairly jolted the life out of one with the constant bump, bump, bump, they gave when driving over them. In the course of a few years they were usually covered over with ground which helped to make them a little more passable. Some of the first main roads running through the country were made of plank; sleepers were put down and six inch planks nailed on them. [M. G. Scherk]

The longevity of some corduroy roads was certainly true, because when the huge primeval tree trunks were used, they took a very long time to rot away. As recently as ten years ago, the remains of these giants were still being found beneath roads in Waterloo County.

A little satirical verse, written years later, sums up the situation of riding on these roads:

Half a log, half a log,
Half a log onward,
Shaken and out of breath,
Rode we and wondered.
Ours not to reason why,
Ours but to clutch and cry
While onward we thundered.
[Carrie Munson Hoople]

The creation of roads was one of the most important
elements of local government (if there can be said to have been such
a thing as 'local government' in pioneer Ontario). Pathmasters were
appointed whose task was to ensure the building and maintenance
of roads in their areas. They had the authority to direct the work,
and from an early period, the whole population was expected to help.

Every male is obliged to work three days annually upon the public
roads, or employ a substitute, or pay the sum of thirteen shillings
and sixpence to the path-master, being the wages of a labouring
man for three days. Heads of families, and persons who keep
teams, are liable to a greater proportion of statute labour. However,
notwithstanding these regulations, the roads throughout the
Province in general are in very bad repair, the path-masters not
being sufficiently strict in exacting the apportioned quantity of
labour from each individual. [John Howison]

Road-making obligations were a form of taxation, and
naturally people did their best to avoid paying taxes. If the
pathmaster was a friend and neighbour who depended on you in
other ways, he would find it difficult to be too demanding as a road-
mender.

Our first experience of statue labor was realized in 1835, when one
day a whole lot of us were notified to be ready one morning at eight
a.m., to go to a certain spot to make a crossway. Well, we mustered
together and marched to the pretty little stream that runs into Mr
Allardice's bush land, and there prepared to crossway said stream.
We had no oxen, and so had not only to cut the timber, but to carry
it out of the swamp, and for some of us It was about as tough a
commencement of hard work as could well be wished for. I think
the late Mr George Skene was our pathmaster, and although we

233

did not get on very fast, yet we did as well as we could, and under his charge laid down a very nice piece of crossway, which, for all I know, may be there yet. Our hands blistered nicely, but we just pricked the little blobs [oozing sap] on the balsam trees, and rubbed them with that, and they healed wonderfully. Our dinner consisted of dried deer ham, which old Mr Black provided, with bread, scones and grog. [Alexander Ferrier]

Long-distance travellers with luggage, or the more delicate and refined, could not walk and may not have wished to go on horseback. That meant that a vehicle was required.

...forthwith booked ourselves for Lake Simcoe, in an open waggon without springs, loaded with the bedding and cooking utensils of intending settlers, some of them our shipmates of the *Asia*. A day's journey brought us to Holland Landing, whence a small steamer conveyed us across the lake to Barrie. The Holland River was then a mere muddy ditch, swarming with huge bullfrogs and black snakes, and winding in and out through thickets of reeds and rushes. Arrived at Barrie, we found a wharf, a log bakery, two log taverns—one of them also a store—and a farm house, likewise log. [Samuel Thompson; the 'day's journey' was a healthy 32 miles.]

We left Darlington in a one-horse pleasure-waggon—so called, or rather mis-called, by the natives. For my part, I never could find in what the pleasure consisted, unless in being jerked every minute two or three feet from your seat by the unevenness of the road and want of springs in your vehicle, or the next moment being soused to the axletree in a mud-hole, from which, perhaps, you were obliged to extricate your carriage by the help of a lever in the shape of a rail taken from some farmer's fence by the roadside. You are no sooner freed from this Charybdis, than you fall into Scylla, formed by half a mile of corduroy-bridge, made of round logs, varying from nine to fifteen inches in diameter, which, as you may suppose, does not make the most even surface imaginable, and over which you are jolted in the roughest style possible, at the expense of your breath and injury of your person. [Samuel Strickland[

234

There were stagecoaches which ran on the important roads.

...The coaches being heavy and cumbersome, and the roads frequently very bad, especially in the spring and fall, they were usually drawn by four horses, a change or relay of horses being made at certain places along the route. They were obliged to travel fast to make good time in order to connect with other lines at the various junctions, and of mail coaches to fulfill their contract with the government for carrying the mails. The trunks and valises, or carpet-bags, were piled on top or on a rack behind.... The stage would often get stuck in mud holes and the passengers were obliged to alight and help pry the coach out with fence rails and wooden bars. [M. G. Scherk]

The stage-coaches in Canada appear in profile all the world like a canoe, with a leathern roof, set on wheels. Indeed, one would think that the idea of them was taken from that species of craft. They are necessarily very strongly built, having a treble connecting bar between the fore and hind axle. They are likewise treble seated inside, having a middle seat with a leathern strap for a back. They are hung on leathern swings.... The drivers generally seem to possess considerable dexterity, which is not a little needed in some parts. Every year, however, the roads are improving. [Henry Christmas]

Whether travelling in one's own gig, on foot or via hired conveyance, there was a need for places to stop, rest, eat, sleep and change the horses. In a place where the roads wandered through wooded areas, there was danger in finding oneself caught en route at night.

I had scarcely met a soul in the 7 or 8 miles I had now ridden, and was passing over a spot where I was hemmed in on either hand by a wild boggy forest, and had no retreat whatever should a bear and wolf simultaneously appear in front and rear; having been assured, however, that all the wild animals are very timid near the settled parts of the country, and avoid man, I rode on without distrust, and was soon overtaken by a thunder storm— seeing a hut in the distance, I took refuge therein, and was hospitably received by the owner and his family, and offered spirits while my horse was led to the stable. [John Thornton]

235

The traveller learned quickly that he would be made welcome at most roadside dwellings, especially in case of emergency.

The old settlers are extremely hospitable and obliging; the wandering stranger is sure of welcome and accommodation for the night, either among the higher or lower classes of settlers; he is certain of admission into the large farmhouse, or of a nook on the already crowded family room of the little log house; every person already settled, seems to remember that he had his own day of difficulty to encounter and feels a sympathy for the necessities of the new comer; in short, the exercise of hospitality is considered a sacred duty, which no one neglects—the circumstances and necessities of the country require it, and even the houseless wanderer can communicate, in exchange for the food and lodgings he obtains, a valuable return in news from the mother country, if he be lately from it, or from the remoter townships with which there can be but little direct and personal intercourse.
[Martin Doyle]

I thought my fatigues almost repaid by the pleasures of a good fire; and it was well I did so, for the house afforded scarcely any other comforts. Its inhabitants had recently come to the settlement, and were of course very poor. They presented me with bread, pork, and tea without sugar, and made a bed for me on the floor. There was, however, no appearance of wretchedness or despondency in the house, its owner and his wife being cheerful, and sanguine about what the future would produce. I have always observed, that the new settlers in Upper Canada are perfectly happy and contented in the midst of their severest hardships; and with reason, for a moment's observation must convince them that prosperity and abundance will, sooner or later, be the result of their labours and exertions. [John Howison]

The government realized that, as the land was opened, the first necessity was an inn along the way at regular intervals. Then, as the settlers arrived, they could be cared for. The arrangements were often minimal, even primitive.

This is James Scott's description of the establishment of the first inns on the Huron Road:

But the trail which had been blazed by John MacDonald, the surveyor, and cleared by Galt's work parties was not of practical use. For at least four or five months during the winter it was buried deep in snow and completely impassable. For its entire seventy-five-mile distance there was not a single tavern or house on it in 1828. But Galt was not discouraged. He made plans for inns to be put up at twenty-mile intervals along the road. These he was going to call, rather picturesquely, "Houses of Entertainment." They were to provide shelter for settlers as they worked their way into the Tract along the Huron Road and provender for their animals. Galt realized that not many men would be interested in keeping an inn in so desolate a country and as a further inducement he determined that, during the winter months when there would be practically no traffic along the road, the innkeepers' incomes from travellers would have to be supplemented. His proposal was that the inn the first twenty miles west should receive $50.00 a month during the winter; the one twenty miles farther on was to get $72.10 per month and the third still another twenty miles west $75.00 per month. For these fees the innkeepers were expected to keep the roads open and in order...

By about Christmas of 1828 he [Anthony Van Egmond] had engaged three men to erect and keep the inns along the road. These were Helmer, Fryfogle and Seebach. Van Egmond says that the task of finding such men was one of the most difficult he had ever undertaken because it required men of great courage, as well as with a keen spirit of adventure to undertake such a chancy venture.

Helmer, who was to keep the first inn, reached his lot and erected his new tavern without much difficulty. It took Fryfogle eleven days' travelling to reach his destination which was approximately one mile east of the present village of Shakespeare. It took Seebach seventeen days on the road to get still twenty miles farther.

But all these men proved to be excellent choices. They did reach their destinations and for many years thereafter all three kept inns as Galt had envisaged. True enough they were not palatial hostelries. Fryfogle's first house—which Dr. Dunlop described as a mere shanty—was eighteen feet by fourteen and the total cost, plus stocking it with food and drink, was $50.00. Seebach put up a larger place—thirty feet by eighteen—which cost him $203.00.

In the ensuing years hundreds and hundreds of pioneer families stopped at these three inns as they made their way into Huron County. Many of them kept records of their travels into the county and not one of them speaks with high praise of what they found. There is no doubt that the fare was most primitive. This was due mainly to the difficulty in getting supplies. It was not at all unusual for a settler to arrive and find the house in charge of the wife of Fryfogle, Helmer or Seebach, as the case might be, and practically nothing to eat. The innkeeper himself would be on the road laboriously bringing back the supplies. The houses were drafty, uncomfortable and possessed absolutely no amenities. The people slept on the floor or on rough bunks in a single large room. There was only a fireplace to keep it warm, and no privacy. In the leanest times the only food which could be obtained at the inns was some sort of mash. Normally this was supplemented by such staples of pioneer diet as turnips and salt pork. It was not the intention, nor was it possible even if it had been, that the inns should provide luxurious entertainment. They were merely the minimum of necessity and convenience...

Having made those dire observations, Scott points out that "anything in the desolation of the primeval wilderness looked good."

For most people, the first experience of the Upper Canadian inn was on the way from Lachine to Kingston. Whether riding on the batteaux or walking on the riverside paths, the immigrants needed to stop to eat, and possibly sleep also. These inns were the equivalents of motels near star tourist attractions today. They knew that travellers were obliged to partake of their services because they had no choice.

For those newly arriving from Britain, the relaxed attitudes and egalitarian nature of Canadian innkeepers were surprising. They often attributed these to American influences; in fact, sometimes they assumed the innkeepers were Americans.

I now, for the first time, had an opportunity of observing the manners of an American innkeeper of the lower order. Gentlemen of this description, in their anxiety to display a noble spirit of *independence*, sometimes forget those courtesies that are paid to travellers by publicans in all civilized countries; but the moment one shews his readiness to be on an equality with them, they become tolerably polite. I found the *maitre d'hotel* at St. Ann's seated at his door, posing his chair on its

238

hind legs, and swimming backwards and forwards. He took no notice of me when I alighted from the calash, nor when I walked into the house; no—not even when I desired him to get breakfast ready. But I had forgot myself—"Will you have the goodness," said I, "to order breakfast for me, if convenient?" "Immediately, squire," replied he, as he rose from his chair and shewed me into an apartment.

In a short time my host returned, and having seated himself beside me, entered into familiar conversation, and inquired into my affairs, respecting which I did not fail to give him such information as put his curiosity upon the rack. At first, the familiarities of the tavern-keepers used to irritate me a good deal... [John Howison]

Here I found an *independent* host, who, in the true American style, answered each question I put to him by asking another, and shewed such extreme curiosity about my affairs, that, I believe, nothing but the fear of violent treatment prevented him from examining the contents of my portmanteau.
[John Howison]

Setting up as an innkeeper required nothing more than to build a suitably spacious building in a spot where people might want to stop.

They had been recently married, as he promptly informed us, had selected this wild spot on a half-opened road, impassable for waggons, without a neighbour for miles, and under the inevitable necessity of shouldering all their provisions from the embryo village [Barrie] we had just quitted: all this with the resolute determination of "keeping tavern."

The floor was of loose split logs, hewn into some approach to evenness with an adze; the walls of logs entire, filled in the interstices with chips of pine, which, however, did not prevent an occasional glimpse of the objects visible outside, and had the advantage, moreover, of rendering a window unnecessary; the hearth was the bare soil, the ceiling slabs of pine wood, the chimney a square hole in the roof; the fire literally an entire tree, branches and all, cut into four-foot lengths, and heaped up to as many feet. [Samuel Thompson]

Eating arrangements were often quite catch-as-catch-can (as Mrs Moodie's experience above[1] testifies) and whatever beds were available had to be apportioned as needed. This meant that you might have to share.

> ...having gone to the wrong hotel, I occupied one eleventh of seven beds. [John Langton]

> Stopped in Brockville all night. It was Court time. obliged to sleep double. [— Johnson]

In the more primitive sites (such as those described on the Huron Road), sleeping on the floor was quite usual. Bush experiences, even in hostelries, were not for the faint-hearted.

> A bed on the floor in a public sleeping-room! Think of that; a public sleeping-room!—men, women, and children, only divided by a paltry curtain. Oh ye gods! think of the snoring, squalling, grumbling, puffing; think of the kicking, elbowing, and crowding; the suffocating heat, the mosquitoes, with their infernal buzzing—and you will form some idea of the misery I endured the first night of my arrival in bush. [Susanna Moodie]

George Head and his servant found themselves travelling in February with a group of shipwrights bound for Penetang-uishene's naval settlement. They stopped for the night in the most basic of places, ate and settled for the night with their own bedding on the floor. It was very uncomfortable.

> However, I fell asleep, and continued so some hours, when I awoke, owing to the cold, and found that one of my neighbours (having felt, I take it for granted, cold too) had deprived me of my buffalo skin, which was tightly wrapped round him, while the fellow was snoring as happily as it if belonged to him. The harder I tugged, the harder he held on and snored; and, as he was a thick-set fellow, I had the more difficulty to recover my property. However, I jumped up, and, invoking the spirit of Archimedes, I placed my foot on his ribs to such advantage,

---

[1] see page 161.

that by one violent, determined pull, I thoroughly uncased and rolled him out on the floor.

Lucky immigrants would have been advised that one or another inn was worthy, and William Cattermole even makes a point of this in his emigrants' handbook:

[Dundas] has an excellent tavern, kept by a Mr. Jones, from Birmingham, and no traveller, desirous of comfort, if near night-time, should pass his door, a good inn being a perfect *rara-avis...*

What was once a good inn might sink into chaos.

...we stopped for the night at what was once a very good inn. It is just now dismantled by a recent distress, which circumstance may also account for the ill-humour of the barmaid. She well nigh threw the viands at our heads because one of the company complained that the toast was burned. All of them laughed to see her make a slop basin of the fireplace. [Mary O'Brien]

Here is a capsule description of a good inn, Hugh Black's two-storey log house at Fergus:

There was one large room in it, one small parlor, the bar-room, and a kitchen behind on the ground floor, and bedrooms above. Besides Mr. Black's family there were some thirty boarders in the house, which was literally crammed, and the bar-room was scarcely ever empty. While the weather was fine the house was pretty quiet and orderly, but a wet day was a misfortune, as the men being off work, they gathered in the bar, and it was a steady system of horning till night.

There was a celebrated character known as the Major, a member of an old Scotch family, who sometimes kept the bar, and when such was the case there was sure to be a fight, which he then managed to bring to an amicable conclusion by a friendly glass all round, and if nobody would fight the Major would get very fired himself, but took care never to get hurt. He was a dangerous associate for idle young men....
[Alexander Ferrier]

The food would vary considerably according to the abilities of the innkeeper, but one writer's references to 'everlasting ham and eggs' shows the typical fare. Anna Jameson had a sumptuous meal which she shared with the other inmates, according to the custom of the country:

> As it was necessary to gird up my strength for the undertaking, I laid a good dinner, consisting of slices of dried venison, broiled; hot cakes of Indian corn, eggs, butter, and a bowl of milk. Of this good fare I partook in company with the two backwoodsmen who appeared to me perfect specimens of their class—tall and strong, and bronzed and brawny, and shaggy and unshaven—very much like two bears set on their hind legs; rude but not uncivil, and spare of speech, as men who had lived long at a distance from their kind. They were too busy, however, and so was I, to feel or express any mutual curiosity; time was valuable, appetite urgent—so we discussed our venison steaks in silence, and after dinner I proceeded.

The silent nature of hotel eating, and its speed, were often remarked on. Even at the more fashionable hotels, such as the Clifton at Niagara Falls, the habit of quick and quiet meals prevailed.

> I found shelter for myself in the Ontario house, where I was comfortably lodged; lived at a kind of table d'hote of fifty or sixty persons; and was much amused to witness the rapidity with which the gentlemen assembled at the ringing of a bell, and the despatch they made in eating, or rather devouring their meals, as if engaged in a match against time, or impelled by the most ravenous hunger. In a quarter of an hour, nearly all had swallowed their food and disappeared, except some few stragglers, who had come in late, and with whom I commonly finished my meal in peace. [James Marr Brydone]

From time to time the nature of sharing extended to more than some travellers would expect.

> We had heard of some rather primitive practices among the steerage passengers on board ship, it is true, but had not accustomed ourselves to "uncase" before company, and

hesitated to lie down in our clothes. After waiting some little time in blank dismay, Mr. Root kindly set us an example by quietly slipping out of his nether integuments and turning into bed. There was no help for it; by one means or other we contrived to sneak under the blankets; and, after hanging up a large coloured quilt between our lair and the couch occupied by her now snoring spouse, the good wife also disappeared.
[Samuel Thompson]

One traveller, returning to the bush from doing business in York, encountered the jealous wife of his recent fellow traveller at an inn near their home. She joined him in the parlor:

She no sooner came into the room, than it was evident, by the way she pulled out her pins and placed her feet upon the fender, that she felt herself perfectly at home where she was. I very soon perceived that American customs were likely to prevail, and that unless chance should throw in a third person to interrupt the *tête-à-tête*, we were doomed to pass the evening in each other's company. This not only proved to be the case, but our landlady positively disposed of us in separate beds in opposite corners of the same room, where we remained till the morning. [George Head]

Weary immigrants would have found it difficult to deal with devious or unscrupulous innkeepers. Those who were being shepherded to their new homes by James Marr Brydone had the benefit of his vigilance.

...we arrived at Vanorman's [Van Norman's] Inn, where we stopped for the night. I procured bread and milk, for the children; tea and beds for the women; and a barn, with plenty of straw, for the men and boys; at the price agreed on with the Landlord.
    The landlady (an American) as soon as the boys had retired to rest, in the barn, carried out eight or ten counterpanes and covered them, as they lay on the straw, in order to charge us, so many additional beds; but, as this was objected to, and she found, on a reference to her husband, the device would not answer, she immediately carried off the counterpanes.
    June 21st. West's wife being taken in labour in the night, I was obliged to leave her here, with a daughter of

Voice's, as her nurse, and we started at an early hour, in order that the house might be quiet, and proper accommodations afforded to the woman: but not before I had ascertained that all was right; that a midwife was at hand: and a medical gentleman near.

In paying the bill, I found that the landlady had doubled the usual charge for milk, which I should have resisted, had I not been apprehensive, that Mrs. West might fare the worse, by the landlady suffering a second defeat at my hand.

Those who lived near a network of lakes and rivers had the option of travelling by water. In the 1820s many settlers stopped at Cobourg or Port Hope and made their way north to Rice Lake and then Peterborough. The area was already partially settled by Peter Robinson's Irish settlers and hence offered some amenities.

...after jolting over thirteen miles of mud and stumps arrived to dinner on the Rice Lake, which, as its name would denote, is a low, muddy, swampy, aguish looking place, covered over with Canadian rice and other aquatic weeds. From thence I proceeded twenty-five miles by steamer up the Otonabee to Peterborough.... [John Langton]

Several early writers find the quality of the water worth mentioning. It's clarity and purity are attractive, both to look at and to drink.

By the way, I never yet have mentioned what is one of the greatest pleasures in the navigation of these magnificent upper lakes—the purity, the coldness, the transparency of the water. [Anna Jameson]

On the large lakes there were steamships. There are many descriptions of voyages on Lakes Ontario and Erie, but perhaps few as picturesque as this experience of William Fraser:

About midnight as our Capt. attempted to pass through the Cut or break which was opened across Long Point on the 7th of January last in order to save the risk & time of going 25 miles round the point—our boat ran aground. Here not withstanding all our efforts to get her off she lay till 8 O'clock next morning when we succeeded in getting through the Cut & proceeded on our voyage—I may remark here the little concern the accident of running aground seemed to give to the master of the Ship. It did not seem to put him the least out of countenance. Whenever she stuck fast which happened 3 or 4 times during the voyage the passengers without distinction were called on deck. In one instance we were all routed out of her. When stationed on the Upper deck we were directed to run simultaneously from one side of the vessel to the other and by this means She was rolled from side to side and made way for herself through the loose sand which seems to compose the bottom in most parts of the coast.

The great bodies of water could accommodate ships, but the pioneers needed smaller boats for moving goods from towns to their clearings, and perhaps the things they had to sell from their farms into the towns. Because of his practical nature, John Langton spends a lot of time describing the technical aspects of his life to his father, including the use of boats. Most of the time he uses a scow, a flat-bottomed boat with deep sides, in which a great deal can be transported. They were not fast nor graceful, but they worked.

The happy discovery for many settlers was the canoe. The indigenous peoples used these in two forms. One was made of birch bark and was both light and quick, but had some disadvantages in handling. The other was a hollowed-out cedar log or dugout, heavy and awkward but more stable than birch-bark.

Langton's father asked about his canoe:

In one of your letters, if not your last, you express some apprehension about my canoe. Now a canoe[2] is certainly a little light affair that you can carry for a mile or two upon your shoulders and which a single false step in embarking or disembarking will upset, but it will carry half a dozen men in safety over a stormy lake and when you get accustomed to the craft you feel as steady as in a seventy-four. Indeed the other day, so much does habit make one unconsciously keep one's balance, that though I

---

[2] Langton himself notes that he means a birch canoe.

245

attempted it frequently I could not upset my canoe when Macredie was out with me in it, and it was not till I had got out that his awkwardness in attempting to do the same enabled me to give him the desired ducking.

Langton makes a comparison between his scow and canoe:

A boat is in most cases a preferable craft, you can carry a greater load, you need not handle it like a new-born baby, you go quicker and defy all winds. In a canoe unless the wind is dead aft it is always in your way, particularly if alone, and even with the greatest care she is constantly getting a leak. But then in fine weather she is so easily launched, and paddled with such ease and silence if you want to steal upon a duck, etc. You cannot take a boat upon your shoulders and carry it over any obstacle such as Cameron's Falls or the pitch at Bobcajewonunk [Bobcaygeon], and in coming up even a practicable rapid in a boat you may indeed put out your whole strength, but you have to keep the middle of the stream with barely room often to ply your oars, whereas in a canoe you may go anywhere which will admit the narrow bark itself, and steal up the sides of the stream taking advantage of the eddy caused by every stone and stump, and by stepping out with one foot keeping her floating in two inches of water. Each has its own advantage and I have both to use as occasion may require.

Langton was aware of the greatest trick necessary in paddling a canoe:

I decidedly have not yet acquired the true Indian twist of the wrist, but I am a very tolerable hand and can face a very heavy swell or stem a rapid much to my own satisfaction.

Because canoes did upset easily and there were few bridges where needed, there were many accidents. People did not know how to swim and if they were dunked might easily drown.

Fortunately we were only a few yards from the shore when the accident happened, so that we all reached it in safety. Had this happened at a distance from the bank, the probability is, that we would all have been drowned, as not one among us could swim. [William Bell]

246

William Bell had earlier described how, when he and his guide came to a deep stream, they removed all their clothes and held them over their heads while crossing.

The making of bridges seems to have been a slow process. Certain places became known as locations for crossing rivers or streams, perhaps because they could be forded or they were narrow. There might be ferries powered by winches or wind-lasses, or horse drawn. A boat could take people across but larger ones powered by horses or winches could manage teams and wagons.

Eventually bridges might be constructed, wooden to start with either above the water or floating on it. Floating bridges were popular in Kawartha, but they tended to be washed away in spring floods. Stronger piers to hold the bridges in place used stones as a base.

Quite soon, the settlers would come to know their own area well. There would be the road, whatever condition it was in, plus paths through the forest to various neighbours and perhaps a shortcut to town. These paths would be quite familiar after a time, but initially there would be a danger of getting lost and anyone who strayed from the path might well lose their way. Since the forest looked the same in every direction it was difficult to know where to go. When night came, there might be animals about, aside from cold and hunger.

> ...he forgot his compass and we lost our way in the forest. After wandering up and down, like the babes in the wood without even a blackberry to console us... [John Galt]

Some settlers learned the tricks of travelling in the bush, such as being able to tell the direction by seeing which side of the tree the moss grew on. However, tales of people becoming lost were so common that Mrs Moodie devotes a whole chapter to tales of lost children.

> Persons, when once they get off the beaten track, get frightened and bewildered, and lose all presence of mind; and instead of remaining where they are when they first discover their misfortune—which is the only chance they have of being found—they plunge desperately on, running hither and thither,

247

in the hope of getting out, while they only involve themselves more deeply among the mazes of the interminable forest. [Susanna Moodie]

William Bell referred to people who were lost in the bush as being 'stupified' and said:

Since that time I have never ventured into the woods without a compass; and I would advise every one else to use the same precaution.

There were two means of summoning people from the bush.

On the horn being sounded at 12 o'clock, which is the usual way of summoning persons at work round a farm to their dinners... [Henry Christmas]

If a guest at a rural inn went out walking and did not return at the expected hour, they would think he was lost. They would fire a gun to guide him back. [Edward Marsh]

Of course men had to eat in those days as well as now, and the blast of the old tin dinner-horn fell on the ear with more melodious sound than the grandest orchestra to the musical enthusiast. Even "Old Gray," when I followed the plough, used to give answer to the cheerful wind of the horn by a loud whinny, and stop in the furrow, as if to say, 'there now, off with my harness, and let us to dinner.' If I happened to be in the middle of the field, I had considerable trouble to get the old fellow to go on to the end. [Canniff Haight]

One other function of the roads was communication, the only means of which was writing. The mails were haphazard and costly.

Our nearest Post Office was Guelph, and Mr Black's wagon generally brought the letters about once a week. Letters in those days came from Britain by way of Halifax, and were generally about two months old before we got them, and postage was very high—2s. 4d. a letter. [Alexander Ferrier]

248

In theory, letters were paid for by the recipient, not the sender, although as we see from Mickle's complaint below, sometimes both had to pay. It was possible that people might not be able to afford letters that came for them, or that the letter might, once opened, not be welcome.

> I have omitted to state that on Friday last week I received a letter from Rev John Johnstone, Glasgow, dated 25th March [he was writing on 25 September] remarkable for nothing but for news which I have been in possession of two months before. It cost me 6/9 currency. [William Proudfoot]

> As it cost me near a Dollar every time I write or receive a Lre I cannot promise you to write so often as you mention. [William J. Mickle]

However, most letters were very welcome. It made a connection with the family so far away at home, a link that was not broken. It must have been that much more difficult for the illiterate, whose family were perhaps illiterate also, to know that they could not communicate with one another no matter how much they wished to.

> This morning a man brought to me a letter from my dear brother Alexander, dated the 3rd of April. What a refreshment a letter from one so dear and so far away. [William Proudfoot]

News from home might tell of a recovery from illness.

> you was wishing to here from Barbras Thomson brother he is with his father at milnathart is better of his health and is going about gathering Dung [Alexander Crichton]

Perhaps the greatest advantage of the mail was that it would bring things from England which were not available in Canada. If other emigrants or visitors were expected, they might also bring things. People asked for, and received, a great variety of parcels.

The Postman: Postal Service in Pioneer Canada, by Adam Sherriff-Scott (Couresty National Archives of Canada, C-004453)

I shall in the first place proceed to thank thee for they very kind present of a Shawl and Comb which I received together with letters... [Mary Mullett]

...I shall be very much obliged if thou wilt send me a Butter-print also—please excuse the freedom I make use of—I think my dear I know thee too well to suppose thou wilt be displeased. [Mary Mullett]

...fetch a little Broom seed and whone seed with you and a few of poor robin's almanacks... [Mary Ritchie]

Please to send 4 sions off the Bakeing Apple and 4 off the wine Apple take them of short shoots of last years with a little old wood. Send me 4 of the scarlit Thorn. James Graham will show you them at my old Dwelling. Roll them in oild paper and tye them close. Send me a pint of spring veches and a dosen of Long pod Beans. Send these with Miss Trimble she will come to this place. [Joseph Carrothers]

I want you to get me some gras seed one kind I want which I dismember the name of but it is the softest and lightest of all the gras kinds I remember us to have it sown on the narrow strip of meadow below the kill the have it in many parts of the country I think Andrew mongomery can eisley get it for you only one pound of it I want let it be very Clean it is jenerly sown on bottoms so you cant mistake it; it produces very soft and light hay I want you to try the seed shopes in eniskilen if the have got any of the Italian rye grass seed and if the have get me a pound of it likewise it is sown and cultivated in england and scotland and far preferible to any other gras; gather me allso a pound of common gras seed of your own stabel loft letting it be clean possible marking the name of each kind on the enclouser we have the timethey and rye gras here the grow well put I dont like them as the dont produce any after groth [Nathaniel Carrothers]

when I resided in the town I wrote you not to send me the news as I co^d always see them in the news papers now it is otherwise. I shall be happy to hear anything & pray let me have a long letter when you write in answer. [William Mickle]

Mrs Traill's description of a box from England makes it sound like Christmas.

Ours I think was more than the half as Mr Woods portion contained some heavy cotton sheeting table cloths and some merino and books for the children, also some German silver spoons and a metal teapot and two coats for the boys, a nice remnant of velveteen and some sundries in small wares, a few needles, cottons, thread and a fine pair of cutting shears, also some towelling very useful and valuable. Agnes sent me a very excellent Scotch plaid winter gown of her own which I was very glad of as it was ready made and fits me well and will be a great comfort to my poor rheumatic arm.... I sincerely hope you may find the contents such as may be useful. I will tell you what mine are, sixteen yds of pale blue calico for frocks for the girls, 12 checked muslin de laine, 14 good grass cloth, about 18 yds white cotton, 12 blue check shirting very useful for the boys, some flannel which I judge to be about ten yds, some red chinzam, a dress, which I shall endeavour to pay old Zinney some washing arrears with, some plain cap net, two chimizetts from Agnes always valuable to poor me and some cap ribbon from Agnes, six pairs of white stockings, some yards of clean striped muslin a good pair of boots for myself most acceptable for I was literally shoeless and bootless, and two small pairs for Will and Walter who were dit, dit [ditto, ditto, i.e. also shoeless]—the four[th] vol of the Queen's and a copy of the new Scrapbook—this with some half pound of cotton a few tapes, and pins and needles, are the contents of our box...

Society

Since many people lived in an area of sparse population, and had a great deal of work to do, their principal society was bound to be their own household. This was one reason why a large family was an advantage, coupled with the fact that many hands made light work.

The only salvation of a man here is to have a wife and children; the poor wife must make up her mind to lead a hard life; but the children are almost sure to do well—that is, if they have intelligent parents: it is the very land for the young, and the enterprising. [Anna Jameson]

He too was prospering with a large farm and a large family,—
here a blessing and a means of wealth, too often in the old
country a curse and a burthen. [Anna Jameson]

they are young looking wives but it is customary for girls to
marry young in this country. The reason is a great many young
men come here and they want wives when they come.
[Robert Wade]

At a young age the young would obtain jobs to augment
the family income. The girls might go out to work as servants in
other homes, unless they were needed to help their mother with
their own younger siblings. Boys were more likely to have day
jobs or to do occasional work for others but continue to live at
home. Very young children would probably have some small
tasks around the house or barnyard but would otherwise run free,
since schoolhouses were rare.

Anna Jameson suggests that women emigrants were
unhappy, and others have said that the first generation often
pined for the old country, its familiar faces and places. The next
generation saw Canada as home and so found the rigours of
pioneer life easier to bear because they knew nothing else.

...I never met with so many repining and discontented women
as in Canada. I never met with one woman recently settled
here, who considered herself happy in her new home and
country: I heard of one, and doubtless there are others, but they
are exceptions to the general rule. Those born here, or brought
here early by their parents and relations, seemed to me very
happy, and many of them had adopted a sort of pride in their
new country, which I liked much. [Anna Jameson]

Even emigrants who set out from home with hope and
excitement would find themselves wishing they could see
familiar places. John Hallas' wife had earlier stated she would be
happy never to see her native city of Leeds again, but

she often thinks & weeps about her Mother and could like to
see her...hopes she keeps well in health as well as her sister
Maria & hopes her mother will live untill she comes to Leeds

which will very likely be a long time that she may have the unspeakable pleasure of Seeing her once more.

It was natural to miss one's parents, and many letters home make references to meeting again in heaven, or urge those left behind to emigrate also.

> do tell them for me they are often, very often, the companions of my thoughts, and the bare idea of our some day or other meeting again gives me pleasure, all tho' the wide Atlantic now rolls between us. I shall live in the fond anticipation of Hope that such a thing may some day come to pass. [Mary Mullett]

> I like America very well, but should like it much better if you were all here; make up your minds and come to us, don't fear crossing the sea, for when you are started you will think of it no more than crossing the Thames...I only wish you were here to live as we do, we want for nothing; but when we sit down, to think how they are all starving at home, it gives me the horrors, especially my poor father and mother... [George Carpenter]

> I think of those whom I shall see
> On this fair earth no more;
> And wish in vain for wings to flee
> Back to thy much-loved shore. [Susanna Moodie]

Once the land began to be somewhat settled, it was not impossible to consider someone coming for a visit from Britain. William Hewgill wrote in 1843:

> Since the countries are become so near together that vessel can cross the ocean in 10 or 12 days, you need not spend such time visiting us, we shall be glad to see you hope you will take Mistress with you and treat her with a visit to Canada, fertile Land, whether you come by New York or Quebeck. the passage to Toronto is very quick and fare low. A gentleman 70 years [old] came from Nova Scotia by way of Boston to see his son one of my near neighbours, a distance of 1200 miles in 7 days...

It was one of the advantages of settling in a group of people that you knew; this kind of loneliness was lessened somewhat.

For the many young men who made the journey to the new country alone, and then settled in splendid isolation, some nights and days must have seemed very long. They had probably set out with more adventure than domesticity on their minds.

> Many young men are attracted to the Backwoods by the facilities they present for hunting and fishing. The wild, free life of the hunter, has for an ardent and romantic temperament an inexpressible charm. [Susanna Moodie]

William Stewart Darling's novel *Sketches of Canadian Life*, which was meant to inform people about Canada as well as entertain, begins with a reference to the "wild romance and adventures of the Backwoodsman's life." If young men in Britain were reading such a thing, there was little to stop them dreaming of a carefree existence in another world.

The reality was different. There was a great deal of work and if a man lived on his own, he had to manage his shack himself, including the cooking. This may have been the greatest handicap in an age when few men knew how to cook.

John Langton mocked his own abilities:

> I certainly did once roast a duck to charcoal, and once burned the pea soup so much it was necessary to give it to the goats, but, upon the whole, when I handed over the frying pan and potato kettle to my boy Willie, I did it with the conviction that nature intended me for a great cook; great, first because I have a genius that way, and secondly because I never could overcome my aversion to washing up dishes, etc.

Actually, Langton did very well for himself and his frequent visitor and co-worker, Alexander McAndrew. McAndrew was also single but had more reliable servants than Langton.

When he had to feed a crew of hired hands, but had only one pot to cook in, Langton still managed a dinner of potatoes, half boiled then fried, beef, half boiled then roasted, stew of porcupine and rice, bread, venison pie, cranberry tart, fried fish,

255

Interior of Cottage looking North

Interior of Cottage looking South

—Drawings by Anne Langton

Two sketches of the interior of John Langton's cabin, by his sister, Anne Langton (From Early Days in Upper Canada*)*

deviled duck, cheese. He described it as 'a very handsome dinner for the backwoods.' It sounds handsome for anywhere.

Although some visitors suggested that the winter was a time of less work, there was always something to do. John Langton gives us a description of his bachelor's winter workday:

> I rise at an hour varying from five to seven. Having dressed I clean the house whilst the kettle is boiling and after breakfast I smoke a cigar and read as long as it lasts; I then wash up the accumulated plates, etc. of the twenty-four hours and set to work at chopping firewood, joinering, or whatever may be in hand at the time. At an hour before sunset, which I have come to calculate very accurately, I begin cooking, bringing in a pile of firewood, sweeping out the house, etc. in the intervals; and I rarely fail to have finished my dinner just as it gets dark. Another cigar's time is then devoted to meditation and digestion, and after reading, writing or sewing for half a candle, I go to bed. My baking, which is performed in a frying pan before the fire, requires constant attention, so I superintend that in the evening, having kneaded the dough during my cooking hour.

Langton was educated and spent much more time reading than most pioneers, but this may still reflect an average day.

Other young men, whose vision of backwoods life owed more to hunting than chopping, and gun dogs than goats, might well have become discontented. One young woman noticed this quality in her cousin:

> I do not think he likes Canada very well. Yesterday he went over to John's on his way to Bath to see a young man that came out with us on some private business we know not what yet. I believe Cousin Edward made use of my name when he wrote home so that I may do the same. if he had not been disappointed I believe he would have settled in Canada as he took a fancy to one of George Bo—ris daughters a very pretty little girl but too young to be married. he has talked of going in partnership with John but he does not seem to know his own mind long together. [Deborah Mullett]

Faced with life alone in a log cabin, single men had two roads they might take. Society knew which they should choose.

> I am dull & stupid—lonely & alone in my own house for the last eight days—I must have a female—a wife to comfort & keep me company, but where shall I find one—who can she be—*nous verrons*—for I do not know... [William Gilkison]

> more should come here with wives for English women are as valuable as the gold of Ophir in this country. [Robert Wade]

The writer speaks more of a companion than someone to share the work, although others giving advice to emigrants stress the need for a helpmeet first. For others, marriage was not so pressing if money was a consideration.

> I fear he has ingered his futuer prosperity like others of the fameley by to earley a marage. [Nathaniel Carrothers]

The alternative was a life of carousing with the other single men in the community. They would congregate at the tavern or one another's cabins.

> the temptations here are of a lower & less expensive nature[3], though I should dread them for a son quite as much as [illegible], drinking & smoking are sadly in fashion. the young man who on first going to the Bush would disdain the thought of the first. by degrees, from working hard & having no employment for the evenings & no superintending society of relatives & friends they care about, soon contract the sad habit & you cannot think the degenerate appearance they have to us, even, who of course see them at their best, when they visit Toronto, after a year's residence on their lot... [Lady Colborne]

> ...those who give themselves entirely up to such pursuits, soon add to these profitless accomplishments the bush vices of smoking and drinking, and quickly throw off those moral restraints upon which their respectability and future welfare mainly depend. [Susanna Moodie]

---

[3] Than in Britain.

So it was clearly a better idea that he should marry. The young people in any community had a limited choice for mates, being confined to their own neighbours unless they had connections in some nearby town where they might visit. There were also conventions of religion and ethnicity which would make a difference in many cases. One difficulty with young people who did not see other people often was they hardly knew how to behave when they met someone new. William Bell found himself staying with a family of strangers, and after remarking that his hostess had 'a great talent for silence' he met her three equally silent daughters.

> My guide afterwards told me, that the young women in that quarter are so shy, that if a stranger call, they often run and hide themselves; and if they remain, they scarcely speak a word. Their education must be very defective, or injudiciously managed.

However, in some quiet way a couple might come to an understanding.

> Thou also wished to be informed what sort of young women John has made choice of for his intended partner for life. She is in my eye better than the generality of the Canadian girls. I think thou would not object to her for a grand-daughter. She has two brothers which I think most likely will become they grandsons. they have not yet made known their intentions to Father and Mother, neither is it the practice of the country till a few weeks before they send in their intention of marriage to the Monthly Meeting.[4] I quite forgot to say their visits are to Sarah & Deborah. The latter desires me to tell thee she have not yet forgot all her old tricks, and for all people tell her she is going to get married she will have a good bit of play with thee any day she can 'get a change', and also tell Uncle Gillett for her we have orchards here in abundance where he may drive her round bare footed without running over so many docks and nettles as there is in the Orchard at Frampton. We have not any in this country. Don't think R [Rachel] is without a beau. no she has had several though neither of them have pleased her fancy.

---

[4] The Mullets were Quakers.

259

They were Irishmen. In my last letter to thee, I think I said I would have nothing myself but an Englishman, and expect thou wilt be surprised to find I am likely to become united with a young Irishman by the name of Wm. Clendenan who came out last summer. His uncle will, I expect, be the bearer of this. You must make much of him. he is a very nice friend. Thou must also consider him a relation by marriage. I should much like to have many of my dear relations to attend my wedding which is likely to take place the twenty first of the fifth month. do tell me how many of my cousins are likely to follow my example, or if any have. I much wish thou couldst see thy intended grandson. he stands by looking over my shoulder, telling me to give his love to his grandmother. [Mary Mullett]

The best possibility was then that the clergyman of choice would come by the cabin to do the wedding. The young couple might go, with a friend or two, to the parson's house instead, but in many areas there was a shortage of clergy.

To remedy this difficulty the Government authorized magistrates to perform the ceremony for any couple who resided more than eighteen miles from church. There were hardly any churches, and therefore a good many called upon the Justice to put a finishing touch to their happiness, and curious looking pairs presented themselves to have the knot tied. One morning a robust young man and a pretty, blushing girl presented themselves at my father's door, and were invited in. They were strangers, and it was sometime before he could find out what they wanted; but after beating about the bush, the young man hesitatingly said they wanted to get married. They were duly tied, and, on leaving, I was asked to join in their wedding dinner. Though it was to be some distance away, I mounted my horse and joined them. The dinner was good, and served in the plain fashion of the day. After it came dancing, to the music of a couple of fiddlers, and we threaded through reel after reel until nearly daylight. [Canniff Haight]

A rural wedding was an event to which most of the community might come. In a small population, it was likely that everyone knew both bride and groom, and may even have been related to one or both. It was the happiest sort of gathering.

260

On February the 12th, we were invited to a wedding and to have a sleigh-drive. The day was not very cold, but it snowed from morning till night. When we reached the house of the bride's father, which consisted of only one large apartment, we found it crammed full of people, all standing, for there was not room for them to sit down. I proceeded to unite the happy couple without delay, and after the usual congratulations, followed by handing round of wine and cakes, we all mounted our sleighs and drove to the house of the bridegroom where we were to dine. We had seventeen sleighs as full as they could be crammed, besides a number of pedestrians who crossed over by a nearer road. The procession formed a long line, and drove on at a rapid rate. Our horse, being a spirited animal, became excited by the noise of so many tongues, as well as the bells, and began to kick and dance in a manner which I did not deem quite consistent with our safety. However as we had four miles to run, I hoped he would get tired by and by; but after we had got half way, some of the foremost began to race, and before you would say Jack Robinson, the whole line was in full gallop; our horse got quite furious, and kicking up his heels like a young colt, I feared that some mischief would happen. Thanks to the kindness of Providence, by cool and steady management, we all got safely on terra firma, at the end of our journey. Dinner soon followed and much provision, excellent in quality, and various in kind, disappeared, before the hunger of all the company was appeased. Eating, drinking and dancing continued all night, but we came away at nine, and got home safe though the evening was dark. [William Bell]

The long line of carriages or sleighs driving through the countryside was a common habit of weddings. The bride and groom led, although the other high-spirited young men would try to pass him. The other gigs might also have couples in them, this being an occasion when prospective spouses might be interviewed privately without interference by elders.

Those who lived near the lakes and the St. Lawrence might slip across the border to be married, where it was a simpler matter. Many couples who wanted to avoid the expense of a wedding, or simply disliked the fuss, might cross to New York or sail to one of the ports on Lake Erie where they could quietly marry among strangers.

In a land where few people had a lot of ready cash, the bridal couple had to decide how to pay the clergyman or Justice. Scherk says he had heard of ashes[5] or turnips as offerings, but in his *History of Leeds and Grenville* Thad. Leavitt tells a prettier story:

> I have frequently heard him mention the circumstance of a young man asking him to perform the ceremony, at the same time confessing that he had no money, but promising to make a good wheat fan. The offer was accepted, and, in due time, the fan was delivered. An old man once came on the same errand, his offer being a corn basket, with oak splints, and so compactly made, that it was 'warranted to hold water.' It is needless to say that he was made happy.

William Bell was approached on the same issue:

> An Irishman called upon me and asked if I would marry a young couple. I told him I would if he brought them forward. He put a number of questions, the drift of which I soon perceived was to ascertain how the thing could be done in the *cheapest* manner. This led me to suspect that he was not the bridegroom, for at these times bridegrooms are not often so attentive to economy as they are afterwards.

As well as weddings, funerals were often a time of community-wide gatherings.

> ...funerals are always very numerously attended. In the present instance every settler from probably three adjacent townships had joined in this procession to manifest his respect for the deceased and sympathy for the survivors. Few are desirous of absenting themselves, especially if there had been any differences in life-time, for fear their so doing should be misconstrued. Not to attend a funeral would be proof of harbouring ill-will towards the family, much more than would the fact of attendance be proof of any strong friendship having subsisted during life-time; but let us not dwell on this negative view of a Canadian interment, as if attendance was all but

---

[5] Which might be used for potash; see below p. 292.

compulsory for the sake of decency. Roman Catholics and Orangemen, all can join, and each has plenty of time for reflection while accompanying the remains of those who have shared his hardships as a fellow-labourer, to their last resting-place on earth. [Mrs Edward Copleston]

This last remark is a reference to the fact that the funeral procession, from the house to the cemetery, might have to cover quite a distance. This was one reason why many people were simply buried in a quiet corner of a field on the farm itself. These plots can be recognized today, if not by surviving gravestones, by the unlikely patches of lilacs and day-lilies which were planted by family members more than a century ago.

The importance of mutual goodwill cannot be emphasized enough. So much of what they had to do required assistance or availability of neighbours, so the pioneers knew they had to keep a close sense of community.

> ...if he has neighbours, he will often be able to get his work done without any direct outlay, it being customary for the inhabitants of a new settlement mutually to help each other, by accepting labour in return for labour. There is thus no outlay on either side, every one affording another a degree of assistance equal to what he has received from him. A man, perhaps, borrows a waggon for a day from his neighbour, and repays him by lending his oxen for an equal length of time. A new settlement is sometimes twenty or thirty miles distant from a mill, and the roads are generally so bad, that the person who carries grain to it waits till it is ground, although he should be detained several days. When this is the case, each individual, by turns, conveys to the mill the grain of three or four of his neighbours, and thus the great waste of labour, which would be occasioned were every one to take his own produce there separately, is avoided. [John Howison]

Aside from weddings and funerals, what did people do to relax and dispel the sense of endless work? Anna Jameson surprises us by saying:

When I was in Upper Canada, I found no means whatever of social amusement for any class, except that which the tavern afforded; taverns consequently abounded everywhere.

She was certainly right that every place had a tavern. It was the centre of every settlement because it was the only public building there for the first few years.

When the first settlers needed to meet and discuss setting up a church or school, founding a club or society, or even to hold a local law-court or elections, it was the tavern which was used. It held the same position as the public house in Britain.

The use of the tavern as a church may strike us as unusual, but there may have been no choice.

> I arrived on Tuesday the 24th of June, and on the following Sabbath preached at the inn, that being the only place in the village where there was a room large enough for the purpose....
> For more than a year I preached in the large room at the inn, there being no other suitable place in the settlement.
> [William Bell]

Another reason for the popularity of the tavern was the fact that alcholic drinks were very inexpensive. They were sold in gallon casks as well as by the glass in taverns, so the liquids were liberally available everywhere. As Katherine O'Brien (one of the Peter Robinson settlers) remarked:

> The rum is very cheap, and a good many of our settlers likes it too well, which may prove their ruin.

> Liquor was a very common commodity in many of the homes in the province. The distiller often lacked ready cash and the settler exchanged his grain for whiskey. The settler in turn sold the whiskey to the innkeeper. In many families, whiskey was served to each member of the household every morning, and thus from infancy the children were accustomed to its taste. Whiskey or cider was usually offered guests or visitors and liquor was served with the meals at many of the inns and on all the boats. [M. A. Garland]

Joseph Abbott observed:

Drunkenness, which is indeed the prevailing vice, the besetting sin of this whole continent, was so rife in our little village, that one could hardly walk quietly through it, especially on a Sunday evening, without being shocked or insulted. Some idea may be formed of the extent to which this vicious habit was carried, from the fact that one-third of the houses in the place were taverns.

You will have heard all the particulars respecting shepherd. ere this he has proved himself a disgrace to the English emigrants, in fact a disgrace to the country. He is a compleat drunkard. Poor Isabella is much to be pitied. What she will do I know not. her prospects I do think must wear a very gloomy appearance.
[Mary Mullett]

In the mind of the pioneer man, drinking and 'bees' (the cooperative gatherings to do large tasks, such as barn raising) went together. If you were having a bee at your farm, you were expected to supply a goodly amount of liquor to get everyone through the day. Those who objected would find that others would be reluctant to attend. From time to time we read of someone who is trying to start a new trend, where bees would be 'dry', but they do not meet with success.

a man came to ask help to put up his barn. It is very inconvenient to spare the hands, but the man is anxious to establish a precedent of having bees without liquor. On condition of his doing so, Edward promised his help.
[Mary O'Brien]

One of the results of the free drinking of whisky was the growth of the temperance movement, which began in the United States but quickly spread to Canada. It was stronger in the evangelical churches, but even the early Presbyterians did not object to drinking. Samuel Strickland was one of those who thought that moderation was better than abstinence. To begin with he thought whiskey-punch had advantages:

...after the soaking we had got, I ordered some whiskey-punch, which I have always found very efficacious on such occasions. Some people recommend tea made from the boughs of the

265

hemlock-pine, which, I dare say, is excellent for some constitutions; but it never agreed half so well with mine as the former antidote, which I can conscientiously recommend—but, like all other medicines, an over-dose may do more harm than good..

He also told a story which ridiculed the hard-line temperance advocates.

A few years ago, when this question was first agitated in Canada, a meeting was held in a school-house on the English line, in the township of Dummer. The lecturer, on that occasion, was an itinerant preacher of the Methodist persuasion. After descanting some time in a very fluent manner, on the evils arising from intemperance, and the great numbers who had lost their lives by violent means, "for my part," said the lecturer, "I have known nearly three hundred cases of this kind myself."

This broad assertion was too much for one of the audience, an old Wiltshire man, who exclaimed, in his peculiar dialect, "Now, I know that 'ere be a lie. Can you swear that you did ever see three out of them three hundred violent deaths you speak on?"

"Well, I have heard and read of them in books and newspapers; and I once saw a man lying dead on the road, and a jar, half full of whiskey, beside him, which, I think, you will allow is proof enough."

"I thought your three hundred cases would turn out like the boy's cats in his grandmother's garden. Now, I will tell thee, that I did know three men that did kill themselves by drinking of cold water. There was John H—, that overheated hisself, walking from Cobourg, and drank so much water at the cold springs, that he fell down and died in a few minutes. Then there was that workman of Elliott's, in Smith, who dropped in the harvest-field, from the same cause; and the Irishman from Asphodel, whose name I forget. So, you see, that more people do die from drinking cold water than whiskey." Then he turned round to a neighbour, who, like himself, was not over-fond of cold water, and said, "I say, Jerome, which would you rather have, a glass of cold water, or a drap of good beer?"

"I know which I would take," exclaimed Jerome; "I would like a drap of good beer best, I know."

This dialogue raised such a laugh against the apostle of temperance, that the meeting was fairly broken up, leaving the Wiltshire man triumphing in his victory over cold water and oratory, in the person of the lecturer. The dryness of his arguments prevailed against the refreshing and copious draughts of the pure element recommended by his discomfited opponent.

John Rowan also saw a funny side to the temperance men, who enjoyed rum sauce too much:

...the temperance men, who make up for no drinking by eating enormously, and who get a little surreptitious stimulant out of the pudding sauce, which the cook, who knows their tastes, furnishes in gallons...

The problems with drunkenness was made worse by the habit of 'treating' which is mentioned by most visitors to Upper Canada at this time. Everyone present was expected to accept a drink from the others and then take his turn as it came.

"Treating" as it is called amongst fellow travellers, is so excessively common, and the drink so freely circulated, as no measurement is required, the cost price of the liquor being perhaps to the publican not above 1s. a gallon. Thus the decanter is put down, and every one is free, for three or four coppers, to dash into his tumbler as much of the dangerous stimulant as he fancies; and he must have a determined will indeed who begins to taste and keeps within anything like moderation. [Henry Christmas]

This habit of whisky treating is far too prevalent, not only in the backwoods, but throughout the province, East and West. My husband often walked to Orillia, and was sure of a friendly lift home; but it was very rarely, indeed, that he was not asked to drive while the owner of the sleigh slept off the effects of the numerous 'treats' he had indulged in during the day.
[Mrs Edward Copleston]

However, people could certainly find other means of enjoyment than the proverbial drinking and smoking. In *Life in the Clearings*, Susanna Moodie includes chapters on amusements and lists fashion, dancing, evening parties, theatre, riding and boating, picnics, the circus, wandering lecturers, singers and musicians. Games were also possible; at Christmas 1840, the Langton family played chess, backgammon and cards. Religious camp-meetings, which had a more serious purpose, also supplied diversion from daily routine.

Of these, several would be confined to the towns. However the most common was the 'evening party.' This is the grand name for what might simply be a gathering of people to eat and talk. If there was room and a musician handy, there would likely be dancing.

As we have seen earlier, dancing was common on shipboard as a way of passing the time. It was also part of any wedding feast. In addition, it was a great attraction in the bush. People would dance all night.

> Balls in Canada are no joke; when one comes forty miles to dance one does not like to make such a journey for a trifle and one takes a spell of dancing sufficient for an average winter at home. [John Langton]

Mrs Moodie remarked on how everyone liked and knew how to dance.

> I never met with a Canadian girl who could not dance, and dance well. It seems born in them, and it is their favourite amusement. Polkas, waltzes, and quadrilles, are the dances most approved in their private and public assemblies. The eight Scotch reel has, however, its admirers and most parties end with this lively romping dance.
>
> Balls given on public days, such as the Queen's birthday, and by societies, such as the Freemasons', the Odd Fellows', and the Firemen's, are composed of very mixed company, and the highest and lowest are seen in the same room. They generally contrive to keep to their own set—dancing alternately—rarely occupying the floor together. It is surprising the goodwill and harmony that presides in these mixed assemblies. As long as they are treated with civility, the lower classes shew no lack of courtesy to the higher. To be a spectator at one of these public balls is very amusing. The

country girls carry themselves with such an easy freedom, that it is quite entertaining to look at and listen to them. At a freemasons' ball, some years ago, a very amusing thing took place. A young handsome woman, still in her girlhood, had brought her baby, which she carried with her into the ball-room. On being asked to dance, she was rather puzzled what to do with the child; but, seeing a young lawyer, one of the *elite* of the town, standing with folded arms looking on, she ran across the room, and putting the baby into his arms, exclaimed— "You are not dancing, sir; pray hold my baby for me, till the next quadrille is over." Away she skipped with her partner, and left the gentleman overwhelmed with confusion, while the room shook with peals of laughter. Making the best of it, he danced the baby to the music, and kept it in high good humour till its mother returned.

"I guess," she said, "that you are a married man?"

"Yes," said he, returning the child, "and a mason."

"Well, I thought as much any how, by the way you acted with the baby."

"My conduct was not quite free from selfishness—I expect a reward."

"As how?"

"That you will give the baby to your husband and dance the next set with me."

"With all my heart. Let us go a-head."

In the country, the small log cabins did not lend themselves to dancing, but the threshing floor of the barn, traditionally the cleanest part of that building, could be swept and used in this way. Both church services and wedding receptions might well be held there. Writing in 1842, Anne Langton tells of a ploughing match held nearby which was to end in their barn with a dance and a feast of buns, rice pudding and gingerbread.

John Howison tells of a village priest who forbade his parishioners to dance. It is puzzling to modern readers why he would do this when it was one of only a few amusements available to them. Their forms of dancing did not involve cuddling, which might have formed the basis for the objection, but perhaps it was the gathering and its inevitable drinking and excitement which were not wanted.

One gathering which was a social occasion even if it were not meant to be was the annual mustering of the militia. Legally all adult males had some obligations to be available to defend the king's honour, but they were not called upon to do so during this time period. The only events which had a military flavour were those brief moments of the rebellion in 1837.

Anna Jameson describes a militia gathering, with the cavalry, or 'lancers,' in a variety of uniforms and as for the infantry:

> Here there was no uniformity attempted of dress, of appearance, of movement; a few had coats, others jackets; a greater number had neither coats nor jackets, but appeared in their shirt sleeves, white or checked, or clean or dirty, in edifying variety! Some wore hats, others caps, others their own shaggy heads of hair. Some had firelocks, some had old swords suspended in belts, or stuck in their waistbands; but the greater number shouldered sticks or umbrellas.
>
> Mrs. M[agrath] told us that on a former parade day she has heard the word of command given thus—"Gentlemen with the umbrellas take ground to the right! Gentlemen with the walking-sticks take ground to the left!"

She concludes by saying, "The parade day ended in a drunken bout and a riot...."

As Mrs Moodie implies, everyone mixed together at social events. In fact, many of the ideas about exclusiveness which dominated social interaction in Britain were left behind there. Religious antagonisms were lessened.

> There in every city or village the Churchman can attend his own church, The roman Catholic, the Presbyterian, and the Methodist can do the same. There is toleration here too, but not carried to excess. There is not war to the knife, as in Ireland, between Protestant and Catholic. Political parties are not divided according to religion; Protestant and Catholic, Churchman and Dissenter, vote together at the polling booth, and yet each loves and supports his own church. [John Rowan]

The familiar objections would occasionally be made, but instead of approval, they would meet with the new tolerance in reaction. Someone criticised a church decorated for Christmas, mostly in greenery from the surrounding forest.

> So strong is the feeling of Ultra-protestantism in many parts, that these harmless (to say the least), and to our mind cheering and appropriate symbols of Christmas, recalling so many happy associations, are considered as so many evidences savouring of Popery, by the same orthodox individuals who would raise the emblems of Orangeism in defiance of the known wishes of their sovereign. [Mrs Edward Copleston]

Each writer (and each settler, too) did bring their own particular prejudices to their observations. The following two conflicting quotations are both based on an assessment of the state of the farms of established settlers:

> The Scottish Highlanders were distinguished as hard workers, but their living standards remained low. Immigrants from the south of Ireland practised a slovenly agriculture, unless they happened to be located among other British groups. Samuel Strickland, who had excellent chances for observation, declared that 'as a general rule, the English, Scotch, and north of Ireland men make much better and more independent colonists than emigrants from the south of Ireland.' Lowland Scots, as we mentioned above, had the highest reputation. [R. L. Jones]

> Most of the settlers might live much more comfortably than they do at present, if they exerted themselves, or had any ideas of neatness and propriety; but they follow the habits and customs of the peasantry of the United States, and of Scotland, and, consequently, are offensively dirty, gross, and indolent, in all their domestic arrangements. [John Howison]

The Irish did have to endure the contempt of the English. As Sydney Smith said during this very time period:

> The moment the very name of Ireland is mentioned, the English seem to bid adieu to common feeling, common prudence and common sense, and to act with the barbarity of tyrants and the fatuity of idiots.

271

However, there were a great many Irish in Upper Canada, and also Scots, who were politically powerful and did not have the same intensity of feeling about the Irish as the English did.

Although Samuel Thompson mentions fighting between Orange and Green Irish on board ship, and McKay cites Irish rioting in Lanark which went on for several days, there are relatively few discussions of this topic in pioneer accounts.

Martin Doyle, in his influential emigrants' guide, suggests that the best thing would be a 'cross in the breeds' mixing Irish, English and Scots which would result in 'an improved character.'

One divide that could not be avoided was that between rural and 'urban' or between our town and any other.

Although we tend to think of our pioneer ancestors in a log cabin in the forest, many lived in towns or at least villages which had some claim to urban life. They still depended on the land for much of what they did, had extensive gardens and kept animals. The differences were similar to those that divided the urban and rural worlds until the advent of television eliminated many of them. For some people, wherever they lived was the best place, bar none.

> To the north-west of Chinguacousy lies the township of Caledon, long looked upon as beyond the verge of civilization, or habitable country by emigrants or land seekers. It was originally peopled by a rough and hardy set, a large number of whom still remain, and retaining their old backwoods, *divil-me-care* manners, seem to think, when they descend to an older settled or more civilized township, that it is necessary to give themselves airs, to show their independence. It is amusing to see some of these gentry at a tavern, when they happen to come down to the village to sell their wheat, or transact other business. Nothing pleases them; nothing is so good as they get in Caledon! There are no potatoes on the table; they can get potatoes for supper in Caledon. They do not like *bread*; they get hot cakes for supper in Caledon. The beef is not as good as they get in Caledon. The tea is not as good. Even the salt is not as salt, the sugar as sweet, nor is the mustard, (even when it brings tears into their eyes) as strong as they get in Caledon! And should any one at table possessing a little more sense of propriety, attempt good naturedly to check their grumbling,

they will probably become sulky, and exclaim loudly that they can talk as much as they like in *Caledon*. [W. H. Smith]

Life in the bush was such that many people rarely got to town. The towns that they had seen were those they encountered on the trip into the province, the stopping places along the water: Prescott, Kingston, Cobourg, Port Hope, Toronto, Hamilton. For those who went on to the west, there might be Niagara and Queenston, Port Dover and Port Talbot.

One of the benefits of the geographical proximity to the United States was that democratic ideas quickly made themselves felt in the new society forming in Upper Canada. This manifested itself in one way which made some visitors uncomfortable.

> I felt my English blood almost boil in my veins when I found myself sitting in company with two servant women at the *table d'hote*, at the same time that their mistress occupied a place at the other end of the table. I could very well accommodated myself to such neighbours in the States, but never expected to have found the levelling system introduced into the British provinces to such an extent. [Edward Coke]

This difficulty—dining with the servants—comes up often with visitors, not only in hotels but also those at table in private homes. It had quickly become a matter of no remark to Canadians.

> Pride of birth was unknown... [Canniff Haight]

> One great comfort is, in the forest you are as well off as your neighbour. [Ellen Steele]

Servants were something of a problem. Many households needed to employ people to help both inside and out. They were often used to having servants at home and expected the same class of people to be available in Upper Canada. They were not. Whole families worked together to maintain their own farms and only a limited few were prepared to live elsewhere. They were usually very young women. Young men often hired themselves out as day workers, particularly as 'choppers,' but were also needed at home too much to be gone long.

273

The young women who hired as servants were often as young as fourteen and consequently their knowledge of some household tasks was limited. Anne Langton remarks on this but says that women married so young that employers had no choice. She does say that her fourteen-year-old maid is a 'capital little scrubber.'

People hiring servants have always tended to sigh and remark that those available are not quite what they wanted.

> Almost all the servants are of the lower class of Irish emigrants, in general honest, warm-hearted and willing; but never having seen anything but want, dirt, and reckless misery at home, they are not the most eligible persons to trust with the cleanliness and comfort of one's household. [Anna Jameson]

Another adjustment was that people whom one regarded as a social equal might be willing to be hired as a menial. While this would not have been possible in Britain, in Canada it simply required a change in the mindset of everyone involved.

> Whilst we were at dinner, one of the young Seagers came in, having failed of getting a permanent place. Fanny and Richard were melted and after much private consultation determined on taking him themselves. The difficulty rested on employing as a hired servant a person whom they could not receive in their family but as an equal. [Mary O'Brien]

Having been plucked from British-Irish society, with its emphasis on class, it is not surprising that some of those in Upper Canada preferred to let on that they came from a higher level than may have seemed evident.

> The affectation of wishing people to think that you had been better off in the mother country than in Canada, is not confined to the higher class of emigrants. The very poorest are the most remarked for this ridiculous boasting. A servant girl of mine told me, with a very grand toss of the head, "that she did not choose to *demane* hersel' by scrubbing a floor; that she belonged to the *ra'al gintry* in the ould counthry, and her papa and mamma niver brought her up to hard work."
> This interesting scion of the aristocracy was one of the coarsest specimens of female humanity I ever beheld. If I called

her to bring a piece of wood for the parlour fire, she would thrust her tangled, uncombed red head in at the door, and shout at the top of her voice, "Did yer holler?"
[Susanna Moodie]

The people who hired out as 'choppers' (those who helped clear the land) were usually rough, tough and we would tend to think of them as exclusively young men. Clearing was so necessary that young women also did it, and Samuel Thompson tells a brave and touching story about one of them.

> Hardworking they were all and thrifty. Mary and her elder sister, neither of them older than eighteen, would start before day-break to the nearest store, seventeen miles off, and return the same evening laden each with a full sack flung across the shoulder, containing about a bushel and a half, or 90 lbs. weight of potatoes, destined to supply food for the family, as well as seed for their first crop. Being much out of doors, and accustomed to work about the clearing, Mary became in time a 'first-rate' chopper, and would yield to none of the new settlers in the dexterity with which she would fell, brush and cut up maple or beech; and preferring such active exercise to the dull routine of household work, took her place at chopping, logging or burning, as regularly and with at least as much spirit as her brothers. Indeed, chopping is quite an accomplishment among young women in the more remote parts of the woods. ...Mary...being a good-looking, sunny-faced, dark-eyed, joyous-hearted girl, was not a little admired among the young axe-men of the township. But she preferred remaining under her parents' roof-tree, where her stout arm and resolute disposition rendered her absolute mistress of the household, to the indignity of promising to 'obey' any man, who could wield no better axe than her own.

Since choppers usually worked in pairs, for safety's sake, Mary found herself often beside a young Scot of 18, who adored her. Eventually she agreed to marry him, but before the wedding she was killed in a chopping accident. The young man never did marry anyone else.

The hired man had a special place. Although he was an employee (not a word that would have been used at the time), he was not regarded as a servant. He ate with the family and interacted with them on an equal level.

In his history of agriculture in Ontario, R. L. Jones also makes a point about the handyman's role within the family. The boys would learn from him, perhaps taking instruction from him more easily than their father, who was also an authority figure. The daughters of the house could flirt with him (also a learning process) and it was not unusual for one of them to marry him.

The same question worked in reverse; the 'master,' as he was called in Britain, was not found in Canada in the same way. He was replaced by an employer, a 'boss.'

> the person I work for came here a very poor hand 10 years ago. had to go about to [sheet torn] wood for a Living. he is an Irishman and is now the greatest master here employing nearly 150 hands, Joiners, Bricklayers, Laborers, &c. I have as good a wage as any Man in the Shop and am well satisfied. I can only say this that if I was a Journeyman in england and buy any means could get as much as would bring me to America I would not stop in england and home but come where a man considers himself as good as his Bos for that is the name they give them here. they never call them master they think it below them [John Hallas]

Visiting one another quickly became a matter more of shared interests and concerns than predetermined social standing.

> We have the honor of visiting at the Judge's and member of Parliament's what many of our English relations cannot say. the former is a very nice family they have a very nice garden and a great many greenhouse plants what is very scarce in Canada. [Deborah Mullett]

Clothing, which was such a mark of social levels in Europe, was less so in Canada.

> This has become a verry fashionable place you would see more silks worn here in one day than you would see in Maguiresbridge in your lifetime and could not tell the difference between the Lady and the Servant Girl as it is not uncommon for her to wear a Silk Cloak

276

and Boa and Muff on her hands and her Bonnet ornamented with artifical flowers and vail and can well afford it wages is so good.
[M. Carrothers]

Soon after, another gentleman came up, whom I had often seen in Edinburgh, and who recognizing me, although we had not been acquainted, accosted me. He had travelled over Europe several years ago, and had at last come to Goderich, and bought land in the township of Colbum [Colborne]. When I met him, he had an ox's chain carrying around his body, and a piece of beef in his hand, which rendered his appearance very different from that formerly presented by him in the character of an Edinburgh dandy. He requested me to inform his friends that I had seen him in chains...
[James Logan]

Crime was not a great problem. Taking someone to court was such a great effort that it was avoided, according to Alexander Ferrier, who said that people in Fergus had to make the two-day trip to Hamilton to go to court.

Fortunately, in those days crime was very uncommon, and in this neighborhood, especially, the settlers were of a very respectable description generally. There might be a black sheep here and there, but they were not numerous. I am sure I never locked my door for years, and slept with the window open, and it was the same even in the village.

The basic fact of society, especially backwoods society, was that everyone depended on one another. They needed one another's assistance. The most obvious example of this is the 'bee.' Henry Christmas tries to make the potential emigrant feel better at the prospect of building his house with the news that his neighbours will come and help put it up. He neglects to mention that you will then be expected to do the same for them.

Bees were not merely a good way of accomplishing large tasks, but also a basic part of social life.

The older colonists about you, if solicited will come and help at what (from the bustle and activity of the work,) is termed a Bee, they first draw the timber together with oxen, (provided that you have it previously felled, cut into the proper lengths and

277

squared,) and raise up your house; this kind of work is called a raising Bee, and in the same way, assistance is mutually given in beating out the Indian corn from its husks, in what is called a husking Bee—the nature of the work always determining the denomination of the Bee.

Such is the friendliness of the more established settler, that they will dispense with your giving them breakfast and dinner, if your circumstances render you really unable to provide them; some whiskey, and the evening frolic are sufficient inducements for the attendance of your neighbours, whose accommodating mode of assisting each other, and of doing as they would be done unto, is highly creditable to their feelings. It will, however, be expected, and very fairly, that you will repay these acts of kindness by giving labour in return, on similar occasions. [Martin Doyle]

This is a logging bee:

There were about six acres to log, and he had collected about twenty of his neighbours, or their servants, as those who could not work were obliged to find substitutes. There were five yokes of oxen, and generally four, but sometimes only three, men to a yoke, with a boy to drive. To the yoke over the necks of the oxen is fastened a long chain, with a hook at the end, and this chain is put round a log, which is thus dragged to the pile. Two of my friends, myself, and a servant, were attached to one of the yokes, which was driven by a boy. When the logs, which vary from ten to fifteen feet in length, and from one to two and a half in diameter, were brought to the pile, we laid them on in a proper manner. After the first layer was arranged, the rest of the logs were hoisted on with handspikes; the heaps vary from four to five feet in height, and are not made too large, so as to burn with facility. This is a very laborious part of the operation, especially when the logs are heavy; and if they should slip, you are in danger of getting your leg broken, or even of losing your life. We worked hard all day from nine, and logged about three acres. At one we had dinner in the barn, masters and servants together, without distinction. Two young Englishmen were present, but did not assist, and were therefore laughed at.
[James Logan]

The drinking and dancing which followed most bees were deplored by some.

> Some people can do nothing without a bee, and as the work has to be returned in the same manner, it causes a continual round of dissipation—if not of something worse. [Samuel Strickland]

However, the formal aspects of a bee (someone making the rounds to ask people to be present, the whisky and dancing afterward) were not necessary. If someone required assistance, people simply did what was required. As Canniff Haight put it, "The sufferings or misfortunes of a neighbour, as well as his enjoyments, were participated in by all."

A fine example is related by Samuel Strickland. When he began his farm in Otonabee, he went alone, leaving his young wife at her father's, pregnant. He was called away when she became ill after the birth of their son, but she died before he could reach her. He remained in Darlington for some weeks in mourning, and expected that his crops would be lost, for his return was made too late to sow. When he arrived home, he found that his neighbours had sown his fields for him, which he terms, "this act of Christian benevolence."

Religion

At the beginning of this period, the Church of England remained the state church of Upper Canada also. As each township was laid out, land was set aside for the church (these were called Clergy Reserves).

However, a good many of the new settlers were not Church of England. There were many Scots, there were Irish Presbyterians and Roman Catholics. At this time the Church of Scotland (which was Presbyterian) was in a state of ferment involving controversy which would, in the 1840s, blossom in actual schism.

After the death of John Wesley in 1791, Methodism also began down a trail which led to many kinds of Methodists who competed with one another for adherents.

A new colony such as Upper Canada offered all these groups opportunities for evangelism. Initially the Church of

279

England did not have a sufficient number of clergy to send as missionaries to the new land and the thinly spread population made the old-country concept of parishes difficult to transfer to the new. In 1820, there were only sixteen Anglican clergy in all of Upper Canada.

Methodist missionaries were active in the area, travelling on horseback and holding services wherever they could. Concentrations of Scots offered the chance for missionaries from Scotland to start churches. Both these groups brought the theological quarrels of their places of origin to the new country.

What did this mean to the settlers? They were used to living in a place where the church was handy, and everyone had some connection with it. This may have been only a thin thread of baptism, marriage and burial, or it may have been a weekly attendance at services. Even for those whose attendance was sporadic, there was probably an underlying belief in the general tenets of Christianity and ties to a specific denomination.

When they came to Canada, they wanted the same situation to continue. Regular attendees wanted to have the services; the others expected to have their children baptized.

> Oh! what a favour I should think it if I could live within the compass of such a nice meeting as Bristol. no person can tell but those that are deprived of it. [Deborah Mullett]

Once a community was founded (with its scattering of houses, a tavern and perhaps a store), it soon had two needs. One was for a schoolhouse and the other for a church. These might be perceived as the same need. The schoolhouse which was used by pupils during the week could serve as a church on Sunday.

> During the winter, with a large stove in the church, if we were not quite so comfortable as we could have wished, we were much more so than we had ever been before. The schoolhouse, at best, was but a miserable substitute for a church; and the tenure by which we held our trifling occupation of it, the whim and caprice of the mixed public, made it still more objectionable; but now our bare walls, with their sheltering room—they could boast of little else—were our own, and we felt ourselves at home. [Joseph Abbott]

The schoolhouse was a public building and use of it as a church might be at the 'whim and caprice' of the public. If there were more than one clergyman to hold services there, then they must each have a chance.

Neighbouring clergy did not feel the need to be friendly. Joseph Abbott, the Anglican priest who wrote the words above, did not have a civil word for his local Methodist counterpart. William Fraser, the Secessionist Presbyterian minister near London, often found himself in unhappy proximity to other clergy. He had to share a schoolhouse in Goderich with an Anglican priest and a pulpit in West Gwillimbury with a Church of Scotland minister.

The Methodists had been in the habit of allowing the Presbyterians to worship in their chapel, but at one point the favour is withdrawn as Fraser records:

> This day the sacrament of the Lord's Supper was dispensed. We were denied the privilege of using the Methodist chapel and were obliged to occupy a private house.

Missionary clergy did not have an easy time of it. They had very little money and no time to farm or garden to grow food for their families. Their congregations expected them to work toward building a church, the funds for which might be difficult to find. They were also away from home a great deal. A single duty might take them away for the whole day.

> Hired a horse and rode out to Dorchester 10 miles—Performed the ceremony of marriage between Julia Ramons & Sarah Manning vexed at being obliged to wait so long. Got home at sunset. [William Fraser]

They could also expect to go on long journeys, staying with strangers and holding services in whatever places offered themselves. Joseph Abbott reports:

> ...but the more distant settlements which were comprised within my extensive charge occupied a large portion of my time. There were six principal ones, each of which now has a church and a clergyman of its own. Two of these I visited once

every winter, and the others once during the summer, so that each had divine service only once a year. ...When I reached my destination I married seven couples, and baptized seventeen children and three adults. I was two Sundays absent, during which time I read prayers and preached in schoolhouses and private dwellings eleven times to crowded and attentive congregations.

Distance and the difficulties of communication also caused problems. Once, the people at Paris expected William Fraser to come and preach, and assembled for the purpose, but he did not know it and did not go. Naturally they were angry and blamed him.

Most settlers wanted to have a church in their midst, as it was part of life. Many would have had strong religious convictions which made the church even more desirable. If the church which was erected was not of the sect which they knew, they might well change to it, for convenience. It was thus that many who had adhered to the Church of England (or Ireland) became Methodists in the new country.

The possibility of having a clergyman at a settlement for the first time was exciting for the settlers.

If I mentioned in my last letter that we had the prospect of a minister settling in this quarter I must now say that the prospect was not realized but we are now more happily situated. The General Assembly has sent us out one and pay half of his yearly stipend. he is to preach at three different stations, one of which is to be Fitzroy Harbour. He preached in my new home some weeks ago when a call which I had previously prepared was signed by heads of families present and afterwards sent round for the Signatures of those who were absent. The other places have done the same, and we expect he will be placed so soon as the sleighing becomes good. He has passed two nights with us since his arrival, and appears to be a very pious and excellent man. [David MacLaren]

Aside from the obvious religious reasons, the people needed the clergy for marrying, burying and baptizing. As we have seen, people were used to going where they could to be married. Burying the dead had to be done with some swiftness, especially in summer, so if a clergyman was not available, it was done by a respected or elder member of the community, who could read a piece of scripture and say a few prayers at the graveside.

The baptism of children was more of a problem. The idea that an unbaptized child who died might be in peril in the next world was still prevalent. Since death was an always present danger, most parents wanted to see their children christened. Also, it was part of their tradition.

In England, the Church of England clergy baptized all who came to them. Roman Catholic priests were also prepared to do this. However, the theological storms in the Church of Scotland had made the baptism of children a contentious issue. William Bell, William Proudfoot and William Fraser all refused to baptize children whose parents were not members of their congregations. In Proudfoot's and Frazer's cases, this meant the parents had to subscribe to their Secessionist views also.

> I was accosted by David McKenzie a man whose face I did not recollect ever to have seen who said that he had a child to baptize. I said to him that it was true that I had baptized Neil Ross' child but that I had since entertained serious doubts of the propriety of having done so. That according to our formalities we were not allowed to dispense ordinances to those who were not church members and that he had better wait a little.
> He immediately got into a towering passion. Said he wd. not wait—that he wd. get it done elsewhere—that at home children were baptized when 8 days old and that he cd. not think of waiting—that our rules were a great deal too strict—and that he saw but little prospect of having a church established on that road. I replied that if the principles by which we were regulated were too strict and required modification it was not for me or for any other individual minister to set them aside altogether, &c. &c. He turned away and went off as he said to stop his wife whom he said was on the road [i.e., on her way for the baptism]. [William Fraser]

William Bell in Perth felt the same way:

> Ignorant or immoral persons would sometimes call at my house with children and request me to baptize them; and it was of no use to tell the former they must be instructed, or the latter that

they must reform their conduct, before I could recognise them as church members or baptize their children.

Still he insisted, but finding it of no use, he altered his tone, and in a most insolent manner told me that I *must* do it, and that I had no right to refuse. [William Bell]

Though I had given public notice that, in ordinary cases, I would baptize no children but in presence of the congregation, and after the parents had received the necessary instructions, or had satisfied me that they had a right understanding of that ordinance, yet ignorant applicants continued to bring children to my house, and insist that I should baptize them there. On the evening of one of the coldest days I have ever felt even in Canada, a man and a woman came with a child nearly frozen to death, and requested me to baptize it. [William Bell]

The parents of this last child were ill, and these were the godparents, probably fearful for the child's health. Bell refused, and the people went to the only other clergyman in the vicinity, the Roman Catholic priest. He performed the baptism. The child and its father both died shortly after.

Bell also records that he refused funerals if he disapproved of the dead person's life.

It may be difficult for us to understand the mindset of clergy who seem so divided from their flocks by the intensity of their beliefs. Perhaps William Proudfoot himself can illustrate it for us, as he wrote about the religious fervour of another clergyman:

Once when travelling he was exceedingly thirsty—he came to a beautiful cool brook—he said to his parched throat—"Now throat I must teach you that Anderson is master of Anderson so you shall not get a drop." He marched without tasting a drop of water. He never but once kissed his only child, a daughter, because the act of kissing produces too much fondness and in this fondness we are apt to forget our duty to our children.

This rigour allowed the clergy to make decisions which divided them from the public, but also seemed to affect every observation they made:

284

> In the evening visited a family of Highlanders of the name of Buchanan from Appin who are Kirkmen. Read & prayed with them. Their expressions of gratitude for the attention were warm & perhaps sincere. [William Fraser]

The result was a division between clergy and people. The ordinary person did not want his life interfered with, while the clergy felt they had a right (or a duty) to do so.

> About mid-day two waggons came to carry loads to Perth, and we were in hopes of getting away, but were disappointed; for they were permitted to choose their own loading, and they preferred government stores. After they were gone, I learned that the reason they assigned for refusing to take my family and luggage to Perth was, that they heard that I was a minister, and expected that I would reprove them for swearing, a vice to which they were very much addicted. [William Bell]

Since the writer had actively admonished the sailors on-board ship on this matter, the carters were probably right. William Bell had even attempted to prevent the Roman Catholic French-Canadian boatmen from saying their evening prayers in their own fashion while he was travelling down the Saint Lawrence with them.

One belief which became a great sore point was 'profanation of the Sabbath' as the Presbyterians called it. It meant that Sunday was to be not so much as day of rest as a day when nothing but religion was possible. Even walking was disapproved of:

> Many well dressed people were walking on the beach, and the Sabbath appeared to be rather considered a day for amusement than any thing else. [William Bell]

William Bell even referred to it as 'the most common vice in this settlement.' He expected everyone to attend service each week; but, people who had had no clergyman for a long time might have lost the habit.

I began with my own servant. On observing, one Sunday morning, very near church time, that he had not his best clothes on, I asked him if he was sick, or what was the reason he was not ready to go to church? He replied, that he had been there two successive Sundays, and that I surely would not insist upon his going *every* Sunday. [William Bell]

The thin population could not support a local pastor in many cases, so much of the work fell on missionaries in every denomination. Because many of these missionaries did not see their flocks often, they may not have known them personally, which was something of a difficulty. In addition, the clergy themselves were paid very little and were constantly faced with straitened circumstances. As an illustration of this, here is a letter written by Father John Cassidy to the Bishop of Kingston in 1839:

Hon. & Right Revd. Dear Lord,

I wish to acquaint you that I have now got no mission unless I consent to go to a place called Thorah, a bush settlement to the back of Lake Simcoe 70 miles from Toronto. I declare to Heaven I have not as much money as would pay travelling expenses even a shorter distance, and I know your Lordship will not hesitate to believe me for various reasons. I need not detail to you the pecuniary sacrifices which my simplicity has brought me to respecting the mission of Guelph. If there be a single priest in the province to receive a portion of Gov't allowance this season I am the one who might look up to you for that privilege, and the last that ought to be excluded. Bishop Gaulin asked me did I not receive a check from you? Indeed I have not, and when I shall, I will be ready to go to Thorah, or to any place where I could be of service, particularly if it were to serve your Lordship to whom I owe great respect and veneration as in gratitude I am bound. I return today from the city to the bush of Puslinsh near Guelph, and if your Lordship should remember me, please to write in care of Daniel Cambell of Dundas...

At this time, the Roman Catholic church in Guelph was served by missionaries from Dundas, who also cared for a mission in Puslinch, long since vanished. Father Cassidy's view of the country near Lake Simcoe as being in the distant bush is reflected in other contemporary writings.

But there were many who agreed with the stringent, upstanding principles and they joined the churches of the ministers they liked. Others went elsewhere and this contributed to the diversity of church life in Ontario as the century progressed. This was a difference between the old and new worlds.

> you can either go to church on a Sunday or play a game at cards wherever you like, nobody says any thing to you [John Hallas]

Evangelism was constant. Camp meetings, in which preachers in tents attracted huge congregations, were very popular. When one came to town, most of the population might be there, to hear a new preacher. Young people were encouraged to go by elders who considered them insufficiently religious.

> William my son has been at their house a few weeks ago all well, he was with them at a camp meeting which began on a Friday and ended on the Tuesday following, it was supposed there were two thousand people present on the Sunday.
> [William Hewgill]

M. G. Scherk states that if the meeting lasted a week or more, as it might, people would come long distances and camp out at the site. Meetings were held throughout the long days, some mass meetings in the big tents, others small groups privately. He states, "The voice of prayer could be heard in all parts of the ground."

Scherk also says these were exclusively Methodist in nature, but this was not necessarily so. In his history of the Disciples of Christ in Canada, Reuben Butchart mentions 'big meetings' of two or three thousand people.

People's attachment to religious life, or lack of it, continued much as it had in the old country. Churches were established early and remained a focus of any community, along with the schoolhouse and the store. The tavern, which had been the first focus, gradually faded in importance.

The lack of regular access to a clergyman continued to have practical effects long after. The James Lunn family in Clarke

287

township were never entirely sure of their ages. Andrew Lunn (of a later generation, but the problem remained the same) explained that by the time his baptism rolled around, his mother was no longer certain when he had been born. The result was that, through a long life, he could only provide an approximate idea of his birthdate.

Illness

In this period, illness was greatly feared. The change in the weather between Britain and Canada made the settlers uneasy.

> God help the poor emigrants who are yet unprepared against the rigour of the season! [Anna Jameson]

Life was very fragile, for medicine was not in a state to heal many illnesses or prevent others.

> Found all my family well with the exception of the dear babe who is rather unwell with a sore mouth. May God preserve her, and sanctify our fears about her. [William Proudfoot]

> Brother and cousins was rejoiced to see us al living; but on the 17th the child Margaret died been worn out on the journey and up the country in the boats and the waggon the most fatigueing of all. James was the stoutest of us we were worn to perfect weakness... if any changes in my old friends by sickness as it did prevail. Sister Jane Died at Lashine 9 miles from Montreal and Thomas Stuart Died since he came to Godrich Brother Thomas's eldest son Died 28th of last month of croop children are subject to it and it is generally fatal George Scott was sent to hospital from the ship and some others and I heard no word of him since. [Joseph Carrothers]

There was a great deal of talk about 'ague' and Anna Jameson even mentions 'aguish vapours.' The ague consisted of muscle pains and fatigue, and probably was the early-nineteenth century equivalent of our 'flu'.

By and large people had to do without doctors. There were few of them, especially in the country.

...there were numerous quacks and 'characters' about the Market who would sell you anything from cure-all salve to flypaper, and whose repertoire comprehended any service from pulling teeth to writing love letters. [E. C. Guillet]

...medical men were difficult to be obtained and many persons without medical education or experience practised on the unfortunate sufferers. [E. C. Guillet]

When one did settle in the country, they might be similar to the 'mad doctor' described by Samuel Strickland. Strickland himself knew about the lack of medical men and got some training before he emigrated.

Before quitting Suffolk I had learned the art of blood-letting from our own medical attendant. Every person intending to settle in a distant colony ought to acquire this simple branch of surgery: I have often exercised it myself for the benefit of my fellow-creatures when no medical assistance could be procured. [Samuel Strickland]

He then used his knowledge when he was settled, even being invited to assist Doctor 'Tiger' Dunlop himself.

We had no medical man in Guelph for some months after my arrival, so, for want of a better, I was obliged to turn physician and surgeon, and soon became very skilful in bleeding and tooth-drawing, and, as I charged nothing, you may be sure I had plenty of customers. And so well pleased was Dr Dunlop with my proficiency, that he invariably sent all his patients to me. [Samuel Strickland]

Any difficulty might have fatal consequences. Samuel Thompson told of some friends in Nottawasaga, but the story had a sad ending.

The next thing I heard of them was many months afterwards, when Malcolm was happy in the expectation of an heir to his two hundred acre lot, in the ninth or tenth concession of the township. But alas! as time stole on, accounts were unfavourable, and grew worse and worse. The nearest

289

professional man lived at Barrie, thirty-four miles distant. A wandering herb doctor, as he called himself, of the Yankee eclectic school, was the best who had yet visited the township, and even he was far away at this time. There were experienced matrons enough in the settlement, but their skill deserted them, or the case was beyond their ability. And so poor Flora died, and her infant with her.

Mary O'Brien writes in her diary of the birth of her second son in 1832, but she is up and about within three days.

> I got up to breakfast and remained up all day only lying down occasionally. I cut out a frock for little Mary, ate a moderate dinner of boiled mutton, and gossiped away the rest of the time.

As Thompson indicated, married women in the vicinity would serve as midwives, and those with special skills or experience would do general nursing as required. It was quite possible that they would be needed if there was an outbreak of something infectious. Mary O'Brien's husband found scarlet fever and measles raging in Toronto, and a friend of theirs sent her children to be with them in the country to try to keep them safe.

Anne Langton described a nurse who had been trying to stave off a fever in their vicinity.

> One courageous woman has been invaluable in both places. She said that she smoked and before going into the house took a little brandy and wormwood and considered herself proof against infection.

Even if you had a doctor—or two—the situation might be uncertain, whether the illness itself was simple or complex.

> ...David has been poorly all winter and from the 23 of Decem till the first of April close confined by getting cold in the church sitting near a window that admitted air. he was seized headach earach and toot ach and high feavered. the Dr Drew a tooth and cut his gum and gave him medicine that Salicated him imedetly unintended as his complaint was Quinsy at first and when recovering of that he was sized with remitant fever. When we got the second Doctor he understood his trouble and treated

290

him accordinly and he has been working all last month but at one time after his mouth burst inside he could not ly more than 5 minutes by the clock till he must be up and have his mouth washed out an amount of discharge running through amongst his teeth which shut nearly closed so much so tht he had to suck all he got and for 9 days he was in that state without one wink of sleep and on the 10 day he lay ten minutes at one time and I thought he Slept for the first...time his neck was open with a lance 6 or 7 times and I do not know how often he was blistered besides other applications out of number. Now thank God he is well again. Margret waited on him with the most unwearied attention and we relieved one another in turns and our Neighbours were attentive and kind. [John Millar]

One problem for single farmers who became ill was that animals still had to be fed. Neglected crops might fail, but the beasts required attention. In January 1841 John Ross, a farmer in Huron, was thrown from his cutter and severely bruised. His diary entry reads:

confined to the house & unable to work. the maid & Dr Hamilton tended the stock

Once again we see the neighbourly idea of everyone pitching in, even the doctor. The following day, Ross was able to feed the cattle and pigs, and by the next day he was cleaning out the shed. Even severe bruises could not keep someone down in 1841.

Of the many illnesses which bothered the settlers, the worst was cholera. A touring circus was said to have spread the disease throughout Upper Canada.

People heard of it and were very afraid, but where could they go to avoid it? William Gilkison wrote:

Yesterday we have learnt the Cholera is at Quebec, Montreal, &c. and every one is fearful of the disease coming to this quarter...20 June at Niagara - Yesterday a man died in a vessel at the wharf & the usual contradictory opinion—medical opinion is given of the case having been Cholera—at any rate the man died in course of a few hours....I think of leaving this place when Daniel arrives—but I do not know where to steer to avoid the coming pestilence—the minds of people are wonderfully agitated by it. We have reports of all sorts—one story that 100 people died at Montreal on Thursday last.

Clergy, doctors and coffin-makers were all worked to their utmost. A Church of England parson describes a scene in a cemetery:

> On the 19th of June, on entering the burial-ground at six o'clock in the evening, the spectacle which met my view was truly appalling. The grass was strewed with coffins; about twenty men were employed in digging graves; and a few mourners stood in groups of three or four, apparently stupified with fear, or absorbed in mournful contemplation of the scene. They all gathered around me: some looked, and other said aloud, "What shall we do?—where will all this end?" After having consigned all the bodies that were there to the grave, I proceeded to the gate with the view of leaving this scene of death, supposing this part of my labours for the day to be ended; but the appearance of three or four carts in the road, each bearing its load of mortality, induced me to return. The same scene was repeated again and again, until the shades of evening began to close around us. [Joseph Abbott]

The Household

The first product which the new farm could produce was potash. The alkali present in ashes produced by the various fires on the farm would be leached out and then boiled until the water was gone. The result was a salt which was cooked and fused. Potash could be shipped to Montreal for export.

> The currency of the day was flour, pork and potash. The first two were in demand for the lumbermen's shanties, and the last went to Montreal for export. The ashes from the house and the log-heaps were either leached at home, and the lye boiled down in the large potash kettles—of which almost every farmer had one or two—and converted into potash, or became a perquisite of the wife, and were carried to the ashery, where they were exchanged for crockery or something for the house. Wood, save the large oak and pine timber, was valueless, and was cut down and burned to get it out of the way. [Canniff Haight]

292

soon as I can get a pot ash ketle will make pot ash which is
always paid in cash and will then get plenty of clothing
[Robert Forrest]

This will explain why a clergyman would accept a sack of ashes
as payment for performing a wedding. One of Mary O'Brien's
neighbours paid the annual instalment for the purchase of his
farm using the ashes from his clearing.

If the pioneer family had followed the advice of the
guidebooks and arrived in time to plant a crop in the fall for
harvest the next spring, they would be well set to begin on the
road to prosperity. There were things they could grow, and there
was the natural harvest of the forest around them. That left them
independent.

Almost every article of provision and clothing is raised upon
their own farms, but the few articles they must purchase from
the merchant, they pay with ashes, timber, staves, wheat, flour,
butter, cheese or butcher meat. [William Bell]

Mother was making candles last week. We make all our own
things most soap, candles, candlewicks, ropes, thread, bed-
linen, blankets—and William and James' shirts for them to
work in also we have a cloth gown apiece for our own spining
and they are very comfortable for this cold country. People are
often froze here. James have had his ears froze. It is also so cold
here that Rachel & myself slept in the stove room all last winter
but we did not intend to do it again or else we shall lose all our
English Colour. [Deborah Mullett]

the farmer is the most independant in this country as the can
have everything with in them selves to make life comfertible
the make their own soap and candles and sugar in abundance.
Thomas made 400 weight of sugar last spring it was as good a
quality as 8d or 9d sugar the mapel from which this is extracted
is in abundance in this part of the country; the make sugar
trakel beer and vinegar out of the mapel in abundance
[Nathaniel Carrothers]

The farmers up there required very little money, indeed they
feed their own pork, have immense flocks of turkeys, geese,
ducks and poultry. They make their own soap, candles, clip,

293

spin and weave their own wool, raise their own flour, meal, Indian corn. Their milk is excellent , and universally living on their own land they have neither rent nor taxes, and are much more apparently comfortable [than] any man may be in the whole world. I never really saw the really independent man till I saw the Canadian farmer. [John Leeming]

What did they have to buy? Few of our writers mention this and the one who did makes it clear that she must have lived in town and not in the country, where most of what she does not have was cheap or even free.

The quantity of fuel we had to buy at a dear rate; the price demanded for all we consumed seemed exorbitant; the difficulty of procuring any good fresh vegetables; to which we might add the cost, and inferior quality of milk and butter—the former always well diluted, and, not infrequently, sour—were drawbacks that daily discomposed us, and made us long for a move into the country, where plenty might abound without so constant a pull on our purse-strings. [Mrs Edward Copleston]

It was also possible that in a remote, new settlement, there might be a shortage of something quite basic, such as flour. In the history of Grey County, E. L. Marsh tell this tale:

After supper father inquired about a Mr. John Frost, a merchant, and, as it was Saturday night, asked if the store would be open. The reply was, 'Yes; like the gates of 'ell, it's always open.' The man-of-all-work around the tavern was sent to guide us to Mr. Frost's store. On arrival at the store he walked in and said, 'Mr Frost, these men want to see you.' Father introduced himself and handed Mr Frost a letter of introduction from merchants in Montreal who had known Mr Frost when he was in business in Bytown (now Ottawa). Mr Frost was delighted to see men coming in, especially with families, but remarked that it was a dull time at the present and there was no flour in the village. Father said that we were prepared for that as we had six barrels at the wharf.

'Six barrels!' exclaimed Mr Frost. 'Will you lend me two barrels for ten days?' When father agreed he said, 'Please write out an order for the two barrels. Dave, take three men on the scow and pole down to the wharf and get the flour as quick as you can. Sam, take this order to Connel's and get him to give Dave the flour, and you come home on the scow.' Two or three boys who were around the store were then sent out to the different homes to tell the people that if they were at the store in about an hour they could get some flour.

We remained to see the residents of the place assemble. Men and women and children soon arrived. When the flour came, it was doled out in five, ten, and fifteen pound lots according to the number in each family. Though late, there were a good number of hot pancakes in the village of Sydenham on the night of May 12th, 1849. We had hot biscuits for breakfast in the Coleman House on the first Sunday morning we were in the County of Grey.

In the country, people might be fortunate if a travelling peddler came round selling things which could not be made on the farm oneself.

After dinner I rode with Fanny through some of the most magnificent woods. Our business was to order some butter tubs to be made by a cooper who lives there. Fanny was startled to see a pedlar with his bag of drapery and little mahogany box in so wild a scene, but I believe no inhabited spot is beyond this class of adventurers. [Mary O'Brien]

R. L. Jones says that peddlers "were probably more important than the country store-keepers in the distribution of minor staple articles, especially in the newer settlements."

Cash money was scarce, but having little was not too much of a problem, for it was universal. Storekeepers gave goods on credit, but charged more for them as a result.

Mr Ferguson was an excellent worthy man, but a very bad store-keeper; he went upon the old Canadian system of enormous profit and almost unlimited credit; this might be almost necessary formerly, but now when cash is more plentiful those who have it are not content to give cash for credit prices.
[John Langton]

Someone in the neighbourhood might have a little cash.

...she had laid by hard cash, and was regarded as a 'banker's wife' in the woods, always having the needful to lend to her more straitened neighbours whose thrift had not been equal to her own. [Mrs Edward Copleston]

Once a year there was certain to be a demand for hard currency.

...barter did very well, except with the tax gatherer, who, of course, required money; however, taxes were very light in those days. [Alexander Ferrier]

Since they did not have much cash, most settlers were glad to sell or barter what they had.

As for cheese and butter, staple market items later, once again it was a matter of eating what you produced. Robert Wade thought that farm people were profligate with their dairy products.

The reason that butter and cheese sell so much better here than other things is the great extravagance of the inhabitants, many of them that keep four or five cows eat all their butter and cheese themselves.

In his history of agriculture in Ontario, R. L. Jones states that cheese-making was woman's work, which may account for its low status in the money-making ladder.

...the old method of cheese making has done more to injure the health of women in cheese-dairying districts than any other cause.

Jones describes how the first suggestion of a cheese factory in Lobo in the 1860s was greeted with derision until it made money, when others quickly joined in. So it was that the settlers had the luxury of their own fine produce which noticed by Mrs Moodie.

The most delicious butter and tempting cheese, quite equal, perhaps, to the renowned British in everything but the name, were displayed in the greatest abundance.

296

As to vegetables, although Copleston says they were not available, the other side of the coin was that the farmers said they could not sell them. John M'Donald's reason was clear, especially given the state of the roads:

> In the first place, they are far from a market to sell their produce, the nearest being Kingston or Brockville, both of which are 60 miles distant at least by the shortest road. The second disadvantage under which the new settler labours, is the scarcity of draught animals, such as horses and oxen, and their consequent high price, and his inability to purchase. He is therefore obliged to hire one from a driver, so that the expence of conveying his agricultural produce from one part of the province to another, or for the purpose of exportation, is equal in value to the original cost.

They had the same trouble with wheat.

> Thus the pioneers near the southern end of Lake Simcoe were only forty miles from Toronto, but the value of their good crops was halved by the cost of transporting them down Yonge Street. [R. L. Jones]

So the settlers grew vegetables they would use themselves, enough that they could either store or preserve to last through the winter, and of a kind which would prosper in the rugged conditions.

The season began later than in Britain, because of late frosts.

> May was a wet month; plums and cherries in bloom on the 10th; apples on the 20th. Wheat was beginning to shoot on the 30th. June has been a remarkably pleasant month; fine breezes with a warm sun has brought vegetation very fast forward. Seed time continues till late here, from 20th of April to the 20th June; they sow peas as early as they can, after peas they plough their land for Indian corn; they begin to plan early in May, they cannot plant sooner for fear of frost as it is so tender. I sowed three acres of Spring wheat on the 27th of May which looks

297

very well; I sowed barley and oats from the 10th to the 17th of June. [Robert Wade]

The common plantings were 'Indian corn', meaning what we call corn (or sweet corn) today. The word 'corn' referred to grain in Britain. Corn was universally grown for both people and beasts, with pumpkins among it.

The way they plant Indian corn is to plough it once and then harrow it, and then take a hoe and plant them in hills four feet asunder, and as soon as it comes up they plough amongst it and till the soil about the roots and then they do the same thing again in summer; two quarts will plant an acre; pumpkin seed is planted along with it, about a hundred seeds will plant an acre, they run along the grain and sprout up and will grow from ten to 12 cart loads per acre; great quantities of them are used in making pies, etc., and they eat them like custard.... There are great quantities of melons and they grow to great perfection. [Robert Wade]

Robert Wade also thought pumpkins were good as fodder:

Pumpkins are very rich feed and make cows give a great deal of milk and butter.

He also advised:

Turnips are very difficult to raise here on account of the great quantities of grasshoppers.

However, James Scott describes "white turnips and swedes which reached a huge size on new land." Certainly turnips are often mentioned in letters and accounts, and the taste for them was universal among pioneer families, so somehow they managed to overcome the grasshopper problem. Turnips were an ideal kind of crop for these farmers, as they were relatively easy to grow in the garden beside the house, they kept well through the winter, and were substantial and filling when served. They could also be used to feed cattle in the winter.

Potatoes were grown everywhere. After the blight which caused the famine in Ireland in the 1840s, new kinds of potatoes had to be developed. North American farmers were also on the lookout for potatoes which would suit their climate better than the European breeds, and tried many.

Writers on emigration mention green and leafy vegetables seldom, perhaps because they were not accorded as much importance then as now, or because the woods offered such a variety of greenery that it required no comment.

Fruit was a matter of greater interest.

> Nearly every kind of fruit found in the temperate zone flourishes here—apple, peach, pear, plum, quince, cherry, grape, apricot and berries of all kinds. [L. H. Tasker]

> Apples are in every variety superior, when carefully raised, to the English; pears not so good, plums, cherries, mostly of the Kentish kind; peaches are so plentiful, the very hogs feed upon them; the peach trees are all standards, but so little care is taken of them, that it is not possible to imagine to what extent they might be improved. Grapes grow in the Niagara district, but are inferior; gooseberries, currants and raspberries grow wild in great quantities, and in the season wild pigeons feed upon them. [William Cattermole]

> Apples, plums and cherries are more certain than in England, but we want more of a variety; we have no gooseberries but currants grow in abundance. [Robert Wade]

> Rasps and brambles [blackberries] are of the same nature; as soon as the large wood is cleared away they never fail to grow. [Robert Wade]

What is not clear from many of these references is whether the writers mean wild or cultivated fruit. Almost everything which they were used to finding in Britain grew wild in Canada, but of course being wild it was smaller and less sweet.

> Their gooseberries are by no means equal to those of our country, being very small and prickly, though very delicious to the taste. [John M'Donald]

Not everyone was as happy with the thought of wild fruit.

This is also the case with gooseberries, currants, strawberries, &c., which are both abundant and good. Those growing wild in the woods are of little use. [William Bell]

The settlers were glad to find food of any kind in the forest, so the wild fruit, along with greens, roots and nuts, would have been welcome. Sometimes they discovered something they had not known before:

> this has been a fine fruit year there is a kind of cherry in the woods that bear fruit in like manner as the currants the grow very large trees from 2 to 3 feet thick and upward of 60 feet high and quite strait, the timber is beautiful and very durable [chokecherries] [Joseph Carrothers]

They also moved the wild plants into the garden:

> Southby and Anthony went into the woods to get some gooseberry plants, of which they find there is a species remarkably good to be used green. They grow in marshes and with them a species of strawberries very much like our scarlet. These two plants are therefore to occupy jointly a bed in the lowest part of the garden. [Mary O'Brien]

John MacTaggart, who had worked on the building of the Rideau Canal, mentions the cranberry plants which grew in bogs in eastern Ontario, and how people would drive miles to pick them.

Herbs for both seasoning and medicine were plentiful.

> We have the same kind of wild herbs as on the wild Land in England, Tansy, wormwood, nettles, thistles, burdock, elder; but we have no white holly or brume; grass and clover grow natural all over Canada. [Robert Wade]

The thistle, mentioned here for its benefits, was generally regarded as a problem because it grew up in the grain and caused trouble at harvest time. Visitors were divided on the subject, however, some of them denying that Ontario had thistles.

the large thistles, some of them seven feet high, caused us great annoyance. [James Logan]

Often have I gazed upon the *Canadian thistle*—that prolific, sturdy democrat of the soil, that rudely jostles aside its more delicate and valued neighbours, elbowing them from their places with its wide-spreading and arms foliage—and asked myself for what purpose it grew and flourished so abundantly? Surely it must have some useful qualities... [Susanna Moodie]

The apple was always the queen of fruits and as the settlers developed their gardens and the other land near their houses, they wanted an orchard also. A few trees were necessary to provide a winter's worth of fruit, which might be stored in barrels or sliced and dried for pie. It was not long before the rule of 'pie three times a day' began in rural life, and applesauce was always on the table.

they have a nice and cheep way of making Apple sauce by only paring them & cutting them in quarter's and boiling them in Cider—The longer they are boiled the better it will keep. They also dry apples and they will keep for seven years. we have dryed a great many this year. [Deborah Mullett]

By 1840 John Leeming was able to write to his uncle,

Orchards are almost universally attached to farm houses in the Upper P[rovince] and Mr Pooles is both very extensive and well arranged.

Mrs Moodie had also noticed the orchards with some surprise when she arrived:

The banks of the St. Lawrence are picturesque and beautiful, particularly in those spots where there is a good view of the American side. The neat farmhouses looked to me, whose eyes had been so long accustomed to the watery waste [the ocean], homes of beauty and happiness; and the splendid orchards, the trees at that season of the year being loaded with ripening fruit of all hues, were refreshing and delicious.

My partiality for the apples was regarded by a fellow traveller with a species of horror. 'Touch them not, if you value your life.' Every draught of fresh air and water inspired me with renewed health and spirits, and I disregarded the well-meant advice: the gentleman who gave it had just recovered from the terrible disease. [cholera]

By the time John Rowan arrived to make his assessment, he could say:

> The apple orchards of Ontario, both as regards the quantities and qualities of the fruit, are second to none in the world. The export of apples has been found such a profitable business, that farmers through the province have been adding largely to their orchards during the last few years. [this is the 1870s] A ten-acre orchard is not an unusual sight, and I have seen orchards as large as forty acres. Many of the so-called American apples that we see in the shops at home [England] are grown in Canada; the following are some of the favourite kinds: Rhode Island Greening, Northern Spy, Baldwins, Swurzes, Pomme Grise Fameuse, Duchess of Oldenburgh, Swaar, Gravensteins, Blenheim Orange, Keswicks' Codling, Holland Pippin, Alexander, American Golden Russet, Red Astracan, Ribson Pippin, Esopus Spitzenburg, and King of Tomkin's County.

The McIntosh had not been introduced yet.

Orchards everywhere meant that cider was freely available. It was "brought on the table in jugs-full, as water would be brought in England." It is not clear from this reference if it is hard cider or simple apple juice, but probably there would have been plenty of both.

The maple tree and its possibilities were a happy discovery for the emigrants. Aside from its obvious value as wood, there was its contribution of sugar and molasses (as maple syrup was known) to the family's cooking.

The wood itself was "highly prized for axe handles, sleigh runners, shafts, poles, machinery and any purpose for which strength and elasticity are required." Having observed this, John Rowan could not understand why it was also used for firewood (where it also shone). The answer was that there was so much of it, the settlers did not value it highly.

302

But maple trees in the forest each year contributed their very sap and the result was used to sweeten the family's cooking for the rest of the year. Both the syrup and sugar could also be sold for cash.

The timing of the sap run was very definite, when the sun was warm in the day but the frost was still sharp at night. The natives had taught the settlers all about the process, including how to make the sugar moulds from birch bark.

Honey was the other source of sweetness.

> ...in the harvast cut it down and take out of it 50 or an 100 wheight of honey if it happens to be an hollow tree where bees can hive. this is not an uncomon case as the are plenty in the woods. bees do thrive and multiply in this country far better than with youes. I have counted 73 hives at a farmers place. the honey is not so well tasted as with yous I think. it is owing to the wild state of the country. [Nathaniel Carrothers]

Soon after the building of the house, and while the chopping was going on in the surrounding forest, some sort of barn would have to be built to accommodate the animals which would be arriving soon if they were not already there. There might be cows for milk and meat, oxen as draught animals, pigs and poultry.

> If a settler had a good yoke of working oxen and a cow, with two or three pigs, he was pretty well off, and was not very particular as to the breed. I think the favorite cattle in old times were the red cattle, which were generally quite hardy, and the cows pretty good milkers, and their origin, I have little doubt, was French, having come from Lower Canada or the French settlements in the West [i.e., near Detroit] [Alexander Ferrier]

After being so kind to these pioneer breeds, Alexander Ferrier then goes on to describe their appearance at the 1836 Guelph fair:

> The show of animals in 1836, with a few exceptions, was miserable. A lot of poor, little, lean beasties represented the cattle in general, and the hogs were the genuine alligator and chipmonk breeds.

R. L. Jones suggests they were probably an indistinguishable mix of old Dutch, English and German breeds, every colour possible.

Taken one with another, they were poor milkers and producers of tough beef, and seem to have been valued mainly according to their hardiness.

The cows were allowed to wander, eating at will.

The cattle are genrly all horned and of a reddish colour. They ly out all winter except some Scotch settlers that has them put up in a house. [John Millar]

We foddered our cattle from the 15th of December until the 20th of April; the customary way here is to keep the horses and cows in pasture and turn the young cattle into the woods, where they live very well and they return twice or thrice in the week for salt, which is very necessary on account of the great distance from the sea, the rains not being impregnated with salt. [Robert Wade]

all the poor people here have a cow or two they can get one for from 3 to 5 pound they keep them for very little. the air is so different here from what it is at home that they require to give the Cattle Salt People will rise in the morning milk the Cow after give her a plate of salt she will then go away into the fields and Lanes pick what she can to eat in the evening she returns home to be milked and take another plate of salt and then goes to rest for the night so that the keeping you see cost them little or nothing compared to what it would in england and so it is with pigs the walk away in the morning stops sometimes weeks away and comes home to their stys again [John Hallas]

The saving, therefore, (of course this is in the case of a family) is very great. On a farm, moreover, the expense of keeping these animals is comparatively nothing. I believe that these "republican cows" who pick up their living by the road sides, are liable to be pounded [impounded as strays], but this is scarcely ever done unless they turn out "breachy," i.e., knock down fences to get at the crops. In Toronto, even cows and pigs are occasionally seen running loose about the town, though contrary to law, frequently pursued by half the dogs in the parish, who seem to consider them a fair game when they trespass on the respective localities of the said canine gentry, to whose objurgations they reply as they beat a hasty retreat by a variety of squealings, lowings, and bellowings, which form now and then in the back streets a whimsical and most unmusical concerto. By the way, talking of concerts, the lovers of ancient music will be pleased to be informed that a very promising society for the performance of the works of the great masters flourishes in Toronto... [Henry Christmas]

Cows might wander too far, however, and not be available for milking. There was a suggestion finding them and ensuring their return:

A bell attached to the neck of one or two, and a good lump of rock salt within their reach near the house, in addition to 'slopping them' or giving them a little meal or bran mash, or a few roots at milking time, are generally amongst the best means of securing their regular and respectful attendance. [Henry Christmas]

Eventually more far-seeing farmers imported purebred cattle from England. News of these breeds spread by means of the newly founded agricultural societies and fairs, but ordinary farmers resisted them. They were happy to leave their cows running free, meeting up with whatever bulls happened to be in the neighbourhood.

Uncles house for some time after we arrived was visited by gentlemen and Farmers to see the Cattle we had brought over with us and the news of our arrival was put in the Newspapers at Port Hope as having arrived with imported Cattle From England; your Uncle and Cousins John and Ralph have taken 17 Premiums this last Summer held at Grafton they have the best breed of Cattle in the Neighbourhood and they certainly have the best farms... [Ralph Wade]

The Wade family made a great contribution to improvement of bloodlines in Ontario in this way.

The government encouraged the founding of agricultural societies, whose principal purpose was the education of farmers and promotion of modern scientific methods. County and provincial agricultural fairs were also sponsored by these organizations. The competitions helped to focus attention on

305

improved breeding, although for most people the fairs were mostly a fine opportunity for a holiday.

As early as 1831, the Kent county annual 'cattle show' was being held in the autumn, but the prizes do not mention breeds. There are simply horses, neat cattle 'of improved Canadian breed,' swine and sheep. By 1850 when the provincial show had started, there were many categories by breed in large animals right down to kinds of poultry and birds.

Since most settlers had no training in butchery, they simply did the best they could.

> ...there is not a regular butcher in the country. The way they kill a beast in this country is to have a bee, viz., five or six of the neighbours to assist them; they take him in the pasture without fastening him and with a little axe they fell him, cut off his head, take off his hide, quarter him and immediately take him to market. [Robert Wade]

As we have seen, the pigs also ran free. They were regarded as predatory, being capable of insinuating their heads (if not more) between fence rails to eat crops growing in fields. Elderly sows were also dangerous around small children.

> Young pigs we have in abundance—a great quantity of poultry such as ducks, Geese, & fowls. We lose a great many when young for want of care, the pigs eat them. [Mary Mullett]

However, they were domesticated and eventually would be rounded up for fattening in fall. This was a good time, as they had generally fed on falling hickory and beech nuts, and if confined for a few weeks and fed on corn, they would be ready for slaughter. R. L. Jones also suggests the pioneer kept them to eat 'buttermilk, potato skins and other things which would otherwise go to waste.'

> Pigs grow very fat while running at large in the woods, especially at the fall of the year... [William Cattermole]

Father killed ten fat hogs last fourth day. they were considered the fatest that had been killed in Adolphustown this year. some of them were four inches thick in fat. [Deborah Mullett]

A day of slaughter—three pigs must bleed today for part of the winter's store and the summer supply of bacon. Southby has his pigs shot, which saves them some suffering and us much annoyance from their dying groans... [Mary O'Brien]

At some point the settler would have to bring a pig or two into the bush from wherever they were bred. This might not be an easy task, if travel on water were involved. John Langton thought his pig was well-trussed.

In the middle of the Lake the pig got her legs loose and dire was the scuffle before I could get her down again and get her manacles adjusted. In her struggles she had kicked out some rags with which a leak had been temporarily stopped up till I can get a supply of oakum and pitch, and I had to stop every ten minutes to bale out, until by shifting my cargo to one side so as to bring one gunwale almost to the water, I contrived to keep the leak above water, not however without imminent danger of drowning my pig in the water which still filled the bottom of the boat. The pig though a bad sailor is nevertheless a good pig, a very tractable animal except for a great fondness for coming into the house. As for want of oxen I have not yet been able to fence in my garden, I cannot fairly object against her the rooting up my onion bed.

The people of Upper Canada consumed so much salt pork, it being their principal meat, particularly in winter, that it had to be imported from the United States.

Pork may certainly be grown as good in Canada as in the States, and the farmers' pork is generally better; but not being yet so well settled a country we use more pork than we grow and Ohio pork can be procured cheaper; they have extensive backwoods there where the pigs run almost wild,—most of the heads in our pork contain a rifle ball. This winter I shall not use much pickled pork; I am going to kill my interesting animal and two of her progeny when the frost sets in. [John Langton]

307

The pigs may have been fleet of foot, but many of them and the wandering cows must have been lost to bears and wolves.

> It is difficult to rear lambs or calves, as the wolves carry them off. My brother lost several in this manner. [James Logan]

Poultry would have been an early addition to the farmyard. The varieties were once again whatever was available. Jones indicates that 'scrub hens and ducks' were the norm until after 1850.

Since the hens wandered freely, they had to be locked up at night to save them from foxes. Their eggs could be anywhere.

> The hens might as well have remained at Peterborough, for the brush heaps afford so many convenient hiding places that I have not yet found an egg; indeed one of the poor creatures would have been much better there, for she this morning served as breakfast to a fox or marten. I have finished the frame of a hen-house but until I get up some of my boards from McAndrew's I cannot give them effectual shelter.
> [John Langton]

The weather also took its toll on the occupants of the barnyard:

> The poultry here must suffer dreadfully from the cold. It is quite a common thing for them to lose their toes. One of ours lost an entire foot, though it is contrived to walk about very well with the stump and the half foot that remined on the other leg. Some of the more weakly birds were frozen to death.
> [Anne Langton]

Geese were kept both for Christmas dinner and their feathers. It might surprise some modern readers to find that they could be plucked more than once:

> The geese were generally plucked 3 or 4 times during the year, or once in every seven weeks, commencing in the month of June. In some places the practise is contrary to law, it being considered a cruelty to animals, but in the early days it was very common many farmers keeping a flock of geese for this purpose. The plucking was done by the women, the down being

308

made into pillows and feather ticks...Grandmother would put a stocking over the head of the goose when plucking it. This was done to keep the goose quiet. [M. G. Scherk]

Sheep were also kept by people who were used to having them in Britain, or who intended to spin and weave the wool. Eating mutton was not as common in Ontario as in Britain, although lamb was popular enough. Goats were rare, which makes it surprising that when John Langton established his bachelor establishment, his first intention was to bring in a pair of goats.

> My provisions and other necessaries are all ready and for stock to my farm I have procured a kiten and am looking out for a goat for milk during winter.

He finds a pair and later says he is surprised that he has had no visitations from wolves, "though one would have thought that the odour of my Billy goat would have attracted them for miles around."

A falling branch hits the billy on the head and for a time Langton is sure the beast will not survive despite the 'surgical assistance' he has rendered. He plans on dragging the carcass through the woods for a mile or two, to attract wolves which Langton can then shoot (the heads were worth a substantial bounty). However, billy recovered.

Langton had success with the plan for milk.

> Tomorrow I go home to make preparations for the rest who are to dine with me on my birthday, and to superintend an interesting event which is about to take place with my venerable nanny-goat, who will now, I hope, supply me with milk.

Langton's cat is one of few mentioned in the emigrants' books. No doubt people had them, but their lives must have been short given the number of predators which would have enjoyed them.

John Langton's sister Anne mentions a neighbour's cat, which goes off to the woods each summer, returning only when the weather turns cold to be a hearth-cat during the winter.

Mrs Moodie tells a cat-tale which starts out being funny:

"If I tolerate our own cat," he would say, "I will not put up with such a nuisance as your friend Emilia sends us in the shape of her ugly Tom. Why, where in the world do you think I found that beast sleeping last night?"

I expressed my ignorance.

"In our potato-pot. Now, you will agree with me that potatoes dressed with cat's hair is not a very nice dish. The next time I catch Master Tom in the potto-pot, I will kill him."

"John, you are not in earnest. Mrs — would never forgive any injury done to Tom, who is a great favourite."

"Let her keep him at home then. Think of the brute coming a mile through the woods to steal from us all he can find, and then sleeping off the effects of his depredations in the potato-pot."

Although Mrs Moodie begs him to leave the cat alone, he does kill it shortly afterwards. The Moodies' own cat, Peppermint, runs off during the course of their move from Douro to Belleville, and they never see her again.

Dogs may have been difficult to bring on the boat, although we do find references to dogs which lived on them. Also, one of the emigrant guides discourages bringing dogs along. As we have seen, Mr. Johnson[6] recorded in his diary, "took my passage in the *Thorntons* for Quebec. Seven guineas in the steerage. paid one guinea for my dog." We also noted that his dog, Grouse, met with hostility from the crew.

Then when they reached Lachine, Grouse was not welcome on the batteau, so Johnson sent his things on the boat and walked with Grouse to Kingston.

Dogs were useful for pioneers, not only as companions but as alarms if wild animals or other people came by. English dogs did not know how to deal with wolves or bears, however. Samuel Thompson's setter, who had recently whelped, dashed past him

---

[6] Johnston's first name is unknown; the earlier references to Grouse's difficulties appear on pages 36 and 65.

when he left his cabin to deal with some circling wolves. He heard her death screams but when they searched for her later, no scrap of her body remained but her heart, which had rolled under a bush.

The dogs that were present needed to be large and strong, for hunting and defence. In her description of 'Brian, the Still-Hunter,' Mrs Moodie sets the scene with his powerful dogs:

> Placing the rifle he had carried on his shoulder in a corner of the room, he advanced to the hearth, and, without speaking, or seemingly looking at me, lighted his pipe and commenced smoking. The dogs, after growling and snapping at the cat, who had not given the strangers a very courteous reception, sat down on the hearth-stone on either side of their taciturn master, eyeing him from time to time, as if long habit had made them understand all his motions. There was a great contrast between the dogs. The one was a brindled bull-dog of the largest size, a most formidable and powerful brute; the other a stag-hound, tawny, deep-chested, and strong-limbed.

Horses were both a necessity and a luxury. Travelling distances or hauling things were made easier by horse-drawn vehicles, but the money to buy a horse might not have been to hand. Eventually, a horse and the equipage to drive it would have become part of the assets of the household. In the meantime it was possible to hire a horse (and a carriage, if required) for special occasions.

> As our route to-day led through a wild and thinly settled tract, we determined on leaving the waggon, and adopting the saddles we had brought for the purpose. It was necessary, however, to procure an additional nag, and I sallied forth in quest of an old tavern acquaintance, Mr Oliver, who I found had retired from the Bar, and now confined his attention to brewing good ale for the lieges. He was unable to supply our wants, but recommended us to a tailor, who transferred us to a butcher, by whom we were introduced to the owner of a Lower Canada pony, and W— finally mounted thereon, at the charge of 3s. sterling per day. [Adam Fergusson]

In *The Canadian Emigrant and Western District Advertiser* in 1833, the editor reprinted some advice for people travelling with horses, perhaps needed because so many people were not used to having their own. It suggested that horses be treated as 'sensible creatures' because "I have seen horses that had more intelligence than the dolts that ride them," and that horses be addressed in Spanish, "most horses have an ear for Spanish." It ended with this tip:

> Never ride your own horse when you can borrow a friend's or neighbor's—especially if you want to travel fast. A horse that knows you won't push himself like one that does not.

Once they joined the family, horses tended to develop personalities, and relationships with everyone concerned. All our families had their special horses. Here is Canniff Haight's tribute to the horse of his childhood:

> I must say a few words in this place about "Old Gray." Why he was always called "Old Gray" is more than I know. His colour could not have suggested the name, for he was a bright roan, almost a bay. He was by no means a pretty animal, being raw-boned, and never seeming to be in first-rate condition; but he was endowed with remarkable sagacity and great endurance, and was, moreover, a fleet trotter. When my father began the world for himself he was a part of his chattels, and survived his master several years. Father drove him twice to Little York one winter, a distance of over one hundred and fifty miles, accomplishing the trip both times inside of a week. He never would allow a team to pass him. It was customary in those days, particularly with youngsters in the winter, to turn out and run by, and many such races I have had; but the moment a team turned out of the track to pass "Old Gray," he was off like a shot, and you might as well try to hold a locomotive with pins as him with an ordinary bit. He was skittish, and often ran away. On one occasion, when I was very young, he ran off with father and myself in a single waggon. We were both thrown out, and, our feet becoming entangled in the lines, we were dragged some distance. The wheel passed over my head, and cut it so that it bled freely, but the wound was not serious. My father was badly hurt. After a while we started for home, and before

we reached it the old scamp got frightened at a log, and set off full tilt. Again father was thrown out, and I tipped over on the bottom of the waggon. Fortunately, the shafts gave way, and let him loose, when he stopped. Father was carried home, and did not leave the house for a long time. I used to ride the self-willed beast to school in the winter, and had great sport, sometimes, by getting boys on behind me, and, when they were not thinking, I would touch "Old Gray" under the flank with my heel, which would make him spring as though he were shot, and off the boys would tumble in the snow. When I reached school I tied up the reins and let him go home. I do not think he ever had an equal for mischief, and for the last years we had him we could do nothing with him. He was perpetually getting into the fields of grain, and leading all the other cattle after him. We used to hobble him in all sorts of ways, but he would manage to push or rub down the fence at some weak point, and unless his nose was fastened down almost to the ground by a chain from his head to his hind leg, he would let down the bars, or open all the gates about the place. There was not a door about the barn but he would open, if he could get at the latch, and if the key was left in the granary door, he would unlock that. If left standing he was sure to get his head-stall off, and we had to get a halter made specially for him. He finally became such a perpetual torment that we sold him, and we all had a good cry when the old horse went away. He was upwards of twenty-five years old at this time. How much longer he lived I cannot say. I never saw him afterward.

The animals at a successful farm might have been numbered like this:

> We have 4 milking cows 8 young Cattle one Yoke of working Oxon one span of horses 13 sheep about 100 fowls 20 Geese 5 pigs. We killed nine hogs two weeks ago we keeped six ourselves for our own consumption. [James Mullett]

In addition to the domestic animals which settlers could use for work or food, they were surrounded by wild animals, many of which could also be eaten. William Bell lists bears, wolves, raccoons, beavers, otters, marten, mink, squirrels, hares, rabbits, muskrats, omitting the very smallest ones, mice and what the earliest settlers called 'chitmunks.'

There were a great many deer who were normally quick to run away. A wise hunter learned how to approach them.

> Deer abound in the woods, all persons capable and willing to hunt them do so, there being no game laws. In the western districts, great quantities of venison is annually killed, the hind quarters of which are preserved and sent to York in the sleighing season. [William Cattermole]

The obvious way to hunt deer was by shooting them. However, there were two other ways which happened often enough to be mentioned by visitors.

> During the long winters these animals, like the moose, make yards in the greenwoods, and feed on the browse. In the deep snow they are unfortunately very easily run down by hunters on snow shoes. I do not know a more pitiable object than a Virginian deer endeavouring to escape from its pursuer in deep snow. When forced out of the well-beaten paths of its yard, the active creature makes a succession of desperate bounds, each one shorter than the one before. At each plunge it sinks to its withers in the snow. The cold-blooded pursuer knows that his game is safe, and does not even waste a bullet. He comes up leisurely behind the totally exhausted quadruped, disregarding the pleading glance of the wild and beautiful eye, and getting on its back, holds it down in the snow till he cuts its throat with his knife. [John Rowan]

If deer entered the water, they could easily be run down by men in a canoe, who would again use a knife rather than a gun for the kill.

> opposite to this house is a little [illegible] to which the young men with their dogs had gone this morning a-deer hunting. While I was at breakfast the deer was started, and I had the pleasure of seeing him secured by a canoe in the river to which he had gone for safety. The mistress of the house told me that her people had taken twenty within a very short space of time. Whenever the deer is pushed by the dogs, he always takes the water. [— Johnson]

It might surprise us to know that the settlers were capable of stealing the game of other hunters. Twice in a short time, John

314

Langton tells of taking a deer which had been chased by wolves. In one case, the deer took to the water, where a settler was able to kill him from a boat. In the other, the wolves had actually done the killing, but were chased off by the settlers' dogs and the men claimed the venison.

> We used frequently to hear the wolves in pursuit of the deer; and two or three times got parts of the deer which they had been unable to devour. [Alexander Ferrier]

When large animals were killed, the meat could be shared with neighbours.

> By the way, the bear's meat is very good to eat but nobody has appetite to eat it. We have sent some as a dainty present to our black neighbour, Mrs. Jackson, who is most delighted.
> [Mary O'Brien]

As for birds, there were pheasant, quail (which the settlers called partridges, to the irritation of English visitors), turkeys, ducks, geese and pigeons. The game birds had little knowledge of hunters with guns, and sat quietly to be shot, even when others of their number had been taken.

> At that place I saw ducks flying in immense numbers, round and over a marsh; when they rose, they made a noise like the roar of very heavy thunder. [Thad. Leavitt]

> partridges may be had at half an hour's warning [John Langton]

One traveller, who had native guides, helped them shoot some ducks for their dinner. The guides took the birds unplucked, pulled them open and sliced off the breasts only, discarding the rest. They were so plentiful there was no need to be frugal.

The most legendary of these were the pigeons, who flew in huge numbers like clouds in the sky.

> I recollect seeing pigeons flying in such numbers that they almost darkened the horizon, and so low, often, as to be

knocked down with fish-poles. I saw where a near neighbor killed thirty at one shot. [Thad. Leavitt]

I have known twenty-five pigeons killed at a single shot; and have myself got a dozen by firing at random into a maple-tree on which they had alighted, but where not one had been visible. [Samuel Thompson]

The enormous flights of pigeons which cover at times whole districts of the North American continent, and which are very good eating, especially in a pie, will always afford fair game for a very moderate shooter—more especially if he happen to have taken up his abode in a newly-settled district, when butcher's meat cannot be regularly had. They generally make their appearance in early spring, and in some of the more western parts, as at Owen's sound, they generally remain during most of the summer, when they for a time disappear, returning again to the southward, though not with such certainty or in equal numbers, in the fall. Their breeding places cover an incredible extent of ground. There was one at the township of Blenheim, not far from Woodstock, in the Oxford district, in the summer of 1847, which covered somewhere about twenty square miles of ground. The trees literally groaned under the weight of the nests, and the earth was strewed with the *debris* of nests, broken eggs, and unfortunate young ones who had tumbled overboard. A party going thither could, if needful, soon load a waggon with the spoils. [Henry Christmas]

It was unnecessary to use guns at all in catching the pigeons.

Another, and much more innocent sport, was netting wild pigeons after the wheat had been taken off. At that time they used to visit the stubbles in large flocks. Our mode of procedure was to build a house of boughs under which to hide ourselves. Then the ground was carefully cleaned and sprinkled with grain, at one of which the net was set, and in the centre one stool pigeon, secured on a perch was placed, attached to which was a long string running into the house. When all was ready we retired and watched for the flying pigeons, and whenever a flock came within a seeing distance our stool pigeon was raised and then dropped. This would cause it to spread its wings and then flutter, which attracted the flying birds, and after a circle or two they would swoop down and commence to feed. Then

316

the net was sprung, and in a trice we had scores of pigeons under it. ...If we captured many we took them home, put them where they could not get away, and took them out as we wanted them. [Canniff Haight]

Game which was unfamiliar might take some getting used to, but there was not so much food available that most people could afford to be choosy. The bounty of the land was seen as all food for the table.

We had several turtle feasts. The mud turtle is by no means a pretty creature, but the eggs are very good, and parts of the body also. One was got in the beaver meadow behind St. Andrew's Church and two or three in the river. Several porcupines were killed. The porcupine is very good eating, very like a rabbit, and we had a fine dish of it once at Mr. J. Webster's, where Mr. James Wilson now resides. Raccoon is not bad, but is rather rich and strong tasted. [Alexander Ferrier]

One day Mr. Drysdale shot a young bear, which was very good eating, very like a young pig; and a good bear ham is a very good dish. [Alexander Ferrier]

The other day I shot a porcupine which upon the second trial I pronounce very good eating, and, what is better, there is a great deal of solid substantial food on them; there is a peculiar smell and taste about the meat which I judged it prudent to mitigate by parboiling, but after that he made a most excellent stew. [John Langton]

Sometimes, it was simply more than people could manage.

...at the same time produced a large piece of the flesh of a bear which some Indians, whom he had met on the way, had given to him. It was a great lump of black looking meat, very much like horse-flesh, without the least particle of fat about it; however, as I knew it was usually eaten in the country, notwithstanding the appearance, I felt not the least objection to make an experiment upon it, and I had it for dinner the same day. But there was something so very disagreeable in the taste, so extremely fusty, as if it had been kept in a close cupboard, or a hot pocket, that with all my inclination to dine on fresh meat, I could not eat an ounce of it. Nor could my servant touch it. But Rover [his dog] had no scruples of any sort, and ate the whole. [George Head]

Catherine White described a fallback position if all other food failed.

> The Bay of Quinte was covered with ducks, of which we could obtain any quantity from the Indians. As to fish, they could be had by fishing with a scoop. I have often speared large salmon with a pitchfork. Now and then provisions ran very scant, but there being plenty of bull-frogs, we fared sumptuously.

Fish were indeed plentiful, and Mrs White's description of scooping them from the water, often with the bare hands, is echoed by others.

As for frogs, they were then perhaps somewhat larger than the ones we know today.

> Some species of frog grow here [the U.S.] and in Canada to a prodigious size. A plain honest Scotsman, with whom I travelled some days in Canada, amused me much with his account of them, when detailing his feats in the slaughter of wood-pigeons. "You never saw the like o' the puddocks, sir; I brought down three dows at ae shot, and afore I could tak' them up, a muckle deevil, wi' a mouth as braid's my loof, gobbled up yin o' them, roup and stoup." Mrs R—, too, assured me that, from her vicinity to the meadows at the river side, she had no chance of rearing ducks, the young brood always falling a prey to the frogs. [Adam Fergusson]

There were Atlantic salmon in Lake Ontario at this time and they could be found in streams near the lake also. They were fished so thoroughly that even by the 1830s, people were complaining that the numbers were depleted. They blamed the newly built sawmills for this change.

Some writers say that these salmon were not true salmon at all and others distinguish between salmon and salmon-trout, but all agreed that they were delicious and plentiful. There were also a good many other kinds.

The rivers and lakes, with which the country abounds, are well stocked with fish of various kinds; such as salmon, chub, carp, pike, black bass, pickerel, and sturgeon, which are both large and good. In catching them, hooks and lines are seldom employed. They are generally speared, or taken in nets in the rapids of rivers. [William Bell]

The days of salmon-spearing by jacklight from birch canoes had passed, but pike, bass, perch, sunfish and an occasional maskinonge could still be caught off the wharves, though lunge were, of course, more plentiful on the Don and Ashbridge's Bay. [E. C. Guillet]

But our great dependence at present is the black bass...having eaten it, I decide that it is an excellent fish. [John Langton]

Last evening gave three Indians and their fish a lift to the village by the cutter for which I levied a toll of six fine salmon trout. [James Thomson]

Spearing fish by torchlight was an exacting sport, because although the fish were plentiful, they were also quick, and the spear-thrower had to judge the angle of the thrust taking into account the refraction caused by the water. Visitors were often dazzled by young native boys whose proficiency made them envious. It continued to be possible elsewhere long after it was no longer done in Toronto harbour as described above.

The other method of fishing which was new to the emigrants was through the ice. In winter, when food was scarce, the idea of fresh fish was appealling.

He sat over a square hole cut in the ice, with a short spear ready to transfix any fish which might be attracted by his bait. The hole was about a foot square, and the bait was an artificial fish of white wood, with leaden eyes and tin fins, and about eight or nine inches long. The ice where he had cut it was about three feet thick. [George Head]

This was another skill which the natives taught to the newcomers. John Rowan, whose book is meant for sportsmen, was interested that women (even old women) had this skill equally with men. He also notes that they spear eels through the ice.

The two species which the settlers feared were bears and wolves. Wolves were seen as enemies: they were destructive of property in the form of domestic animals; they competed with the settlers for food; they might even kill humans.

There was a bounty on the head of wolves, so anyone shooting them would bring in the proof to a local court and be paid. They were often heard but not seen, which was more frightening. The danger from them was considered a constant threat.

> Mr. M. shewed me the place in the forest where one of his sons, while felling timber, was suddenly beset by a pack of 7 or 8 wolves, only a quarter of a mile from their hut. He had the presence of mind to seize a large branch and jump upon the trunk of a felled tree, and brandish the branch about, which intimidated the wolves, and they retired. He made for the hut, the wolves again turned upon him, but he had given the alarm and *escaped*. Out of his three dogs only one stood and shewed fight. [John Thornton]

Bears were feared, but not so much, perhaps because they might turn away as soon as they would fight. Given a choice, the bear might well keep to himself. It was possible that bears and humans might live near one another in a casual way.

> A Bear also during the summer had made a lair, or bed, very near the hut, which was not discovered till harvest-time, though things were missed which had been its prey.
> [John Thornton]

> Mrs. S. and her daughters, on going out one day for a walk, at the season when the wild cherries and raspberries were ripe. saw a bear march leisurely out of the forest across this field without taking any notice of them; and on after examination, the footsteps of the beast were evident round the fruit trees.
> [John Thornton]

> We have had a few bears in our neighbourhood this summer but they were soon destroyed; they live on berries and Indian

320

corn; they seldom attack any animal but pigs, and then when they are pinched with hunger. [Robert Wade]

People became used to bears, and eventually legends would grow up about how people bested bears they met, or found that meeting a bear was nothing much at all. One visitor told a tale of a man walking through the woods reading a book and who bumped up against something, glanced up and said, "Oh, a bear," walked around him and kept going.

Even if the meeting of man and bear had an element of danger, it might be described in a humorous tone:

A solitary settler was sitting very quietly just inside the door of his shanty, taking a rest and smoking his pipe, when a black muzzle was very quietly poked in at the door. Thinking it might be some stray dog that had come to pay him a visit—for the dogs and cats of Canada lead a remarkably free and easy republican sort of life, frequently leaving their own masters to pay a visit of weeks or months, as it may suit them—he peeped out, and, to his intense horror and dismay, found that it was none other than an enormous brown bear, that had come to pay him the 'compliments of the season'; whereupon the poor fellow, frightened out of his wits, made one hop, skip and jump across the narrow floor, and darted up the chimney, out of the way of the unwelcome intruder. This would, in reality, have been but small security for him, had Bruin been inclined to pursue him; but, as it happened, he contented himself with sniffing round the place, when, perhaps not approving of the recent aroma of the 'dudheen,' he forthwith walked off again to his quarters in the forest, greatly to the relief of the gentleman for whom he had left his card... [Henry Christmas]

The same writer tells of a pair of youngsters, home with no adults about, who see a bear and two cubs swimming from an island toward the mainland. They immediately call the dogs and make for a boat. Approaching the swimming bruins, they set the dogs on the mother (they jump on her back and hold her under water) while the boy shoots the cubs. The mother drowns and they haul her back to land beside the boat. In this tale, even children can best a bear!

As for birds, many writers mention the woodpecker (then called 'cocks of the woods'), which was vividly easy to see and hear. The winter birds near Penetanguishene were referred to as 'Snow Fools' by a Scottish sailor. Anna Jameson mentions a number of different birds, including American goldfinches (which she describes but cannot name), bluebirds, eagles and robins, of whom she is particularly fond.

The large North American robin is very different from its European counterpart, which is tiny. Early settlers in the United States named the American robin as a reminder of the familiar bird which lived around their houses in England. It is touching to think that pioneers in Canada might have taken some comfort from having a robin of their own to listen to and watch for in spring.

The settlers were much plagued by even smaller animals. Of these the worst may have been the mosquito, whose effects were mentioned earlier.

> Could not sleep for the mosquitoes. John says they only came a day or two before us and will leave in August. I am sure I hope they will. Life is not worth living in their company. They are the only drawback we have found in this country. [Ellen Steele]

> You would laugh to see us as soon as evening closes in, running to shut the windows, and then beginning our work of destruction no our inveterate enemies—the mosquitoes. We run round the room clapping our hands together, and are sure to enclose one or two every time. We despatch them with the greatest eagerness. A gentleman who crossed the lake with us told us not to kill them for we should only bring more about us to see what had become of their companions. I am sure nothing could induce us to spare one of them. They are very delicate and easily killed. John does not mind them at all this year.
> [Ellen Steele]

Most writers also mentioned flies, blackflies in the spring and early summer, and sand flies or gnats when it was hot.

Fly bites are always more annoying in the heat, and the British, used to their cool climate, found the combination of heat and insects unbearable. Both William Bell and George Head, for example, give long treatises on the difficulties of fly bites and how to deal with them.

Head arrived in Ontario in the depths of winter and was driven along the side of the St. Lawrence on a cold sunny day by a Scot from Glengarry.

> There I asked him, à-*propos* to nothing, whether he thought he would be able to wear the kilt in Canada? "Na," said he, "the flies wad nap a body." I thought it was rather odd he should be thinking of flies at a time when the frost was biting so particularly sharp; but still he insisted upon it, that the flies, of the two, were the worst.... [George Head]

The other bugs which caused the early travellers problems were fleas. Beds in many of the makeshift inns were dubious in many ways, and since people often had to share them with strangers, the situation might be that much worse.

> Set out early, found myself not much reanimated from my rest, no wonder. my bed was full of fleas and my shirt had the appearance of a butcher's lodgings. [— Johnson]

> The night before I had attempted to sleep at what seemed to be the headquarters of the flea race. This evening I had no sooner retired that I discovered that I had brought sufficient along with me to found a new colony. [William Bell]

> ...at this hour of half past ten, I find myself sitting by the fire with nothing to do, and I know, from dire experience, that, unless I sit up till one or two to get very, very sleepy, the fleas will have commenced their attacks before I get fairly asleep and then there will be little rest for me, for when once they begin they come on in such armies, that even in the dark I have caught a dozen or two in the course of the night. [John Langton]

There were times when the question of bugs did cause social embarrassment, as when the Lieutenant-Governor came to Peterborough.

323

By the Bye, the said house is so full of bugs that they dared not invite his Excellency to sleep in it and had rigged up a tent near it, under which his bed was prepared. [John Langton]

Crickets were also plentiful. Their song might be pretty, but William Bell said they ate clothing.

I find they have been feasting lately on my shoe leather. The noise of them at night is unceasing, but this we get accustomed to... [Anne Langton]

Bell did praise the butterflies, however.

Squirrels were very destructive, as Bell detailed, but their smaller cousins mice and chipmunks were both great trouble in the house and barn, making inroads on the grain supplies in the latter and in any foodstuffs left out in the former. Mrs Moodie describes mice running over the family while they lay in bed and 'cutting a thousand capers on the floor.' A cat was the solution for this, in both barn and house.

The farmer depended on field crops for feeding his family and his animals, as well as the possibility of selling some for cash. Wheat was the first of these, sown when he had first cleared the land, between the remaining stumps. Ontario, especially the area between Lake Erie and Lake Huron was thought of as one of the best grain-growing areas on the continent.

Oats were also grown, especially in areas settled by Scots and for horses, plus Indian corn and peas, which did well and were good for pig farmers.

Whatever they grew, many of the farmers did not come from grain-growing backgrounds and had little idea of what the land required to remain at its peak. A common practice was a two year rotation of wheat—fallow—wheat—fallow, which was exhausting to the soil. It was many years before some of these bad practices were eliminated by education.

Since the omnipresent stumps made working the land difficult, farmers used a harrow which could wend its way between them.

Our farming utensils are not the same as some of yours, but we have not so many kinds. The harrows used in new ground among the stumps are made in the shape of the letter "A." they are drawn by the sharp point so that they are not so ready to catch upon roots and stumps. [Daniel Stewart]

Although the most primitive of grain harvesting techniques were necessary for the pioneers, who had little equipment, the first threshing machines appeared in the 1830s, and by 1850 the flail had disappeared.

When some form of blight appeared, such as the wheat midge, which made its way from Montreal westward through the province from 1827, there was little the farmers could do but wait it out. Eventually it would kill off all it could and then depart. Then farmers could either start again or find a new strain of grain which could withstand it. The potato blight which had caused so many Irish to flee to North America came to Ontario in 1845 and 1846 and it was not until the introduction of hardier varieties from the United States in the 1860s that the crop recovered.

New technology caused as much interest then as now, with those eager to try it and those who preferred the tried-and-true. In 1843 William Hewgill reports that 'a great part of wheat has this year been cut with the Cradle.' The Scottish emigrants had already been recommending this innovation to their brethren back home. With it, one man could then do the work that had previously been done by three or four.

It is a rare thing indeed to see a Canadian woman working in harvest. Sickles are very rarely used except in back settlements. The principal instrument in use here in harvest is called a cradle, but I cannot describe it very well. It consists of a scythe with a frame fixed on the swath that catches the grain as it is cut, so that it can be laid in neat regular swaths, with the heads all one way. With this machine I have heard that an expert hand will cut 2 or 3 acres a day, but this is in ground that is free of stumps; in the back settlements we cannot do so much. Another person with a rake gathers the grain and binds it up as fast as the cradle cuts it... [Daniel Stewart]

To ensure that the field crops were allowed to grow, fences were necessary. They kept out large animals (such as the farmers' own oxen and horses) but small wild things were certainly able to penetrate.

As we have seen, the first fences were made of uprooted stumps. Once a farmer was established he would begin to make split-rail fences, often of white cedar because it was plentiful and lasted a long time. These rail fences (or snake fences) were familiar sights in Ontario until well into this century.

It required some skill to build these fences, ensuring that the rails were straight enough and that they sat together properly and would not fall down. They were usually six rails high, but the top one 'was inevitably getting knocked off.' Some people might use wire but it was a mistake, because it rusted out and then the fence fell down. A properly balanced all-wood structure was better.

A white pine or cedar of two and a half feet in diameter would be split into four, six or even eight rails; thicker rails were needed at the bottom.

A farmer might be known for his fences.

A glance at road fences will usually reveal the sort of farmer who tills beyond them. Upstanding, well maintained fences indicate progressive yeomen, well cultivated fields and contented livestock, whereas neglected fences go with tumble down barns, undernourished cattle, weedy fields, poverty and general inefficiency. [Harry Symons]

Later a farmer might build log and stone structures, with boulders at the bottom topped with intimidating logs.

The snake fences had spaces in each bend which encouraged the growth of small trees, berry-bearing shrubs and tall grasses. Here many animals lived: bobolinks and meadow-larks, rabbits, quail (or partridge), pheasants, woodchucks. Squirrels were famous for using the fencetops as runways.

Domestic animals often learned how to knock gaps in rail fences to get at the crops growing behind them. Rails which dipped provided spaces for pigs to thrust in their snouts, and

326

larger animals simply knew they could use their body-weight against the flimsy rails.

> The cross zigzag fences, being rails laid upon each other, are very convenient, as they can be taken up and down at pleasure. Sometimes, however, the oxen get a practice of knocking them down, when they are called breach oxen. In purchasing a yoke, care should be taken to ascertain whether they have this habit or not. [James Logan]

People could also move the rails; when the following writer says, "the owners have no objections indeed at any time," the reader might be a little skeptical.

> At first sight I did not like the looks of the rail fences and stumps but the stumps will soon be burnt up, or rot away and I think the Canadians would not like any fences so well as the rails, they are so very easily moved from one place to another, in the winter when the roads are full of snow it is very convenient to be able to take down the fences and drive in the fields, the owners have no objection indeed at any time.
> [William Wade]

In the growing of field crops the interdependence of the population was also apparent. In some cases, people who had cleared land did not have the means to keep grain growing in it. It was a better idea to have someone working the land, otherwise nature would soon reclaim it with small trees and shrubs. One possibility was simply to let the neighbours use it until you had a son old enough to work it.

> Opposite my House a Mr Rutlege owns 20 acres of land and he gave me the liberty of it for 8 years until his son is of Age, to Clear and crop and pasture as I please for the time.
> [Joseph Carrothers]

A second was to go 'on shares' with each participant taking some of the results. This could be done with things other than land.

We picked thirty-eight bushels of apples this fall on shares as we have not many on our own farms. [Deborah Mullett]

We shall have a great deal of wool [to] spin next summer as Mother intends having William Faulkner on Shares he keeps about a hundred and fifty Sheep so you may think we shall not have much time for play [Deborah Mullett]

Thomas has saved 30 or 40 pounds this last year; he has taken a farm on shares, a hundred acres of land with six or seven cows on it, 50 sheep, a yoke of oxen and two horses; he has it for three years, has half the produce of the farm and stock and half the wood and sheep for working it. [Robert Wade]

The arrangement for 'shares' circumvented a more straight-forward tenancy in which rent would be paid. The difficulty there would be finding the cash money to pay the rent; shares meant the landlord's fees could be paid in kind, and in clearly established amounts.

Those who offered services required by farmers could also work on a kind of 'shares'. For example, the Gonder family of Niagara ran a tannery. People brought in their skins and the tanners kept part for doing the work. In one example, a farmer brought in two sheepskins and a calfskin; the tanner returned the fleeces when done, but kept the calfskin for his share.

Perhaps the most common of the arrangements for 'shares' was the grist mill, which kept a part of all the flour it ground.

Inside the house was a hive of activity. It was quite small, a simple living area with a minimum of furniture. The most common remark made by the pioneers, who retained visions of their warm and cosy cottages in Britain, was of the cold. The logs, even if their chinks were filled with moss and mud, let in the cold, and the inexpertly constructed chimneys also let out the heat.

We have had a very trying winter indeed. the cold very intense—now the sixth of the fourth month and the snow not off the ground and the ice on the Bay sufficient strong to bear foot passengers... [Mary Mullett]

328

Sarah and Maria carry hot bricks to bed with them, so you may think how cold it is in Canada. [Deborah Mullett]

James tells us that he got his nose frozen on the first day last, which much frightened him, at the prospect of leaving a nose in this cold country. [Deborah Mullet Haight]

Early on the inadequacies of chimneys in the Canadian winter led to the widespread use of stoves.

the Canadians keep their houses warmed by *stove heat* up to a degree that few Europeans could support, we have thermometers placed in our suite of sitting room, and by placing stoves in passages every where, since we arrived, we can keep the whole house to the temperature of 64 at which degree it is very agreeable and healthy, and I assure you that I have never felt a sensation of cold [Lady Aylmer]

First and foremost, we deemed it essential to take a home in which there were open fire-places. Rooms heated by stoves were, to me, most suffocating and stifling, and I imagined, must be injurious. I could not understand how people could exist in them—a doubt long since solved; for without them, I do not believe any human being could equalize the temperature of a room, so that every bit of you feels warm, which cannot be said in favour of open grates, however cheerful a blaze may be— your face is apt to be scorched while your back is shivering. [Mrs Edward Copleston]

The cold was secondary to some people, however, who felt that a little cold was worth it to be free of the landlord.

At the remote cabin in the woods, the fire was important because it was used every day for cooking, even in summer. It had to be kept going all the time, whether banked down to coals covered in ash, or flaming high. Allowing it to go out would be uncomfortable if not disastrous.

I went to see Fanny and found her thawing her tablecloth which had frozen during breakfast. Unfortunately, she and Richard are bad fire-makers and this is the first severe frost we have had.

329

[Mary O'Brien]

It was necessary to carefully cover up the live coals on the hearth before going to bed, so that there would be something to start the fire with in the morning. This precaution rarely railed with good hard-wood coals. But sometimes they died out, and then some one would have to go to a neighbour's house for fire, a thing which I have done sometimes, and it was not nice to have to crawl out of my warm nest and run through the keen cold air for a half mile or more to fetch some live coals, before the morning light had broken in the east. My father usually kept some bundles of finely split pine sticks tipped with brimstone for starting a fire. With these, if there was only a spark left, a fire could soon be made. [Canniff Haight]

The other side of this was that burning logs frequently gave off sparks with a snap, hurling them into the house. This might cause a conflagration which burnt the house down in minutes, or it might simply cause constant holes in the hearthrugs and tablecloths, despite the fenders.

The plainness of the house might be alleviated by a little decoration, perhaps a picture brought from home (as we saw above, Mrs Traill had engravings of military heroes on her walls), or something made from nature's bounty outside.

We went to a cedar swamp and there I gathered some branches of cedar to form the background of a flower pot, the front of which is to be occupied by white everlastings. The whole will be stuffed into a little Indian basket and hung up against the wall. The rest of the cedars are to be tied together to form a hearth brush. This is much superior to any other inasmuch as it is never used without diffusing a most agreeable odour. [Mary O'Brien]

Native-made baskets, which could be traded for various things, were both useful and decorative additions to the settlers' homes.

Although someone might bring a much-prized watch with them,

Clocks were not common. It is true, in most of the better class of old homes a stately old time-piece, whose face nearly reached the ceiling, stood in the hall or sitting-room, and measured off the hours with slow and steady beat. But the most common time-piece was a line cut in the floor, and when the sun touched his meridian height his rays were cast along this mark through a crack in the door; and thus the hour of noon was made known. [Canniff Haight]

Clocks sold by peddlers were very expensive and people continued to rely on their experience of looking at where the sun was in the sky.

Aside from sleeping, the principal activity in the log house was cooking. It might be surprising that anyone felt it necessary to say so, but Copleston feels it necessary to say that every woman who emigrated with the idea of starting out in the backwoods needed to know how to cook, as well as any number of other domestic skills. She had obviously encountered some who did not know how, and she herself said that her own education could have been better. It is unlikely that many potential emigrants would stop to take a course (or the equivalent) before setting out. The result was that people learned by doing, succeed or fail, and consulted with their more knowledgeable neighbours.

Anne Langton's diary is full of references to failures in the kitchen. Her bread does not rise; she and her mother cannot do the blood puddings correctly or roll their hams as needed, and their cream has a bitter taste. Worse, a ham which has been hung in the chimney to smoke comes crashing down into the fire, where it is covered with soot and seared with flames. Meat was scarce enough that the Langtons cleaned it off and used it anyway.

At the beginning, cooking was rough and ready. The men, especially, enjoyed telling tales of cooking with unusual utensils. Here is Tiger Dunlop's own recipe for boiling green peas:

Put them in a large pot full of water, boil them till they burst. Pour off one half of the water, leaving about as much as will cover them; then add about the size of your two fists of butter, and stir the whole round with a handful of black pepper. Serve in a wash-hand basin.

In the bush, they used whatever was to hand.

There nobody was at home but we took possession, and, thinking the spade looked cleaner than the frying pan, I broiled some venison we had with us on it finding some ears of corn we roasted them also and made an admirable breakfast.
[John Langton]

...his ingenuity, by its assistance, provided me the same evening with a very good loaf of bread. He had placed the iron pot on hot embers, having laid a large piece of tin, taken off one of the packages, over the mouth as a lid, and upon this he had strewed more embers. The loaf was supported in the middle of the vessel, between the two fires, upon cross sticks, and in this way a tolerably good oven was constructed. [George Head]

Everyone's powers of invention were activated in the backwoods. From the natives or old-timers, the settlers learned to use things from nature which could be converted to something practical.

The bass tree has remarkably tough, stringy bark, which rips easily from the trunk, and is so strong and flexible, that it serves all common purposes of rope. [George Head]

He forged the iron of the spear in my fire, beating it with a hammer against a large stone; and he made a very neat splice to mend the gunstock, which he cemented with a sort of glue he carried in his pouch, and made by boiling the bones of fish.
[George Head]

Or, they simply manufactured using what they had.

After the first year, we raised a supply of Indian corn, but had no mill to grind it, and were, therefore, compelled to pound it in a large mortar, manufacturing what we called 'samp,' which was made into Indian bread, called, by the Dutch, 'suppawn.' The mortar was constructed in the following manner: We cut a log from a large tree, say, two and a half feet in diameter, and

six feet in length, planted it firmly in the ground, so that about two feet projected above the surface; then carefully burned the centre of the top, so as to form a considerable cavity, which was then scraped clean. We generally selected an ironwood tree, about six inches in diameter, to form the pestle; and many a time have I pounded at our mill, until the sweat ran merrily down my back. Although this simply contrivance did well enough for corn, it did not answer for grinding wheat.
[Thad. Leavitt]

Your Cousin John will be about the same height of yourself, and the greatest genius I have seen. The greatest part of the Furniture has been made by him, the House has been enlarged this Summer and all the wood work was done by himself, as Joiners work is so very high in this Country it is necessary to try to do a little of the work, he shewed me a turnip drill of his own making, a Potato Washer of his own making, he showed me the machine, the water wheel his own making and a good deal more of the wood work of his own doing, he has a circular Saw, attached to it he has invented two locomotive rakes which takes the straw from the Machine and conveys it off a considerable distance. I think this machine will do as much work as 2 at home. [Ralph Wade]

We have a washing machine that helps us great deal for we used to be two days washing and now we are but one.
[Deborah Müllett]

And so, with making do and taking advantage of what was available, and keeping a positive frame of mind about it all, the log cabin in the backwoods became more than merely a shelter. It was a sanctuary, a castle.

McAndrew was spending Xmas with me; we had worked hard all day, flooring the loft and reducing everything to order; a table had been manufactured out of a door and two empty barrels, a table cloth was airing at the fire, silver forks, mustard and such-like almost forgotten luxuries were ready to grace it, and last—not least—we were almost longing for bed time to luxuriate once more in the novelty of a pair of sheets. Such were the prospects of enjoyment before us when Robert returned with a handful of letters for each, and a bundle of old

newspapers which some kind friend at Peterborough had sent to enliven our solitude. Imagine what an evening we spent.
[John Langton]

Advice on the subject of clothing was contradictory. Some people said to bring little, others said it was difficult to obtain. Perhaps it depended on where you lived.

our greatest difficulty is getting Cloaths ware very badly off for clothing [Robert Forrest]

We cannot afford for they [grasshoppers] to eat up our Cloths as clothing of every description is very dear in Canada.
[Deborah Mullett]

He traded one of his coats about two months ago with William Clendenan for two hundred acres of land, now he has traded one hundred away since he have been out for a pair of trowsers and he have traded them away for five bushels and half of weat
[Deborah Mullett]

Mary O'Brien describes a woman's typical dress as a handkerchief over the head and a dark flannel gown in winter. People owned few clothes, having a 'good' set for Sundays and funerals, and another for working in. These last might have holes and stains, but everyone was the same so it did not matter. All women wore long aprons while working about the house.

I made seventy five yards of flannel this last summer. I have two gowns out of it for every day wear it would look coarse to my friends in England, but alas they know but little of Canada.
[Deborah Mullett Haight]

O'Brien also describes in detail an outfit she has created so her brother can ride in the cold, which begins with a flannel 'case' as she calls it (meaning underclothes) which extends from throat to toes. The shirt is calico and the breeches corduroy. The coat has several layers, soft cloth on the outside, serge inside with silk between. He then wears sealskin overalls, with the hair outside and lined with leather, and fleece inserts in his boots. It all sounds quite uncomfortable but no doubt kept him warm.

the people here wear mostly home made shirts of flannel. Linen some of which is home made is worn in the Summer at wch time it is more durable than cotton as it stands the perspiration better but in the winter the cold cuts it to pieces on which account Calico is then worn & lasts far longer than in summer. Coarse Linen fustian & other durable articles of the same description are worn in the Summer. Home made cloth & coarse cloths in the winter. Best Suits are made of Broadcloth which is cheaper in England than in this Country—a Tailor from Oxfordshire & a man of property liv^g within 4 miles works at a very reasonable rate for this part of the world. Boots & Shoes are cheaper here than in Eng. 2 pr of good Home made socks will last me one a year... [William Mickle]

Clothes were made at home, and for those who kept sheep, the whole process of shearing, carding, spinning and weaving might be done there.

I have sent thee a ball of thread of our own manufacturing that I thought would do for knitting [Rachel Mullett]

Aunt Martha queries if I can spin sufficiently to be able to spin thee some caps. No my dear Grandmother I can not. I can spin fine enough for sheets &c of which I shall send thee a sample which will do for thee to sew a coarse work with.[Mary Mullett]

Deborah Mullett boasts to her grandmother, "We make our own starch...we have been clear starching today," but Anne Langton and her family did not care for Canadian starch (made from arrowroot), it being too blue, and they had theirs imported from England. Most families would, like the Mulletts, learn to make do with what was available here.

Even shoes might be made at home:

I have learned to make shoes since we have been heare and I have made all they shoes since I have been able to. they men's shoes in this Country are not made as they are there the bottom instead of being sown on are peged with wooden pegs. [James Mullett]

With so many tasks, everyone helped, including the children. The following letter from a young boy to his grandmother in England demonstrates that even the smallest members of the family had some jobs to do.

> I fetch the cows morning and evening for Sisters to milk them. I also feed Williams Oxon; Father was so kind as to give me an axe, and I take great pleasure in chopping the wood for the fires. In the summer I plough and drive the oxen. Henry and me have learnt to skait this winter an amusement we are very fond of. I have a hen and 8 chickens that Henry gave me; I had a pig that I let Father have for a dolar. I took it to the store and got three knifes for it. Father intends to let me learn the Blacksmith trade. [Arthur Mullett]

As mentioned earlier, once a settlement was established, the pioneers would begin discussions about founding a school and a church.

> A few years ago schools were so far apart, and the tuition of children so expensive, that none but the very better class could scrape money enough together to send their children to be instructed. Under the present system, every idle ragged child in the streets, by washing his face and hands, and presenting himself to the free school of his ward, can receive the same benefit as the rest. [Susanna Moodie]

From the above we might conclude that Mrs Moodie does not necessarily approve of universal education. It was part of what people began to expect of life in the new world, and so each township was divided into school sections and a primitive structure installed for teaching.

People had aspirations for their children, even in the backwoods. David MacLaren described his children's situation to a relation:

> Our boys are all with us as yet, but they are fast advancing into active life, and it may be looked for that they will not all be long so. Jamie is 22 years of age, John 20, David 18, Henry 16, William 12, Alexander 8. The three oldest with a hired Hewer, and occasionally an additional hand have commenced the

winter operation of making timber. A business we shall probably close this season, as it interferes, I find somewhat with farming operations particularly with clearing the land. And is besides a kind of business I do not much admire. The two next boys does partly the threshing attends to the cattle and chops the firewood. Alexander the youngest I must set down as doing nothing. I may say that none of them have ever been at school. There has been none within our reach, and the deficiency has had to be supplied in the best way we could by my tuition. James has gone very succesfully through common and decimal arithmetic and trigonometry. Knows a little of Geometry and Georgraph—none of the others are so far advanced as James, they have all however a tolerable share of natural ability and want only time for study And a good teacher to make passable scholars. [David MacLaren]

The reply he received offered a home for one of the boys in Scotland so he could go to school. In April 1842 David MacLaren wrote:

...I thank you for the kind offer of a home for one of my boys in the event of my sending him over to school. I may perhaps yet avail myself of your good offer but I am for the present inclined to wait untill I shall see the result of our new school Act. The Provincial Legislation have voted fifty Thousand Pounds Annually for Common Schools, and the people are to be taxed to raise a like amount for the same object and each child attending school will have to pay 1/3 [one shilling and threepence] per month.... It is intended to have one of the schools for this township in my 'old clearance' where I have offered an acre of land to build on. The number of children in the neighbourhood are too few however to enable us to support a teacher such as would be desirable, but they are increasing and we look forward with hope. the demand for teachers, in consequence of this Act will, I think, be very great. Have you any to spare?

If both a schoolhouse and a teacher could be found, then children were sent, but perhaps erratically.

The school house was a small square structure, with low ceiling. In the centre of the room was a box stove, around which

the long wooden benches without backs were ranged. Next the walls were the desks, raised a little from the floor. In the summer time the pupils were all of tender years, the elder ones being kept at home to help with the work. ...In the winter time the small school room was filled to overflowing with the larger boys and girls. This did not improve our condition, for we were more closely packed together, and were either shivering with the cold or being cooked with the red-hot stove.
[Canniff Haight]

Most tales of these one-room schools tell of harsh discipline and wild antics, as well as some learning.

I next sat under the rod of an Irish pedagogue—an old man who evidently believed that the only way to get anything into a boy's head was to pound it in with a stick through his back. There was no discipline, and the noise we made seemed to rival a Bedlam. We used to play all sorts of tricks on the old man, and I was not behind in contriving or carrying them into execution. One day, however, I was caught and severely thrashed. This so mortified me that I jumped out of the window and went home. An investigation followed, and I was whipped by my father and sent back. [Canniff Haight]

Perhaps the best summary of pioneer education in the country would be that its availability was haphazard, and the children's attendance was the same.

Once it became general, however, the new land had all the elements of society: commerce, religion and education. The pioneers became merely inhabitants of an established place, and Ontario as we know it had begun.

Becoming Canadians

English visitors in the late Georgian period made a distinction between themselves and 'Canadians.' Modern-day readers cannot help but ask: when did the immigrants become Canadian?

There was no magic day, and for most, they would always have a sense of being a displaced Scot or Englishwoman or Irishman. There were some who could not bear the cold, the mosquitoes or the rough work, and returned home.

But the sense of freedom and healthy economics of the new country convinced many that they would not want to be anywhere else. Perhaps that is what being Canadian meant to them.

> I still am well pleased with this country and with this part of it as I am sure there is no better in it. the climate good and land of a most excellant quality and I may say I never wrote anything of this country but the truth and I am sorry at nothing so much as that I did not come sooner to it
> [Nathaniel Carrothers]

> In short, Sir, it's a fine country for a poor man, if he be industrious, and, were it not for the ague, a good country, and a rich one, though to be sure it is rather out of the way, and the roads are bad and winter very cold; yet there is always plenty to eat and sure employment, and good pay for them that like to work. [Martin Doyle]

> A man who owns a well-cultivated farm in Ontario is as comfortable and independent as a farmer can be. His farm gives

him and his family all the necessaries and most of the comforts of life, and in a new and rapidly growing country he has the satisfaction of knowing that each year as it rolls away adds to the value of his property, and that every hour a well-directed labour spent on his land will be entirely for his own advantage and that of his heirs. [John Rowan]

I am now come to that part of my letter, where I must give you my own opinion of this place, which is shortly this, were I to get a free house & shop in Parkhead, and one hundred pounds besides, I would not exchange, I value my present situation more than that. I can see men here, who have not been more than two or three years on their land, who have now 5 head of cattle, & 40 fowls about their doors, and living in the greatest plenty, now only compare this with that of the weavers at home, and you will be able to judge for yourselves,—we would all be pleased exceedingly, were every one of you to come to this place, should you do so, I will do every thing in my power to make you comfortable, by next fall or harvest I think I shall have provisions enough to satisfy all our wants.
[William Dowie]

Appendix I

The Diary of Leah Purkiss

As an example of an emigrant's diary in full, we print here the diary of Leah Purkiss, a schoolteacher, who emigrated with her husband George from Portsmouth, England, in 1844. The original diary is in the Thomas Fisher Rare Book Room, University of Toronto.

April 2nd: We sailed from the docks on Tuesday about 5 o'clock a.m. laid in the hamble the whole of the day. [Footnoted: we had a prayer meeting on deck by moonlight], the Captain and Mrs Brown coming on board about six P.M. We sailed at ten P.M. got as far as Yarmouth [Isle of Wight] that night.

3rd: Weighed anchor this morning at ten. Mr Brown went on shore. A boy who joined the Ship the day before from Portsmouth fell down the hole and was carried on shore at Yarmouth. We had a prayer meeting in our berth.

4th: Still on our passage to Plymouth, rather alarmed this morning with a cry of "Fire!" on board which turned out to be the passengers cooking hearth, the brick work having become red-hot caught the deck. It was soon extinguished but caused great inconvenience as the passengers are obliged to cook in the galley. Many are very sick. I am not yet only a little giddy—George is quite well. We had a prayer meeting in our berth.

5th Good Friday: On awakening this morning we were told we were at Plymouth, Stonehouse & Davenport [Devonport].

We had a prayer meeting in our berth this morning. Many are anxious to go on shore but the Captain will not permit.

6th: Still lying at Plymouth, the [word missing] passengers went on shore and came on board quite intoxicated. The Doctor came on board in the same state went to see a sick child, he upset a pan of water and broke a chair. We had a prayer meeting.

7th: Weighted anchor this morning at seven. we had a part of the Church Service at eleven and a young man of the Wesleyan connection preached from Romans 8th chap. 32 verse a great many attended. In the evening we had service on deck. another man preached from John 19th chap 9, 19-20 verses the cabin passengers & the sailors attended.

8th.: Still beating about near land withhout any wind to carry us on. A child died in the night 15 months old it was cast overboard at 11 this morning. the Doctor read the service. We had a prayer meeting in our berth in the evening.

9th. Tuesday : Still calm, not far from land, a boat put out to us this morning from Penzance with fish. I kept a school on the deck for an hour or two, we had some singing on deck and a prayer meeting in our berth in the evening.

10th.: More favourable today, we had made considerable progress.

11th: very rough all the women in bed from sickness. I went on deck but was soon glad to go to bed—very sick for the first time—George is also sick.

12th Friday : Much the same as yesterday. all in bed. the ship in incessant rocking. George is better today.

13th: The weather is better today, many are able to go on deck. I am not sick today but feel very unwell.

14th Sunday: Very rough wind not able to have any service in the forenoon. George kept school on the deck. There was preaching in the steerage in the afternoon but I was not able to attend from indisposition.

15th: We find we have been preserved through a heavy storm during the night the wind continued high all the day but not fair. We finished the day generally by singing and prayer in our corner, thus we feel the presence of the Lord with us.

16th : Still a heavy sea and not favourable, the only consolation is—the Lord knoweth best He is too wise to err.

17th Wednesday : A Brig was keeping us company this morning, sailing as fast as us and in the same direction, this seemed to vex our Captain, he remarked that there must be a Jonah on board and he would cast lots, however to his great joy we gained considerably on her before night. The Northern Lights were seen which the Captain hoped would send us a fair wind.

18th.: Rather calm this morning, the invalids are on deck, the wind still unfavourable.

19th: No change of wind a very fine day—

20th : A very wet day—obliged to remain below all day

21st. Sunday morning: We have passed a restless night the vessel lurched much but to our great joy there was a cry of fair wind this morning which proved correct. the Lord has not forgotten to be gracious. There are three other vessels in sight. The Doctor read the Church Service this morning in the afternoon we had a little meeting and one in the evening The wind is again contrary.

22nd: A very fine day, we had the company of four other vessels one left Plymouth on Friday as we left Sunday but we sailed faster than any of them. We are now abreast of Fayal or the Azores, where the St Michael oranges come from. This brings to my remembrance "Bullars visit to the Azores" a book I read with much interest while with Miss Fowke. I should now enjoy an orange as our water is very bad today and I am very thirsty. The wind is still contrary.

23rd: A fine day a great number of porpoise in sight and some sharks

24th : Very rough this morning, many are very sick. I went on deck but was so tossed about that I was sick and obliged to go to bed. The Captain was expecting a storm and ordered every sailor to take in the sails, when all of a sudden the wind ceased, it was an awful sight, the vessel appeared in a bason and wall of water all around her, there was a whirlwind at a distance but we escaped it the sudden ceasing of the wind caused the ship to roll from side to side. I was in bed it nearly tossed me out. I jumped up to see what was the matter, such a sight. I could not help laughing, pots, boxes, potatoes and everything all rolling

343

about, women and children tossed upon each other. I did not then know the danger we had been placed in until George came down and told me.

25th: There has been another theft committed during the night a young man's pocket cut out, with 4 sovereigns in it. We are sailing better but it is very cold.

26th: A fine breeze today sailing on the right course.

27th: We have spent a restless night such continual rocking. The day is very unpleasant and we are obliged to keep below. the wind is contrary.

28th: A Sunday morning, a memorable Sabbeth morning. We have been spared through a tremendous gale which came on about eleven Saturday night, the wind and sea were very high, the darkness was illuminated with flashes of lightning followed by peals of thunder. I did not venture on deck during the morning it abated about noon. We have not been able to have our accustomed services owing to the rocking of the ship. in the evening we had a prayer meeting and raised our Ebenezer "Father by Thy help we've come". The wind was rather in our favour.

29th: I have spent a good night and the day is very fine. the sea is calm and seems to have forgotton all its troubles of the preceding night. We have a side wind and sailing pleasantly.

30th: We have had another heavy gale through the night, higher wind and sea than Saturday night but no hail or thunder, the vessel is laying to—that is without any sails up, not been able to sail under the gale. I have been on deck this morning to see it, and oh what a sight the sea was terrific it was truly sublime. George thought beautiful but I can scarcely think so, except when viewing the mountain top of each wave. the colour was a beautiful green fringed with its snow white foam.

May 1st: We hail the month of May in the hope that it may be more favourable for us although we have many mercies to record during the past month. the weather is fine today and we are sailing better but not a fair wind.

2nd: The sea is tolerably calm but no fair wind.

3rd: We have had no sleep since 11 last night; we were awoke by another heavy gale of wind, the rocking of the ship was worse than ever, there are no females up today, our berths are thoroughly swamped from the spray of the sea coming down the hatch way. I am thankful to say that our beds are dry, and with the use of a few of the ships swabs or mops our deck will soon be dry too, it is much calmer this evening.

4th: A very fine morning, and a fair wind, we are sailing well today, we trust the Lord will continue it.

5th. Sunday morning: We were awoke this morning with a cry of fair wind I went on deck to see the sun rise, it was a delightful morning but it is come on very foggy. which indicates we are near the banks of Newfoundland. We had service in the afternoon George delivered a short discourse from John 1st verse 36 and in the evening another young man preached from Ephesians 2nd chap 8-9 verses. A large number attended it is very foggy and we are on the banks.

6th: We were awoke this morning about 1/2 past 2 by a heavy blow against the vessel & then a grating sound and another blow, fear seized every one and the cry of "what's that?" soon resounded through the berths. That we were struck on this banks was the thoughts of most the Captain was in his berth he was soon on deck and they who were on the deck soon called out to us that all was well it was only a piece of ice. The Captain seems much annoyed he says it is the first time his ship was struck. The sailors are of opinion that if he had been on watch it would not have occurred. There is a vessel close to us, the Captain spoke to them, they sailed from Waterford on the 8th of April and was bound for Quebec. It continues very foggy and there are many immense pieces of field ice floating past us. There is now a man stationed at the bow to prevent our running against it.

7th: We have slept well tonight. There was a cry of a quantity of ice ahead early this morning; many went up to see it, it was an immense field 1 1/2 miles along. there was a second field during the morning longer than the first with a variety of fantastic forms, one minute you could imagine a Loo[7] Table another like a vessel dismasted some like the stumps of old trees then you could fancy a Stonemasons Yard indeed it was truly sublime but too varied to describe I would only say "Are these thy works Parent of good, Thyself how wonderous then?" There is a

---

[7] Loo was a popular card game.

beautiful sight this evening at a little distance another vessel which looks dark and a beautiful white Iceberg beside it.

8th: I have spent a wakeful night and found that we met ice all night. The Captain was on deck all night and early this morning he cut the ship through a large field one piece was higher than the bulwarks, about 11 oclock A.M. there was another cry of ice and in a moment we were fairly surrounded with it, as the Captain cried out rather despairingly fear seized many but the Chief Mate who was on duty cried out all was right and we soon cut through it, but the weather is wet and foggy and we present a miserable appearance we are steering south which is much out of our course, but if we trust all is right.

9th: It is a fine clear morning we passed a Schooner this morning it is very cold, this Evening about eight we met a vessel they spoke to us, and said we had better not go far on that tack as there was much ice ahead but as it was a fine clear night the Captain kept on until one Oclock in the morning and made a good run

10th: A very foggy morning, but about twelve it cleared away, and we were on deck the whole of the afternoon there were a number of Porpoises playing around us, it was very cold.

11: We heard a cry of fair wind this morning about 5. Mrs Roberts confined about seven with a Son, at three this afternoon we passed a Bark close enough to speak without a trumpet the Albion from Newport, bound for Boston, it had been out 54 days the wind continues fair and we are sailing better than 9 miles an hour it is bitter cold and we shall be glad to get away from Newfoundland, there was an immense Iceberg in sight this morning at a distance, in the evening there were 5 one very close it appeared like one point of the needles, it was aground on the banks, we had a snow storm, which cleared the atmosphere.

12 Sunday: A very fine morning but the wind is again contrary. Mrs Roberts is doing well, it is a fine Boy there are a number of fishing vessels around us at anchor and many small boats are crossing from one vessel to another. we have fair wind this afternoon and are sailing too fast to stop to take Cod Fish. We had service in the afternoon and evening Roberts child was taken to the Cabin and named Richard Arnold Rainbow!

13: I have spent a wakeful night Rock Rock Rock the whole of the night the winds increased after 9 Oclock, but as the wind was fair we went very rapid, 11 1/2 knots an hour until 12 at midnight when the Captain feared that from the darkness of the night he might run down a fishing vessel hove to until day break, it is a wet morning the wind not quite so fair, we passed two brigs one homeward bound and one bound for Quebec. In the Evening there were 4 in sight all appeared to be bound the same way.

14: A very cold morning we had a snow storm, it cleared away about noon the Evening was very fine and not so cold.

15: A beautiful morning and we were sailing pleasantly there are many vessels around us and a great many porpoises.

16: A May morning indeed finer than in England Land was discovered at day break it is Cape Ray its Mountains are covered with Snow it is 5 weeks yesterday since we lost sight of land.

17: A very fine morning but quite a calm we are opposite the bird Islands they appear like long black rocks in the sea. There are a vast number of birds on them, the Captain says the Islands are wasting away.

18: We have lost sight of the Islands the wind is contrary and we are sailing much out of our course, the wind is fair this afternoon and we are in our right course.

19: I have spent a wakeful night some Christian friends near our berth, has lost a beautiful little girl during the night 3 years and a half old from inflamation on the Chest it was sown up and committed to the deep at eleven this morning, very many tears were shed. The wind is fair and we are sailing right but slow, more land is in sight, Anti Costa [Anticosti Island], its name. We had two services to day.

20: We have had rather a rough wind during the night, and it is foul it changed about noon and we have sailed well this afternoon from 6 knots an hour which increased to ten, we are surrounded by a number of vessels we have lost sight of Anti Costa.

21: A contrary wind again this morning it changed about noon and until the evening we sailed well we are out of sight of Anti Costa and are in sight of Main Land

22: The wind is contrary so we are beating about in the river. A Pilot came on board during the night. We were all anxious to go on deck to see the wonderful being from the long desired shores the foul winds continued all day the evening was calm and we presented the appearance of a ragatta.

23: Wind still contrary so we are making but little progress we have land both sides of us and there is smoke on the islands which looks very cheering, in the afternoon the wind was more favourable and we gained a little. Camela Mountain is in sight.

24: A very fine morning and we are told that the wind became fair about twelve last night so we are all in high spirits as we are drawing near the quarintine station, all we hope are well enough not to detain us. we are surrounded by more than 50 other vessels the river St. Lawrence is truly beautiful the foot of the mountains on the left side have very many villages. we have had fair wind the whole day and have made 14 knots an hour.

25: We were awoke very early this morning with the cry that all berths were to be cleaned as we were closer to the quarintine station, we all bustled up and Oh what a consternation the Doctor was expected, at least he came and we all passed before him and thought all was well but to our grief we found that one child [of] Mrs Bile's of Canford near Poole was to be sent on shore to the Hospital and all our berths were to be white-washed. the Child was soon taken on shore and we soon passed on after being well washed with lime water

We are now safely anchored at Quebec you must excuse the bad writing as it was sometimes dark and always very shaking.

Appendix II

Emigrants Admitted into the Temporary Houses at York, 1 May 1831 to 1 May 1832

On the following five pages are the names of some indigent or poor immigrants who required assistance from charities in York (Toronto) in this one-year period. The information is given in tabular form, exactly as in the originals. The information given is the name, numbers in the family, when they arrived and departed, and some comments, which may be the place of destination or may be a personal observation by the overseer on the character of the person involved. This last was not uncommon by people who dispensed charity in the nineteenth century.

Name spellings may be unusual, depending on the person writing. The calligraphy is usually clear, although one or two names caused difficulty.

The original document is at the Archives of Ontario, MU 2105 1831 #7 F775 (Miscellaneous collection #7, Emigrants admitted into temporary houses at York).

No.	Name					16 Apr. 1831	16th May 1831	Behaviour Good
1	Willm. BRUCE	2	1	4	1	16 Apr. 1831	16th May 1831	Behaviour Good
2	Niel MCLEAN	1	1	1	2	1 Jany. 1831	27 April 1831	General conduct good
3	Dunn. MCLEAN,	1	1	1	2	1 Jany 1831	Ditto	Do
4	John MCGREGOR	1	5	3	3	16 Apr 1831	24th May 1831	Ditto (appears indifferent as to cleaning their apparel.
5	Jas. MCGREGOR	1	1	3	3	15 Apr 1831	24th May 1831	Ditto ----- Do ----- which they occupied.) Well behaved and particularly attentive to cleanliness and safety of appart.
6	Andw. GRAY	1	1	5	4	25 Apr 1831	24 May 1831	General conduct good
7	Thos. CALLAR	1	1	6	5	21 Apr 1831	2nd May 1831	General conduct good
8	John CAMPBELL	1	5	1	2	7 May 1831	20th May 1831	Well Behaved
9	John MURRAY	4	1	7	1	8 May 1831	13 May 1831	General good conduct chiefly industrious
10	Hugh MURRAY	1	1	2	1	11th May 1831	3rd June 1831	Behaved well
11	Hugh BELLAMY	1	1	3	1	11th May 1831	4 June 1831	Gone to the country in search of work, Poor.
12	James STARES	1	1	4	3	13 May 1831	17th May 1831	Behaved well
13	Steven HILES	1	1	5	3	13 May 1831	17th "	Ditto
14	James LONGE	1	1	8	5	13 May 1831	17 "	Do
15	John MUNRO	1	1	"	5	14 May 1831	3 June 1831	Do
16	John BRUCE	1	1	5	5	14 May 1831	1st June	A moral good man
17	George FORTH	"	1	5	5	29 May 1831	9 June 1831	Gone to the township of Oro. A well behaved man
18	William PARKEN	"	1	"	2	29 May 1831	1st June 1831	Got work at Mr Kitcheys the Carpenter
19	John WILLIAMSON	1	1	"	2	29 May 1831	20 June 1831	gone to the States
20	Geoe. UNDERWOOD	1	"	"	2	29 May 1831	9 June	gone to the States
21	Geoe. GREEN	1	"	"	2	29 May 1831	3 June	Got work in the town, a very steady man
22	Thos. SWADALE	1	"	"	2	29 May 1831	20 June	gone to the States
23	John SWADALE	1	"	"	2	29 May 1831	20 June	Do
24	John HAZLEWOOD	1	1	1	3	29 May 1831	31st "	Gone to live with Mr. Ketchum
25	John PAGET	1	1	1	3	29 May 1831	21 June	gone to Oro
26	John WATSON	1	1	1	3	29 May 1831	23 June 1831	Gone to Oro
27	John HOMBLEY	1	"	2	3	29 May 1831	15 June 1831	Got work in York
28	Joseph PEARS	1	1	2	4	29 May 1831	9th June 1831	Gone to the township of Oro
29	Geoe. TOMLINSON	1	1	5	4	29 May 1831	9 June 1831	Do
30	Geoe. COWLWELL	1	1	3	4	29 May 1831	9 June 1831	Do
31	Sarah CHAPPELL	"	1	"	4	29 May 1831	9th June 1831	Do [Gone to Oro]

No.	Name				June 2nd	June 9th	Notes
32	John PROCTOR	1	1	6		June 9th	By the Packet Alciope. Gone to the States. Dissatisfied.
33	David COPLAND	1	1	6	" 2	June 9	Do. Do. Do.
34	Wm. MOORE	1	"	6	" 2	June 9	Do Gone to the States
35	James BIRD	1	"	6	2	9-Jun	Do. Gone to the States
36	Robt. NAGGS	1	"	6	2	9-Jun	Do. Gone to the States
37	Wm. BILTON	1	2	6	2	9-Jun	Do. Do. Dissatisfied
38	John BARKER	1	3	3	2	23-Jun	Do. Gone to Oro. a very steady man but very poor
39	Thos. HARDWICK	1	2	5	4th	June 9th	By the Great Britton Packet / Taylor, Gone into Toronto
40	John HAYMAN	1	"	4	4th	June 4	Do / Poor man had 1/3 when landed at York
41	John ATKINSON	1	"	4	4	June 9th	Do Gone up Young St to Mr. Lackie
42	Willm. BROWN,	1	1	2	7th	June 14	Per Quenston - gone to the States
43	John MORTIMER	1	1	5	7	June 14	Gone to the States
44	Geo WILSON	1	3	3	7	June 11	A very steady man. got work in York
45	Geo Osborne	1	"	3	7	June 15	Do Do
46	Thos CARTER	1	"	3	7	June 15	Gone into the country
47	James SYLAS	1	"	6	9th	June 15	Per Great Britton - Gone to Oro
48	Joseph CLARK	1	"	6	9	June 15	Do. Gone to Oro Shoe Maker
49	Stephen CLARK	1	"	6	9	June 15	Do. Gone to Oro
50	John SEAGAR	1	"	6	9	June 15	Do. Gone to Oro Farmer
51	Geo STEDMAN	1	"	6	9	June 15	Do. Gone to Oro Carpenter
52	Thos. DOWSWELL	1	8	6	9	June 15	Do. Gone to Oro Saddler
53	Noah CORTON	1	7	1	9	June 13th	Do. Gone to Oro Farmer
54	Henry CROWFORD	1	"	1	9	June 13	Do Do Do
55	Claudus LAUGHLAN	1	1	1	9	June 23	Do gone to the Country
56	Robt. SWANN	1	"	1	June 14	June 18	Per Great Britton - Basket Maker. Gone to Oro. 600 passengers dirty.
57	Jno GOSLING	1	"	1	14	June 18	
58	Saml. GERMAN	1	"	1	14	June 18	Gone to Oro
59	Geo. BRETT	1	"	1	14	June 18	Gone to Oro
60	Wm. SYMPSON	1	6	1	14	June 28	Shoemaker - gone to Oro
61	James PUSLEY[?]	1	"	1	14	June 18	Gone to Oro
62	John COLSON	1	"	2	14	June 18	Gone into the Country
63	Thomas COLSON	1	"	2	14	June 18	Gone into the Country

No.	Name							Remarks
64	Wm. RICHARDSON	1	"	"	2	14	June 17	A very Steady Young Man }
65	Thomas DUFFEY	1	"	"	2	14	June 17	Do. } Both Farmers
66	John HESSEY	1	1	6	5	June 16	June 20	*Alciope* Gone into the township of Albion. passengers 200
67	John HARPER	1	2	1	6	June 16th	27th June 1831	By the Alciope Settled in York.
68	Benj. FOX	1	"	"	6	June 16	18th June 1831	gone to the States Stone Cutter
69	John MCGUIRE	1	1	4	4	16	29 July 1831	Sick
70	John FRANKS	1	1	3	1	June 18	28 June 1831	Got a house in York By Niagara 150 pas.
71	John WETHERALL	1	1	6	1	June 18	June 20 1831	Gone Into the London District
72	John MOORE	1	1	1	2	June 18	July 25 1831	Gone to the Township of King. A Drunken Man
73	Joseph ROBSON	1	"	"	2	June 19	June 23	Gone into the Country By *G. Briton* 350 pas.
74	John SIMPSON	1	1	5	2	June 18	June 21	Gone up the Country to the Canada Company Land
75	Robt. STOCKDALE	1	"	"	2	June 19	June 23	Gone up the Country
76	John BUGG	1	"	"	2	June 19	June 23	Do
77	Jno SHERWOOD	1	"	"	2	June 19	June 23	Do
78	Wm. LANGLEY	1	"	"	2	June 19	June 21	Got work in Town, being a Shoe Maker & Lame
79	Richd. PERRY	1	1	3	5	June 20	July 8	Gone to the Township of King
80	John MOORE	1	1	6	2	June 20	Augt 30	
81	James EMMS	1	"	8	3	June 24	28th June 1831	Gone up the Country. A very Dirty people. *Alciope* 150 pass.
82	Wm. EDWARDS	1	"	"	3	June 24	28 June 1831	do
83	John SMITH	1	"	"	3	June 24	28 June 1831	do
84	Wm. LEITCH	1	1	8	4	June 24	June 24	gone up the Country *G. Briton* 200 pas
85	John BOYD	1	1	6	6	June 28	August 2nd 1831	Gone up Younge Street - Weaver
86	Geo ROBERTSON	1	1	4		June 28	July 7 1831	Gone to Oro A good Man *Queenston* 100
87	James ORMSBY	1		1	3	June 28	July 6 1831	Gone to Oro
88	Thos. HOLDWORTH	1	1	4	5	June 20	28 June 1831	Gone to Oro. Very Poor, not as much as to get 1 loaf of bread.
89	David BROCK	1	"	"	6	June 28	7 July 1831	Gone to Oro. Scotch Very Moral Family
90	John WARE	1	1	4	1	June 30	5 July 1831	Got a house in York but intends to settle in Oro
91	Wm. BASKERVILE	1	1	11	4	July 1st	6 July 1831	Gone to Oro
92	James TABER	1	1	4	3	July 1st	6 July 1831	Gone to Oro
93	Gilbert DOUGLASS	1	"	1	5	July 4	9 Augt 1831	Gone to Drummer very steady Scotch
94	John ROBB	1	1	6	5	July 4	9 Augt 1831	Gone Do very steady Do

No.	Name							Remarks
95	Wm. BROWN	1		8	6	July 4	7 July 1831	This man lost on the Packet 6 Sovereigns Gone to Oro Carpenter
96	Alex NALLY	1		9	2	July 4	8 Augt 1831	got Lodging in town
97	Patrick HOLYGHAN	1		4	4	July 4	6 July 1831	Gone to Oro
98	James HASTY	1		4	1	July 7	12 July 1831	Gone to Oro
99	Robert Moore	1		4	3	July 9	16 Augt 1831	Gone to Oro
100	Hugh MURRAY	1		4	4	July 19	July 25 1831	Gone to Esquesing Very Moral People
101	Wm. HICKERBOTTO	1	2	5	3	July 22	Augt 12 1831	Gone to the Head of the Lake
102	Wm. PEYTON	1		4	5	July 22	July 23 1831	Settled in York
103	Chs. WARD	2		1	6	July 22	Augt 3 1831	Gone up Yong Street
104	Peter CURREY	1		4	5	July 25	Augt 8 1831	Do
105	Henry SHAW	1		5	4	July 29	Augt 6 1831	Gone to the country
106	John GORDEN	1		3	1	July 30	Augt 8 1831	Got lodging in the Town Scotchman
107	Willm. CHISHOLM	1		4	4	July 30	Augt 8 1831	
108	Angus MCDONALD	1		4	4	July 30	Augt 20 1831	
109	Geo MCDONALD	1		3	2	July 30		
110	Ken KEMP	1		7	6	Augt 4		
111	John MONRO	1		2	6	Augt 4		
112	Danl. PEACOCK	1		5	2	Augt 5	Augt 11 1831	Gone to Scarborough
113	I. MCQUINN [?]	1		5	1	Augt 8	Augt 24 1831	
114	James COATES	1		1	1	Augt 8	Augt 20 1831	Gone to Esquesing
115	John HENRY	1		"	1	Augt 8	Augt 24 1831	
116	Niel SHARP	1		"	1	Augt 8	Augt 24 1831	
117	Peter MCPHEE	1		"	1	Augt 8	Augt 24 1831	
118	Duncan MCKECHIN	1		9	4	Augt 9	Augt 12 1831	Settled in York
119	Angus FLETCHER	1		3	4	Augt 9		
120	Danl. CAMERON	1		4	5	Augt 12	Augt 17 1831	Settled in Oro]
121	Fras. BUCHANAN	1		5	5	Augt 12	Augt 17 1831	Settled in Oro]Scotch very Moral People
122	John HARDY [Note]	2		"	5	Augt 12	Augt 17 1831	Settled in Oro Scotch
123	Duncan MCPHERSON	1		6	3	Augt 12	Augt 20 1831	Settled in Oro Scotch
124	John HUNTER	1		"	3	Augt 12	Augt 20 1831	
125	John MCKENZIE	1		"	3	Augt 12	Augt 20 1831	

126	Douglass CAMPBELL	1	1	4	3	Augt 21	Augt 29 1831	gone up Yonge Street
127	Donald CAMERON	1	1	6	3	Augt 21	Augt 29 1831	Do
128	John BELL	1	2	3	3	Augt 29		
129	Donald CAREY	1	1	1	3	Augt 29		
130	John MCALLUM	1	1	3	3	Augt 29		
131	John MCCARTNEY	1	"	"	3	Augt 29		
132	Murdo MCARTNEY	1	"	"	3	Augt 29		
133	Neil BLOOMFIELD	1	1	3	2	Augt 29		
134	Arh. MCCLEVAN	4	3	4	2	Augt 29		
135	Henry HERRINGTON	1	1	4	5	Augt 29		

Appendix III

Unterricht

Für Einwanderer in Ober Canada

A four page broadside printed for the Canada Company
English translation by Michael Zimmermann

Information for Immigrants
To Upper Canada

The many kinds of inquiries about Canada that have come from various parts of England and the United States, have compelled the Canada Company to put these inquiries into print for general instruction, persuaded that the facts therein contained, which have been provided by men of understanding and experience, will be of use and interest to all those who are of a mind to immigrate to Upper Canada; the same will offer those already settled with a way of giving information to friends left at home, who would like to follow.

Question Nr. 1—About the Holdings of the Company, their Location, roads, Navigable Waters, etc.?

Answer: The Company owns properties in almost every part of western Canada: they exist in scattered parcels/

355

lots of 200 acres, as well as larger parcels or so-called blocks: the main block of about one million acres is the Huron district, situated on Lake Huron, which borders it for 60 miles. Effort and cost were not spared for the construction of two main roads which cut through the land (see the report regarding the Huron district, contained in the special note, and the report of the company for the year 1847, which can be obtained at the Bureau of the company). The other blocks of 3000 and 9000 acres are situated in the Western District and are usually within six or eight miles of navigable waters. Because the district is near navigable waters, its roads have not been as well maintained as in other parts of the province. Excellent corduroy/plank roads have already begun. The scattered lots are comprised of between 80 and 200 acres and can be found in almost every township, municipal district and province and are usually surrounded by settlements.

Question Nr. 2—Price Per Acre of the Lands of the Company?

Answer: The price of land varies a great deal, but the following can be taken as the average prices per acre in the various parts of the province:

	Sh.	Ps.		Sh.	Ps.
Huron District	12	6	to	20	0
Western District	9	9	to	20	0
London, Brock, and Talbot Districts	20	0	to	30	0
Gore district	11	3	to	20	0
Wellington District	11	3	to	20	0
Home and Simcoe Districts	8	9	to	17	6
Newcastle, Colborne, Midland and Victoria Districts	8	9	to	15	0

Johnstown District	2	0	to	15	0
Bathurst, Eastern, Ottawa and Dalhousie Districts	2	0	to	12	6

Prices of some lots in the various areas are somewhat higher.

N.B. 3 shillings 1 1/2 Pence equal 1 Prussian, Saxon Thaler, etc. and 2 Shillings equal 1 Gilder

The conditions of payment according to which the Company transfers its lands to settlers are very favourable and are arranged to that they suit the various circumstances of the immigrants; no cash is necessary for the purchase.

The settler can rent land for a duration of ten years, whereby his rent is not more than the interest of the amount of the sale price, and which is always due on the first of February of each year. The leaseholder thereby secures for himself all advantages of the improvements he has made to his land, as well as the yearly increase in value of the land, that he can sell, at any time during the ten years for the fixed purchase price contained in the lease agreement. For not more than a low yearly interest he thus has the full use of the land for ten years and can then buy it for the price contained in the lease agreement or can transfer it again, whatever he liked.

Should the lease holder wish to purchase the land before the end of the ten-year lease, the Company will make a deduction from the price stated in the lease agreement and the leaseholder will pay no more interest, making the land entirely his own.

Settlers' Savings Bank

In order to provide the industrious and economical settler with all possible support, the Canada Company receives from the lessee small and unused sums of money that the settler wishes to save, and gives him six percent interest per year. The lessee can, however, at any time he wants and without notice, request the return of the entire amount of money with interest for the time that the money was in the hands of the Company. The thrifty and cautious settler can, by dint of this arrangement, easily save money to buy the land that he has rented. Should an unforeseen misfortune befall him or should he have a crop failure, he can use the money that he has deposited into his savings account to help him at any time. The company only receives money from the leaseholders of its lands and only during the period of their leases.

Question Nr. 3—Regarding Land Clearing Costs and How the Land is to be Deforested?

Answer: Under the term "clearing" of wild land is always to be understood the deforestation and fencing of land in fields of 10 acres, such that only the stumps and roots of the trees remain (to be removed in time), in order to prepare the land for sowing. The prices vary and change according to conditions, but can be estimated at about 10 dollars or 2 pounds 10 or 16 Prussian Thaler for moderately wooded land, the price of which would increase to between about £3 0 0 to £4 10 0 per acre once it is situated in or near remote settlements. The clearing costs must always be paid in cash unless otherwise stated in a written agreement. Heathland which is more sparsely wooded, costs less to clear; its development is, however, more costly; on the other hand, it rewards its cultivator's efforts much sooner. Heathlands (called plains) are usually sandy but yield regular and sure harvests. They require greater capital to begin cultivation than wooded lands.

Question Nr. 4—Regarding the General Cultivation of Crops?

Answer: Because wheat (the pride of the province) thrives best on newly deforested and burned land, it is usually planted first on such land. Farmers who have capital sow new land with grass and leave it five or six years like this, but the farmer with only a small amount of capital sows the land immediately in the next year either with potatoes or spring wheat and then with wheat every second year until he has the ability to clear enough land every year for his wheat crop, in which case he leaves the old land in grass or sows it with something else, without observing the general rules of cultivation until the stumps have rotted and the land can be ploughed. The first sowing is always just harrowed under.

Question Nr. 5—Average Yield Per Acre?

Answer: For all fruit the yield varies from one year to the next, especially because of spring and fall frosts. On the average, however, it may be roughly accepted as follows: wheat, 25 bushels; barley, 30 bushels; oats, 40 bushels; rye, 30 bushels; potatoes, 250 bushels per acre—Swedish roots, mangelwurzels, and other similar roots are not planted frequently enough to be able to give an average yield; one may surmise that the yield would be similar to that in England. Flax and hemp also thrive here very well, although not much has heretofore been planted; it is to be hoped that it will not be neglected any longer, as many parts of the province are in every respect suitable for its cultivation.

Question Nr. 6—Costs of the Customary Buildings and Furnishings

Answer: A comfortable log house of 16 by 24 feet with two floors and a shingle roof costs £9 (6 1/2 Prussian Thaler equal £1); log barn 24 by 40 feet £10; a frame house, that is, one of the same size which is finished and covered all round with boards, £50; a frame barn, £70. Tables from 10s. to 17s. 6p.; bedsteads 15 to 20s.; a dozen chairs £1 50; cooking pots, pans, kettles, forks, knives, etc. are also to be had cheaply. The settler usually constructs his buildings himself and is usually helped by his neighbours. The cost of a settler's furnishings seldom exceeds £10 and is often not even half that much. Many make their own until they can afford better.

Question Nr. 7 and 8—Costs of Cattle? Farmer's Kitchenware? Clothing? Food?

Answer: A yoke / team of oxen costs £10 to £12 10; cows £2 10 to £3 10; horses £10 to £20 each,—also cheaper in some districts. Sheep are 10 or 20s. each.

Wagons; £15 to £20; double harness, £6 to £7 10; saddle and bridle, £3 15; harrow, £1 10; plough, £1 15; wind mill for cleaning fruit, £6 to £6 15; water pail, 2s.; fruit sacks, 1s. 3p to 3s. 9p.; American scythe, 4s.; sickle, 12s. 9p.; farmer's sledge, £7 to £7 10; spade, 3s. 9p.; feathers, 1s. 10 1/2 p. per pound; wool, 1s. 2p. per pound; hay, £2 10 per ton; oats, 1s. per bushel.

Clothing is only a little more expensive than in England. Earthen dishes and ordinary ironware are very inexpensive.

Food—Pork, 15s. to 20s. per hundredweight; fine flour, £1 10 per 196 pound barrel; cheese, £1 10 per hundredweight; butter, £2 10 per hundredweight; eggs, 5 to 6p. per dozen; beef, from £1 to £1 5 per hundredweight, often cheaper; oatmeal, 7s. per hundredweight; spirits, 1s. 3 pence to 1s. 9p. per gallon.

The following table shows the average price per 60-pound bushel for wheat or corn in Toronto, from 1832 to 1847.

1832	4 6		1840	4 1.5
1833	4 2		1841	4 5
1834	3 4		1842	4 .5
1835	3 9		1843	3 8
1836	5 0		1844	4 2
1837	8 0		1845	3 11
1838	6 6		1846	4 7
1839	6 0		1847	5 4

Question Nr. 9—Beginning and End of the Winter Frost?

Answer: The arrival and the end of the winter frost, signalling the end and the beginning of work in the fields, varies from year to year. The careful farmer should never count on doing anything in the fields after the first of November or before the first of April. The farmer must also not forget to put away enough feed for the livestock, so that there is at least enough until the second week of May, because it is always better to have a little left over than not enough as spring often begins almost an entire month later (after April 17). Many farmers have suffered much loss because of carelessness in this regard.

Question Nr. 10—Activity of the Farmer in the Winter?

Answer: The activity of new immigrant farmers during the winter months is usually spent caring for livestock and in the felling and cutting up of trees, to be ready for burning in the spring. Bushes have to be cleared away before the snow falls. The women can spend time at spinning or other womanly activities. Since they must do most of the things that contribute to the comfort of the family, one can well imagine that the duties of the farm wives and their grown daughters are by no means insignificant. The comfort and welfare of the house depends almost entirely on their industry and skill. In the summer, because of the frequent shortage of workers, all help in the fields, and even children of five can make themselves useful. It is therefore regrettable that many of the Canadian farmers pass the winter in vanity and unnecessary visits, thereby neglecting their farm work and contributing to their own impoverishment.

Question Nr. 11—What Kinds of Fruit and Vegetables Are There in Canada?

Answer: All fruit that is to be found in England also thrives in Canada, especially plums, apples, strawberries, raspberries, and melons, and in small areas grapes grow fairly well. Peaches also thrive, although one seldom finds good grapes or good-tasting peaches, something which is attributable more to the neglect of the culture of the fruit and not the climate. Garden plants grow as well or better here than in England or Germany.

Question No. 12—Wages of Farm Labourers and Farm Maids and the Daily Wage of Artisans?

Answer: Farm hands receive £2 monthly with board, £3 monthly without board. Farm girls, £1 with board. Day labourers, 3s. 9p. per day, without board. The daily wage of carpenters, cabinet makers, and other artisans varies greatly, depending on the skill of the worker and runs from 5s. to 10s. per day. These are the prices for farm labourers and artisans who are experienced working in the country; newly arrived immigrants do not receive as much.

Question Nr. 13—Payments That Settlers Have to Make?

Answer: Large changes have recently been made regarding taxes; the entire authority has been assumed by the district councils and taxes are levied at a certain rate according to the estimated value of property. The aforementioned district councils are always elected by the people of the district, so that in actual fact the people tax themselves. All taxes raised in one district are spent in that district. This is a great thing and should, in a short time, bring about important internal improvements to the country. The taxes are quite insignificant (in amount) as they do not amount to more than 1 1/2 pence of each pound of the estimated value of the property.

Question Nr. 14—Offices Held by Settlers?

Answer: It may fall to each settler to have to serve the following offices in his township (city district), namely: Pfandstallhalter [livestock inspector], Fence inspector, Road Master, township writer, assessor, and school superintendent. District councillors must, according to the law, possess real property valued at £300; members of parliament £800. Only owners of land and householders are able to vote in the elections for members of the provincial parliament.

Question Nr. 15—Churches and Schools?

Answer: There are many houses for public worship in all regions of Canada. As evidence of this one might only mention that in the city of Guelph there are 7 churches and chapels and in Chatham, in the Western district, there are 4 churches, even though both of these places are new settlements. Each individual denomination has its own church. As regards schools, instruction in cities and more heavily populated areas is very cheap and good. In the country, and especially in the newly settled areas, the circumstances are not as good, although good schools do exist in these areas and children can receive inexpensive instruction.

Question Nr. 16—Climate of Canada West and the Highest and Lowest Temperatures?

Answer: The question is best answered with reference to the following weather table from the government observatory in Toronto, for the years 1840 to 1846

table omitted

Question Nr. 17—Family of Five or Six Grown People Until It Can Feed Itself From the Land?

Answer: Until an able family (of mentioned size) can support itself, the cost of maintaining such a family for 12 months can be calculated to be about £36. It depends mainly on the needs and uses of the family, because many are satisfied with half of what others need. From the food costs mentioned above, one can judge for oneself.

Question Nr. 18—Are Wild Animals an Annoyance to Settlers?

Answer: If wolves are driven to it by the ravages of winter, they can sometimes bring losses to the farmer. Sheep are usually protected from these animals by pens. Sometimes a farmer may lose a pig to a bear. There are farmers who have lived in this country ten years and have still seen neither a bear nor a wolf.

Question Nr. 19—What Kind of Wild Game is there in this Land?

Answer: The game in some regions is very abundant and consists mainly of deer, partridges, quails, rabbits (commonly called hares), in addition to a large number of wild ducks and geese. Wild turkeys are also numerous in the London and Western districts. Wonderful fish are also in abundance in all rivers and lakes. A remark made by an old and well-to-do farmer deserves to be cited here because it is very meaningful and true: "if only a new settler could earn a quarter of beef in the time it takes to hunt a quarter of game."

Question Nr. 20—Transportation Costs on the Navigable Waters and By Land to the Various Company Settlements?

Route and distance from Quebec and Montreal to Kingston, Toronto, and Hamilton.

From Quebec to Montreal 180 miles by steamship, each day at 5 o'clock, docking at Three Rivers, Port St. Francis, and Sorel.

From Montreal to Kingston on
the St. Lawrence River

	Miles
Lachine, per wagon,	9
Cascades per Steam Boat	23-32
Coteau du Lac, per wagon	12-44
Lancaster per Steam Boat	18-62
Cornwall	16-78
********	20-104
Matilda	8-112
Prescott	15-127
Brockville	12-139
Gananoque	32-171
Kingston	18-189
Toronto	180-369

Passengers depart each day at 12 o'clock from Montreal and arrive in Kingston the following afternoon. a cabin is 60 sh., on deck 12 sh. 6 p.

From Montreal to Kingston by way of
Bytown and Rideau Canal

Miles

Carrillon, per steam boat or
barge..54
Grenville 12-66
L'Orignal 7-73
Bytown 56-129
Kemptville by Rideau Canal...28-157
Merrickville......." 18-175
Smith's Falls....." 15-190
Oliver's Ferry...."....................9-199
******......................." 17-216
Jones's Falls......" 10-226
Kingston.........." 29-255
Steam ships depart each day from the
Lachine Canal. Passenger fare to
Bytown 10 sh. For baggage 2 sh. per
hundredweight. Fare to Kingston or
any other destination on the Rideau
Canal 15 sh. Baggage 2 sh. Per
hundredweight.

Children under 12 are half price and under 3 are free.

Passenger fare for a cabin from Rochester to Toronto 17s.
6p, on deck 7s. 6p; for a cabin from Lewiston to Toronto
7s. 6p., on deck 3s. 9p.

Hauling Over Land—i.e. a wagon with two horses and a
driver with a load up to 18 hundredweight, can cost on
the average 8p. per mile to the place of destination; it is
assumed that the wagon would have to travel back empty;
one can travel more cheaply, depending on the kind of
contract one can arrange.

Communication with the United States:

Steamships go daily from Lewiston, Queenston, and
Niagara to Toronto and Hamilton, a distance of 36 miles.

Two steamers go regularly three times per week from Rochester to Toronto, Kingston, and Hamilton. The distance by rail between Buffalo and Lewiston is 28 miles. The steamers "London" and "Canada" travel between Buffalo and Detroit and dock at all landing places on the Canadian shore of Lake Erie, in conjunction with the steamer "Brantford" that travels from Dunnville to Brantford and the steamer that travels every day between Detroit and Chatham. On this route one can travel easily and cheaply to the districts of Gore, Brock, London, and the Western district. Fast carriages travel to and from the steamships at Port Stanley, and from London and Goderich. The steam ship "Emerald" travels between Buffalo and Chippawa, and from there a train travels to Queenston.

The distance from Hamilton to Guelph is 30 miles; two fast carriages and a mail wagon go back and forth daily.

Steamships go daily between Kingston and Toronto. Passenger fare for a cabin, 20s.; on deck, 10s.; and from Toronto to Hamilton twice daily: passenger fare for a cabin, 7s. 6p.; on the deck. 3s. 9p.

Note: The quoted prices are in Halifax currency, in which $1 or 5s., 8 York shillings. or 4s. Sterling are equal.

Friedrich Widder, Commissioner

Canada Company Office
Frederick Street, Toronto,
July 1, 1847

Printed by Heinrich Eby, Berlin, Canada West

The German-language original of this document is in the Archives of Ontario, MU2110, F775, Miscellaneous Manuscripts 1847, #10.

Bibliography

This listing includes all materials consulted during the course of research, whether the final result includes any material from them or not. In the case of often-reprinted materials, the original date of publication is given, perhaps with a reference to a recent edition.

Published sources

Abbott, Joseph. *Memoranda of a settler in Lower Canada: or, the emigrant to North America, being a compendium of useful practical hints to emigrants...by an immigrant farmer.* Montreal: Printed for the author by Lovell & Gibson, 1842.

Abbott, Joseph. *Philip Musgrave, or, Memoirs of a Church of England missionary in the North American colonies.* new edition. London: J. Murray, 1850.

Adams, William Forbes. *Ireland and Irish emigration to the New World from 1815 to the Famine.* New Haven: Yale University Press, 1932. [reprint Baltimore, 1980]

Bachelor, Diana. *Early memories : Mrs. Diana Bachelor's childhood days among the Indians in the wilds of Canada, and her later life.* Red Wing, Minn. : Journal Job Printing, 1892 [1985 printing].

Bell, William. *Hints to emigrants: in a series of letters from Upper Canada.* Edinburgh: Waugh and Innes, 1824.

Bonnycastle, Sir Richard H. *The Canadas in 1841.* London: H. Colburn, 1841.

Brydone, James Marr. *Narrative of a voyage, with a party of emigrants sent out from Sussex in 1834, by the Petworth Emigration Committee, to Montreal, thence up the river Ottawa and through the Rideau Canal to Toronto, Upper Canada, and afterwards to Hamilton....* [Petworth, England? : s.n., 1834]

Buchanan, A.C. *Emigration practically considered: with detailed directions to emigrants proceeding to British North America, particularly to the Canadas.* London: Henry Colburn, 1828.

Burkholder, Mabel. *Out of the storied past.* Hamilton: s.n., 1968.

Butchart, Reuben. *The Disciples of Christ in Canada since 1830.* Toronto: Churches of Christ (Disciples), 1949.

Butchart, Reuben. *Old Everton and the pioneer movement amongst the Disciples of Christ in Eramosa township, Upper Canada from 1830.* Toronto: Butchart, 1941.

Butler, Samuel. *The emigrant's complete guide to Canada: hand-book of facts, collected with the view of guiding intending emigrants in their proceedings; together with much practical advice.* New edition. Glasgow: W.P. M'Phun, 1848.

Byerly, A.E. *Fergus, or the Fergusson-Webster settlement.* Elora: Elora Express, 1934.

Calvin, D.D. "Atlantic Crossing, 1835," in *Queen's Quarterly*, v. XLII, no. 1 (Spring 1935).

Carter, Floreen Ellen. *Place names of Ontario.* London: Phelps, 1984. [microfiche edition, London: Information Graphics]

Cattermole, William. *Emigration: the advantages of emigration to Canada*. London: Simkin & Marshall, 1831.

Charbonneau, André. *1847, Grosse Ile: a record of daily events*. Ottawa: Parks Canada, 1997.

Christmas, H. *Canada in 1849: pictures of Canadian life, or the Emigrant churchman, by a pioneer of the wilderness*. London: Richard Bentley, 1850.

Cobbett, William. *The emigrants' guide; in ten letters, addressed to the tax-payers of England*. London: Cobbett, 1829.

Cobbett, William. *Rural rides in the counties of Surrey, Kent, Sussex, Hampshire, Wiltshire, Gloucestershire, Herefordshire, Worcestershire, Somersetshire, Oxfordshire, Berkshire, Essex, Suffolk, Norfolk, and Hertfordshire*. London: Cobbett, 1830.

Coke, E.T.. *A subaltern's furlough: descriptive of scenes in various parts of the United States, Upper and Lower Canada, New Brunswick and Nova Scotia during the summer and autumn of 1832*. London: Saunders and Otley, 1833.

Copleston, Mrs. Edward. *Canada: why we live in it, and why we like it*. London: Parker, Son and Bourn, 1861.

Counsel for emigrants with interesting information and original information and original letters from Canada and the United States. Aberdeen: John Mathison, 1834.

Craig, Gerald M. *Upper Canada: the formative years*. Toronto: McClelland and Stewart, 1963.

Darling, William Stewart. *Sketches of Canadian life, lay and ecclesiastical, illustrative of Canada and the Canadian church*. London: David Bogue, 1849. [Fiction]

Dickens, Charles. *American notes*. London: Hazell, Watson & Viney, 187-? [Originally published 1842 by Chapman & Hall.]

Dictionary of Canadian biography. Toronto: University of Toronto Press, 1965-

Dixon, James. *Personal narrative of a tour through a part of the United States and Canada, with notices of the history and institutions of Methodism in America.* New York: Lane & Scott, 1849.

Dobie, W.C. "Sailing across the Atlantic sixty years ago," in Thunder Bay Historical Society *papers & annual reports,* 1914.

Doyle, Martin. *Hints on emigration to Upper Canada, especially addressed to the middle and lower classes in Great Britain and Ireland.* Dublin: William Curry, 1832.

Drummond, J.C. & Anne Wilbraham. *The Englishman's food: a history of five centuries of English diet.* London: Jonathan Cape, 1939.

Dunlop, William. *Statistical sketches of Upper Canada for the use of emigrants.* London: John Murray, 1832. Reprinted in *Tiger Dunlop's Upper Canada* (Toronto: McClelland and Stewart, 1967).

Elliott, Bruce S. *Irish migrants in the Canadas: a new approach.* Kingston: McGill-Queen's University Press, 1988.

Elliott, John K. "Crime and punishment in early Upper Canada," *Ontario Historical Society papers and records,* v. 27 (1931).

An emigrant's experience in Canada, Cuddy Peggy, &c., by a Roxboro' farmer. London: s.n., 188-.

Fergusson, Adam. *Practical notes made during a tour in Canada....* Edinburgh: William Blackwood, 1833.

Ferrier, A.D. *Reminiscences of Canada and the early days of Fergus.* 2d ed. Fergus: Fergus Heritage Group, 1992. [Reprint of 1923 edition.]

Fidler, Isaac. *Observations on professions, literature, manners and emigration in the United States and Canada, made during a residence there in 1832.* London: Whittaker, Treacher, 1833.

Finan, P. *Journal of a voyage to Quebec in the year 1825 with recollections of Canada during the late American War, in the years 1812-1813.* Newry: Printed by A. Peacock, 1828.

Fraser, William. "Diary of William Fraser, August, 1834-July 1835," in *Transactions of the London and Middlesex Historical Society*, no. 14 (1930).

Frye, Northrop. "Conclusion to a 'Literary History of Canada,'" in *Literary History of Canada*. Toronto: University of Toronto Press, 1965. [Reprinted in *The Bush Garden: Essays on the Canadian Imagination*. Toronto: Anansi, 1971.]

Garland, M.A. & J.J. Talman, "Pioneer drinking habits and the rise of the temperance agitation in Upper Canada prior to 1840," *Ontario Historical Society papers and records*, v. 27 (1931).

Gibson, David. "Conditions in York a century ago (written in a letter to a friend in Scotland)," in *Ontario Historical Society papers and records*, v. 24 (1927)

Gilkison, William. "The diary of Captain William Gilkison, 28 May 1832-31 March 1833," *Western Ontario Historical Notes*, vol. xvi, no.2 (September 1960)

Godfrey, Charles M. *The cholera epidemics in Upper Canada, 1832-1866*. Toronto: Seccombe House, 1968.

Gouger, Robert. *Emigration for the relief of parishes practically considered*. 2d ed. London: Ridgway and Sons, 1833.

Graham, Conrad. *Mont Royal, Ville Marie: early plans and views of Montreal*. Montreal: McCord Museum, 1992.

Gray, Leslie Robb. *Proudfoot to pepperbox to prosperity, 1833-1983*. London: New St. James Presbyterian Church, 1983.

Guillet, Edwin C. *The great migration: the Atlantic crossing by sailing-ship since 1770*. Toronto: University of Toronto Press, 1937.

Guillet, Edwin C. *Toronto, from trading post to great city*. Toronto: Ontario Publishing Company, 1934.

Haight, Canniff. *Country life in Canada fifty years ago : personal recollections and reminiscences of a sexagenarian*. Toronto: Hunter, Rose, 1885. [Reprint edition, Belleville: Mika, 1986]

Harrison, Jane E. *Until next year: letter writing and the mails in the Canadas, 1640-1830*. Waterloo: Wilfrid Laurier University Press, 1997.

Haw, William. *Fifteen years in Canada, being a series of letters on its early history and settlement; its boundaries, divisions, population and general routes....* Edinburgh: Charles Ziegler, 1850.

Head, George. *Forest scenes and incidents in the wilds of North America, being a diary of a winter's route from Halifax to the Canadas, and during four months' residence in the woods on the borders of Lakes Huron and Simcoe*. London: John Murray, 1829. [reprint edition, Coles, 1980]

Howison, John. *Sketches of Upper Canada*. Edinburgh: Oliver and Boyd, 1821.

"Impressions of Canada West in the 1850s," *Western Ontario Historical Notes* v. XVII, no. 1 (March 1961).

Irish emigrants' letters from Canada, 1839-1870. Belfast: E.N. Carrothers, 1951.

Jameson, Anna Brownell. *Winter studies and summer rambles in Canada*. London: Saunders and Otley, 1838. [many later editions]

Johnston, Stafford. "Hessian migration to the Canada Company's Huron Tract," *Families*, v. 15, no 4 (1976).

Jones, Elwood H. *Intermittent ambition: bridges over the Ontonabee since 1825*. Peterborough: Peterborough Historical Society, 1991.

Jones, Robert Leslie. *History of agriculture in Ontario, 1613-1880*. Toronto: University of Toronto Press, c1946, reprinted 1977.

Kingsford, William. *History, structure and statistics of plank roads in the United States and Canada*. Philadelphia: A. Hart, 1852.

Kingston, William H.G. *The emigrant voyager's manual*. London: Trelawney Saunders, 1850.

Lamond, Robert. *A narrative of the rise & progress of emigration, from the counties of Lanark & Renfrew, to the New Settlements in Upper*

Canada, on government grant.... Glasgow: Chalmers & Collins, 1821. [facsimile, Ottawa: Canadian Heritage Publications, 1978]

Langton, Anne. *A gentlewoman in Upper Canada: the journals of Anne Langton.* Toronto: Irwin, 1950.

Langton, John. *Early days in Upper Canada: letters of John Langton from the backwoods of Upper Canada and the audit office of the province of Canada.* Toronto: Macmillan, 1926.

Leavitt, Thad. W.H. *History of Leeds and Grenville Ontario, from 1749 to 1879.* Brockville: Recorder Press, 1879.

Legget, Robert Ferguson. *Rideau waterway.* Toronto: University of Toronto Press, 1955.

Lewis, Joyce C. *From Douro to Dublin: the letters of Frances Stewart.* Peterborough: Peterborough Historical Society, 1994.

Logan, James. *Notes of a journey through Canada, the United States of American, and the West Indies.* Edinburgh: Fraser and Co., 1838.

Lynch, John. "Report of the agricultural condition and prospects of the county of Bruce," in *Journal and transactions of the Board of Agriculture of Upper Canada, 1855-1856.* Toronto: 1856.

M'Donald, John. *Narrative of a voyage to Quebec, and journey from thence to New Lanark in Upper Canada.* Edinburgh: Printed for the author by Andrew Jack, 1823 [facsimile, Ottawa: Canadian Heritage Publications, 1978]

McKay, Donald. *Flight from famine: the coming of the Irish to Canada.* Toronto: McClelland and Stewart, 1990.

MacTaggart, John. *Three years in Canada: an account of the actual state of the country in 1826-7-8.* London: H. Colburn, 1829.

Marsh, E.L. *A history of the county of Grey.* Owen Sound: Fleming Publishing, 1931.

May, John. "Bush life in the Ottawa valley eighty years ago," in *Ontario Historical Society papers and records* v. 12 (1914).

Medicine for heroes: a neglected part of pioneer life. Erin: Mississauga South Historical Society in association with the Boston Mills Press, c1981.

Middleton, Jesse Edgar. *The municipality of Toronto, a history.* Toronto: Dominion Publishing, 1923.

Miller, Audrey Saunders. *The journals of Mary O'Brien, 1828-1838.* Toronto: Macmillan, 1968.

Moodie, Susanna. *Life in the clearings versus the bush.* London: Richard Bentley, 1853. [many later editions.]

Moodie, Susanna. *Roughing it in the bush, or, Forest life in Canada.* London: Richard Bentley, 1852. [many later editions]

Muir, Elizabeth Gillan. *Petticoats in the pulpit : the story of early nineteenth century Methodist women preachers in Upper Canada.* Toronto: United Church Publishing House, c1991.

Murray, John. *The emigrant and traveller's guide to and through Canada by way of the river St. Lawrence, as well as by way of the United States of American, with some friendly advice on embarkation....* London: Smith, Elder, 1835.

O'Gallagher, Marianna. *Grosse Ile: gateway to Canada, 1832-1937.* Ste-Foy: Carraig Books, 1984.

Proudfoot, William. "The Proudfoot papers, 1833," in *Ontario Historical Society papers and records,* v. 26 (1930), continued in v. 27 (1931)

Radcliff, Thomas. *Authentic letters from Upper Canada.* Dublin: William Curry, 1833. [reprint, Toronto: Macmillan, 1953]

Ray, Hugh. "Reminiscences of the Highland pioneers in Eldon, Victoria county," in *Ontario Historical Society papers and records* v. 24 (1927)

Read, Gordon. *Emigration from Europe to USA & Canada via the port of Liverpool.* Liverpool : Winston Churchill Memorial Trust/National Museums and Galleries on Merseyside, 1985?-1996.

Read, Gordon. *Through Liverpool to North America, 1830-1907: a selection of emigrant narratives.* Liverpool: National Museums and Galleries on Merseyside, 1998.

Robertson, Norman. *The history of the county of Bruce.* Toronto: William Briggs, 1906.

Rolph, Thomas. *The emigrants' manual: particularly addressed to the industrious classes and others who intend settling abroad, together with 'The memoranda of a settler in Canada.'* London: Cunningham and Mortimer, 1841.

Rowan, John J. *The emigrant and sportsman in Canada.* London: Edward Stanford, 1876.

Sansom, Joseph. *Travels in Lower Canada: with the author's recollections of the soils, and aspect, the morals, habits and religious institutions, of that country.* London: printed for Richard Phillips and Co., 1820.

Scott, James. *The settlement of Huron county.* Toronto: Ryerson Press, 1966.

Shirreff, Patrick. *A tour through North America: together with a comprehensive view of the Canadas and United States, as adapted for agricultural emigration.* Edinburgh: Oliver and Boyd, 1835.

Skelton, Isabel. *A man austere: William Bell, parson and pioneer.* Toronto: Ryerson, 1947.

Smith, W. H. *Canada: past, present and future, being a historical, geographical, geological and statistical account of Canada West.* Toronto: Thomas MacLear, 1851.

Smith, W. L. *The pioneers of old Ontario.* Toronto: George N. Morang, 1923.

Statements from settlers on the Canada Company land in the Huron district. [Stratford, Ont.? : s.n., 1842?]

Stephenson, Gerald F. *John Stephenson and the famous Peterborough canoes.* Peterborough: Peterborough Historical Society, 1987.

Stuart, Charles. *The emigrant's guide to Upper Canada, or, Sketches of the present state of that province.* London: Longman, Hurst, Rees, Orme and Brown, 1820.

Stuart, Will [William Stuart Cameron]. *Some we have met, and stories they have told.* s.l. : s.n., 1967.

Symons, Harry. *Fences.* Toronto: McGraw-Hill Ryerson, 1974.

Tasker, L.H. "The United Empire Loyalist settlement at Long Point, Lake Erie," in *Ontario Historical Society papers and records,* v. 2 (1900)

Taylor, Andrew W. *Our Todays and Yesterdays.* Galt: North Dumfries and Ayr Centennial Committee, 1970.

Thompson, Samuel. *Reminiscences of a Canadian pioneer for the last fifty years, 1833-1883, an autobiography.* Toronto: Hunter, Rose, 1884. [more recent edition, McClelland and Stewart, 1968]

Thornton, John. *Diary of a tour through the northern states of the union, and Canada.* London: F. Barker/Simkin & Marshall, 1850.

Trace, Mary Kearns. *Footsteps of a highland emigrant, John McCorkindale.* Calgary: Traces, c1987.

Traill, Catharine Parr. *The backwoods of Canada : being letters from the wife of an emigrant officer, illustrative of the domestic economy of British America.* London: C. Knight, 1836. [many later editions, most recently & definitively Ottawa: Carleton University Press, 1998]

Traill, Catharine Parr. *I bless you in my heart: selected correspondence of Catharine Parr Traill.* Toronto: University of Toronto Press, 1996.

Unterrich für Einwanderer in Ober Canada. Berlin, U.C. : Heinrich Eby, 1847. (Archives of Ontario, MU 2110, F775, Misc MSS 1847 #10, Catechism of information for intending immigrants [English translation by Michael Zimmermann]) for the complete text of this item, see Appendix III.

Walpole, K.A. "The humanitarian movement of the early nineteenth century to remedy abuses on emigrant vessels to America," in *Transactions of the Royal Historical Society* (1931).

White, Catherine. "Reminiscence of Mrs. White, of White's Mills, near Cobourg, Upper Canada, formerly Miss Catherine Chrysler, of Sydney, near Belleville, aged 79," in *Ontario Historical Society papers and records*, v. 7 (1910)

Whyte, Robert. *Robert Whyte's 1847 famine ship diary: the journey of an Irish coffin ship*. Cork: Mercier Press, c1994.

Williams, E. Wynn. *Britain's story: from the age of Elizabeth to modern times*. Toronto: J.M. Dent, 1947.

Wilson, James. *Narrative of a voyage from Dublin to Quebec in North America*. Dublin: James Wilson, 1822.

Newspapers

Canadian Emigrant and Western District Advertiser (Sandwich, Ontario)
Dublin Evening Post (Dublin, Ireland)
Illustrated London News (London, England)
Orillia Packet (Orillia, Ontario) [diary of Ellen Steele, 1898]

Manuscript sources

"Account of emigrants admitted into temporary houses at York from the 1st of May 1831 to 1st May 1832." (Archives of Ontario, MU 2105, 1831, #7, F775) for the complete text of this item, see Appendix II.

Aylmer collection (National Archives of Canada, MG 24, A 43)

Baker collection (National Archives of Canada MG 24 I 172)

Diary of Aitcheson Brown (National Archives of Canada MG 24 I 135)

Joseph Brown collection. (National Archives of Canada, MG 24 I 41)

A.C. Buchanan. "Notice to settlers and emigrants from the United Kingdom" signed by A.C. Buchanan, resident agent for the Superintendence of Settlers and Emigrants in the Canadas, Quebec, 4 May, 1830. (Archives of Ontario, MU 2105, 1830, #4)

Reminiscences of Joseph Carder (Wellington County Museum & Archives, MU 294, A995.19)

Letter of Fr John Cassidy, 15 February 1839 (Archives of the Roman Catholic Archdiocese of Toronto, M AB07. 13)

Letter of Elizabeth, Lady Colborne to John Yonge (National Archives of Canada MG 24 I 186)

Connon collection (Archival and Special collections, University of Guelph Library)

Journal of Robert Cromar (Wellington County Museum and Archives, 975,821 aMan. 377A. MU 8)

William Dow collection (National Archives of Canada, MG 24 I 185)

Diary of Sarah Hallen Drinkwater (Archives of Ontario, MU 843 1-D-3)

Reminiscences of James Edwards (Archives of Ontario, MU 7786, #5)

John Forrest collection (National Archives of Canada, MG 24 I 158)

Diary of John Frazer (National Archives of Canada, MG 24, I 197)

Great Britain. Treasury Civil Establishments 1842, no. 130-V (Archives of Ontario Library, Imperial Blue Books, Box 14, N. 130-V).

Letter of John Hallas (National Archives of Canada, MC 24 I 175)

William Hewgill (National Archives of Canada, MG 24, I 77)

Papers of Andrew Hunter (Archives of Ontario, MU 7824, #2, F830)

Diary of — Johnson (National Archives of Canada, MG 24 I 35)

John and Sarah Leeming collection (Archives of Ontario, MU 47817)

Diary of Julia Bird Mann (Archives of Ontario, Mann Family Papers, MU 2003, envelope 1)

David MacLaren, letters 1836-1846 (National Archives of Canada MG24, I 164)

W J Mickle collection, 1830-1832 (National Archives of Canada, MG 24 I 53)

John Millar (National Archives of Canada, MG 14 I 67)

Mullett family letters, 1821-1859 (Archives of Ontario, MU 4563, #7); the National Archives of Canada version of these materials, from which our photograph of William Mullett is taken, is called the "Hannah Clothier Papers," (MG24 I 132) from the recipient of the letters.

Reminiscences of Mary Hutchinson Orr (Wellington County Museum & Archives, A989.7 MU 102)

Diaries of William and Elizabeth Peters (National Archives of Canada, MG 24 I 131)

Diary of Leah Purkiss, 1844 (University of Toronto, Thomas Fisher Rare Book Room, MS coll 123) for the complete text of this item, see Appendix I.

James Ritchie Papers. (National Archives of Canada, MG 24 I 199)

Diary of George Robinson, 1832 (Archives of Ontario, MU 7824, #9)

M.G. Scherk, Memoranda on early life in Upper Canada (Archives of Ontario, MU 2096, F775, Misc MSS Box 2, #79)

Diary of John Boyd Taylor (Archives of Ontario, MU 846, I-T-1)

Diary of John Thomson (Archives of Ontario, MU846, I-T-2)

Letters of Henry Tyler and Thomas Cather, 1836 (Archives of Ontario, MU 2107 Misc Coll 1836, #12)

Robert Wade letters 1819-1842 (National Archives of Canada, MG 24 I 127)

Diary of John Walker (National Archives of Canada, MG 24 I 181)

Diary of Joseph Wilson (Archives of Ontario, MU 847)

Notes

To avoid intrusive footnotes and many superscript numbers in the text, the notes below are arranged under their respective pages. It should be a simple matter for the reader to find references for the various quotations by locating the page number and then the brief reference given below. Full references for both published books and manuscript materials can be found in the bibliography.

page 4
"Working in their own..." Guillet, *Migration*, p. 3.
page 5
"The labourers seem..." Cobbett, *Rural*, p. 16-17.
"Between 1847 and 1856..." Jim Rees' brochure for his database, "The
       Fitzwilliam Estate Clearances, 1847-1856." jrees@gpo.iol.ie
page 6
"It is a melancholy thing..." *Dublin Evening Post*, 30 April 1818.
"To those who are..." Doyle, p. 5.
"Those who are instrumental..." Murray, p. 12.
page 7
Emigrant societies: This story is told in some detail in *A narrative of the rise
      & progress of emigration from the counties of Lanark & Renfrew to
      the new settlements in Upper Canada*, by Robert Lamond, Secretary
      & Agent for the Glasgow Committee of Emigration; material on the
      meeting of 24 October 1820 is on p. 18-19.
page 8
"Having with many of my..." M'Donald, p. 3.
page 9
"I had a personal..." Fergusson, p. 311.
"At noon, reached Lachine..." Brydone, p. 14-15.
page 10
"We answer, the..." Gouger, p. 4; "that the time of..." same, p. 7.
page 11
"Emigration has taken place lately..." *Illustrated London News*, 18 August
      1849, p. 115.
"wild romance and..." Darling, p. 3.
"From a very early age..." Christmas, v. 1, p. 1; "so sanguine were we..."
      Thompson, p. 17.

page 12

"The hardships necessarily..." Gouger, p.3.

Emigration statistics: Guillet, *Migration*, p. 20.

page 13

"My picture of..." Copleston, p. 5.

"'Martin Doyle' was..." Thompson, p. 17.

"That all the truth..." M'Donald, p. 2.

"Upper Canada has been..." Shirreff, p. 374.

"If there be means..." Stuart, p. 316.

page 14

Low crime rate: Sansom, p. 15; his impression is borne out by official court
    statistics of the time, quoted in John K. Elliott, "Crime and
    punishment in early Canada," *Ontario Historical Society papers and
    records,* v. 27 (1931), but docks and travelling vessels are notorious
    haunts of thieves.

"You will expect me..." letter of Robert Wade, 1819.

"I think there is little..." letter of John Wade, 9 September 1835; this was
    Robert Wade's son writing to Robert's brother Ralph, who did
    eventually emigrate.

page 15

Nathaniel Carrother's note: *Irish emigrants'*, p. 4.

"We take this favourable..." letter of Mary Ritchie, 26 January 1847.

page 16

"That a man who..." R.L. Jones, p. 67.

page 17

"I worked steadily..." Taylor, p. 35.

"Brother Arthur I expect..." letter of William Gillett, 4 March 1821 from the
    Mullett papers.

page 18

Tools: Lanark list from Lamond, p. 22-23; Doyle's list from p. 46.

page 19

"You ask about bringing..." letter of W.J. Mickle, 27 January 1831; writing in
    1850, Henry Christmas made a point of saying that things had
    changed in the last fifteen years, and that taking agricultural
    implements was no longer advisable, since Canadian ones were
    available (v. 2, p. 245).

"Dear brother if you..." letter of Robert Wade, 6 July 1820.

Feather-beds: Buchanan, p. 87.

"A pair or two..." *Counsel for emigrants*, p. 56.

page 20

"You should also have..." Doyle, p. 46.

"The kind of apparel..." Wilson, p. 7-8.

"You should have a..." *Counsel to emigrants*, p. 59.

page 21

"No heavy or cumbrous..." MacTaggart, v.2, p. 305.

page 22

"Cooking utensils, crockery..." *Counsel for emigrants*, p. 56; Mathison says of the logging chains, "In Canada such chains cost about from 15 to 25 dollars per 100 lbs."

"But curtains, carpets..." Christmas, p. 247.

page 23

"It is necessary to..." James Wilson, p. 8.

"You must have all..." *Counsel for emigrants*,p. 55-57.

page 24

Currency: Charles Stuart explains that the "New York shilling, or the shilling of the practical currency, is worth seven-pence halfpenny of the legal currency; and the pound of the practical currency, is worth only twelve shilling and six-pence of the currency which is legal. The eight shillings of the practical currency to the dollar, are equal to the five shillings of the legal currency." (p. 311-312). In addition, there were quarter dollars and eighth dollars; a more complete discussion of this complex subject can be found in *Money and exchange in Canada to 1900*, by A.B. McCullough (Toronto: Dundurn Press for Parks Canada, 1984).

"I wrote a letter to brother..." letter of John Millar, 14 November 1834.

page 25

"mechanics, particularly carpenters..." Stuart, p. 65.

Do not bring maids: Dunlop, p. 132; "For the last five..." letter of David MacLaren, 12 December 1840.

"There is one other quality..." Cobbett, *Emigrants Guide*, p. 33.

"From what I have seen..." letter of Thomas Cather, 10 November 1836.

page 26

"I was invited..." Trace, p. 6.

"one old lady came..." Taylor, p. 35.

page 27

"There were two covered..." *Illustrated London News*, 21 Dec. 1844, p. 398.

page 28

Expenses to America: diary of John Walker, 17 September 1835.

page 29

"Left Guisboro..." diary of Joseph Wilson, 5 April 1831.

page 30

"We travelled from Manchester..." Shirreff, p. 2.

"We arrived...." diary of George Robinson, 19 June 1832.

The *Comet*: not to be confused with the sailing ship of the same name, which plied the Le Havre-New York route in 1819.

page 31

"The passage on these..." Williams, p. 225-226.

"Sailed from Glasgow..." diary of John Frazer, 13 May 1837.

page 32

"6 O'Clock A.M...." diary of John Frazer, 14 May 1837.

"When Sir George..." Edwards, p. 1.

page 33

"Left Annan..." diary of William Hunter, 5 May 1849, p. 1, in Andrew Hunter
     papers.

"June 25th, Michael..." *Illustrated London News*, 6 July 1850.

page 34

"...was directed by the mate..." diary of John Frazer, 14 May 1837.

"The person employed..." *Illustrated London News*, 17 April 1847.

page 35

"Make your bargain..." Buchanan, p. 86.

page 36

"Having agreed for a..." Calvin, 21 July 1835.

"took my passage..." diary of — Johnson, 14 July 1819.

page 37

"Monday 15 May..." diary of John Frazer.

Journey via Halifax: For an account of a journey to Halifax, then overland to
     Quebec (in winter!), see the early section of Head.

page 38

Temporary accommodation in York: see Appendix 2.

page 40

"Those to whom..." Doyle, p. 63.

Fares: Doyle, p. 63.

page 41

Offer to German settlers: Stafford Johnston, p. 160-167; an English translation
     of the prospectus is given in Appendix 3.

"the only vessel..." Traill, *Backwoods*, p. 27.

"bought a cheese..." diary of — Johnson, 19 July 1819.

page 42

"Mr Buchanan, government..." Butler, p. 44.

"Those who have been..." Doyle, p. 64.

page 43

"48 stone of potatoes..." Buchanan, p. 87.

"trusting to potatoes..." Butler, p. 44.

"By authority from..." Fergusson, p. 385.

page 44-45

"The baby which..." letter of Sarah Leeming, 5 May 1840.

"To preserve new..." Wilson, p. 7.

"—bread, 2/3 lb..." Cattermole, p. 81; "a few pounds...' same, p. 81.

"The next thing, after..." Dobie, p. 35-36.

"...it was whispered..." *Illustrated London News*, 29 July, 1848, p. 54.

page 47

"All now appear to be..." Trace, p. 9.

page 48

"April 27th 1833. Went on board..." diary of Millicent Steele, 27 April 1833.

page 49

"Now the little steamer..." Trace, p. 9.

"We arrived at Glasgow..." diary of John Boyd Taylor, p. 36.

"the vessel removed..." diary of P. Finan, 20 April 1825.

page 50
"We hauled out from..." diary of William Hunter, 8 May 1849.
page 51
"A woman, also, with the tact..." Coke, p. 5.
"On the third day..." Fergusson, p. 12-13.
page 52
"After a detention..." Coke, p. 1.
"Came on board on Monday..." diary of Elizabeth Peters, April 1830.
page 53
"we sailed immediately..." Thornton, p. 5.
"On the date of sailing..." Dobie, p. 36.
page 54
"after a lapse..." Fergusson, p. 384.
"At noon, on the 24th..." Shirreff, p. 5.
page 55
"Went on board of..." diary of John Frazer, 21 May 1837.
page 56
Irish versus Liverpool fares: Adams, p. 153; for more information about
        Liverpool as a point of emigration, see Gordon Read's *Emigration
        from Europe to USA & Canada via the port of Liverpool* and his
        Through Liverpool to North America, 1830-1907.
page 57
"After setting sail..." Muir, p. 60; Padstow is a small port in Cornwall.
"It is reported that..." *Illustrated London News*, 9 July 1842, p. 135.
"...the Captain came on..." diary of Elizabeth Peters, 3 May 1830.
page 58
"I was not long..." letter of Thomas Connon, 21 August 1852.
page 59
"All the cooking utensils..." Dobie, p. 35-36.
"We went down into..." *Illustrated London News*, 29 July 1848, p. 54.
page 60
"Go in good time..." *Counsel for emigrants*, p. 54.
"Choose then, if you can,..." Christmas, v.2, p. 242.
"We have had a fine night..." diary of John Walker, 13 October 1835
page 61
"A rough day followed..." diary of John Walker, 13 October 1835.
"On each side..." Bell, p. 3.
page 62
"...to give you an idea..." Diary of Robert Wade, 27 May 1819.
"Persons who have never..." MacTaggart, v.1, p. 4.
"A ship would come..." Dobie, p. 36.
page 63
"On Sunday August 27..." Carder, 27 August 1833.
page 64
"...stormy, strong wind..." et seq., diary of Robert Wade, May 1819.
"The coast is gliding..." Miller, p. 3; the writer became Mary O'Brien several
        years later.

"A tyrannical or rude..." Butler, p. 49.

page 65

"Much depends on the man..." MacTaggart, v. 1, p. 3.

"Certainly courage is..." Thompson, p. 19.

"Grouse having offended..." diary of — Johnson, 9 August 1819.

page 66

"In serving out..." diary of — Johnson, 17 August 1819.

"On the whole the voyage..." letter of William J. Mickle, undated [June 1830].

page 67

"It was our Captain's..." letter of Sarah Leeming, 20 May 1840.

"....our Captain has turned..." letter of Sarah Leeming, 30 May 1840.

page 68

"a nice gentlemanay..." Calvin, July 1835.

"Except one or two..." Calvin, 3 August 1835.

"This was the Sabbath..." diary of William Hunter, 13 May 1849.

"Oh, it is pitiable..." diary of William Hunter, 16 May 1849.

page 69

"the first sabath at..." diary of Joseph Wilson, 17 April 1831.

"A quarrel arose..." Finan, undated.

page 70

"Strangers soon become..." MacTaggart, v.1, p. 4.

"...a row occurred..." diary of John Frazer, 13 June 1837.

page 71

"...our progress to the West..." diary of Robert Wade, 4 June 1819.

"In a calm, the Welsh..." Coke, p. 2.

A French scientist: Drummond, p. 373.

page 72

"I was very unforunate..." letter of Thomas Connon, 21 August 1852.

"The cooking department..." Trace, p. 16.

page 73

"Two women quarrelled..." Trace, p. 19.

"...on Tuesday morning..." letter of Thomas Connon, 21 August 1852.

page 74

"The ship allowance for..." diary of William Hunter, 18 May 1849; "The ship allowance was..." diary of William Hunter, 29 May 1849.

"Generally we have been..." diary of Elizabeth Peters, undated 1830.

page 75

"You can form no..." letter of Sarah Leeming, 5 May 1840.

page 76

"We have had a poor...." letter of Sarah Leeming, 5 May 1840.

"We have bought a..." letter of Sarah Leeming, 22 May 1840.

"...I will give you..." diary of Robert Wade, 29 May 1819.

page 77

"Towards evening..." diary of William Hunter, 11 May 1849.

"Jenny's bisquits are quite..." diary of Joseph Wilson, 3 May 1831.

"Biscuit is much used..." James Wilson, p. 7.

page 78

Eating porpoise: Calvin, 27 & 28 July 1835.
"A very fine day..." diary of Ellen Steele, 2 June 1833.
page 79
"As soon as we were..." Skelton, p. 66.
Table of food rations: Brydone, p. 4.
page 80
"Coffee is much preferable..." James Wilson, p. 6.
"My sister Mary..." diary of Elizabeth Peters, 1 May 1830.
"The tea I cannot..." diary of Elizabeth Peters, undated.
page 81
"I cannot omit to..." Radcliff, p. 33.
page 82
"Yesterday we were cut..." James Wilson, p. 9.
"We are put upon..." diary of John Walker, 6 October 1835.
"Finding that all the people..." Brydone, p. 6.
page 83
"The crew consisted..." Fergusson, p. 385.
"We bought a quart..." diary of William Hunter, 17 May 1849.
"Rather more calm..." diary of Julia Bird, 3 May 1833.
page 84
"The ship rolling much..." Brydone, p. 5.
"Sunday 7 May 1831..." diary of Joseph Wilson, 7 May 1831.
"6 A.M. still squally..." diary of John Frazer, 17 June 1837.
page 85
Burning of the *Ocean Monarch*: *Illustrated London News*, 16 September 1848,
    p. 167.
"...called the Mate down..." diary of John Frazer, 18 June 1837.
page 86
"Scarcely a breath of wind..." diary of John Frazer, 25 June 1837.
"A passenger applied..." diary of John Frazer, 26 June 1837.
page 87
"I cannot express..." letter of Sarah Leeming, 5 May 1840.
"I was informed last..." diary of John Walker, 12 October 1835; "Last Friday
    night..." same, 13 October 1835; the comet was Halley's Comet.
"Mr Woodward's ewe..." diary of Joseph Wilson, 28 April 1831.
page 88
"Constant excercise..." Kingston, p. 25.
"A variety of very..." Kingston, p. 21.
"The weather much finer..." diary of Millicent Steele, 11 May 1833.
page 89
"Mrs Keating does nothing..." diary of Millicent Steele, 13 May 1833.
"Many of the women..." Logan, p. 2.
Cap-making: diary of Robert Wade, 22 May 1819; hat-making, Calvin, 10
    August 1835.
"...as we get in..." diary of Robert Wade, 27 May 1819.
page 90
"Though we have been..." Traill, *Backwoods*, p. 29.

"I have already formed..." Traill, *Backwoods*, p. 30.
page 91
"...while we were on the lookout..." Logan, p. 9.
"This is the very Temple..." diary of Ellen Steele, 27 May 1833.
"Still lovely and calm." diary of Ellen Steele, 28 May 1833.
page 92
"Stewart and I..." Logan, p. 2.
"It is now five days..." diary of John Walker, 13 October 1835.
Danish pirate: Logan, p. 6.
page 93
"In some cases, the use of..." Shirreff, p. 5.
"It is said that the shark..." MacTaggart, v.1, p. 8.
"I have not shaven..." diary of — Johnson, 8 August 1819.
"we had 348 second..." letter of John Hallas, June 1842.
page 94
"Keep yourselves clean..." Buchanan, p. 87.
"Old Beersley..." diary of William Hunter, 26 May 1849.
page 95
Doing chores on Sunday: Bell, p. 21.
"Every day the Captain..." M'Donald, p. 4.
"The captain caused the..." Logan, p. 8.
page 96
"This has been another..." diary of William Hunter, 10 May 1849.
"I used to make it..." Christmas, v.1., p.6.
"Report comes from below..." Trace, p. 17.
page 97
"Those who had young..." Bell, p. 7.
"An inquiry was set on foot..." Bell, p. 9.
"...a cabin passenger gave birth..." Shirreff, p. 6; Emperor Napoleon I of France,
        after whom the ship was named, had as his first wife (and greatest
        love) the Empress Josephine.
page 98
"A remarkably fine..." Brydone, p. 7.
"our passengers are all..." diary of Robert Wade, 3 June 1819.
page 99
"It has been an awful..." diary of William Hunter, 12 May 1849.
"Ship rolling fearfully..." Trace, p. 13.
"After the two first..." letter of Lady Aylmer, 24 February 1831.
page 100
"I have neglected..." diary of Elizabeth Peters, undated, May 1833.
page 101
"took a draught..." Bell, p. 5.
"most of our neighbors..." diary of Joseph Wilson, 21 April 1831.
"Wine or ale..." diary of Joseph Wilson, 1 May 1831.
"A most happy change..." Miller, p. 5.
"Most of our family..." diary of George Robinson, 28 June 1832.
page 102

"I was called upon..." diary of George Robinson, 28 June 1832.

page 103

Recipe for cholera beverage: A. Soyer, *The Modern Housewife* (1849), quoted
in the *Illustrated London News*, 1 September 1849, p. 158.

page 104

"I think it my duty..." James Wilson, p. 16.

"Several people sick..." diary of John Frazer, 2 July 1837; "the body of the..."
same, 3 July 1837.

page 105

"Child belonging to..." diary of Robert Cromar, 26 June 1836.

"the child put overboard..." diary of Robert Cromar, 27 June 1836.

page 106

"a child belonging..." diary of Robert Cromar,12 August 1835; "a child died..."
same, 20 August 1836.

"This morning one of..." diary of — Johnson, 11 August 1819.

"many of our company..." letter of Joseph Brown, 10 January 1835.

page 107

"I visited Phoebe Dagg..." James Wilson, p. 11.

page 108

"...a small black..." Calvin, July 1835.

"A fine morning &..." diary of Joseph Wilson, 27 April 1831.

"Several,however, of the..." Christmas, v. 1, p. 22.

"Cod-fish are caught..." MacTaggart, v.1, p. 7.

page 109

"...there has been a herd..." diary of John Walker, 6 October 1835.

"Fogs off Newfoundland..." MacTaggart, v. 1, p. 5.

"On a fine, mild..." Coke, p. 6.

page 110

"We were roused..." letter of Sarah Leeming, 22 May 1840.

"At 9 A.M. a mass..." Bell, p. 28.

page 111

Stuck in the ice: *Ravenscrag: the Allen Royal Mail Line*, by Thomas E.
Appleton, p. 41-45.

"This cold state..." M'Donald, p. 4.

"A very fine morning..." diary of Joseph Wilson, 18 May 1831.

"Newfoundland on the north..." diary of William Peters, 2 June 1830; "By this
morning...", same, 4 June 1830.

page 112

"But Canada has..." Frye, p. 217.

Anticosti: "It might be an..." Christmas, v. 1, p. 18; "It does not appear..."
Trace, p. 19; in a letter of 28 September 1819, Robert Wade describes
the island as being 100 miles long, but McCorkindale states it is
'more than 200'—the difference perhaps reflecting the effect it had.

page 113

"Ships coming up..." MacTaggart, v. 1, p. 27-28.

"...we are now sailing..." diary of Robert Wade, 1 July 1819.

page 114
"...with seven ships..." diary of Robert Wade, 6 July 1819.
page 115
"A great many sick..." Trace, p. 12.
page 116
"Oh! the sea..." diary of Ellen Steele, 1 June 1833.
page 117
"To the emigrants..." Coke, p. 2.
page 118-119
"After a stormy day..." diary of John Walker, 28 September 1835.
"Towards noon the sea..." diary of John Walker, 1 October 1835.
"When fully out to sea..." MacTaggart, v. 1, p. 11-12; "We have some
         Stormy..." diary of John Walker, 21 October 1835.
"Awoke between 12..." diary of Joseph Wilson, 24 April 1831.
page 120
"No cooking could be..." Bell, p. 24; 'partly alive' indicated it was already
         maggoty..
"The wind rose..." M'Donald, p. 3-4; the season was May, 1821.
"A great lurch..." diary of Julie Bird Mann, 20 April 1833.
page 121
"After this we had..." letter of Sarah Leeming, 20 May 1840.
"Very stormy indeed." diary of Julia Bird, 1 May 1833.
"As we felt much..." diary of Ellen Steele, 20 May 1833.
page 122
"The Hottinguer sailed..." unidentified newspaper clipping.
The Irish Coast: private information from Jim Rees.
Loss of the Exmouth : Illustrated London News, 8 May 1847, p. 295.
page 123
Loss of the Charles Bartlett : Illustrated London News, 7 July 1847, p. 2;
         personal losses, p. 10.
The Europa : Illustrated London News, 29 January 1849, p. 2.
Loss of the Great Britain : Illustrated London News, 20 May 1843, p. 345.
page 124
"early on the morning..." letter of Joseph Brown, 10 January 1835.
"found the voyage..." McKay, p. 212.
page 125
Narrative of the Hebe : The Canadian Emigrant and and General Advertizer,
         28 September 1833.
page 127
Epigraph: as quoted at the head of Chapter XIV of Guillet's The Great
         Migration; this diary was later published under her married name,
         O'Brien (see under Miller in the bibliography)
"We are now at..." diary of Joseph Wilson, 21 May 1831.
"This is a noble..." Trace, p. 26.
"smooth lawns..." Traill, Backwoods, p. 39.
page 128
"We reached Grosse Ile..." Traill, Backwoods, p. 40.

Ferrier background: Byerly, p. 55.
page 129
"...sad were the scenes..." Ferrier, p. 7.
"We have already seen..." Traill, *Backwoods*, p. 41.
page 130
"Believe me, in this..." Traill, *Backwoods*, p. 42.
Figures for 1834: Murray, p. 61.
"Here we counted..." Brydone, p. 8-9.
page 131-132
Cholera statistics: Godfrey, p. 42; O'Gallagher, p. 38.
"After encountering some..." letter of Joseph Brown, 10 January 1835.
"Got up to..." diary of Robert Cromar, 24 August 1836; "Got up at 5..." same,
      25 August 1836; "Got up early..." same, 26 August 1836.
"Nothing but scrubbing..." Logan, p. 14.
page 133
"Having conducted the people..." Brydone, p. 11-12.
House of Commons funding: Treasury Civil Establishments 1842, No. 130-V.
page 134
Deaths in 1847: Charbonneau, p. 1, p. 15.
"Every vessel having..." *Illustrated London News*, 6 May 1848, p. 289.
"the greatest variety..." letter of John Leeming, 10 June 1840.
page 135-136
"On leaving the..." Murray, p. 15.
"At ten last night..." Traill, *Backwoods*, p. 43.
"At a bend of..." Bell, p. 38; "Quebec consists of two..." Strickland, p. 8.
"I never was in..." Trace, p. 27; "I don't like..." same, p. 29.
"The ship anchored..." Finan, undated June 1828.
Duty on guns: diary of — Johnson, 16 July 1819.
"Anchor got up..." diary of Robert Cromar, 27 August 1836.
page 137
"...the Captain and several..." M'Donald, p. 5.
"On monday forenoon..." letter of Thomas Connon, 21 August 1852.
"Elizabeth and I..." letter of Sarah Leeming, 10 June 1840.
page 138
"Upon reaching the quay..." Fergusson, p. 75.
"The influx of emigrants..." Fergusson, p. 79.
"Things, however, seemed..." Christmas, v. 1, p. 34.
page 139
"It costs a good deal..." Radcliff, p. 96.
"Quebec contains several..." Strickland, p. 10.
Buchanan's background: Guillet, *Migration*, p. 23.
"Dress yourself in..." Buchanan, quoted in Fergusson, p. 350-351.
page 140
"Accordingly having an..." James Wilson, p. 21.
page 141-142
"We arrived safe..." James Wilson, p. 19.
"On leaving the ship..." *Counsel for emigrants*, p. 57.

"John and Joseph..." letter of Sarah Leeming, 10 June 1840.

"The French language..." letter of John Leeming, 10 June 1840.

"We arrived at Quebec..." M'Donald, p. 5.

page 143

"The emigrant before going..." Rolph, p. 90.

Times of steamship departures: *Unterrich für Einwanderer in Ober Canada.*

"Steamer started for Montreal..." diary of Robert Cromar, 28 August 1836.

"The steam boat sailed..." James Wilson, p. 23.

page 144

"Set sail for Montreal..." diary of Joseph Wilson, 24 May 1831; "The prospect up the..." same, 25 May 1831.

"The vessel in which..." Dickens, p. 180.

page 145

"After leaving Quebec..." Murray, p. 18.

"At present, comparatively few..." Howison, p. 3.

"When we had got..." Christmas, v. 1, p. 41.

page 146

"since sabbath till last..." letter of Thomas Connon.

"Landing was neither..." Copleston, p. 7.

page 147

"We arrived this morning..." Trace, p. 31.

"We arrived at Montreal..." James Wilson, p. 23-24.

page 148

"Montreal has a most brilliant..." Thornton, p. 74.

"We arrived in Montreal..." Radcliff, p. 53.

"Having a few hours..." letter of Mary Mullett, 10 July 1821.

page 149

Bringing farthings: *Counsel to emigrants*, p. 56-57; "some soap..." same, p. 57.

"The change to this..." diary of Joseph Wilson, 26 May 1831; use of the form 'batteau' conforms with contemporary usage in this period. It is now, and correctly, 'bateau.'

page 150

"Went into Montreal..." diary of Joseph Wilson, 27 May 1831.

"If on your arrival..." Murray, p. 20.

"When we arrived..." *Counsel for emigrants*, p. 53.

page 151

"Here we arrived in 24 hours..." M'Donald, p. 6.

"It is highly injudicious..." Howison, p. 241.

page 152

"When I was in Quebec..." Howison, p. 62-63.

Naive emigrants: Mackay, p. 200.

page 153

"you will see I intend..." letter of William Mickle, 22 November 1830; in his letter of 6 July 1831, Mickle tells his father than he earned £10 and his passage to the interior while waiting.

"Having a letter from..." James Wilson, p. 24-25.

page 155-156

"In travelling from Montreal..." Howison, p. 6-7; "On Saturday 31st..." Letter
of Robert Wade, 28 September 1819; "We are going..." letter of Mary
Mullett, 10 July 1821; "they are of the..." Radcliff, p. 55.

page 157-158

"14 Seper..." diary of — Johnson, 14 September 1819.

"I took my passage..." Strickland, p. 11; "We were charmed..." Thompson, p.
27; "From Lachine to Prescott..." letter of Robert Wade, 28 September
1819.

Boatmen: see Howison, p. 42; "I may here inform..." Bell, p. 58.

page 159

"15 Sep I stopped..." diary of — Johnson, 15 September 1819.

"here allow me to say..." letter of Joseph Brown, 10 January 1835.

"the house was situated..." Howison, p. 11.

page 160

"...the Rapids of Les Cedres..." Howison, p. 15.

"Nothing of interest..." letter of John Leeming, 9 December 1840; "We
afterwards passed..." Head, p. 344.

page 161

"At La Chine we deserted..." Radcliff, p. 56.

"The hotel at Cornwall..." Radcliff, p. 57.

"It was unanimously voted..." Moodie, Roughing, p. 70.

page 162

"At all the poorest..." Radcliff, p. 58; the Radcliff letters' claims to be
'authentic' are put in doubt here, for no traveller would have
encountered currants, strawberries, raspberries and cherries at the
same time anywhere, since they do not ripen at the same time.

page 163

"After sailing a few..." James Wilson, p. 26.

"Being uneasy to get..." James Wilson, p. 27.

page 163

"In the morning..." Brydone, p. 20-21.

page 164

"Notwithstanding the dangerous..." Howison, p. 16; "The steamer
'Passport'..." Illustrated London News, 21 July 1849; by this time, the
steamers were coming much farther up the river than in other
examples.

page 166

Prescott: "Prescot is a fine..." M'Donald, p. 8-9; "I remained two..." Strickland,
p. 11.

Length of journey: Howison, p. 37; Robert Wade, letter of 28 September 1819;
diary of — Johnson.

"If I were ever..." Coke, p. 326.

page 167

"We arrived at Prescott..." letter of John Leeming, 9 December 1840; "very
conspicuous objects..." same.

Thousand Islands: Logan, p. 59; "the most perfect..." Dixon, p. 138.
"At Kingston we..." Christmas, v.1, p. 59.
page 168
"on our arrival..." letter of William Dowie, 25 November 1821, John Forrest
Collection; "here our little William..." letter of Robert Wade, 28
September 1819.
page 169
"Those who go to..." A. Bell, quoted by his father William Bell, p. 212; "The
water of the river..." Howison, p. 29; the word 'flux,' here and in the
Dowie letter above, was the common term for diarrhoea.
"The evening of the 28th..." Gilkison, p. 41.
page 170
"you have acquantance..." letter of Nathaniel Carrothers, Irish Emigrants', p.
4.
"For emigrants of small..." Murray, p. 34.
"On leaving Lachine..." Murray, p. 36.
page 171
"The first adventure..." W. L. Smith, p. 195-196; Smith is paraphrasing from
John Treffry's diary.
"Proceeding up the Rideau..." Murray, p. 37.
page 172
Various lakes: Murray, p. 38.
"In the summer of 1828..." MacTaggart, v. 2, p. 21.
"This infernal place..." MacTaggart, v. 2, p. 13.
Dimensions of canal: Legget, p. 17.
page 173
"On Thursday morning..." letter of Robert Wade, 28 September 1819.
Steamboat routes: summarized by Roberts in Middleton, v.1, p. 459-461.
Quality of accommodation: Cattermole gives a lengthy description of the
luxury parts of the steamers, p. 54-56.
page 174
"I have lived in..." quoted from an unknown source by E.V. Roberts, "Toronto
Harbour," in Middleton, v.1, p. 456; statistics of the lighthouse come
from Guillet, Toronto, p. 60.
"The general aspect too..." quoted by Roberts in Middleton, v. 1, p. 443.
page 176-178
"The general appearance..." quoted by Scott, p. 12; also the description of the
hotel.
"...jostled almost..." Bonnycastle, v.1, p. 146.
"Toronto is a very..." Letter of John Leeming, 9 December 1840; "the society
in York..." Cattermole, p. 17; "Toronto at this time..." Ferrier, p. 13.
"It is a matter of much encouragement..." Cattermole, p. 98-99; "Any person,
however humble.." Christmas, v.1, p. 88.
"When the emigrant reaches..." Howison, p. 242-243; Charles Stuart
specificies that the house must be eighteen by sixteen (p. 54).
page 179
"The casually impending..." Stuart, p. 54.

"Everyone is dressed..." diary of Ellen Steele, 12 June 1833; in the *Orillia Packet* for 14 April 1898, this quotation is from an entry dated 11 June, but this is corrected to 12 June in the later publication of the diary; the newspaper has two 11 June entries.

page 180

James Buchanan: Craig, p. 126.

"When we landed..." letter of John Hallas, June 1842.

"I saw and tasted..." Dobie, p. 38.

page 181

"By this time..." reminiscences of James Edwards, p. 1.

"While the navigation..." Dobie, p. 38.

page 182

"At 7 o'clock..." diary of Ellen Steele, 21 June 1833.

"The Erie canal..." Cattermole, p. 79.

page 183

Routes from New York via the railway: Haw, p. 32.

"On Monday 28th May..." diary of William Gilkison, 28 May 1832.

page 184

"Landed in Rochester..." diary of William Hunter, 22 June 1848.

"we arrived here by the..." Fraser, p. 90; storm on Lake Erie, p. 91.

"We arrived in..." Carder, 27 August 1833.

page 185

"At last the boat..." diary of Ellen Steele, 26 June 1833.

page 187

"Suppose, for instance..." Rowan, p. 15.

page 188

"To all the Highlanders..." diary of William Bell, quoted in Skelton, p. 169.

John Howison, p. 240-242 (quoted above in the chapter on Quebec and Montreal)

The fifty-acre size: Scott, p. 92

One hundred acres: Rowan, p. 32

Land values: Howison, p. 234

page 189

Take care before investing: Rowan, p. 12

"Contrary to an impression..." Jones, p. 67.

"When you arrive..." letter of W. J. Mickle, 8 December 1831.

John Stuart's journal: from Will Stuart's transcription, pp. 1-2. Will Stuart's note about John Stuart's initial journey: "by horse and foot and boat from Montreal to west of Peterborough and return, Aug. 27th to Sept. 15, 20 days."

page 191

"Let us try to follow..." Robertson, p. 24

"At Owen's Sound..." Christmas, v.2, p. 221.

page 192

"The ground is measured..." M'Donald, p. 14-15.

"I arrived here a week ago..." Mickle, letter of 6 July 1831

page 193

Kinds of trees: "The best land is timbered..." Strickland, p. 162; "When you are upon it..." Christmas, v.2, p. 222; the same sentiments are echoed by Cattermole who lists oak, maple, beech, ash, black walnut, hickory, basswood, cherry, cedar, elm, birch, pine; 'superior quality', Cattermole, p. 39.

page 194

"My visit to this spot..." Christmas, v.1, p. 120.

Cedar swamps: John Langton, p. 30.

"There are always plenty..." John Leeming, letter of 9 December 1840

"Settlers, with capital,..." Cattermole, p. 31.

page 195

"Some fifteen years prior..." Abbot, p. 91

"It has been remarked.." Board of Agriculture of Upper Canada, 1856, p. 615.

page 196

"The original settlers in Ontario..." Rowan, p. 29.

page 197

"I must not omit telling thee..." Letter from Mary Mullett, 10 July 1831

"'I guess,' quoth our Yankee driver..." Moodie, *Roughing*, p. 111.

"At length we arrived..." Copleston, p. 41.

page 198

"half a mile from..." Robert Wade, letter of 28 September 1819.

"Though the road is..." diary of Ellen Steele, 1833.

page 199

"This will not, however, prevent..." M'Donald, p. 13; "Either a mink..." Ferrier p. 27

page 200

Mosquitoes: "In addition to these difficulties..." M'Donald, p. 15; "For three days I had been disgusted..." Howison, p. 42; "There is only one drawback..." Rowan, p. 379.

page 201-202

Getting lost: "We soon left the cleared land..." Letter of John Leeming, 9 December 1840; "A story from another part..." Marsh p. 299.

First shelters: "A settler upon getting..." Cattermole, p. 86; "About an hour before nightfall..." Radcliff, p. 8; "A bundle of spruce..." Head, p. 189 (he had previosuly given a detailed description of the hut made for him by sailors); "Wretched habitations indeed!..." M'Donald, p. 13.

"I prepared our bed..." Strickland, p. 231.

page 203

Methods of clearing: A good explanation appears in Scott, p. 93-95, and a definition of a slack in Abbott, p. 47; "Some persons take..." Cattermole, p. 86; a more detailed explanation of girdling in Jones, p. 71; "I began & chopped..." Mickle, letter of 29 July 1831; a very lengthy version of the whole process can be found in Radcliff, p. 92-93.

page 204

"When ye burn..." Abbott, p. 47; timing explained by Strickland, p. 165-166.

Demanding work: Christmas, v.2, p. 220; underdone partridge leg, p. 235.
Dangers of fire: Strickland, p. 22.
Fence rails: Symons, p. 30.
page 205
Labour: "Labour will always..." Robert Wade, letter of 28 September 1819;
    Scott, p. 94
Rates of clearance: Radcliff, p. xiv; "We have cleared..." Wade, letter of 7
    November 1820; "I have abt 3/4..." Mickle, letter of September 1831.
page 206
Axe wounds: "John Plews..." Wade, letter of 6 March 1821; Strickland, p. 108f.
"I have been working..." Letter of William Singer, quoted in Doyle, p. 83.
"The MacPhersons were strong..." Ray, p. 464.
page 207
Stumps: "I believe most land..." Cattermole, p. 111; "Scott's 'monkey',..."
    Ferrier, p. 19; stumping method, Symons, p. xliv. Christmas,
    however, recommended the stump extractor, v.2., p. 223.
page 209
Placement of house: discussed briefly in James Scott, p. 93
Water: letter of Robert Forrest, undated.
page 211
"Their method of building..." John M'Donald, p. 20
"I have a well-finished..." letter of John Kelly, 20 September 1842, quoted in
    Statements from settlers... p. 13.
page 213
"The roof was formed..." Doyle, p. 31-32.
"The usual dimensions..." Cattermole, p. 86.
Size of house: Robert Forrest, undated letter
page 214
Peeling elm bark: E.L. Marsh, p. 316.
"...then in place of slates..." M'Donald, p. 21.
"A log shanty, twenty-four feet..." Strickland, p. 165.
"I could have bought..." letter of Robert Wade, 7 November 1820.
page 215
"We have had a..." letter of Robert Wade, 3 September 1825.
"As soon as the settler..." Strickland, p. 170-171.
"Dear Willy..." letter of Joseph Carrothers, 23 October 1848.
page 216
Chimney: "...built of split cedar..." W.J. Mickle letters, March 1832;
"Everything froze..." Ferrier, p. 26.
Beds: E.L. Marsh, p. 299-300; moss, p. 317.
page 217
"a house was built..." Haight, p. 3
"We began with nothing..." Diary of Sarah Hallen Drinkwater, 20 December
    1840, Archives of Ontario MU 843 1-D-3. Despite the fact that Sarah
    came from an educated background and even her husband could read,
    they have only a single book.

page 218
The house's surroundings, Haight p. 111-112.
page 219-220
The second house: its appearance, Haight p. 79-80, grandfather's comforts, p.
9. The 'Dutch' qualities of these houses, which include both the
general appearance and the double door, probably arose from the fact
that many of the first settlers in Quinte came from New York state,
which was originally Dutch. Many of them also had Dutch ancestors
among the early inhabitants there.
page 221
"...amongst the farmers..." Christmas, v.1, p. 103.
page 222
"In the parlour we are kept warm...": Traill, *I bless you in my heart*, p. 41
"Women of refinement..." Jones, p. 82.
page 224
"We are all looking forward..." letter of James Clothier Mullett, 16 January
1825; "We had two..." letter of Deborah Mullett, 21 January 1825;
her references to 'friends' means 'Friends,' i.e., Quakers.
page 225
"We lived about a mile..." Strickland, p. 20
"On foot and alone..." Abbott, *Philip Musgrave*, p. 9.
"I immediately set out..." William Fraser, p. 144.
page 226
"It may be observed..." Doyle, p. 9
"Although the air..." Head, p. 167; "The weather was fine..."Head, p. 171.
"I returned trembling..." Jameson, p. 6; throughout the early stages of his
journey, George Head also remarked constantly on the cold and its
effects.
page 227
"The wood-sleighs are my delight..." Jameson, p. 11
"It is the favourite afternoon drive..." Moodie, *Clearings*, p. 181; for a
technical description of the kinds of sleighs, see Cattermole, p. 6.
"The Bay is now..." Fraser, p. 100. This is actually a description of Toronto
harbour on Christmas Day 1834; despite its happy sound, the writer
disapproved of the frivolity because he did not believe there was any
scriptural justification for Christmas.
page 228
"On the morning of..." Diary of William Fraser, p. 93.
"Drove all the cattle..." Diary of Aitcheson Brown, 31 December 1840.
"The sleighing, about which..." John Langton, p. 60.
"Sometimes, indeed, they were bad..." Abbott, *Philip Musgrave*, p. 30, 32.
The fact that he was an Anglican clergyman and the settlers with the
shovel were Presbyterian may have made a difference in their atittude.
page 229
"As there appeared to be..." Howison, p. 218.
page 230
"Bushwalking..." John Langton, p. 69.

Primitive roads: Logan, p. 51

page 231

"Next day, I started..." Ferrier, p. 16-17.

Plank roads: fully described in Kingsford. The statistics about early plank roads in Upper Canada are given on p. 5-6.

"The place in Hamilton..." Burkholder, p. 79.

page 232

"In swampy marshy places..." Scherck, p. 172.

Corduroy roads: A picture of the remains of one appeared in the *Kitchener-Waterloo Record* on 21 July 1961; it was reprinted in a good descriptive article by Ellis Little about these roads in the annual volume of the Waterloo Historical Society for 1989.

page 233

"Half a log..." Carrie Munson Hoople, "The corduroy road," from *Along the way* (1909), quoted in E.C. Guillet, *Pioneer travel in Upper Canada*, epigraph to chapter VIII.

"Every male is obliged..." Howison, p. 236.

"Our first experience..." Ferrier, p. 29.

page 234

"...forthwith booked ourselves..." Thompson, p. 29.

"We left Darlington..." Strickland, p. 55.

page 235

"The coaches being heavy..." Scherck, p. 183.

"The stage-coaches in Canada..." Christmas, v.1, p. 100.

"I had scarcely met..." Thornton, p. 41.

page 236

" The old settlers are..." Doyle, p. 27.

"I thought my fatigues..." Howison, p. 218.

"But the trail which had..." Scott, p. 46-48.

page 238-239

"I now, for the first time..." Howison, p. 9-10; "Here I found..." Howison, p. 118.

"They had been recently married..." Thompson, p. 31; the innkeeper in question was David Root.

page 240

"...having gone to the wrong..." John Langton, p. 5; "Stopped in Brockville..." diary of — Johnson, 20 September 1819.

"A bed on the floor..." Moodie, *Roughing*, p. 98.

"However, I fell asleep..." Head, p. 183.

page 241

"has an excellent tavern..." Cattermole, p. 28; *rara-avis* means 'rare bird'.

"We stopped for the night..." Mary O'Brien, 20 October 1829/Miller, p. 74.

"There was one large room..." Ferrier, p. 22-23.

page 242

"As it was necessary..." Jameson, p. 91; there is some dispute over whether her bowl of milk was literally that or a rum drink.

"I found shelter..." Brydone, p. 22.

399

"We had heard of some..." Thompson, p. 32.
page 243
"She no sooner came..." Head, p. 277.
"We arrived at Vanorman's..." Brydon, p. 27; this inn was between Hamilton and Brantford.
page 244
""...after jolting over thirteen..." John Langton, p. 5.
"By the way, I..." Jameson, p. 258.
"Abour midnight as our Capt...." Diary of William Fraser, p. 92.
page 245-246
"In one of your letters..." John Langton, p. 102. In his description of his scow (p. 56) he includes a drawing, and says it can carry 'a ton or two.' Hauling goods from Peterborough required steamship passage to Bobcaygeon, by scow to the rapids, and then hauling upstream through the bush until some could be placed in a rowboat. The more unwieldy things, such as doors, were carried by hand all the way from the rapids. The plentiful use of canoes by the natives transferred to the settlers, and the result was a canoe factory in Peterborough, see Stephenson for details. Langton's 'twist of the wrist' reference is from p. 55. Another settler attempted making a dugout but it would never sit level in the water and in the end he sank it in disgust.
"Fortunately, we were only..." Bell, p. 142.
page 247
Bridges: this information is from a useful summary of bridge-building in Elwood H. Jones' *Intermittent ambition: bridges over the Otonabee since 1825* (1991), p. 2-3.
"...he forgot his compass..." John Galt, writing in *Fraser's Magazine*, November 1830, quoted in Scott, p. 23; the man who forgot his compass was Tiger Dunlop.
Mrs Moodie devotes a chapter to this topic: *Clearings*, "Lost children", chapter 13; "Persons, when once they..." p. 243; there are more stories of people lost in the bush in Christmas, v.2, p. 232ff.
page 248-249
"Since that time..." Bell, p. 135.
"On the horn being..." Christmas, p. 123.
"If a guest at a rural..." Marsh, p. 298.
"Of course men..." Haight, p. 50.
"Our nearest Post Office..." Ferrier, p. 24; "I have omitted..." Proudfoot, p. 439; "As it cost me..." Letter of W.J. Mickle, 8 December 1831; "This morning a man..." Proudfoot, p. 441. More information about the growth of the post office in Canada can be found in Jane Harrison's *Until next year: letter writing and the mails in the Canadas, 1640-1830.*
"you was wishing..." Letter of Alexander Crichton, 13 August 1845 (Baker Collection)

page 251

"I shall in the..." and "...I shall be very..." both from Letter of Mary Mullett, April 1823; "fetch a little Broom seed..." Letter of Mary Ritchie, 26 January 1847; "Please to send 4..." Letter of Joseph Carrothers, *Irish Emigrants'*, p. 12; "I want you to get..." Letter of Nathaniel Carrothers, *Irish Emigrants'*, p. 3; "when I resided..." letter of W.J. Mickle, September 1831. The Carrothers' and Mary Ritchie wanted seed from Ireland, but whether it would grow in the harsher Ontario climate was another matter. A butter-print was a wooden mold for making designs on butter after it was produced; their grandmother must have responded to this hint, for Mary's sister Deborah acknowledges the gift of a butter-print in her letter of January 1825.

page 252-253

"Ours I think..." Traill, *I bless you*, p. 58. This is from a letter to her sister, Susanna Moodie; 'Agnes' is their sister, Agnes Strickland. 'Fourth volume of the Queen's' refers to *Lives of the Queens of England*, a famous series written by their two sisters, Agnes and Elizabeth Strickland, which eventually reached twelve volumes.

"The only salvation of a man..." Jameson, p. 274; "He too was prospering..." p. 82; "they are young looking..." letter of Robert Wade, 8 May 1825.

"I never met with so many..." Jameson, p. 89.

"she often thinks & weeps..." Letter of John Hallas, June 1842.

page 254

"...do tell them for me..." Letter of Mary Mullett, April 1823.

"I like America..." letter of George Carpenter, 29 January 1831, quoted in Doyle, p. 81.

"I think of those..." Moodie, *Clearings*, p. 239.

"Since the countries are..." Letter of William Hewgill, 15 September 1843.

page 255

"Many young men are attracted..." Moodie, *Clearings*, p. 11.

"wild romance..." Darling, p. 3.

"I certainly did once..." John Langton, p. 59; his later menu is given on p. 114.

page 257

"I rise at an hour..." John Langton, p. 93.

"I do not think..." Letter of Deborah Mullett, 21 January 1825.

page 258

"I am dull & stupid..." Gilkison, p. 66

"more should come here..." Letter of Robert Wade, 6 July 1820.

"I fear he has..." Letter of Nathaniel Carrothers, *Irish migrants*, p. 2.

"the temptations here..." Letter of Elizabeth Lady Colborne, 1 June 1835.

"...those who give themselves..." Moodie, *Clearings*, p. 11.

page 259

"My guide afterwards..." Bell, p. 129.

"Thou also wished..." Letter of Mary Mullett, April 1823.

page 260

"To remedy this..." Haight, p. 73.

page 261

"On February the 12th..." Skelton, p. 171; the narrator is William Bell.

The wedding carriage-ride and New York marriages: Scherck, p. 143-5.

page 262

"I have frequently heard..." Leavitt, p. 19.

"An Irishman called upon me..." Skelton, p. 170.

"...funerals are always..." Coplestone, p. 63.

page 263

"If he has neighbours..." Howison, p. 253.

page 264

"When I was in Upper..." Jameson, p. 95.

Taverns as public building: some good examples are given in Tasker, p. 48, 49.

"I arrived..." Bell, p. 102, 106.

"The rum is very cheap..." quoted in MacKay, p. 71.

"Liquor was a very common..." Garland, "Pioneer drinking...", p. 342.

page 265

"Drunkenness, which is..." Abbott, *Musgrave*, p. 135.

"You will have heard..." letter of Mary Mullett, April 1823; Ebenezer Shepperd
        married Isabella Swetman.

Presbyterian temperance: William Proudfoot's view was that alcohol was a gift
        from God, and hence could not be disapproved of. William Fraser,
        who was born in Nova Scotia, was a temperance advocate, but this
        was attributed to American influences.

"A man came..." diary of Mary O'Brien, 29 June 1833, quoted in Miller, p.
        13.

"...after the soaking..." Strickland, p. 58.

page 266

"A few years ago..." Strickland, p. 142-144; the author goes on to say "A good
        joke is not, however, a good argument," and endorses abstinence for
        habitual drunkards, while chiding the temperance societies for having
        zeal without charity.

page 267-268

"...the temperance men..." Rowan, p. 52.

"'Treating' as it is called..." Christmas, p. 105.

"This habit of..." Coplestone, p. 49.

Amusements: Moodie's chapter on this topic begins on p. 88; the Langton
        Christmas is described in Anne Langton's letter of 1 January 1841 (p.
        142).

"Balls in Canada..." John Langton, p. 132.

"I never met with..." Moodie, *Clearings,* p. 89.

page 269

Threshing floor: the earliest recorded communion service in Kitchener was
        held in the Joseph Schneiders' barn, and a list of communicants
        survives; Anne Langton's letter of 29 June 1842 can be found on p.
        163 of *A Gentlewoman....*

Forbidden dancing: Howison, p. 215.

page 270
"Here there was no..." Jameson, p. 51.
"There in every city..." Rowan, p. 50.
page 271
"So strong is the feeling..." Copleston, p. 56.
"The Scottish Highlanders..." Jones, p. 59-60, his quotation from Samuel
    Strickland is from v.1, p. 138; "Most of the settlers..." Howison, p.
    172. Jones' earlier reference said, "As in the United States, they [the
    Pennsylvania Germans] shared with the Lowland Scots the reputation
    of being the best farmers." (p. 53). Doyle makes similar comments, p.
    29.
"The moment the very..." first written in the *Edinburgh Review*, 1807 (v. XI),
    quoted in MacKay, p. 117. This attitude is evident in the writings of
    Moodie, Strickland and Howison, and was still prevalent in Jones'
    history of agriculture, written a century later.
page 272
Irish fighting: Thompson, p. 24; MacKay, p. 75. MacKay had earlier described
    the religiously mixed settlement at Richmond, implying a lack of
    antagonism. In his *Irish Migrants in the Canadas*, Bruce Elliott
    suggests that the Irish protestants and Roman Catholics tended to
    settle in their own areas, however (p. 143f), so the mixing may not
    have occurred as readily as some observers thought.
"a cross in breeds": Doyle, p. 29.
"To the north-west..." W. H. Smith, v.1, p. 279.
page 273
Dining with servants: "I felt my English..." Coke, p. 303; Christmas discusses
    the matter in detail, v.2, p. 185.
"Pride of birth..." Haight, p. 104; "One great comfort..." diary of Ellen Steele,
    printed 19 May 1898, p. 1.
page 274
Youth of servants: Anne Langton, p. 87, 89.
"Almost all the servants..." Jameson, p. 40.
"Whilst we were at..." Diary of Mary O'Brien, 12 September 1830, quoted in
    Miller, p. 133.
"The affectation of wishing..." Moodie, *Clearings*, p. 63; also mentioned by
    Doyle, p. 29.
page 275
"Hardworking..." Thompson, p. 41.
page 276
Hired men: Jones, p. 56.
"the person I work..." letter of John Hallas, June 1842.
"We have the honor..." Letter of Deborah Mullett, 25 January 1825.
"this has become..." Letter of M. Carrothers, *Irish Emigrants'*, p. 5.
page 277-279
"Soon after, another..." Logan, p. 63; 'in chains' would mean in prison in
    British terms, but the Scotsman here is joking about his having to
    carry a heavy chain by winding it around his body.

"Fortunately, in those days..." Ferrier, p. 39.

Bees: Christmas, p. 225; "the older colonists..." Doyle, p. 45; "there were about..." Logan, p. 45; "Some people can..." Strickland, p. 37, this comes after his description of a haying-bee.

"The sufferings or..." Haight, p. 104; the story of Strickland's neighbours' kindness is at v.1, p. 100.

page 280

16 Anglican clergy: cited in Middleton, v.1, p. 149.

"Oh! what a favour..." Letter of Deborah Mullett, 21 January 1825.

"During the winter..." Abbott, *Musgrave*, p. 20.

page 281

William Fraser's experience: with the Anglican (p. 155), with the Kirk minister (p. 114) and "This day the sacrament..." p. 106. The editor of the diary notes, "To be denied the use of a meeting-house was rare in those days when preachers were few and far between." Fraser's viewpoint can be seen from his language, where he says he 'preached' but the Kirk minister 'harangued.'

"Hired a horse..." William Fraser, p. 153. The groom's name was actually Julius Raman.

"...but the more distant..." Abbott, *Musgrave*, p. 35.

page 282

Incident in Paris: William Fraser, p. 154.

"If I mentioned..." Letter of David MacLaren, 12 December 1840

page 283-284

"I was accosted.." William Fraser, p. 144; similar incidents can be found in Proudfoot, p. 443. Proudfoot refused baptism, but was then angry with those who had another clergyman perform the rite.

"Ignorant or immoral..." Bell, p. 120; "Still he insisted..." p. 121; "Though I had given..." p. 122 (the smug tone of this last story, involving the deaths of two people, is startling); Skelton quotes another example, even more vehement, on p. 165.

"Once travelling..." Proudfoot, p. 486.

page 285

"In the evening..." William Fraser, p. 108.

"About mid-day two..." Bell, p. 62.

Sabbath profanation: Bell, p. 46, 145; see also Fraser, p. 91.

page 286

"I began with my own..." Bell, p. 78.

"Hon & Right Revd..." letter of John Cassidy, 15 February 1839.

page 287

"you can either..." Letter of John Hallas, June 1842.

Camp meetings: Scherk MS, p. 155; Mrs Moodie devotes a chapter to them, *Clearings*, p. 138ff.

"William my son..." letter of William Hewgill, 15 September 1843.

page 288

Andrew Lunn story: conversation with Doug Taylor, 29 September 1998.

"God help the poor..." Jameson, p. 12.

"Found all my family..." Proudfoot, p. 437.

"Brother and cousins..." Letter of Joseph Carrothers, *Irish Emigrants'*, p. 7.

page 289

"There were numerous quacks..." Guillet, *Toronto*, p. 40; "for medical men..." same, p. 39. The Market referred to is the St. Lawrence Market in Toronto.

"Before quitting Suffolk..." Strickland, v.1, p. 2; "We had no medical..." same, v.2, p. 207. This is followed by a humorous story about Dunlop's treatment of new arrivals. The 'mad doctor' appears on v.2, p. 208-209.

"The next thing..." Thompson, p. 72.

page 290

"I got up..." diary of Mary O'Brien, 15 August 1832, quoted in Miller, p. 197.

Mary O'Brien's friend: Miller, p. 171.

"One courageous woman..." letter of Anne Langton, 16 September 1842, quoted in *A Gentlewoman....*

"David has been poorly..." letter of John Millar, 1 June 1842.

page 291

"confined to the house" diary entry for John Ross in Aitcheson Brown papers.

Cholera: "seventy or eighty..." Ferrier, p. 7; "Yesterday we have...", Gilkison, p. 42; "On the 19th..." Abbott, *Musgrave*, p. 118; more information can be found in *The cholera epidemics in Upper Canada, 1832-1866*, by Charles M. Godfrey (1968).

Potash: the process is fully explained in Bell, p. 226; "The currency of the day..." Haight, p. 106; "soon as I can..." Letter of Robert Forrest, 1824; Mary O'Brien's neighbour in Miller, p. 171.

"Almost every article..." Bell, 183; "Mother was making..." Letter of Deborah Mullett, 21 January 1825; "the farmer is the most..." *Irish Emigrants'*, p. 2; "the farmers up there..." Letter of John Leeming, 9 December 1840.

page 293

"The quantity of fuel..." Coplestone, p. 73.

"After supper father..." Marsh, p. 315; the story is related by John P. Miller, son of Edward Miller.

page 295

"After dinner I rode..." Diary of Mary O'Brien, 11 June 1829, quoted in Miller, p. 53; Jones mentions this in a note on p. 57 and quotes extensively from Timothy Dwight's *Travels in New England and New York* (1821).

"Mr Ferguson was..." John Langton, p. 119.

page 296

"...she had laid..." Copleston, p. 46.

"...barter did very well..." Ferrier, p. 27; in 1820, Robert Wade stated his taxes to be '8s. 7d. and a man five days on the highway.' Discussion of the statutory road work is above, under Transportation. By 1850, people were paying money for road-tax instead of statutory labour (cf. Letter of Nathaniel Carrothers, *Irish Emigrants'*, p. 13.)

The reason that..." letter of Robert Wade, 7 November 1820.
"...the old method..." *Canada Farmer*, 15 April 1864, p. 102.
Cheese factory: Jones, p. 250, quoting from an article in *Canada Farmer*, 15
    January 1867, p. 29. He also notes, "Little butter in Ontario was
    made in factories before 1880," p. 263.
"The most delicious butter..." Moodie, *Clearings*, p. 283; she was referring to
    seeing them at an early agricultural exhibition.
page 297
"In the first place..." M'Donald, p. 17; Haight states unequivocally,
    "Vegetables were unsaleable," p. 108.
"Thus the pioneers..." Jones, p. 81.
"May was a wet..." Letter of Robert Wade, 6 July 1820.
page 298
"The way they plant..." Letter of Robert Wade, 7 November 1820; Bell
    describes the same process, p. 231, giving statistics of one acre
    producing thirty to forty bushels of corn, a thousand pumpkins and
    the stalks which will be a ton of fodder.
"Pumpkins are..." Letter of Robert Wade, 25 December 1822.
"Turnips are very difficult..." Letter of Robert Wade, 7 November 1820,
    repeated in his letter of 13 October 1823; "...white turnips..." James
    Scott, p. 95.
page 299
"Nearly every kind..." Tasker, p. 36; "Apples are in every..." Cattermole, p. 11;
    "Apples, plums and cherries..." Letter of Robert Wade, 13 October
    1823; "Rasps and brambles..." Letter of Robert Wade, 7 November
    1820.
"Their gooseberries..." M'Donald, p. 18.
page 300
"This is also the case..." Bell, p. 183.
"this has been a..." *Irish Emigrants'*, p. 10; "Southby and Anthony..." Diary of
    Mary O'Brien, 6 November 1828, quoted by Miller, p. 23.
"We have the same..." Letter of Robert Wade, 13 October 1823.
page 301-302
"The large thistles..." Logan, p. 48; "Often have I..." Moodie, *Clearings*, p.
    280.
"they have a nice..." letter of Deborah Mullett, 21 April 1825.
"Orchards are almost..." Letter of John Leeming, 9 December 1840; "The
    banks of the St. Lawrence..." Moodie, *Roughing*, p. 67; "The apple
    orchards of Ontario..." Rowan, p. 39.
"brought on the table in jugs-full..." Fidler, p. 212.
Maple sugar: information from Rowan, p. 281-283, which includes a good
    detailed (but not too detailed) description of the process; also Bell, p.
    228.
page 303-304
"...in the harvast..." *Irish Emigrants'*, p. 2.
"If a settler..." Ferrier, p. 34; "the show of animals..." p. 30.

"Taken one with another..." Jones, p. 142; "the cattle are genrly..." Letter of
John Millar, 14 November 1834; "We foddered..." Letter of Robert
Wade, 6 July 1820; "all the poor people..." Letter of John Hallas, June
1842; "The saving, therefore..." Christmas, v.1, p. 71.

page 305
"A bell attached..." Christmas, v.2, p. 231.
"Uncles house..." Letter of Ralph Wade, 17 December 1845.
Cattle shows: a list of the 1831 Talbot Agricultural Society show can be found
in *The Canadian Emigrant and Western District Advertiser*, 19
January 1832, p. 3; the complete list of winners of the 10th provincial
show, in Coburg in 1856, covers several pages in the transactions of
the agricultural board for that year.

page 306-307
"there is not a..." Letter of Robert Wade, 7 November 1820.
Pigs: running free and dangerous, Jones, p. 77, 140; "Young pigs we have..."
Letter of Mary Mullett, April 1823; hickory nuts, Gibson, p. 361.
"Pigs grow very fat..." Cattermole, p. 88; "Father killed ten..." Letter of
Deborah Mullett, 21 January 1825; "A day of slaughter..." Mary
O'Brien, 24 November 1828, quoted in Miller, p. 26.
"In the middle of the Lake..." John Langton, p. 107.
"Pork may certainly..." John Langton, p. 129.

page 308
"It is difficult..." Logan, p. 50.
"The hens might as..." John Langton, p. 107.
"The poultry here..." Anne Langton, p. 87.
"The geese were generally plucked..." Scherck, p. 98; Steve Leeson of the
Ontario Agricultural College observed that in theory, geese could be
plucked up to four times, but the quality of their feathers would not be
very good. It was best to do it only once or twice. He suggested the
summertime so that re-growth would occur before winter. This
practice, although barbaric, was never banned. It stopped around 1920
because of an increase in commercial goose raising and a greater
availability of feathers. He also mentioned that people in the north
collected goose feathers from the nests of wild geese. Since Scherck's
family was Mennonite, the authors asked some Old Order
Mennonites how widespread this practice was; they said they had not
heard of it.

page 309
"My provisions and other..." John Langton, p. 34; billy goat odour, p. 61;
interesting event, p. 94.

page 310
wandering cat: Anne Langton, p. 180.
"If I tolerate..." Moodie, *Roughing*, p. 451.
"took my passage..." Johnson, 14 July 1819; not allowed on batteau, 14
September 1819.
Samuel Thompson's dog's death: p. 50.

page 311-312

"Placing the rifle..." Moodie, *Roughing,* p. 215.

Horses: for more discussion of horse breeds in Ontario in this period, see Jones, p. 143-144; " As our route..." Adam Fergusson's diary for 6 October 1833, quoted in Byerly, p. 32; the hints for horse owners come from *The Canadian Emigrant and Wester District Advertiser,* 23 November 1833, p. 2.

"I must say a few..." Haight, p. 51-53.

page 313

"We have 4..." letter of James Clothier Mullett, 16 January 1825.

William Bell's list of animals is found on p. 184.

page 314

"Deer abound..." Cattermole, p. 10.

"During the long..." Rowan, p. 65.

"opposite to this house..." Diary of --- Johnson, 18 September 1819.

page 315-316

Stealing deer from wolves: John Langton, p. 106, 94; "We used frequently..." Ferrier, p. 26.

"By the way, the bear's..." Diary of Mary O'Brien 28 August 1832, quoted in Miller, p. 198.

"At that place I saw..." Leavitt, p. 19; "partridges may be..." John Langton, p. 115.

Pigeons: "I recollect seeing..." Leavitt, p. 19; "I have known..." Thompson, p. 53; "The enormous flights..." Christmas, v.1, p. 177.

"Another, and much more..." Haight, p. 76.

page 317-318

"We had several..." Ferrier, p. 26; "One day Mr Drysdale..." *ibid.*; "The other day I shot..." John Langton, p. 115; "...at the same time..." Head, p. 234; "The Bay of Quinte..." White, p. 154.

"Some species of frog..." Fergusson, p. 44-45.

Salmon: Jameson, p. 53, says they are not true salmon, but "Atlantic salmon" in *Freshwater fishes of Canada* (1973), p. 193, confirms that they were. There have been recent attempts to re-introduce them in Lake Ontario.

page 319

"The rivers and lakes..." Bell, p. 185; "The days of salmon-spearing..." Guillet, *Toronto,* p. 68; "But our great..." John Langton, p. 115; "Last evening gave..." Diary of John Thomson, dated as '15th Thursday' only.

Spear fishing: a good description can be found in Christmas, p. 255.

Ice fishing: "He sat over a..." Head, p. 201; Rowan's description is longer, p. 299-300.

page 320-321

"Mr. M. shewed me..." Thornton, p. 43.

"A bear also..." Thornton, p. 43; "Mrs S. and her..." Thornton, p. 50; "We have had a few..." Letter of Robert Wade, 25 December 1822; "A solitary settler..." Christmas, v.1, p. 288; shooting bears in the water, Christmas, v.1, p. 125.

page 322

Birds: Head, p. 192; Jameson, p. 79.

Robins: Although they are related, the American and European robins are different in size, appearance and behaviour. The European robin is closer in size and appearance to the bluebird. *Birds of the world* (1993), pp. 286, 294.

"Could not sleep..." "Journey to Canada in '33" *Orillia Packet*, 12 May 1898; "You would laugh..." same, 19 May 1898.

Insects: Bell, p. 186; Head, p. 288.

page 323

"There I asked him..." Head, p. 169.

Fleas: "Set out early..." Diary of --- Johnson, 18 September 1819; "The night before..." Diary of William Bell, quoted in Skelton, p. 156; "...at this hour..." John Langton, p. 26.

page 324

"By the Bye..." John Langton, p. 36.

Crickets: William Bell, p. 186; "I find they have..." Anne Langton, p. 105.

Bell on squirrels, p. 184; Mrs Moodie on mice, *Roughing*, p. 206.

page 325

"Our farming utensils..." letter of Daniel Stewart, 10 October 1836 (for publication history, see below under Cradle).

Grain: more extensive discussion of these ideas can be found in Jones, pp. 85-99. Following p. 99 is a technical description of the kinds of wheat grown and why they succeeded or failed.

Blights: Jones, pp. 137ff.

Cradle: Letter of William Hewgill, 15 September 1843; "It is a rare..." letter of Daniel Stewart, 10 October 1836, published in the *Erin Advocate*, 23 March 1939 and quoted in Butchart, *Everton*, p. 55; more details in Scherck, p. 132.

page 326

Fences: all this information comes from Symons, which is a comprehensive source on the history of fences in Ontario; "A glance at..." p. viii; Scherck also has a section on rail fences, but it may reflect the ideas of a later period (p. 161).

page 327

"the cross zigzag..." Logan, p. 49; "At first sight..." Letter of William Wade, 26 July 1846.

"Opposite my House..." Letter of Joseph Carrothers, *Irish Emigrants'*, p. 9.

page 328-330

"We picked thirty-eight..." and "We shall have..." Letter of Deborah Mullett, 21 January 1825.

"Thomas has saved..." Letter of Robert Wade, 7 November 1820.

Tannery: from "An old family account book," *Ontario Historical Society papers and records*, v. 7, pp. 120-139; Jones contains an account of shares when the pig or cow is killed in the fall, quarters being taken by the blacksmith, tailor and shoemaker as well as the family, p. 80.

"We have had..." Letter of Mary Mullett, April 1823; "Sarah and Maria..." Letter of Deborah Mullett, 21 January 1825; "James tells us..." letter of Deborah Mullett Haight, 9 February 1830.

"the Canadians keep..." Letter of Lady Aylmer, February 1831; "First and foremost..." Copleston, p. 64; cold and the landlord, MacKay, p. 70

"I went to see Fanny..." diary of Mary O'Brien, 18 December 1828, quoted in Miller, p. 29; "It was necessary..." Haight, p. 40; observation about sparks and holes, Anne Langton, p. 136.

"We went to a cedar swamp..." diary of Mary O'Brien, 5 December 1830, quoted in Miller, p. 143.

page 331

"Clocks were not..." Haight, p. 108.

Learning to cook: Copleston, p. 69f.; Anne Langton, bread failure p. 76, black puddings and ham-shaping, p. 83, ham improperly hung, p. 120, cream has a bitter taste, p. 124.

Peas: Dunlop, p. 99.

page 332-333

"There nobody was..." John Langton, p. 38; "...his ingenuity..." Head, p. 193.

"The bass tree..." Head, p. 191; "He forged..." Head, p. 305.

"After the first year..." Leavitt, p. 20; "Your Cousin John..." Letter of Ralph Wade, 17 December 1845; "We have a washing..." letter of Deborah Mullett, 21 January 1825.

"McAndrew was spending..." John Langton, p. 51.

page 334-335

"our greatest difficulty..." Letter of Robert Forrest, undated; "We cannot afford..." Letter of Deborah Mullett, 21 January 1825; "He traded one..." same, this cousin had recently come from England and everything the Mulletts say about him indicates he had little talent for pioneer life.

Clothing: women's, diary of Mary O'Brien, 28 January 1829, quoted in Miller, p. 33; her brother's outfit, diary of 26 November 1834, quoted in Miller, p. 234; "I made seventy five..." letter of Deborah Mullett Haight, 9 February 1830; "the people here..." Letter of W.J. Mickle, 27 January 1831.

"I have sent thee..." letter of Rachel Mullett, 17 January 1823; "Aunt Martha queries..." letter of Mary Mullett, April 1823.

Starch: letter of Deborah Mullett, 21 January 1825; Anne Langton, p. 84.

"I have learned..." letter of James Clothier Mullett, 16 January 1825

page 336

"I fetch the cows..." letter of Arthur Mullett, 16 January 1825.

"A few years ago..." Moodie, *Clearings*, p. 77.

"Our boys are all..." letter of David MacLaren, 12 December 1840, followed by his of 21 April 1842; this concerns Tarbolton.

page 337-338

"The school house..." Haight, p. 17; "I next sat..." Haight, p. 18.

page 339

"I still am well..." Nathaniel Carrothers, *Irish Emigrants'*, p. 1.

410

"In short, Sir..." Mr Cornelius quoted in Martin Doyle, p. 31.
"A man who owns..." Rowan, p. 32.
page 340
"I am now come..." letter of William Dowie, 254 November 1821, from Forrest
    collection #6.

Index

Women are indexed under their maiden names, if those names are made clear in the text.

417

Robert 14, 19, 63, 64, 71, 76,
    90, 98, 114, 156, 158,
    166, 168, 173, 198,
    205, 206, 214, 215,
    221, 253, 258, 296,
    298, 300, 304, 306,
    321, 327
William 168, 327
Wagons 230-231
Walker
    Duncan 105
    Elizabeth see Hextall
    John 27, 28, 61, 82, 87, 92,
        109, 118, 119
    Mary 150
Walking 225, 229, 230
War of 1812 7, 166, 167
Ward, Chr. 353
Ware, John 352
Water 43, 79-82, 169, 209, 244
Waterloo County 40, 187, 232
Watson, John 350
Webster, J. 317
Weddings 259, 260, 269
Weldrick, John 216
Welland Canal 166, 173, 184
Welsh 68, 71
West
    Mrs William 243
    William 9
Wetherall, John 352
Whales 87
Whisky 41, 83, 202, 258, 264-
        267, 279
Whitby township 187
White
    Catherine 318
    Mr 157
Widder, Friedrich 367
William and Matthew (Ship) 62
William Osborne (Ship) 63
Williams, Mr 78
Williamson, John 350
Wilson
    Charles 144
    George 351
    Hannah 144, 149, 157

James 20, 23, 44, 77, 82, 104,
    107, 108, 140, 144,
    147, 163
James (of Fergus) 317
Joseph 29, 69, 77, 84, 87, 98,
    101, 111, 119, 127,
    144, 149, 150, 157
Robert 144
Winter 226, 227
Wolves 216, 308-310, 315, 320
Women 25, 69, 137, 252, 253,
    258
    Employment 14, 25, 253, 273,
        275
Woodward, Mr 87
Woolsey, Mr 91
Yonge, Mr 33
York (Ship) 180
Young, James 31

423

ABOUT THE AUTHORS

Frances Hoffman was born and raised in the north of England. She came to Canada in 1966 and lives in a log house overlooking the Grand River.

She has edited a number of genealogical aids, including church records, an index to the *Elmira Signet*, and pre-1850 Ontario naturalization records.

As a genealogist and oral historian, she has considerable experience in historical research and in presenting the life experiences of others in their historical setting. She has lectured extensively on these topics.

Her current project is the Hoffman Photo Index, a unique idea to link lost photographic images with their relations.

In 1996, she and Ryan Taylor published *Much To be Done: Private Life in Ontario from Victorian Diaries*. She followed that with *Steeped in Tradition: A Celebration of Tea* (1997).

Ryan Taylor is a genealogical librarian at the Allen County Public Library in Fort Wayne, Indiana. He was born in Oshawa, Ontario and has worked as a librarian for more than twenty-five years in Manitoba, Ontario and Indiana.

He has written or edited many genealogical aids, including spending time as editor of the Ontario Genealogical Society's journal, *Families* (1988-1997). His book publications include *Much to be Done* (1996, with Frances Hoffman), *Books You Need to do Genealogy in Ontario: an Annotated Bibliography* (1996) and *Important Genealogical Collections in Ontario Libraries and Archives* (1994).

Since 1993 he has written a genealogy column in the *Kitchener-Waterloo Record*. The columns were collected in *Routes to Roots* (Global Heritage Press, 1997).

Ryan lectures extensively on genealogical and historical topics in both the United States and Canada.